FORGING SOUTHEASTERN IDENTITIES

A DAN JOSSELYN MEMORIAL PUBLICATION

FORGING SOUTHEASTERN IDENTITIES

SOCIAL ARCHAEOLOGY, ETHNOHISTORY, AND FOLKLORE OF THE MISSISSIPPIAN TO EARLY HISTORIC SOUTH

EDITED BY
GREGORY A. WASELKOV AND MARVIN T. SMITH

THE UNIVERSITY OF ALABAMA PRESS
TUSCALOOSA

The University of Alabama Press
Tuscaloosa, Alabama 35487-0380
uapress.ua.edu

Hardcover edition published 2017.
Paperback edition published 2026.
eBook edition published 2017.

Typeface: Scala, Scala Sans, Gill Sans, and Herculanum

Cover image: Fabric fragment, Spiro, Oklahoma; courtesy of Department of Anthropology, Smithsonian Institution, catalog no. 423,373
Cover design: David Nees

Paperback ISBN: 978-0-8173-6274-4

A previous edition of this book has been cataloged by the Library of Congress.
ISBN: 978-0-8173-1941-0 (cloth)
E-ISBN: 978-0-8173-9078-5

For Judith Knight,
in appreciation for all she does for southeastern archaeology

CONTENTS

ILLUSTRATIONS

Figures

Tables

PREFACE

This volume grew from a suggestion in February 2013 by Curtis Clark, director of the University of Alabama Press, that one of us (Waselkov) should organize a volume of essays to honor recently retired UAP editor Dr. Judith Knight for her decades-long contribution to archaeological publishing. Waselkov asked Marvin Smith whether he would coedit the volume. Together, the two of us developed a substantive theme for the proposed book, and solicited chapters from 10 colleagues, from the hundreds of potential authors who had published under Judith's editorial guidance (in the end, we added three more colleagues as coauthors). We asked each contributor or team of contributors to submit an original piece that would highlight important new research, while also serving to thank Judith for all she has done for the field of Southeastern North American archaeology. We have assembled a volume focusing on the Mississippian and post-Mississippian Southeast, our own periods and region of principal interest; we could as easily have done a Woodland or an Archaic volume, given Judith's far-reaching editorial hand.

Dr. Knight has had a major impact on Southeastern archaeology through her work with the University of Alabama Press. Her efforts to publish the best research on Southeastern archaeology, and her singular success in marketing and promoting the volumes, have had a far greater impact on the discipline than the work of any individual researcher.

Judith Knight's career spans five decades. In her first jobs in archaeology, she served as a docent at the Moundville Museum in 1969, participated in excavations at site 1MG72 on the Tennessee River that same year, and later worked at site 1AU28 in Jones Bluff Reservoir on the Alabama River. After the birth of her first child, Judith left fieldwork behind. In the early 1970s, while employed as David DeJarnette's secretary, she typed all of the contract reports produced by a salvage archaeology team led by DeJarnette (based at Moundville and administered through the University of Alabama's Department of Anthropology), and all issues of the *Journal of Alabama Archaeology*. In the late 1970s, Judith became the archaeological lab director for the Columbus Museum of Arts and Sciences.

Judith began her long association with the Southeastern Archaeological Conference (SEAC) book room in 1976 at the Tuscaloosa meeting, selling back issues of the *Journal of Alabama Archaeology* and archaeological reports produced by DeJarnette's Moundville team. The following year she began bringing University of Alabama Press books to SEAC. Over the years, Judith became the unofficial bookroom coordinator, encouraging participation by a wide range of exhibitors whose presence considerably enhanced the value of the conference for all attendees, students as well as professionals.

Judith was also a key player in organizing the Southeastern Archaeological Conference Student Paper Award, which has grown into a multithousand-dollar prize of books, handcrafted replicas, and other items intended to encourage the professionalization of our best students. According to Judith's husband, Jim Knight, Steve Williams started the Student Paper Award in the late 1970s, but it lapsed shortly afterward—until Jim revived it in 1992. Judith would badger university press representatives, and Jim would work on everyone else. It was Judith's idea for each exhibitor in the book room to contribute at least one prize item, and she coordinated the prize display in the book room.

Judith attended graduate school at the University of Florida, where she earned her M.A. (and was elected to the Phi Kappa Phi honor society) in 1979 and her Ph.D. in Education in 1984. She returned to Alabama and worked for the University of Alabama Press from 1985 to 2010, rising to the position of senior editor. During her tenure there, she acquired and ushered into print more than 400 books, the vast majority of them in her specialty areas of archaeology, anthropology, linguistics, Caribbean studies, and Native American studies. The archaeology titles alone total well over 200.

To appreciate the difference Judith Knight made to Southeastern archaeology over the course of those twenty-five years, consider how few books on any area of North American archaeology were published in the preceding decade. Academic Press was publishing a few titles a year since the early 1970s, but generally at prices only libraries and full professors could afford. The University of Tennessee Press picked up Southeastern archaeology titles with some regularity, although its interest in that subject was waning by the 1980s. Only the University Presses of Florida (as it was then known) had a series devoted to archaeology, the Ripley P. Bullen Series, edited by Jerald Milanich, with five books in print when Judith started her career in publishing. The University of Alabama Press had issued just three archaeology titles (DeJarnette's volume of Walter F. George Reservoir fieldwork, Dick Krause's *The Clay Sleeps*, about African pottery production, and John Walthall's perennial bestseller, *Prehistoric Indians of the Southeast*). Their successes surprised the press director, who decided that expanding into archaeology might be a good idea!

In other words, archaeologists working in the Southeast had little chance of seeing their dissertations or their research monographs published by a scholarly press until Judith Knight took on that cause at the University of Alabama Press. Her realization that archaeologists buy books and that the market demand for archaeology titles was far greater than other press editors knew, as well as her hard work to bring quality books to print, often as reasonably priced paperbacks, sparked an enormous expansion of that previously tiny corner of book publishing.

Judith Knight retired from the University of Alabama Press in January 2010, but she remains active in the publishing arena, where we are sure she is bringing imagination and energy to bear on the many modern challenges facing academic publishing. We join our fellow authors in wishing her continued success, and we hope this volume reflects the depth of our gratitude for her distinguished career.

INTRODUCTION: FORGING SOUTHEASTERN IDENTITIES

Gregory A. Waselkov and Marvin T. Smith

Throughout the nineteenth and early twentieth centuries, popular and scholarly uses of the phrase "Southern identity" referred, virtually always, to Americans of European descent born and raised in the Southeastern region of the United States. Only with the civil rights movement of the 1960s were critics of the old order emboldened to question such a one-sided notion. Society as a whole, with popular culture in tow, has now generally acknowledged the more complex reality of the Southern past and the intertwined histories of the many peoples who have lived in Southeastern North America.

Of course, archaeologists, anthropologists, and folklorists working in the Southeast have always recognized the region's social diversity; indeed, recognition of social diversity lies at the very hearts of these disciplines, which have as their central purpose the study of peoples overlooked by the mainstream. Yet the ability to define and trace the origins of a collective social identity—the means by which individuals or groups align themselves, always in contrast to others—has proven to be an elusive goal. Identity is, as many have learned to their dismay, a slippery concept. Yet we all know that humans excel at creating groups, identifying us versus them. Social identities bind people together, while simultaneously providing a basis for ethnocentrism, the deep-seated (and frequently destructive) sense that one's own group is superior to others. It takes no more than a moment's reflection to realize there is hardly a need more pressing in this world than to understand the nature of human social identity.

Fortunately, we now have some effective analytical tools to explore the processes of identity creation and maintenance. Since this book examines Southeastern identities primarily from archaeological perspectives (with one contribution by a folklorist at the volume's end), this introductory discussion focuses specifically on the archaeologist's analytical toolkit.

Recent advances in the archaeological study of social identity build on the theory of relational sociology, an approach that distinguishes two complementary forms of identity. We can all recognize that each of us juggles multiple social identities. Some identities are thrust upon us (for instance, our sex, age, family, and ethnicity), whereas others (such as our social status, occupation, and place of residence) are results of choices made in the courses of our lives from among the range of social roles open to us at different times. These personal multiple identities are constructed in social contexts; they are complexly interrelated—consider the variety of kin relationships each of us holds simultaneously with different members of our own family; and they remain in flux throughout our lives as we age and have different life experiences. Of course, individuals as members of groups have traditionally attracted most interest from archaeologists, whether as representatives of lineages, social classes, ethnic groups, states, and so on. As a member of multiple groups, our personal identities form and operate in communities of varying levels of complexity and integration, which provide engaged individuals with other opportunities for identification (Barth 1969; Calhoun 1995; Díaz-Andreu et al. 2005:1–7; Meskell 2001:187–189; Somers 1994; Tilly 2005).

Relational sociologists suggest this complex web of identity results primarily from two processes, relational identification and categorical identification. A Southwestern archaeologist, Matthew Peeples, has summarized the distinction in this way: "*Relational identification* refers to a process in which individuals identify with larger collectives, often informally, based on networks of interactions or relationships, such as exchange or kin ties. In contrast, *categorical identification* refers to a process through which individuals identify with more formal units such as political organizations, religions, states, or genders, based on perceived similarities with others in those groups. Categorical identities, unlike their relational counterparts, can be defined without reference to direct interaction and, thus, can include far greater numbers of individuals" (Peeples 2011:4). This distinction has great utility in archaeological analyses. Individuals participating in a relational network maintain social ties through direct contact (whether intermittent or continuous), face-to-face interactions that have material consequences in the form of shared practices, shared goods, and shared domestic spaces. In contrast, broad social categories need to be symbolized, often in material ways across considerable geographical spaces, for members to recognize each other in the absence of prior personal interaction (Brubaker and Cooper 2000; Gardner 2007:15–20, 203–217; Jenkins 2004; Peeples 2011:17–22).

Evaluating the interplay between relational social ties and categorical commonalities through time is just one way that archaeologists can track social continuity and change during the dynamic Mississippian and post-Mississippian eras of Southern history. This volume's contributors have deployed an eclectic range of approaches to social identity.

In our first chapter, Adam King and Johann A. Sawyer discuss the symbolic character of five engraved shell gorgets excavated with remains of a woman buried in a very public space, the summit of Mound C at Etowah, the largest Mississippian site in northwestern Georgia. Polly Wiessner (1983) first defined artifact styles that actively express categorical group identity as "emblemic." With their Etowah example, King and Sawyer argue that a mixture of engraved styles publically displayed in this elite burial symbolized the hybrid origins of a revived Etowah society. By consciously drawing inspiration from two historical and spiritual traditions, the rulers of Etowah created a new community identity, a process of hybridization that coincided with reoccupation of an already ancient mound center.

Along with many of the volume's contributors, King is building upon years of study, specifically his long-term reanalysis of Mississippian iconography, at Etowah in particular (King 2007). Similarly, Penelope B. Drooker continues her research into late prehistoric textiles. Building on her groundbreaking *Mississippian Village Textiles at Wickliffe*, Drooker (1992) investigates the use of textiles in Mississippian politics and ritual. In this important overview of textile production and use in the Southeast, Drooker shows how pliable fabrics and basketry were used to signal power relationships in the Mississippian world. In the form of clothing, cloth particularly embodies and signals personal identities and group affiliations. Her wide-ranging survey documents how Mississippian commoner and elite fabric makers, "who," she thinks, "most likely were women," wielded creative power in the production of textiles deployed to draw power from and exercise power in social, political, economic, and spiritual realms—all important venues of identity formation and maintenance.

Building on her twin interests in the pottery and Native peoples of the Georgia coast (Saunders 2000; Saunders and Hays 2004), Rebecca Saunders examines radical changes that occurred around A.D. 1350 at the Irene site. She argues that a revitalization movement overturned the earlier Mississippian social order, as evidenced by "obliteration" of the Savannah-period platform mound under an enormous dome-shaped earthen cap, shifts in burial practice and public architecture and subsistence regimes, as well as replacement of ceramic motifs redolent of the Upper World by those invoking This World. As Saunders argues, this shift in lifeways at Irene was an egalitarian-driven reinvention, a revitalizing communalization of an earlier elite-centered Mississippian pattern. The people of Irene literally created a new social identity by redefining the symbolic values of ancient cosmograms displayed prominently on ceramic vessels.

Robbie Ethridge continues her systematic reinterpretation of the transition from Mississippian to post-Mississippian societies (Ethridge 2010; Ethridge and Shuck-Hall 2009; Pluckhahn and Ethridge 2006) with her wide-ranging discussion of the infrastructure of the Mississippian world during its most severe challenge, the invasion of the Southeast by Hernando de Soto's Spanish army. Borrowing the "infrastructure" concept from modern lexicon, she considers the means and impediments to movements of people, goods, information, and services in the mid-sixteenth century, as well as the human agents (guides, burden bearers, and interpreters) who facilitated travel, whether undertaken by Native Southeasterners or by interlopers. In the process, Ethridge finds, as did the Spaniards, that the limits of Mississippian infrastructure coincided quite closely with the limits of the Mississippian world. She discerns a Mississippian identity "writ large," the Southeast unified by intersocietal movement and interaction on a geographical scale seldom articulated by generations of scholars.

Marvin T. Smith continues his research into the early Contact period (Smith 1987, 2001, 2005; Smith and Barnes Smith 1989) by looking at the types of Native-made marine shell ornaments circulating in the late/post-Mississippian Southeast. By mapping distributions of different engraved shell motifs across the late Mississippian Southeast, stylistic boundaries do, in at least some instances, correspond with societal borders. Smith demonstrates that, in the aftermath of Soto's traverse of the region, engraved shell disappeared by the early seventeenth century, but ornaments such as shell beads and ear pins continued to be produced and used into the eighteenth.

David G. Moore, Christopher B. Rodning, and Robin A. Beck's long collaboration at the Berry site reflects a convergence of their individual research programs exploring the late Mississippian and early colonial peoples of the southern Appalachians and Piedmont of the Carolinas and Tennessee (Beck 2013; Beck, Rodning, and Moore 2016; Moore 2002; Rodning 2015). Their recent success in identifying remains of Fort San Juan and associated Spanish residences, situated for a brief time in the Native town of Joara, is enabling them to discern "the landscapes of colonial interaction and identity in the sixteenth-century Southeast." Although the Spaniards at Fort San Juan failed to impose a Spanish colonial identity on the people of Joara, unraveling the relationship between Spanish fort and Joaran platform mound is revealing efforts by each side of this colonial encounter to control the contested landscape. Spanish attempts to impose a colonial identity on Joara first met negotiation, then resistance and reaffirmation of Joaran separateness. Monumental construction by the people of Joara evidently claimed the day by reasserting a dominant Native authority over the former landscape of Spanish "Cuenca."

Drawing on long experience with the archaeology and ethnohistory of coastal Georgia and northern Florida (Worth 1995, 1998, 2000, 2009b, 2014), John Worth tackles the phase concept in North American archaeology. Developed in an earlier day, before modern applications of social theory to archaeology, the phase concept has been roundly critiqued over the years (e.g., Plog 1974; Stoltman 1978; O'Brien and Lyman 2000) but remains in wide (and generally uncritical) use by archaeologists throughout the eastern United States. Worth ruefully notes that archaeologists have been "prone to make the leap between the material culture (generally ceramics)" characteristic of a phase and the ethnic identity of the people who produced those objects. Worth maintains that any correspondence between an archaeological phase and an ancient social group must be demonstrated, not assumed, and he provides many examples of such assumed correlations that are demonstrably erroneous. He recommends that we disentangle communities of practice from collective social identity, and he argues vehemently for ceramic assemblage analyses that take into account the complex interrelationships between the two. Worth's extensive critique of the assumption that pottery is "a reasonably good indicator of political affiliation and ethnic identity" should encourage Southeastern archaeologists to develop more sophisticated approaches to social identity. He builds on Suzanne Eckert's (2008) distinction between communities of practice and communities of identity to develop what he terms a landscape of practice, which more appropriately describes the colonial Southeast with its numerous coalescent and immigrant Native towns that brought together previously distinct peoples.

Building on her earlier study of Paleoindian and early Archaic subsistence (Hollenbach 2009), Kandace D. Hollenbach compares three Native American plant assemblages from a single site on the Savannah River, one occupation dating to Early Mississippian and the others from the seventeenth and eighteenth centuries (the last probably being a coalescent community of Apalachees, Savannahs, and Yuchis abandoned by 1715). As she notes, foodways are "tightly wound into culture and identity." The first two components indicate considerable continuity in subsistence practices across the centuries, well into the period of intermittent contact with Europeans. The last inhabitants, on the other hand, radically readjusted their foodways, abandoning traditional foods like acorns and many native cultigens, while adopting Old World orchard crops like peaches and retaining traditional medical remedies, such as bearsfoot seeds. Hollenbach suggests this displaced coalescent group's management of the local landscape underwent substantial change. By shunning age-old wild foods and establishing Old World–style orchards, these resilient Native peoples perhaps intended to bring their farming practices more into accord with those of their new colonial neighbors.

Although no doubt better known for their Mississippian research in Alabama (Brown 2003; Knight and Steponaitis 2007; Steponaitis 2009), Ian W. Brown and Vincas P. Steponaitis have also made major contributions to the archaeology of the Natchez area (Brown 1979, 1985, 2007; Steponaitis, Brain, and Brown 1983). Here they look at the Grand Village of the Natchez, as described in historical written accounts and depicted on several detailed French colonial maps. In contrast to Ethridge's consideration of social identity at the macro scale of region, Brown and Steponaitis examine the other extreme, the identity and makeup of individual Natchez towns in the cartographic records of their French neighbors and eventual conquerors. Their reconstruction of the Fatherland site landscape reveals that this important site had as many as six earthen mounds, although not all remained in use by the Natchez in the early eighteenth century. Brown and Steponaitis document the mounds' continued role in the area's economy and landscape, as sources of soil for a massive flood control levee and as targets of early scientific/antiquarian investigations in the nineteenth century.

George E. Lankford, a consummate folklorist, contributes our final chapter. His accomplishments extend into the disciplines of archaeology and anthropology, with major books on Native American myths, Mississippian cosmology and iconography, and African American slave narratives (Lankford 2006, 2007, 2008, 2011). In particular, Lankford has contributed profoundly to recent studies of Mississippian iconography, a specialized field of archaeological analysis that has benefited immensely from methods borrowed from art history and from folklore. Judicious application of these "new" analytical approaches is enabling researchers to draw inferences from the core beliefs of Mississippian descendant peoples that inform us about religious practices dating centuries earlier. Many of the preceding chapters in this volume draw on studies by Lankford and other "iconologists." Here, Lankford examines legends from three groups who have lived in the South—Native Americans, European immigrants, and African slaves—to show how folklorists extract historical insights from such stories. Specifically, he demonstrates the role of legends in building community identity and giving a public voice to issues of contention. Lankford's interpretation of French colonist Antoine Le Page du Pratz's retelling of a Natchez legend, which Le Page heard from the chief guardian of their temple, is a folkloric tour de force of historical analysis. His discussion of legendary history, as practiced through oral recitation and performance by all three major groups of people who have inhabited the South over the last few centuries, also touches on the ways identities are formed, maintained, and altered with narrative, an important theme of modern identity theory (Somers 1994; Somers and Gibson 1994; Brubaker and Cooper 2000).

Although none of the contributors to this volume claims to have pinned down absolutely that slippery concept—identity—we hope that readers will find much of interest and value in the innovative and instructive ways that some of the myriad Southeastern identities forged in this region's past are analyzed.

FORGING SOUTHEASTERN IDENTITIES

1

SHELL GORGETS, HYBRIDITY, AND IDENTITY CREATION IN THE HIGHTOWER REGION

Adam King and Johann A. Sawyer

In 1927 Warren K. Moorehead's (1932) excavation crew recorded the grave of a woman (Burial 6A) while removing the summits of Mound C at the great Mississippian site of Etowah in Georgia. She was buried with a necklace containing five engraved shell gorgets (Figure 1.1). What makes the necklace particularly intriguing is the combination of themes found on the gorgets. Four of them depict what is known as the turkey cock theme, showing a pair of birds, in some cases flanking a striped pole. The fifth depicts the image of a spider. Jon Muller (1989) has argued that all five gorgets were made in the Hightower style of eastern Tennessee. Although Hightower artisans frequently made gorgets with the turkey cock theme, this example is the only one attributed to them showing the spider theme. In fact, spiders are only commonly found on gorgets of the McAdams style (Classic Braden) made in the central Mississippi Valley.

Viewed in isolation, Moorehead's Burial 6A presents an interesting, if not idiosyncratic, juxtaposition of different gorget themes. Their presumed places of origin hint at a blending of local and nonlocal practices at Etowah. In this chapter, we argue that this apparent blending is the result of a cultural process known as hybridity, initiated by the influx of new people to Etowah. In fact, this burial is not unique in its blending of themes and traits. We show that it is part of a broader process of hybridization visible in shell gorget themes and associations throughout the Hightower region (southeastern Tennessee and northwestern Georgia) starting as early as A.D. 1200. Through that process, new personal and community identities were negotiated that incorporated new ideas and people into existing conceptions of identity, history, and belief.

Hybridity

We see in the shell gorgets of the Hightower region a process of introduction of new symbols and ideas and their transformation of existing com-

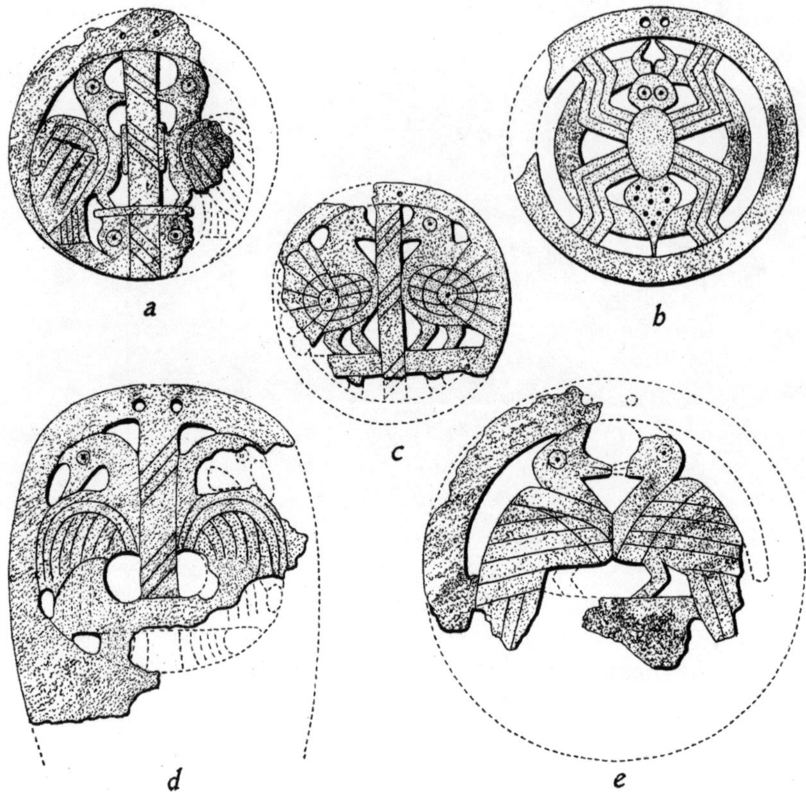

Figure 1.1. Shell gorgets from Moorehead's (1932:60, Figure 32) Burial 6A: (a, c–e) turkey cock theme; (b) spider theme.

munities and traditions. We might call this assimilation or acculturation, but those concepts lack some key elements of the process we think we see. They imply the selective accepting of cultural traits and their integration into existing traditions. In the Hightower region, we see new identities, practices, and traditions emerge from this process—more than just mixing. Concepts like syncretism and creolization can describe how these new things are created but still tend to focus on mixing and borrowing rather than the generative nature of this process. We think what happens in the Hightower region is that entirely new identities and traditions emerge. It is an active process that results from the movement of people.

Hybridity, as introduced by Bhabha (1990, 1994) and used recently by archaeologists like Alt (2006) and Loren (2010), provides an interpretive lens that explicitly embraces the active and generative nature of this process. Although the idea was developed to conceptualize colonial and postcolonial encounters, Bhabha (1990) makes it clear that hybridity is continuous and a part of all culture process—it is always happening. Specifically, hybridity focuses on particular places or moments in time when existing ideas, identities, or practices can be examined, questioned, and ultimately modified to create something entirely new. This does not require encounters on a large and dramatic scale—only that difference be recognized. As a result, hybridity as a process could result from interactions as personal as those between people of different social segments within a community to as broad as colonial encounters.

Hybridity happens in places and at moments when differences are recognized but also can be reconsidered, negotiated, and altered. These are liminal spaces, what Bhabha (1990) called "thirdspaces." These might be actual spaces like cultural frontiers, no-man's-lands, or the edge of town. They also can be moments in the histories of communities or social segments such as a crisis or period of abandonment when traditions and practices are open to alteration (Cobb and King 2005). The key is that this process might alter material culture, but in doing so might create entirely new concepts of self, community, history, and identity.

Shell Gorgets and Identity

Made from the outer whorl of whelk shells and engraved with imagery, shell gorgets have long been recognized as markers of social status. Hatch's (1974, 1976) seminal study of mortuary patterns in the Dallas area of Tennessee clearly linked these markers of status to women, presumably relating primarily to household and kin groupings that were defined through the female line (Sawyer 2009). More recently, Sullivan (2007) reexamined these data and was able to refine Hatch's original observations. After normalizing gorget counts to the numbers of ages and sexes actually interred in Dallas area contexts, she found that the close association with women and children held for gorgets made only before A.D. 1400. Later gorget styles were equally likely to be found with men or women. When those later gorget styles were examined more closely, Sullivan found that only certain forms (Williams Island–style gorgets and shell masks) were more closely associated with men while the various rattlesnake gorget styles (Lick Creek and Citico styles) were exclusively found with women. The results of both Hatch and Sullivan lead us to infer that the gorgets made and used both a century before and after the interment of Moorehead's Burial 6A in Etowah's Mound C are closely associated with women and children.

Women and children are emblematic of the domestic sphere, and, in matrilineal societies, they represent the continuation of families, lineages, clans, and communities. As is well known, Native Southeastern women traditionally owned houses organized along female lines and controlled agricultural production, social group reproduction, and the selection of political decision-makers (Hudson 1976; Swanton 1946). In fact, the power of women was held in high regard by many Southeastern Native societies. Female power derived from the fact that Indian women were revered by their communities as the mothers of the people (Perdue 1998:41–55). For many Southeastern groups, homes and households held by matrilineal lines were a source of power (Wesson 2008). Homes (through their architecture) and their households (membership) are cultural microcosms where individuals become aware of sociocultural values, including a defined set of kinship rules and practices. Homes not only protect the family, but also are the place where the family resides, where new children are cradled, and where the deceased are laid to rest. Households are the heart of kinship systems and sociopolitical organization, without which men or women could not reaffirm their social roles or rights to social or political offices. Houses unite individuals through blood and the central hearth, the embodiment of the central communal fire (Waring 1968), an *axis mundi* that unites family lines and, by extension, the community.

The relationship between women, power, and kinship is embodied in Southeastern gorget symbolism at various places and times. In eastern Tennessee, the earliest (A.D. 1100–1200) gorgets all exhibit the crib theme (Sawyer 2009), which nests a cross-in-circle or simply a circle within a square (Figure 1.2). In Mississippian iconography, a cross-in-circle represents the sacred fire that connects This Earthly World to the Above World. The sacred center in This World can be activated anywhere the sacred fire is kindled (Lankford 2007b; Reilly 2004; Waring 1968). Surrounding the sacred fire symbol by a square reinforces the earthly association, because This World is conceived of as an island, round or square, floating on the primordial sea (Sawyer 2009).

This same basic symbolism is replicated in Mississippian houses, communities, and ritual spaces, and it persists with variations in traditional Southeastern square grounds today. As Antonio Waring (1968) points out, the Muskogee word for the early historic period Square Ground translates as "the big house," which linguistically and symbolically draws sacred and community space back to the domestic space, and reinforces the concept that women and their reproductive powers form the fundamental basis of society and its continuation.

Later eastern Tennessee gorget styles (A.D. 1200–1300) are also dominated by themes that carry cosmological models. For example, George Lank-

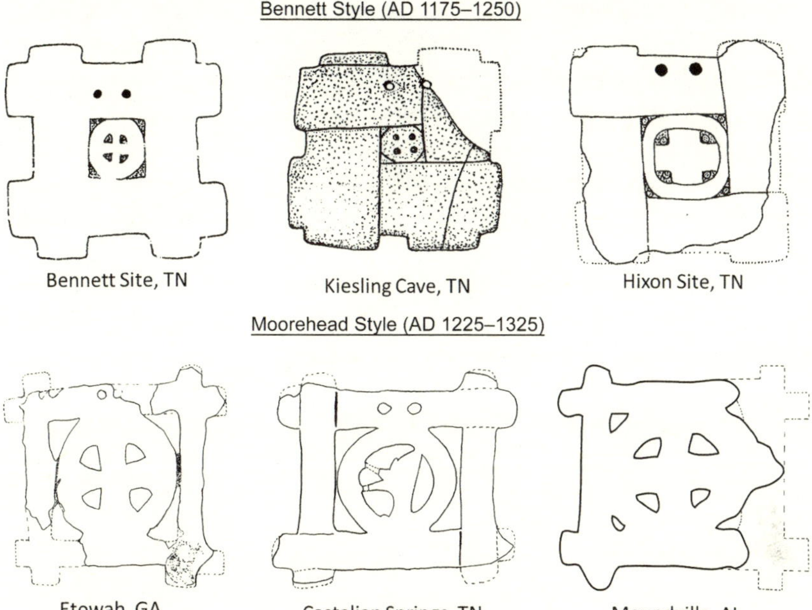

Figure 1.2. Crib gorgets of eastern Tennessee (courtesy of Johann A. Sawyer).

ford (2007b) argues that the turkey cock theme represents a view of the cosmos from the side. The spider and later rattlesnake motifs (A.D. 1400–1600) are all cruciforms, representing the sacred center, although the central symbols differ. Even the anthropomorphic-themed gorgets that appear in the region after A.D. 1250, one can argue, represent a version of the sacred center (Reilly and Garber 2011). Since, with few (albeit important) exceptions, all of these various gorget styles and themes are found most often with women in domestic spheres, in graves beneath house floors, we think they reflect the crucial sacred social role of women in these societies.

This close relationship invites us to think of shell gorgets as emblems of some kinship-related social unit—lineages, clans, or communities. At any given site, at least until the dawn of the historic period, shell gorgets are comparatively rare in the archaeological record. For example, only 19 gorgets were found in the 350 graves excavated from Etowah's Mound C (King 2007), and 16 were found in the 518 graves excavated at Toqua (Polhemus 1987). As such, it seems likely that over the history of any site, only a few individuals per generation possessed a gorget.

As David Hally (2007) has shown, shell gorget styles across the Southeast and Midwest seem to have fairly consistent geographical distributions that are about the size of an archaeological phase. This means the imagery on particular gorgets represented symbolic conventions shared among clearly defined, culturally related sets of communities. Individual families, lineages, or clans did not have their own gorget styles and themes. Rather, gorgets represented particular female-related or domestic sphere–related statuses or roles that were shared by multiple communities. From this perspective, we can infer that most engraved shell gorgets were emblems of shared ideas of community and kinship. Perhaps some were even symbols of personal identities, such as town matriarch. Manipulation of imagery on those gorgets was a modification of conceptions of identity. Shell gorgets were just one object form that acted as a power metaphor in the marking of personal or collective identities. The active manipulation of these objects, their symbols, and the contexts in which they are found reveal the choices that people made to reinforce those identities.

Mound C and the Remaking of Etowah

Etowah's Mound C is arguably one of the most famous contexts in Mississippian archaeology. Over the course of three separate excavations spanning 1884 to 1961, some 350 human burials were excavated, many containing elaborately decorated ritual objects and regalia (King 2007). The mound and its mortuary record were created during the Wilbanks phases (A.D. 1250–1375), representing the Middle Mississippi period of Etowah's history (King 2003). This was a significant period in the history of the site. Starting around A.D. 1200, the site was abandoned. When people returned after A.D. 1250, material practices were substantially transformed. Pottery traditions, architectural styles, and mortuary practices all changed dramatically, and mound construction began at an unprecedented pace.

In Mound C, the honored dead of Etowah were placed into the summits and around the margins of the earliest stages, beginning during the Early Wilbanks phase (King 2007). Prominent among the objects found in those graves were embossed copper objects, pottery vessels, and shell gorgets made both in the local region and in places as far away as the central Mississippi Valley. Some of the earliest objects placed into Mound C graves were the famous copper plates found by John Rogan, which depict the well-known birdman theme executed in the Classic Braden style (Brown 2007). Brown (2004; Brown and Kelly 2000) has argued that Classic Braden originated in the American Bottom (possibly at the great site of Cahokia) during the twelfth century, making the Rogan plates both foreign and ancient when buried at Etowah.

At about the same time those plates (and the ideas they carried) arrived at Etowah, local crafters began making their own birdman-themed compositions on Hightower shell gorgets (King 2011). Revealing the generative nature of hybridization, those new compositions are not replicas of the images on the Rogan plates. They are instead images that take ideas and practices from the Hightower region and meld them with Classic Braden ideas and practices to create something entirely new. In Mound C, this process is visible in more than just shell gorget crafting. The appearance of the Rogan plates inspired a new copper working tradition at Etowah as well as the creation of some pottery vessels that seem to combine local and foreign decorative modes.

As Cobb and King (2005) discuss, periods of abandonment present points in a community's life where traditions, history, and identity all can be reconsidered and rewritten. Because the nonlocal materials appear in Mound C immediately after a period of community abandonment, it seems likely that new people (likely from the central Mississippi Valley) were part of Etowah's reoccupation. The combination of the reestablishment of a new community and the inclusion of new people, practices, and identities creates the third space in which hybridity happens. In this case, we see hybridization resulting in placemaking, where Etowah's inhabitants rewrote their history and redefined their community identity to include both ideas and people from the central Mississippi Valley (Sawyer and King 2015).

This placemaking is apparent in the material symbols found in Mound C and the purposeful arrangement of people and objects. In the Early Wilbanks stages of Mound C, some gorget themes and styles are limited to specific quadrants of the mound, while others are not (King 2005). The Hightower-style gorgets depicting the turkey cock theme are concentrated on the northwestern quadrant of the summits (including Moorehead's Burial 6A). This is the earliest of the Hightower themes (ca. A.D. 1200), and it was most likely made in southeastern Tennessee at an important center like Hixon. In the southwestern quadrant of those summits are graves with cruciform-, annular-, and fylfot-themed-gorgets—themes connected to the central Mississippi Valley. It has been argued that these two gorget clusters represent groups of people from eastern Tennessee and the central Mississippi Valley who helped reestablish Etowah after its early thirteenth-century abandonment (King 2010). In contrast, the birdman-themed Hightower gorgets are fairly evenly distributed across the summits of Mound C, including within the quadrants where eastern Tennessee and central Mississippi Valley gorgets cluster. As mentioned, this theme appears after Etowah is reoccupied and is intimately associated with the site.

The Early Wilbanks stages of Mound C can be viewed as an intentionally created composition. In that composition, two distinctive symbol sets appear in discrete areas of the mound, each associated with different regions contributing members to the newly established Etowah community. At the same time, a third gorget theme that represents a hybrid of eastern Tennessee and central Mississippi Valley crafting produced at Etowah crosscuts those discrete areas. We think this reveals an attempt to unite multiple sets of beliefs and material culture during the creation of a new Etowah community—the process of remaking Etowah.

Shell Gorgets and Identity Alteration in the Hightower Region

Moorehead's Burial 6A connects to another process of hybridity that occurred throughout the Hightower region. This process was surely connected to the events just described at Etowah, but likely predated them, and is most apparent in the appearance of the spider and cruciform-themed gorgets in eastern Tennessee (Figures 1.3a-b, d-e). As noted, the spider theme is uncommon in eastern Tennessee but is very common in the corpus of McAdams-style gorgets made between 1100 and 1200 in the central Mississippi Valley. Cruciform gorgets also are uncommon in eastern Tennessee but are found in the central Mississippi Valley, often in association with McAdams spiders. In fact, the cruciform (see figure 1.3b), the McAdams spider (see figure 1.3a), and the Eddyville-style birdman (Figure 1.3c) themes all appear in contemporary contexts, forming a closely linked set of themes in that region (Brain and Phillips 1996).

In eastern Tennessee, the same set of themes (anthropomorphic, spider, and cruciform) appears after A.D. 1200. Importantly, many of the gorgets exhibiting those themes are not made in central Mississippi Valley styles. Instead, they seem to be local creations with foreign themes. Long ago, Jon Muller (1966, 1989) recognized that the anthropomorphics of the Hightower region were made in the local Hightower style. Extensive use of fenestration and a blank border bounding compositions—conventions most commonly used in eastern Tennessee—suggest to us that the various spider gorgets found in the Hightower region were made locally as well (Muller 1989). The cruciform gorgets that cluster in eastern Tennessee sites do not have extensive fenestration, which makes them stylistically distinct from those made in the central Mississippi Valley (Brain and Phillips 1996:28–33). As at Etowah, in the wider Hightower region, central Mississippi Valley themes and local gorget crafting practices were combined to create entirely new symbolic sets.

Like at Etowah, we think this process in the wider Hightower region was sparked by an influx of new people, at least some of whom came from the

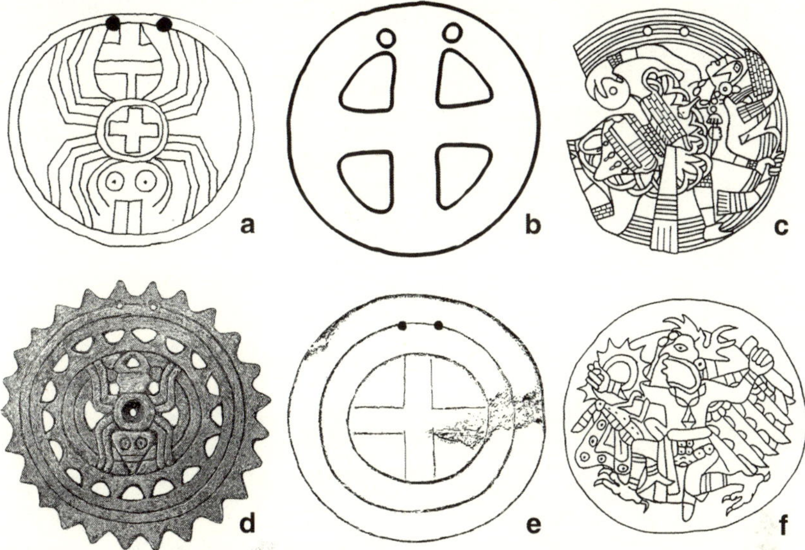

Figure 1.3. Gorget themes and styles referenced in chapter 1: (a) McAdams-style spider, St. Clair County, Illinois (Lankford 2011: Figure 11.2, courtesy of the University of Texas Press); (b) cruciform, Crable, Illinois (courtesy of Johann A. Sawyer); (c) Eddyville-style human figural, St. Mary, Missouri (Brown 2007: Figure 4.4, courtesy of the University of Texas Press); (d) spider, Fains Island, Tennessee (Holmes 1883); (e) cruciform, Hixon, Tennessee (courtesy of Johann A. Sawyer), (f) Hightower-style human figural, Etowah, Georgia (courtesy of F. Kent Reilly III).

central Mississippi Valley. That sustained contact is evident in the small number of pots, gorgets, and copper from that region found at sites like Bennett Place, Toqua, and Hixon (Lewis and Lewis 1995). It may also be confirmed by the presence of people buried in the mound at Hixon who were biologically distinct from eastern Tennessee populations (McCarthy 2011). The webs of relationships that developed through interaction ultimately led, to some degree, to a sharing, entangling, and hybridization of local ideas, histories, and practices.

In Burial 6A from Etowah's Mound C we see another aspect of this process—a pairing of local and nonlocal gorget themes (Table 1.1). The local turkey cock theme of the Hightower style is often found paired in individual graves with nonlocal themes, most frequently with local variants of the cruciform and spider themes. Based on the Hixon sequence, we infer that the turkey cock predates all other themes, including the anthropomorphic theme, in eastern Tennessee (Sullivan 2007). As such, it represents the original materialization of that style and its imagery carries the original

Table 1.1. Turkey Cock Gorgets and Associated Gorgets from Sites in Eastern Tennessee

				Gorget 1		Gorget 2	
Site	Burial	Age	Sex	Style	Theme	Style	Theme
Citico	Mound			Hightower	Turkey Cock		Cruciform
Talassee	113	I		Hightower	Turkey Cock		Spider
Talassee	116	I		Hixon	Turkey Cock		Spider
Toqua	BAE 13			Hightower	Turkey Cock		
Toqua	265	A	F	Hightower	Turkey Cock		
Hixon	47	A	F	Hightower	Turkey Cock		
Hixon	95	A	F	Hightower	Turkey Cock		
Hixon	45	C (4-11)		Hightower	Turkey Cock	Hightower	Turkey Cock
Hixon	52	C (4-11)		Hightower	Turkey Cock	Hightower	Turkey Cock
Hixon	58	A	F	Hightower	Turkey Cock	Hightower	Anthropomorphic
Hixon	72	Infant		Hightower	Turkey Cock		Cruciform
Hixon	68	C (4-11)		Hightower	Turkey Cock	Hightower	Anthropomorphic
Etowah	M-5	Unknown	Unknown	Hightower	Turkey Cock		
Etowah	M-6A-2	A	F	Hightower	Turkey Cock	Hightower	Turkey Cock
Etowah	M-67	Unknown	Unknown	Hightower	Turkey Cock		
Etowah	L-227	C	Unknown	Hightower	Turkey Cock		
Etowah	L-216	A	F	Hightower	Bird		
Etowah	L-143	A	F	Hightower	Turkey Cock		

meanings the turkey cock gorgets were intended to carry. From this perspective, we see the pairing of Hightower turkey cocks with the spider and cruciform themes as another way that people in the Hightower region negotiated and materialized new notions of identity brought about by the relocation of central Mississippi Valley people to the area.

We cannot be sure precisely what these gorgets meant and why they were included in the graves of particular people. As discussed earlier, we think the Hightower turkey cock gorgets were somehow associated with the domestic and kinship spheres. This conjecture arises out of inferred meanings of the imagery on eastern Tennessee gorgets and their close associa-

Gorget 3		Gorget 4		Gorget 5		
Style	Theme	Style	Theme	Style	Theme	Reference
						Lewis and Kneberg 1957
	Cruciform		Plain			Kneberg 1959
						Kneberg 1959
						Polhemus 1987
						Polhemus 1987
						Sullivan 2007
						Sullivan 2007
	Spider		Spider			Sullivan 2007
	Spider		Cruciform			Sullivan 2007
						Sullivan 2007
						Sullivan 2007
						Sullivan 2007
						Moorehead 1932
Hightower	Turkey Cock	Hightower	Turkey Cock		Spider	Moorehead 1932
						Moorehead 1932
						Brain and Phillips 1996; Blakely 1975
						Brain and Phillips 1996; Blakely 1975
						Brain and Phillips 1996; Blakely 1975

tion (in mortuary contexts) with adult women and children. It is possible that the gorgets buried with individuals reflect their social status in life, perhaps their affiliation with a community or kin group or even social role such as clan matron. We see it as also possible that gorgets, and particular combinations of gorgets, were placed in graves with individuals as part of a ritual act carried out for purposes other than signifying the status of the individual. In much the same way that different kinds of gorgets were arranged in the Early Wilbanks graves in Mound C, maybe sets of gorgets were buried with individuals as part of ritual acts or performances intended to materialize the creation of newly altered identities.

Place Matters

While we see the appearance of ideas and symbolism from the central Mississippi Valley across the Hightower region, how objects were used to alter personal and community identities appears to differ depending on place and the historical formation of those places. In particular, Etowah contrasts with other centers in eastern Tennessee like Hixon.

At Hixon, people and goods were found associated with a stacked set of mound stages and buildings, gorget themes and styles were not segregated horizontally, and most of the Hightower turkey cock gorgets were paired with other themes (Lewis and Lewis 1995). Unlike at Etowah, two of the three Hixon graves contained a Hightower anthropomorphic gorget paired with other gorgets, in both cases a turkey cock. Finally, across these themes and styles, gorgets in the Hixon mound were found primarily with women and children.

In many respects, this same patterning applies to other places in eastern Tennessee producing Hightower-style gorgets. For example, salvage excavations conducted at the Mississippian cemetery at the Talassee site recorded two graves containing Hightower turkey cock gorgets. Both were associated with infants and both were paired with spider-themed gorgets (Brain and Phillips 1996:223; Kneberg 1959). A similar pairing was found in salvage excavations conducted at the Citico site in 1957–1958. There a burial recorded in the site's mound contained a Hightower-style turkey cock gorget paired with a gorget made in an unidentified style depicting the cruciform theme (Brain and Phillips 1996:245–246; Hatch 1976:82–85; Lewis and Kneberg 1957).

The pairing of Hightower gorgets at the Toqua site was less common, but the burial patterning appears similar to that seen at Hixon—graves interred in stacked sets of buildings placed on mound summits. Emmert's Bureau of American Ethnology excavations into Mound A in 1882 (Polhemus 1987; Thomas 1894:378–388) recorded two separate burials (Graves 8 and 18) containing Hightower anthropomorphic gorgets, while a third (Grave 13) contained a Hightower turkey cock gorget. In subsequent work at the site, Polhemus (1987:155) excavated Burial 265 on the final summit (summit C) of Mound B at Toqua and in it was a second Hightower turkey cock gorget. It also was not paired with other gorgets.

The patterning in Etowah's Mound C is distinct from those at any of these other sites. In the Early Wilbanks graves, pairing of gorgets is comparatively rare, and this is especially the case for the Hightower turkey cock gorgets. Instead, those gorgets are buried in a particular area of the mound that was spatially distinct from another set of gorgets whose themes connect to the central Mississippi Valley. Those symbolically and spatially distinct sections of the mound seem to be united by an even distribution of Hightower anthropomorphic gorgets, themselves a product of Hightower and central Mississippi Valley practices and ideas. In general, the Hightower turkey cocks are found mostly with adult women and children, as is the pattern throughout the rest of the Hightower region. The central Mississippi Valley gorgets are found almost equally with adult men and women, running counter to practices in the Hightower region and the central Mississippi Valley.

The high incidence of nonlocal goods, clustering of gorgets from different regions, and a relatively high percentage of men with gorgets all set Etowah's Mound C apart from the Hixon mound and other burial contexts containing gorgets in eastern Tennessee. It seems likely that the clusters of people buried in Mound C with gorgets from eastern Tennessee and the central Mississippi Valley were groups of people from those other regions (King 2005). Given the many ways Mound C departs from regional patterns, we must leave room to accept that, in Mound C, objects and people were used in ways that diverged from their original meanings and regional traditions of age and sex association.

Identity Realignment and Placemaking in the Hightower Region

These differences between Etowah and other eastern Tennessee sites provide some clues as to why the process of hybridization at those places may have differed. We believe local history is the key determining factor. If we use the well-dated sequence from the Hixon mound (Sullivan 2007), it appears that new people and ideas began to appear in the Hightower region sometime shortly after A.D. 1200. That is when the first pairing of a Hightower turkey cock and locally made spider appears in the archaeological record of the region.

Current dating of sites in eastern Tennessee shows that important places like Hixon, Citico, and Toqua were all established communities by A.D. 1200 and that a gorget-crafting tradition was firmly in place (Sawyer 2009; Sullivan 2007). At that time, the predominant style in the region was Hightower, and the only theme known was the turkey cock. Not long after A.D. 1200, new symbolic themes appeared in local gorget-crafting traditions that we argue are the product of the thirdspaces created by the arrival of new people and ideas. As a further expression of the new conceptions of community and personal identities created, those new gorget themes were paired with the local turkey cock theme in mortuary settings. We see this as one way that the process of hybridity could operate on identities within already established communities.

It is less clear where the Hightower gorgets and central Mississippi Valley themes appear in the history of the Talassee site because it is not as completely understood. At Talassee, the gorget sequence represented by excavated burials seems to begin in the fourteenth century and extend into the early fifteenth century. If this holds, then Talassee may have first become occupied at a time when central Mississippi Valley ideas and people already had been integrated into Hightower region crafting traditions and societies.

The situation appears very different at Etowah. Between A.D. 1200 and 1250, when new people and symbols enter the Hightower region, the site was not occupied. By the time people did return to Etowah, the process of identity negotiation had already begun at Hixon and Citico. We can see evidence of this process in Mound C in the presence of Moorehead's Burial 6A. She was a woman buried in the same portion of the mound as others interred with Hightower turkey cock gorgets, but she had four on a necklace that also included a single spider-themed gorget. We interpret this grouping of people buried with Hightower gorgets as representing (symbolically, if not actually) people from southeastern Tennessee who helped refound Etowah. Among those people was a woman whose burial accompaniments suggest that her personal and/or community identity had already been altered to accommodate ideas and people from the west.

The reestablishment of Etowah presented an opportunity for the creation of an entirely new community where the local and nonlocal could be integrated at the outset. We can see that attempt to integrate those differences in the distribution of things and people in the Early Wilbanks stages of Mound C. In Mound C, at least some artifacts are associated with people and arranged in ways that do not follow the same rules that apply elsewhere. This may be because those objects and people were combined and arranged in new ways for a specific reason. With the last set of mortuary activities at Mound C (associated with the Late Wilbanks-phase mound stages), we see a set of rituals designed to remake Etowah, purposefully combining people with objects and arranging them to replicate a new vision of the Etowah community within a model of the cosmos (King 2011; Sawyer and King 2015). In essence, these ritual acts constitute an intentional realigning of concepts of identity and community.

Summary and Conclusion

In the Hightower region, we see biological evidence indicating that new groups entered the area sometime around A.D. 1200. Based on the concurrent influx of material culture and symbolism directly connected to the central Mississippi Valley, we think at least some of those new people came from that region. The encounters that resulted created the thirdspaces where hybridity happens—identity, history, and practice all were changed as a result. We can see this clearly in the shell gorgets made and buried with people in southeastern Tennessee and northern Georgia.

Although hybridity seems to have taken place across the Hightower region, we see it being enacted and materialized in different ways depending on site histories. At centers such as Hixon and Citico, contact with those thirdspaces of cultural innovation occurred when they were vibrant communities with established notions of history and practice. In these instances, changes in ideas of self, community, and the other were reflected in the creation of new symbolic forms (spider- and cruciform-themed gorgets) and their active combination with older gorget themes (Hightower turkey cock-themed gorgets) in individual graves. At Etowah, the creation of new community and individual identities was encoded into landscape and history by the arrangement of people and objects in mortuary contexts of Mound C. Because this happened with the reoccupation of Etowah after A.D. 1250, it was part of the process of community building or placemaking.

We do not know what shell gorgets meant and how they were used, but we are confident in stating that they were widely shared symbols intimately connected to notions of female-based kin groups and community. Whatever the exact relationship of women and children with gorgets might have been, the individuals buried with them carried symbols that embodied community identities at specific points in time. The manipulation of gorget symbolism and their use in mortuary ritual reveal the ways that material objects played an active role in the changing of local communities. The differences between Etowah and other important centers in the region have to do with local histories, and those local histories constitute an ongoing process of identity formation and placemaking, of (re)defining the bond between people and the spaces in which they lived.

2

THE FABRIC OF POWER

Textiles in Mississippian Politics and Ritual

Penelope B. Drooker

A significant body of literature highlights power relations and their archaeological manifestations in Mississippian society, often in connection with ceremonial centers such as Cahokia (e.g., Barker and Pauketat 1992; Emerson 1997; Emerson and Pauketat 2002; King 2004; Knight 2010; Marcoux 2007; Muller 1997; Pauketat 1992, 1994; Pauketat and Emerson 1997; Payne 2002; Trocolli 2002; Welch and Butler 2006; cf. e.g., Brown 2006). Many of the archaeological hallmarks of Mississippian peoples, including settlement pattern hierarchies, ceremonial center organization with plazas surrounded by burial mounds and substructure platform mounds, complex iconography, and mortuary practices indicating multilevel ranked societies with ascriptive status differentiation, have been interpreted in terms of dominance and power relations. So has the rich variety of exotic materials and finely crafted prestige[1] and ritual objects from Mississippian contexts, such as iconographic pipes, figurines, and effigy vessels; engraved marine-shell cups and gorgets; embossed copper symbol badges; finely crafted stone weapons and palettes; and carved wooden masks and figurines.

Mississippian pliable fabrics and basketry have rarely been at the forefront in discussions of Mississippian power relations or of objects interpreted as embodying sacred or secular power. For instance, the aforementioned publications typically do not even include fabrics, textiles, or basketry in their indexes, and the most compelling recent exhibition featuring Mississippian art, "Hero, Hawk, and Open Hand: American Indian Art of the Ancient Midwest and South" (see Townsend and Sharp 2004), included no fabric or basketry objects. Nevertheless, a plethora of evidence exists—from ethnohistorical accounts to depictions in Mississippian iconography to remnants of actual fabrics—that these materials, too, served as manifestations of power within Mississippian societies, used in conjunction with objects in other media but contributing unique qualities of their own.

What Is Power?

To support this chapter's discussions, a brief comment about "power" as a concept is in order. Theorists have proposed three modes of power: "power to," that is, the ability of an individual to act or do something (Emerson 1997: 19; see also Pauketat 1994:2; Sweely 1999:11); "power over," that is, the coercive ability to control or prevent others' actions (Emerson 1997:19; Kehoe 1999:17; Wolf 1990:586–587); and "power with," that is, persuasive, noncoercive influence toward obtaining a desired goal (Spencer-Wood 1999:179).[2]

It is simplistic to think of power as a static hierarchy of domination. Spencer-Wood calls it a "dynamic negotiation between individuals" (1999: 180). It is both multiscalar, simultaneously existing at different levels (Levy 1999; Wolfe 1990), and multidimensional (Sweely 1999:12). Some arenas of power include religious or spiritual power; political power, which may be coercive or persuasive, or both; military power, manifest as physical domination; economic power; and social power. A given individual or group may wield power in one area rather than another, or in multiple overlapping areas.

Ideology, which in Marxian theory serves to obscure the reality of material inequality in hierarchical societies (Emerson 1997:22–25), can be an important persuasive force in power relations. Iconography often serves as visual shorthand of ideological principles.

Markers of Power in Mississippian Society

Cahokia, the earliest, largest, and probably the best-known of the Mississippian "temple mound" ceremonial centers (Figure 2.1), evokes superlatives in most descriptions of its material culture and the social fabric that supported it. The "overarching civil and religious authority of Cahokia's central government" (Hall 2004:103) and the enduring influence of the "Cahokian Expression" on the ritual imagery of the Southeastern Ceremonial Complex (SECC) (Brown 2004) make this center, together with contemporaneous communities and centers in the American Bottom, the poster child for the local, regional, and inter-regional power relations that are often highlighted as typical of Mississippian society.

Thomas Emerson summarized the manifestations of political power at Cahokia as (1) architecture that includes elaborate and large structures, ritual facilities, specialized storage facilities, and recreated sacred landscapes; (2) evidence of status and wealth in concentrations of prestige goods and wealth goods; and (3) mortuary patterns that differentiate elites from commoners. Religious power is manifest as (1) architecture that includes

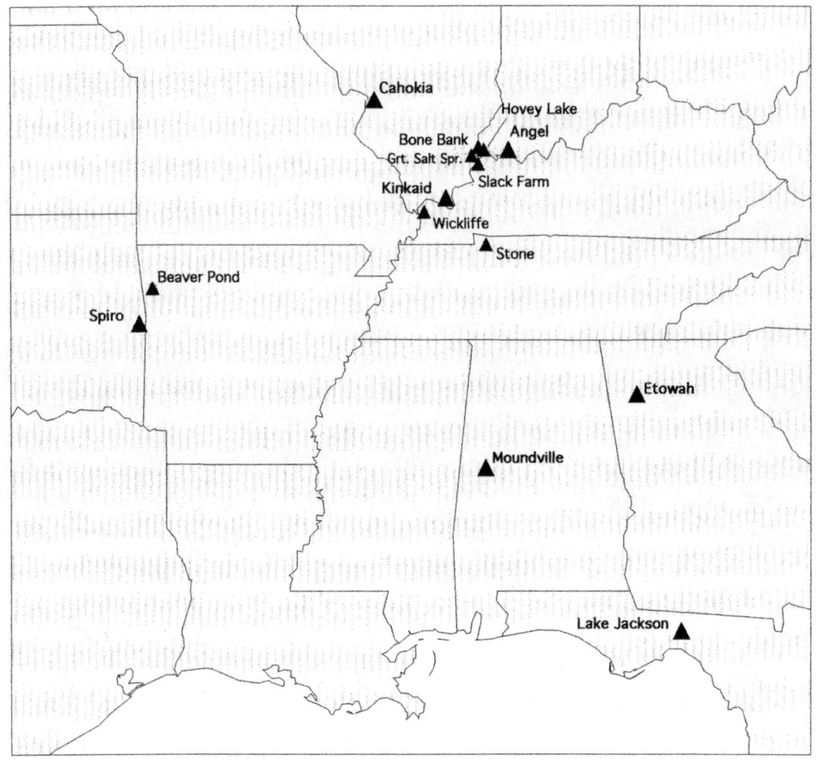

Figure 2.1. Locations of sites mentioned in chapter 2.

temples and charnel houses, specialized ritual structures, and recreated sacred landscapes; (2) concentrations of religious and symbolic artifacts and ritual plants; and (3) special mortuary patterns (Emerson 1997:37). Such markers also characterize later Mississippian ceremonial centers such as Spiro, Etowah, Moundville, Lake Jackson, and the historically known chief village of the Natchez, although exact manifestations differ over time and space (see, for instance, the papers included in Butler and Welch 2006, particularly the critical comparison of Cahokia and early Moundville [Wilson et al. 2006]).

Emerson singled out prestige goods as "symbols of individual power," describing them as "exotic, ritually charged durable materials (associated with elite positions) that circulate through extensive . . . exchange networks that touch distant places and foreign elites" (Emerson 1997:33; see also Helms 1988; Renfrew 1986). They are seen as "critical links in carrying out social transactions and paying debts," both among elites and down the social ladder (Emerson 1997:33; see also King 2004:165). Jon Marcoux (2007) argues, based on evidence from the Moundville chiefdom, for the importance of locally derived goods as well as nonlocal materials and objects as "display goods" within the chiefdom.

Prestige/display goods may serve as status markers such as badges of office, rank, or kin group, which are restricted in use to a particular social segment, or they may serve as wealth items, which anyone can own, and which are "quantifiable in that more, larger, or better made items represent greater wealth" (Prentice 1987:198–199). Examples of Mississippian status markers (for individuals or groups) include large copper symbol badges portraying birds, birdmen, and other iconographic images (Strong 1989); distinctive headplates associated with warriors (Brown 1989:201–202); certain styles of marine shell gorgets associated with particular corporate kin groups at Etowah (King 2004:163; Marceaux and Dye 2007:184); and marine shell mask gorgets typically found with burials of men and children who are assumed to be male (because of their proximity to these gorgets) even though their remains can not be sexed (Smith and Smith 1989). Marine shell beads—found in amounts from one to thousands in burials of elite and nonelite men, women, and children—provide an outstanding example of wealth goods (Prentice 1987). However, masses and/or caches of prestige/display goods, including shell beads, associated with burials may signify collective ritual performance rather than elite wealth, prestige, and/or dominance (e.g., Brown 2006; cf. Emerson and Pauketat 2002:114–118)—manifestation of a different sort of "power."

Emerson and other archaeologists privilege durable materials such as marine shell, copper, quartz crystals, redstone, and exotic cherts in their definitions and examples of Cahokian prestige goods (Emerson 1997:33; Pauketat 1992; see also Brown 2004), undoubtedly because fabrics and other perishables were an insignificant part of the archaeological record there. However, fabrics did function as wealth items, status markers, and ritual objects in Mississippian society. Their special impact derives particularly from their use as clothing, embodying and signaling personal and ceremonial identity (Wobst 1977, 1999), and as easily transported prestige goods (cf. Schneider 1977), important in elite peer polity interaction (cf. Renfrew 1986).

Mississippian Fabrics

Because objects made from organic materials are subject to rapid deterioration under most archaeological conditions in the Midwest and Southeast, our evidence for Mississippian pliable fabrics and basketry comes not only from primary evidence—actual objects or fragments of them—but also from a broad array of secondary evidence (Drooker 2001b).

Figure 2.2. Clay cast of "octagonal openwork" (plain twining combined with transposed interlinked warp elements) fabric impressed on pottery, Wickliffe Mounds site, Kentucky.

Attributes of Fabrics and Fabric Objects

Objects in everyday use, such as skirts, shawls, headbands, sandals, mats, bags, baskets, and hunting and fishing nets, sometimes have been preserved as charred fragments or under dry conditions in caves and rockshelters (e.g., Drooker 1992:58–93; Horton 2010; Kuttruff 1987; Kuttruff et al. 1998; Scholtz 1975). Much evidence also has been preserved as impressions on pottery (e.g., Drooker 1990, 1992, 1993, 2001a, 2003; Henderson 2004; Kuttruff and Kuttruff 1996; Pappas 2008; Spanos 2006; Stathakis 1996). Mats and baskets were interlaced in twill patterns using cane or bark strips. Pliable fabrics were produced through the techniques of twining, interlacing, and knotting, with no evidence for the use of mechanical looms. Plant fibers, twisted or spun into yarn, were the most common materials in these ordinary or "subsistence" fabrics. Decoration of everyday fabrics was in the form of simple stripes (created by grouping twining rows and/or using colored yarns) and through lacy geometric designs created by manipulating selected warp elements (Figure 2.2) (see also Drooker 1992: Figures 9, 24–29, 50, 51). Impressions on pottery provide evidence that a type of twined fabric capable of producing bicolored figurative designs like those on eighteenth- to twentieth-century Great Lakes storage and "medicine" bags was being made and used in Mississippian and Caborn-Welborn contexts (Drooker 1992:107, Figures 9d, 17, 26; Pappas 2008: Figure 6–7).[3]

Examples of very fine-scale and elaborate fabrics and basketry, requiring much skill and time to produce, have survived primarily in elite mortuary contexts at Spiro, Etowah, and a few other locations, and occasionally as impressions on ceramics (e.g., Brown 1996:413–416, 422–425, 619–631, 2014; Burnett 1945; Byers 1964; Drooker 1991, 1992 and references therein, 2001a, 2011; Horton 2014; Horton and Sabo 2011; King and Gardner 1981; Kuttruff 1987; Kuttruff and Drooker 2001; Sibley and Jakes 1994; Sibley et al. 1996; Webb and McKinney 1975; Willoughby 1952). Structurally decorated fabrics have also survived as impressions on stone palettes and as pseudomorphs[4] on copper plates, again primarily in mortuary contexts (e.g., Drooker 2004a, 2004b, 2007; Jones 1982: Figure 7a, 1994:130; Steponaitis et al. 2011:94, 96–98). Their functions include large mantles, both plain and feathered, elaborate sashes, portions of headdresses, and containers or wrappings for bundled objects. Some were decorated with painted or resist-dyed designs and others with added elements such as bone or shell beads (e.g., Drooker 1992: Figure 6; King and Gardner 1981: Figure 4; Moorehead 2000 [1932]: Figure 34; Willoughby 1952: Plates 147, 148). Types of pliable fabrics besides those mentioned include very elaborate openwork designs similar to European bobbin lace, made with white or natural plant-fiber yarns, which have come from Spiro, Etowah, and the Stone site in Tennessee (Drooker 1991, 2011:178–181 and references cited), and twined tapestry, in which different-colored wefts are used to build up mosaic-like designs, which is known only from Spiro (e.g., Brown 1996:623–624, Figures 2–155, 2–156; Burnett 1945: Plate 88; King and Gardner 1981: Figures 5, 6; Willoughby 1952: Plates 140, 141). Baskets can be double-walled, and both baskets and mats from burial mound contexts display elaborate geometrical designs (e.g., Brown 1996:420, Figures 2–43 to 2–46; Horton and Sabo 2011; Moorehead 1932: Figure 64; Webb and McKinney 1975), although complex patterned float weave basketry also has come from rock shelters and caves (e.g., Scholtz 1975:87–107). Yarns of both plant fiber and animal fiber are found in fabrics from elite mortuary contexts such as at Spiro and Etowah, as are mixed-fiber yarns such as rabbit hair and plant fiber, or plant fiber, animal fiber, and feathers/down (King and Gardner 1981:124, 126, 128–130; Willoughby 1952: Plates 142, 143). Both their contexts of disposition and the amount of time and skill required to produce them provide evidence that such fabrics can be considered "prestige goods," as opposed to "subsistence goods."

It is worth noting, for reasons explored below, that one technical attribute typical of Mississippian fabrics is the preference for a particular twist direction in yarn construction and twined fabric construction. Over much of the Mississippian world, particularly in the "Middle Mississippi" region, both single- and double-ply yarns, as well as weft twining rows, overwhelmingly tend to be twisted in the "S" direction (Drooker 1992:207); that is, if the yarn or row is held vertical, the slant of the twisted elements is in the direction of the center portion of the letter "S." The opposite twist is known as "Z." Although yarns and fabrics from Spiro and Caddoan Ozarks sites display significantly more "Z" twisting than in regions farther east (Drooker 1992:201–203, 207; Kuttruff 1988a), recent research by Elizabeth Horton has demonstrated a shift over time in Ozark Plateau fabrics from Late Woodland to Mississippian, to larger proportions of final "S" twist in yarns and twining rows for plant-fiber fabrics, but a retention of "Z" twist construction in feather cloth, considered a continuation of an earlier local tradition (Horton 2010:34, 471–478, 485).

Two- and three-dimensional images of Mississippian people provide additional valuable information about garments and adornment made from perishable materials. Representations of Mississippian elites, ancestors, and anthropomorphic supernatural beings in media such as carved and/or engraved stone, engraved shell, copper, and pottery depict elaborate regalia including items made of both durable and perishable materials, the latter incorporating what appear to be woven and twined fabrics, some highly decorated (e.g., Drooker 1992:76–79). Some extant fabrics can be matched to particular images. Together, they can tell us much.

Spanish chroniclers were notably impressed with the quality of Late Mississippian fabrics, writing of the fine mulberry-fiber yarns and "very pretty blankets" made by the women of Ichisi (Rangel in Clayton et al. 1993:I:271) and of "feather mantles (white, [green], vermillion and yellow) . . . rich and elegant for winter" stockpiled near Cutifachiqui (*aka*, Cofitachequi; Elvas in Clayton et al. 1993:I:83).

Fabric Production

Economically, fabrics embodied a large amount of time, energy, and skill. From replication studies, we know that even ordinary garments required on the order of 150 hours or more for gathering and processing materials, spinning the yarn, and constructing the fabric (Drooker 1992:164–170, 226–234, 2011; Ericksen et al. 2000). Smaller-diameter and/or multifiber yarns, structural patterning in fabrics, applied ornamentation such as feathers or beads (e.g., Drooker 1992: Figures 6, 27, 51, 52; Willoughby 1952: Plates 142, 143), and dyes or pigments to add color (e.g., Brown 1996: Figure 2–155; King and Gardner 1981:130, 132; Sibley and Jakes 1994) would multiply that time expenditure greatly, as well as requiring additional skills. It is quite likely that most of this work was accomplished by women (Drooker 1992:11–12, 237). Their expertise, the "power to" fashion a wide range of yarns and fabrics not only exactly suited to their functions but also, in some cases, strikingly elaborate, constituted an important, and sometimes overlooked, contribution to the social economy of their communities and polities.

Was there specialization in Mississippian fabric production? Although each household would have been responsible for producing pliable fabrics and basketry for everyday use, it is quite possible that different tasks, such as plant fiber preparation, yarn spinning, and fabric construction were carried out by different age groups, as is typical, for instance, in the Andes (e.g., Franquemont 1986). Very likely at least part-time specialists—highly experienced craftspeople—created the most elaborate fabric items (Drooker 1991:231–232, 2011:178–182). In the case of ceremonial items (see below), such practitioners likely also would have been ritual specialists.

Because even the most intricate Mississippian fabrics required little in the way of production equipment (at most, a simple frame), it is not surprising that, to date, archaeological evidence for localization or control of fabric production by any particular group has not been found. However, ceramic spindle whorl sizes and clustered distribution in and around the American Bottom do provide evidence for increased and quality-controlled yarn production at particular locations, perhaps indicating "that fiber production was carried out by a few people with an intent to increase production" (Alt 1999:132). In her study of fiber perishables from Ozark bluff shelters, Horton notes a change over time, from Late Woodland to Mississippian, to finer bast fibers for skirts and mantles (2010:505–506). Although the bluff shelter assemblages contained no ceramic spindle whorls, one intact wooden spindle rod with a gourd whorl did survive, and Horton suggests that the combination of finely processed bast fibers and weighted spindle spinning would have made "the production of significant quantities of cloth," including "complex, intricate and high-quality cloth," more feasible (2010:498–499). Spindle spinning is also a viable hypothesis for the large quantities of cloth, including notable amounts of fine-scale and decorated fabrics, impressed on pottery at Mississippian and later Caborn-Welborn sites in the lower Ohio River valley region, where (for instance) more than 200 perforated discs were excavated at the Angel site (Black 1967:457; Drooker 1992: 159, 226–228; Drooker 2007).

Rather than a purely economic concern or a control of prestige-goods production by elite patrons, as some have proposed (e.g., Pauketat 1997a, 1997b), loci of concentrated craft production may be related to reciprocal obligations of corporate groups within the larger society (Kelly 2006). An historical account by a priest accompanying a French expedition on the lower

Mississippi River may give the flavor of Mississippian communal fabric production. During a visit to an Ouma village in 1700, he spent the day in a cabin "filled with women who spin bark and work at the looms. Some of them are wives of the great chief who has been dead for some months" (du Ru 1934:29).

Fabrics and Socioeconomic Power in the Mississippian World

Social, political, economic, and ritual functions of Mississippian fabrics undoubtedly overlapped, like the multiple social identities of their makers and users. I have chosen to discuss fabrics likely associated with social/political/economic relations among humans in "this world," separately from fabrics likely associated with rituals or ceremonies marking relations between humans and other nonhuman beings in the cosmos as a whole. There is some inevitable overlap.

Items of Status, Display, and Wealth

One key function of fabrics, the world over, is that of clothing. Clothing, in turn, is a key item in signaling social identity (or identities), boundaries, and interactions (e.g., Wobst 1977). Colors, symbols, and unique stylistic features associated with a person's clothing can signify age, gender, social or kin group affiliation, and other attributed or acquired statuses. Greater numbers and greater complexity of labor-intensive garments associated with an individual or group can serve as indicators of wealth. Clothing that incorporates highly visible nonlocal objects or materials, such as marine shell or copper, can objectify sociopolitical ties to other polities, and the power(s) that this may imply, on a personal level.

As might be expected, high-ranking Mississippians tended to be associated not only with durable status and wealth items, but also with elaborate fabrics. It is no accident that the largest known assemblages of very high quality (fine-scale, elaborately patterned/decorated, labor-intensive) organic Mississippian fabrics have been associated with elite burial contexts, with the greatest variety and numbers coming from the Great Mound at Spiro (e.g., Brown 1996; Horton 2014; King and Gardner 1981; Kuttruff 1988a, 1988b; Willoughby 1952). Jenna Kuttruff developed and used an index of production complexity to compare fabrics from elite versus nonelite Caddoan Mississippian burials, finding a significant correlation of more-complex fabrics with elite burials (Kuttruff 1988a, 1991, 1993). Fine-scale and elaborate fabrics also are known from elite burials in Etowah's Mound C (e.g., Byers 1964: Figure 14; Drooker 1991: Figure 4; Sibley et al. 1991: Figure 6; Willoughby 2000 [1932]: Figure 34; personal examination). For example, an intricate lace-like fabric was among the wealth of objects accompanying Burial 57, an adult male, which included "8 large conch shell bowls, an engraved shell gorget bearing a representation of an 'eagle warrior,' 2 copper axes, 5 or 6 embossed sheet copper plates, a profusion of shell beads, and 2 copper covered wooden ear discs" (Larson 1971:64; Sibley et al. 1991).

Claudine Payne notes that maintenance of power and authority requires "advertising," which "is most effective when it is easily understood, highly visible, and reaches the largest possible audience" (2002:193). The power of regalia incorporating such "advertising" was not lost on early Spanish visitors. According to Rangel, the cacique of Tascaluça greeted Soto "on a . . . mound to one side of the plaza, about his head a certain headdress like an *almaizar* [type of turban], worn like a Moor, which gave him an appearance of authority, and a *pelote* or blanket of feathers down to his feet, very authoritative" (Rangel in Clayton et al. 1993:I:290).

Other symbolic aspects of ceremonial dress might or might not have been understood by Europeans. For instance, leaders greeting nonlocal visitors often were described as wearing white, the color of stability and peace (cf. Lankford 2008:73–97). The chief of Taensa in Louisiana, visiting a French delegation in 1682, "was clothed in a white robe" (Tonti in Parkman 1892: 281–282), and both the cacica of Cutifachiqui in South Carolina and the cacique of Coosa in Georgia were carried to meet Soto on litters covered with white cloth (Rangel in Clayton et al. 1993:I:278, 284).

A number of extant garments from Mississippian ceremonial center mortuary contexts clearly were designed to convey symbolic information from a distance, some perhaps related to personal status/social persona, others evidently ceremonial or ritual in nature (see discussion below), and many likely serving both purposes. For instance, nine garments from Spiro—five mantles and four woman's skirts—included three mantles featuring very large, repetitive resist-dyed or painted motifs in a contrasting color (Willoughby 1952:117–118, Plates 145–149). Close up, the rabbit hair yarn of all nine garments would signal their difference from the far-more-common garments made from plant fiber. Beyond any symbolism related to color or motifs, coloration and decoration of these fabrics would have required special skills and extra production time, indicative of "wealth"/"prestige" objects. Another example with similar properties came from an elite burial at Etowah: a fine-scale animal-fiber fabric in dark red, decorated with contrasting resist-dyed motifs (Willoughby 1932: Figure 34; personal examination).

Feathered mantles, an eye-catching class of garment also requiring significant investment of time and skill (Drooker 1992:73–74), may or may not have been exclusively, or even primarily, associated with higher-ranking people. Virtually all examples that survived in the archaeological record of

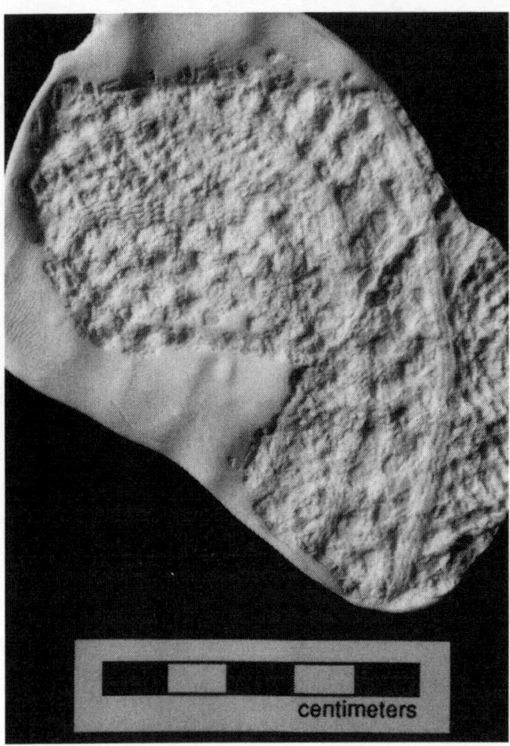

Figure 2.3. Clay cast of decorated fabric impressed on pottery: Roundel design (approx. 10 cm diameter) from an elaborate lace-like fabric, Stone site, Tennessee.

the Southeast were associated with burials, but some of these burials were in caves or rock shelters rather than burial mounds or "elite" cemeteries (e.g., Holmes 1896:29–30; Horton 2010: Table 10.1). Besides feathered fabric fragments and cordage from Spiro's Great Mortuary (e.g., Willoughby 1952: Plates 142–143), about a dozen feathered robes and many fragments, dating from Late Woodland to Mississippian, have come from Ozark rock shelter burials (Horton 2010:344–345, 357, 479–487). Although recognizing historical accounts that clearly link feather robes to "high status individuals, such as male leaders," Horton draws attention to an apparent association in the Ozarks of women and children with feather robes as burial shrouds (Horton 2010:484).

Fabrics from nonelite contexts, such as those impressed on pottery vessels in the lower Ohio River valley, include a variety of structure types that could produce unique motifs suitable for marking social identity (e.g., see figure 2.2; Drooker 1992: Figures 9, 26, 27, 28, 51; Pappas 2008: Figures 5-4, 5-15, 5-18, 5-27, 5-28, 5-29, 6-7). Large numbers of these types of decorated fabrics were produced (Drooker 1992:211, 216–217, 2007). However, except for one notable example from the Stone site in Tennessee (Figure 2.3) (Drooker 1991, 1992:190–192; see discussion below), they did not require levels of skill and time equivalent to those needed for the most elaborate fabrics from Spiro and Etowah, or to robes incorporating feathered cordage. As well, their delicate designs would not have been visible at any great distance.

Fabrics in the Chiefdom Economy

In his analysis of the Moundville economy, Paul Welch considers several models of production, distribution, redistribution, and internal and external exchange of subsistence and prestige goods (1991:6–22). The model that best fit Moundville (1991: Figure 6.1) incorporated (1) subsistence goods produced by local households and distributed to local centers and thence to the paramount center, (2) local prestige goods produced in the paramount center and distributed to local centers as well as being used for external exchange, and (3) nonlocal prestige goods coming in to the paramount center and being redistributed to local centers. Welch notes that this model was specific to Moundville, and that certain lingering questions might be due to the lack of preservation of items made from organic materials. Whether other Mississippian polities conformed to this particular model (see, e.g., Wilson et al. 2006, for a comparison between Moundville and Cahokia), their economies likely all involved internal and external movement of subsistence and prestige goods. Despite the rarity of fabrics in the archaeological record, clearly they were a significant component of this social economy. Their production and distribution would have paralleled those of other goods circulating within and between polities.

Fabric "blankets" made from plant fiber yarn and worn as mantles by both women and men were collected as tribute within sixteenth-century polities such as Cutifachiqui (Elvas in Clayton et al. 1993:74–75). These would have been common fabrics, of the sort likely produced in every household. Their distribution could easily have conformed to that noted for subsistence goods in the Moundville polity. In a number of towns, Spanish chroniclers commented on large *barbacoas* or elevated storage buildings containing shawls, skins, feather mantles, maize, and other items. Stockpiles of clothing, pearls, and weapons also were found in mortuary temples (Elvas in Clayton et al. 1993:75, 83, 87–88). The presence of labor-intensive items such as feather mantles hints at the inclusion of other types of elaborate fabrics that might be considered local prestige goods (e.g., Drooker 1991) among the stored items.

Spanish accounts reveal that the volume of stockpiled fabrics was notable. Caciques and cacicas alike gifted Soto with large quantities of shawls and feathered mantles (e.g., Hodge and Lewis 1907:173, 174, 210), and after Soto's death, the remnants of the *entrada* were able to obtain more than enough blankets to use as sails on the seven brigantines they built to carry themselves down the Mississippi and back to New Spain (Bourne 1904:1:187–191; Clayton et al. 1993:I:151; Hodge and Lewis 1907:173, 174, 209–211). As noted, this large volume of fabrics may have been made possible by the adoption of weighted spindle spinning, which significantly speeds up yarn production, as well as making it easier to produce a consistent product.

Emphasizing the economic, and probably symbolic, importance of stored fabrics is the fact that they were targeted and seized as booty by Native warriors. For instance, during a raid jointly conducted by Soto and the cacique of Guachoya against neighboring Nilco in eastern Arkansas, while the Spaniards butchered Nilco villagers, Guachoya warriors loaded their canoes with clothing from the houses (Elvas in Clayton et al. 1993:135–136). Exhibiting "power over" their enemies undoubtedly involved not only pillage per se but also the element of humiliation. Seizure of clothing might add a very personal insult to that humiliation, as well as an economic blow to local stockpiling.

Although Spanish accounts of "tribute" imply a one-way path for these stockpiled items from lower- to higher-ranking people, they also could have functioned as "communal wealth" (Horton 2010:498). Stockpiled shawls, feather mantles, and other fabrics might have been used in a number of ways; for instance, to clothe high-ranking individuals within a polity, to wrap the honored dead, for upper-level or general redistribution within a polity, and for external gifts and exchange. Whatever the nuances of the system within a given polity, fabrics moving within it, particularly clothing, with its intimate relationship to particular individuals, groups, and statuses, would embody its social and power relations.

Both historical accounts and the archaeological record provide evidence for fabrics as external exchange items. The Soto entrada encountered Natives west of the Mississippi who made salt from local salines to "carry it into other parts, to exchange for skins and shawls" (Hodge and Lewis 1907:218). Spanish leaders also participated in elite-level ceremonial exchanges, of the sort that might take place between leaders of peer polities. Across the entire Southeast, fabric blankets or mantles frequently were presented to Soto by local caciques in greeting ceremonies (e.g., Elvas in Clayton et al. 1993:83, 106, 115, 118, 119, 121, 122, 123, 132, 140; Rangel in Clayton et al. 1993:270). In at least one encounter, feather blankets were presented to the horses (Cañete in Clayton et al. 1993:I:308), which probably were viewed as extraordinary beings worthy of particularly elaborate gifts. (No mention is made of a feather mantle ever being presented to Soto himself.)

Evidence of very long-range movement of fabrics in external exchange networks is provided by a few fragments of plain-weave cotton cloth from Caddoan Mississippian contexts. Cotton fiber was produced no closer to this area than the Rio Grande Valley (Teague 1998: Figure 1.12), more than

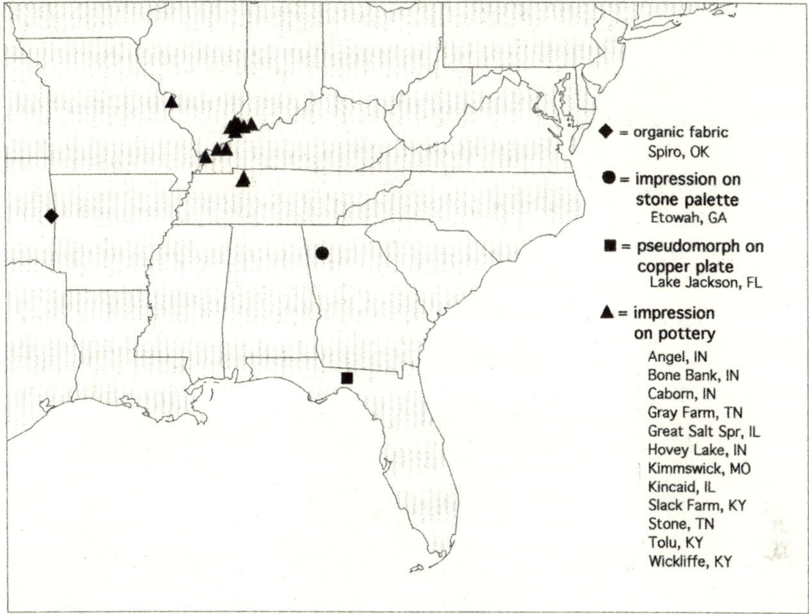

Figure 2.4. Locations of sites from which "octagonal openwork" fabrics are known.

1,000 km away. The best-known transported examples of cotton fabric came from Spiro, where they were located under a stack of copper plates (Brown 1996:621, Figure 2–158). At thirteen single-ply warps and wefts per cm, they are extremely fine-scale. Two additional fragments came from the Ozarks Pine Mountain region Beaver Pond site, a location relatively close to the Arkansas River, which has been suggested as part of a Trans-Plains exchange network (Horton 2010:53, 213–214, 479). These are much coarser than the Spiro example (five doubled or double-ply elements per cm) and are not known to have come from a mortuary context.

Fabric exchange within the Southeast might be represented by the geographical distribution of a distinctive type of twined fabric with structural decorative patterning that is sometimes called "octagonal openwork" (see figure 2.2), which was quite common at Mississippian settlements around the confluence of the Ohio and Mississippi Rivers, such as Wickliffe, Kincaid, and Angel Mounds, and persisted in Caborn-Welborn contexts near the confluence of the Wabash and Ohio Rivers after the mound centers were abandoned (Figure 2.4) (Drooker 1992:41, 101, 108–111, 118–120, 158, 164, 168, 179, 182, 183, 185–191, 198–199, 202, 203, 205, 211, 215–218, 221–222, 225, 228, 230, 236, 240; 2007; Hoyal 2005). In that region (and in a few scattered instances in the Cumberland River valley), octagonal openwork patterns were preserved as impressions on "salt pan" pottery. These impres-

Figure 2.5. Interior surface of copper "hawk man" plate from Burial 16, Mound 3, Lake Jackson, Florida, with adhered "octagonal openwork" fabric, probably preserved as pseudomorphs. Note presence of fabric on both sides of plate (courtesy of Florida Division of Historical Resources).

sions were most likely made from nonelite fabrics originally used as skirts and mantles. Outside that region, however, the few known occurrences of this fabric structure are from elite burial contexts: organic fragments from the Great Mortuary at Spiro (Brown 1996:624, Figure 2–154b); impressions on a ritual stone palette at Etowah, probably from use as a bundle wrapper (Steponaitis et al. 2011:96–97); and fragments preserved on both sides of an elaborate copper "hawk man dancer" breast plate associated with an adult burial in Mound 3 at Lake Jackson, Florida (Figure 2.5) (Drooker 2007; Jones 1982: Figure 7a, 1994:125–126; see also Trocolli 2002:176–178). Again, this fabric probably served as a wrapper for the plate. It seems possible that the octagonal openwork fabrics found in elite burial contexts at the three Mississippian paramount centers may have been made elsewhere, travelling to their eventual ritually charged resting places through high-level exchange. Although relatively easy to make and common in their homeland, these lacy, decorative fabrics could have been highly valued in distant regions where they were not being produced.

Fabrics and Ritual Power in the Mississippian World

Since Antonio Waring and Preston Holder's seminal discussion of Southeastern Ceremonial Complex (SECC) objects and motifs (1945), much research, analysis, speculation, debate, and consultation has been lavished on the study of SECC and other Mississippian iconography and what it, together with ethnohistorical information, can tell us about Mississippian peoples' belief systems and (power) relationships between themselves and other beings in their cosmos (e.g., Galloway 1989; King 2007; Lankford 2008; Lankford et al. 2011; Reilly and Garber 2007a). In discussing the history of SECC studies, Kent Reilly and James Garber note that "this Mississippian Period artistic tradition consists of the artifacts, symbols, motifs, and architectural groupings that provide the physical evidence for the ritual activities practiced by the numerous ethnic groups comprising the demographic and cultural landscape of the Mississippian Period. It is also the discernible cosmology, ideology, and political structures of those various Mississippian Period groups" (Reilly and Garber 2007b:1).

Vernon James Knight has made the case that Mississippian "symbolic objects for ceremonial display, or *sacra* . . . suggest a triad of coexisting types of cult institution: (1) a communal cult type emphasizing earth/fertility and purification ritual, (2) a chiefly cult type serving to sanctify chiefly authority, and (3) a priestly cult type mediating between the other two, supervising mortuary ritual and ancestor veneration" (Knight 1986:675). Mississippian fabrics have a special niche in this ritual landscape.

Fabrics can serve as objects or markers of ritual power through visual characteristics that indicate their association with particular important ceremonies and/or powerful beings, as well as through subtle inherent characteristics that embody particular aspects of the cosmos. Certain fabrics might have physical characteristics with obvious ritual connections, and/or their depositional contexts might hold the key to understanding their ritual significance. Two important functions that fabrics served in Mississippian ritual life were as ceremonial regalia and as containers or wrappings for ritual objects, but even everyday fabrics may have manifested ritual aspects of a broadly shared worldview.

Recognizing Ritual Power from a Distance

Ceremonial garments are significant for their ability to signal the roles of their wearers as communicators with powerful beings or as actual embodiments of such beings. Both chiefly and priestly roles can be embodied.[5] Attributes of ceremonial garments and related fabrics that can signify particular meanings include form, color, and motif. Large-scale, highly visible attributes are typical of fabrics worn or used in public ceremonies.

The most spectacular examples of likely ceremonial garments come from the Great Mortuary at Spiro. Intricate, labor-intensive tapestry fragments depicting feathers, weeping eyes, and the "tied animal" motif in yellow, red, and black are described by King and Gardner as "the first known instance

Figure 2.6. Twined tapestry fragment, Great Mortuary, Spiro, Oklahoma. Eye motifs, probably bird heads (courtesy of Department of Anthropology, Smithsonian Institution; catalog no. 423,373).

of truly representational design in Spiro textiles" (1981:132, Figures 5, 6) (Figure 2.6). They suggest that these might have been remnants of "capes with large, full human figures," like those depicted on some birdman copper plates and marine shell objects (Brown 2007; King and Gardner 1981: Figure 7; Strong 1989). James Brown provides a slightly different interpretation, noting that a particular large fragment depicting feathers (Figure 2.7) (Brown 1985: Figure 23; Burnett 1945:45, Plate 88;) could have been part of "a suitable cloak or mantle to simulate the wings of a bird, such as the falcon. This sort of garment could easily have been used in the costumery implied in the depictions of the falcon impersonator" (1996:623). Its design, rendered in contrasting colors, would have been strikingly visible from a distance. Brown notes that this cloth fragment was associated "with falcon copper plates in a high status copper plate burial (A6a)" (1996:624). Yarns included both plant and animal fibers (Brown 1996:623).

Fragments of feathered garments were recovered at both Spiro and Etowah (Brown 1996:622–623; Sibley et al. 1996). Although none of the Etowah fragments was large enough to distinguish whether particular motifs were present, it is possible that some of them, too, were designed to depict symbolism related to birdmen. At a minimum, comparable colors were present. For instance, chemical analysis of a feathered Etowah fabric from an extremely rich burial showed that the feathers were dyed red and gold (Sibley and Jakes 1994). That is, the colors did not come simply from collecting feathers of a particular hue, but by expending effort and skill to produce exactly what was required or desired.

One aspect of the birdman concept relates to conflict (Brown 2007:85–87).

Figure 2.7. Twined tapestry fragments, Great Mortuary, Spiro, Oklahoma. Feather motifs; largest fragment 31.75 cm (12.5 in) wide (courtesy of the National Museum of the American Indian, Smithsonian Institution [18/9351]; photo by NMAI Photo Services).

The master of ceremonies for the interment of the Great War Chief of the Natchez in 1725 wore a headdress with red feathers and a knee-length garment ornamented with feathers in alternate rows of red and black (Willoughby 2000 [1932]:42). It is possible that this priestly role involved regalia specific to the chiefly role of the deceased.

Brown mentions other motifs rendered in twined tapestry excavated at Spiro, including "flag" and "key" designs that "would be appropriate for a serpent cloak, which is often so rendered in engraved shell representations" (1996:624).

The five dark red, rabbit hair mantles from Spiro included one with a highly visible crenelated design and two that featured motifs of large

(~15–38 cm diameter) concentric circles or half circles in yellow or off-white. The latter originally were interpreted as sun symbols (Willoughby 1952:145–148) but appear to have multiple associations in Mississippian art, including serpents, winged serpents, and piasas (e.g., Lankford 2007a: Figures 5.1, 5.6; Phillips and Brown 1978: Figures 254, 257, 260, 262), among many other contexts. Concentric circles also were a prominent design feature in an extremely elaborate lace-like plant fiber fabric from the Stone site, a stone-box-grave site in Tennessee's Cumberland River valley (see figure 2.3) (Drooker 1991, 1992:190–192; 2011: Figures 9, 10).

On a somewhat smaller scale, but still visibly striking, is a dark red, animal fiber fabric from Grave 19, Mound C, Etowah, decorated with 6–7-cm diameter cross, circle, and cross-in-circle motifs in yellow or off-white (Willoughby 2000[1932: Figure 34; personal examination]). The cross-and-circle motif, common in Mississippian iconography and related to core cosmological concepts (e.g., Brain and Phillips 1996:25–37; Hall 1997:98–100; Lankford 2007a; Phillips and Brown 1978:150; Waring and Holder 1945: Figures 2, 4), is incorporated into a number of elite mortuary fabrics that could have functioned as ritual garments. Besides being realized in contrasting colors on the surface of the Etowah fabric, it occurs in a much subtler, smaller-scale version (approximately 1-cm diameter motifs), worked into the structure of a complex lacy fabric from Spiro (Brown 1996:624, Figure 2–157; Drooker 1991: Figure 3).

Colors as well as symbols in these garments undoubtedly were significant. For instance, Tom Emerson and Tim Pauketat draw attention to the ubiquity of white and, particularly, red pigment in public spaces at Cahokia after the metaphorical "Big Bang," (2002:113–114; see also Lankford 2008: 73–97 on the ethnohistorical significance of these colors).[6]

In addition to tapestry mantles that perhaps replicate the garb of powerful birdmen or serpent men, other known Mississippian fabrics might replicate clothing associated with particular mythical beings depicted in stone, metal, shell, or clay. A possible example comes from the middle Cumberland Valley in Tennessee.

Pottery effigies of women depicted as wearing patterned shawls were deposited as grave goods with many subadult burials in Cumberland Valley stone box graves. These include both older and younger versions of what is probably a single personage. A recent study by members of the Mississippian Iconography Workshop included more than two dozen examples of this effigy figure, concluding that it "is without doubt the single most important subject in the pottery of the Middle Cumberland Culture," who might represent a "possibly supernatural personage who was venerated or invoked in the practices of a mortuary cult complex across the Cumberland

River basin" (Sharp et al. 2011:178, 195–196). The negative-painted garment on these figures is distinctive, typically incorporating shoulder roundels, parallel vertical or diagonal lines, and a prominent crosscutting horizontal stripe(s) (e.g., Sharp et al. 2011: Figures 8.4–8.6; see also Drooker 1992:77, 79, Figure 19). It can be distinguished from a depiction of body paint or tattoos by the fact that its design is continuous across arms and body.

Although this design is complex, it could have been rendered in "octagonal openwork" (see figure 2.2), a fairly straightforward technique that was common in fabrics impressed on pottery in the region surrounding the Ohio-Mississippi River juncture (see figure 2.4). This technique is known from at least two Cumberland Valley sites in Stewart County, Tennessee, one of the seven counties from which the effigy figures have come (Sharp et al. 2011:178). However, contrast between the two textures in this type of fabric would not have been strong, so that even large-scale designs would not be prominently visible from a distance.

A better candidate can be seen in the elaborate lace-like fabric from the Stone site in Stewart County, which actually included a prominently visible roundel of the correct scale (~10 cm diameter) (see figure 2.3), as noted by Sharp et al. (2011:183). Unlike other known complex fabrics from the Southeast, this one was preserved as an impression on a pottery vessel discarded in a pit lined with charcoal and containing a variety of food remains, which the excavators tentatively interpreted as "some kind of cooking pit later filled in with the garbage from the feast" (Coe and Fischer 1959:48). Replicating the shawl designs depicted on Cumberland Valley female pottery figures using this technique certainly could be done, but only with a very large investment of time and skill (Drooker 1991:80–82, 1992:190–192, 2011:178–181). If such effigy figures indeed represent a supernatural personage invoked during mortuary practices, particular women might have worn shawls of similar design during funerary rituals, honoring and perhaps embodying this personage. To speculate wildly, the Stone site fabric, which seems incongruously elaborate to have been employed in the production of a pottery vessel, could have been deliberately impressed on a vessel associated with funerary feasting.

In historical times, a double-faced twining technique using two contrasting yarn colors was employed to depict symbolism of This World, the Upper World, and the Under World on Great Lakes medicine bags. One side often would show an Upper World symbol or being such as Thunderbird, and the other a This World being such as a deer or an Under World being such as Underwater Panther (Drooker 1992:69–72; Phillips 1989; Whiteford 1977a, 1977b; see also Krutak 2013:137–138). A similar double-faced fabric structure has been found impressed on pottery from thirteenth-century contexts at the Wickliffe Mounds site in Kentucky, although the fragment was not large enough to infer any depiction (Drooker 1992:106–108, Figure 9c), as well as on a sherd from the ca. fifteenth-century Caborn-Welborn Slack Farm site, Kentucky (Pappas 2008:23, Figure 6–7, third image). Such a fabric might have been used to produce thirteenth-century medicine bags, but the technique did afford a means of depicting representational motifs of symbolic power by a more economical method (in terms of time and materials) than twined tapestry.

"Secret" Symbolism in Mississippian Fabrics

Symbolism in Mississippian fabrics went beyond visible colors and motifs. For instance, yarn materials and subtle details of yarn and fabric construction may also have embodied significant aspects of Mississippian beliefs with respect to ritual power.

Mississippian fabrics made of animal hair or containing combinations of animal and plant fibers are known primarily from elite mortuary contexts (see above). All yarns analyzed from Spiro twined tapestry fabrics consist of mixed fibers, always including animal hair (Kuttruff 1988a:224–231, 254–261). Fiber combinations could be due to technical considerations, since animal hair such as rabbit is slippery and difficult to spin alone. However, an in-depth analysis of a variety of samples from Spiro found surprising fibers and combinations of fibers in most of them (King and Gardner 1981:126–130). Feather fragments and down were spun together in some yarns, with down coming from turkeys (or other gallinaceous birds) and geese. Most analyzed yarns contained mammal hair (probably mostly rabbit), small amounts of plant fiber, and down. Unfortunately, the published information from this study does not provide data about the fabric sources for the analyzed yarns, so any connection between symbolic meaning and ritual function cannot be considered. However, it certainly seems likely that these laboriously constructed yarns objectify some relationship between This World and the Above World, perhaps related to powerful composite beings such as birdmen. Fiber from particular animals and birds might well hold very specific ritual meanings (e.g., turkey as a war symbol [King and Gardner 1981:132]).

As noted before, Mississippian yarns, both single- and double-ply, consistently exhibit a final "S" twist, as do rows of twining within fabrics. Double-ply yarns typically were formed by twisting together two single-ply yarns twisted in the "Z" direction, so the choice of final twist direction obviously was not driven by a technical limitation. Where temporal differences could be compared, an increase of "S" twisting over time was apparent (see Drooker 1992:201–231, particularly 207, 218, 220, 227; Horton 2010:354, 471–478). What might have been the significance of this attribute?

The ethnohistorical record does include some instances of ritual choice for particular directions of yarn spinning, such as Peruvian yarns that were counterspun to avert black magic (Kerner 1963). However, I was unable to develop a specific hypothesis for this widespread and consistent "community of practice" (cf. Minar 2001) in Mississippian yarn and fabric production. I was intrigued, then, to learn of research by Laura Kozuch (1998), who suggests that the overwhelming presence at Mississippian archaeological sites of sinistrally coiled whelk shells, rather than equally available large marine shells coiled in the opposite direction, might be, at least in part, an ideational choice. She demonstrates a congruence among the whelk spiral direction, clockwise-spiraling ramp access to the tops of certain Mississippian mounds, Creek sacred fire construction, and the inward-spiraling clockwise direction taken by male dancers described in early European accounts (1998:122–145). Kozuch notes that "ethnohistoric and ethnographic accounts in the Southeast indicate that sinistral spirals were sacred, akin to the clockwise path of the sun" (1998:133). This spiraling direction is also congruent with the visible lines in S-twisted yarns and twining rows. The consistent, widespread occurrence of S-twisting in both ordinary and ceremonial fabric items thus may express a basic aspect of the Mississippian belief system, perhaps providing access to ritual power for all who used them.

Mississippian Fabrics from Ritual Contexts

Fabrics from the archaeological record may incorporate attributes that immediately signal their significance in Mississippian ritual life to modern researchers. However, as with other types of artifacts, contexts of deposition can tell us much, and ethnohistorical accounts can provide potential models for testing.

Mortuary contexts, with their direct associations between individuals and objects, are perhaps the most evocative, and a number of instances have been discussed above. In her study of Ozark Plateau fabric traditions, Horton (2010) draws particular attention to feather cloth associations with burials, but she also notes strong evidence that most if not all burials in this region were wrapped in some way, whether by "hide, cloth or basketry." She further observes that "shrouding, bundling, and containing are mean[s] of both respecting ancestors and protecting descendants from the dead" (2010: 480–481). Although some people wore recognizable clothing, many more were wrapped in a sequence of textiles and hides, with bundles tied by fiber or hide cords, and placement on "beds" of matting or grass (Horton 2010:481–483). Here and elsewhere it is unclear whether such wrappings were specially prepared "burial shrouds" or materials that happened to be on hand, but their ritual importance is clear.

Fabrics also often "clothe" objects of power. Wrappers and containers for ritual objects and bundles may have some parallels with ritual wrappings for the dead, serving as both a protection for the objects and a shield for the people who might inadvertently come in contact with them. Some examples from the Mississippian archaeological record include a repoussé "hawk dancer" copper plate interred with a burial at Lake Jackson, Florida, which was wrapped in "octagonal openwork" fabric (see figure 2.5; see above for additional information); copper turtle-effigy rattles and copper-covered bone items wrapped in fabric, matting, and animal viscera or skins from the large Mitchell Mound near Cahokia (Pauketat 1994:84; Winters 1974: 39–41); objects such as a headdress and copper plates, some wrapped with hide, associated with elaborate, distinctive lidded baskets at Spiro (Brown 1996:414, 416; Horton and Sabo 2011); and four stone palettes bundled with minerals and pigments with impressions of five different twined fabrics on sides and bottoms (Steponaitis et al. 2011; the authors also note additional bundles from Mississippian contexts, including Etowah, the Pickwick Basin, and elsewhere [2011:101]).

Again, it is not always clear whether such wrappings were specially created for that purpose. For instance, the palette bundles from Moundville appear to have been wrapped with a variety of typical everyday fabrics, one of which might have been an import, but otherwise with no particular distinguishing features (Drooker 2004a, 2004b; Steponaitis et al. 2011:96–97). Only their placement indicates their significance. Although historical bundles often incorporate specially constructed wrappings for contained objects (e.g., Kelly 2006: Table 12–1; Krutak 2013:137–139), in some cases European machine-made cloth was used (e.g., Gilmore 1932a:45, 46). Whether such cloth was chosen because it was deemed "special" or its use was merely expedient is not clear.

The recent discovery, through re-analysis of the disturbed archaeological record at Spiro, of a "Spirit Lodge" within the Craig Mound (Brown 2014; Horton 2014) might be thought of as a macro sacred bundle. This defined space, a late addition to the mound that contained sacred bundles and regalia, appears to have been hung with colorful tapestries (some previously interpreted as garments) that might have been made specifically for the Spirit Lodge. Both unique, labor-intensive fabrics and unique, labor-intensive double-woven cane baskets featured prominently in this sacred space.

Conclusion

Just as with other, more durable types of materials and artifacts, fabrics can be demonstrated as actively participating in many aspects of Mississippian social, political, economic, and ritual power relations.

The examples discussed here only scratch the surface of the intimate association of constructed fabrics with social, political, economic, and spiritual "power over" and "power with" within the Mississippian world. Fabric producers, who most likely were women (Drooker 1992:11–12; Kehoe 2001), wielded the "power to" create these important objects. Through both primary and secondary evidence, Mississippian fabrics can provide multifaceted insights into the power relations of their makers and users.

Acknowledgments

This chapter is based on a 2001 presentation, "Mississippian Fabrics as Power Symbols," which was part of a Society for American Archaeology (SAA) conference symposium, "Textiles and the Negotiation of Power," sponsored by the Fiber Perishables Interest Group (FPIG) and organized by Linda Neff and Penelope Drooker. It also incorporates aspects of a 2007 SAA paper, "'Octagonal Openwork' and Mississippian Boundaries," that was part of another FPIG-sponsored SAA symposium, "A New Look at a Common Dilemma: Perishables and the Definition of Boundaries," organized by Christina Pappas. My sincere thanks to everyone involved with these symposia, particularly discussants Mary Helms and James M. Adovasio.

I am deeply and sincerely grateful to Judith Knight, who shepherded my novice manuscript for *Mississippian Village Textiles at Wickliffe*—the initial product of my fascination with Southeastern fabrics—through multiple rounds of what felt like crushing critical review. Her tough but positive guidance was essential to the finished product and stands as my ideal for editorial direction.

Notes

1. Prestige goods, display goods, and skillfully crafted goods are terms often but not always used synonymously to signify "artifacts that are rare, non-utilitarian, and ornately crafted," often of nonlocal production and/or made from nonlocal materials (quotation from Marcoux 2007:243, who prefers to use display goods for such objects in the Moundville political economy). Although the term "prestige goods" comes with some baggage—in that it is sometimes explicitly associated with nonlocal objects/materials (e.g., Pauketat 1994:20–21)—I have chosen to use it throughout this chapter for both local and nonlocal "luxury" goods.

2. For additional theoretical overviews and perspectives, see also, e.g., Emerson and Pauketat 2002:119–120; Feinman 2002; Miller and Tilley 1984; O'Donovan 2002; Payne 2002:190–195.

3. For more information on particular materials, techniques, tools, and fabric structures, see, e.g., Drooker 1990, 1991, 1992, 1993; Kuttruff 1988a, 1988b.

4. A pseudomorph is "a mineral, usually a metal corrosion product, that completely

covers and replicates the form of a perishable object such as a yarn or feather" (Drooker and Webster 2000:272).

5. In some Mississippian polities and time periods, ritual power and politico-economic power/authority may have been so closely connected that they, and their markers, might be indistinguishable. For instance, during the development of the Moundville polity, elites were increasingly distanced from nonelites, symbolized by their "restricted access to a cosmologically charged, ceremonial regalia" representing chiefly cult symbolism (Beck 2006:32–33; see also, e.g., King 2004; Marceaux and Dye 2007; Payne 2006:104–106; Trocolli 2002; cf. Brown 2006).

6. The "Big Bang" pertains to a "rapid political consolidation at Cahokia" ca. A.D. 1050—"archaeologically, a virtually instantaneous and pervasive shift in all things political, social, and ideological" (Emerson and Pauketat 2002:109).

3

REVITALIZATION MOVEMENTS IN THE PREHISTORIC SOUTHEAST?

An Example from the Irene Site

Rebecca Saunders

Mississippian expansion from ca. A.D. 1050 to 1200 involved major realignments in many aspects of Native American life. Mississippianization at Cahokia involved dramatic changes in material culture, architecture, organization of space, large-scale population resettlement, mound construction, public feasts, and public deaths (Pauketat 2002). By A.D. 1050, these ingredients coalesced, perhaps around a religious leader, producing an "explosive flashpoint"—Pauketat's (1991, 2002) metaphorical "Big Bang." These changes reverberated throughout much of eastern North America. Although complex political and ritual hierarchies, most notably those involved in the Hopewell phenomenon, had emerged previously in the East, the scale and depth of social change involving subsistence, settlement patterning, the built environment, and strict political and social controls were unparalleled. Although never static, even in its birthplace, recognizable aspects of Mississippian culture ramified from Cahokia to most regions of the Southeast, including the Georgia coast, by A.D. 1250 (Figure 3.1). In some areas, Mississippian traits spread rapidly. Philip Phillips (1970b) refers to this movement down the lower Mississippi River as *Sturm und Drang*, for the dramatic social upheaval it apparently represented. Phillips's appraisal is a reflection of limited excavation and more recent interpretations are more nuanced. Indeed, in some areas, such as the Plaquemine region of central and southern Louisiana, Mississippian characteristics sat lightly indeed.

On the Georgia coast, Mississippi-period sites were less centralized, and political hierarchies were "less developed and less permanent" than at interior sites (Pluckhahn and McKivergan 2002:149). Although a loose affiliation with Middle Mississippian cultures of northern Georgia is apparent in the surface decoration of coastal Savannah Complicated Stamped pottery, only a single site on the coast—the Irene site (ca. A.D. 1150–1450)—contains a substantial platform mound. In addition, at Irene, after some 150 years

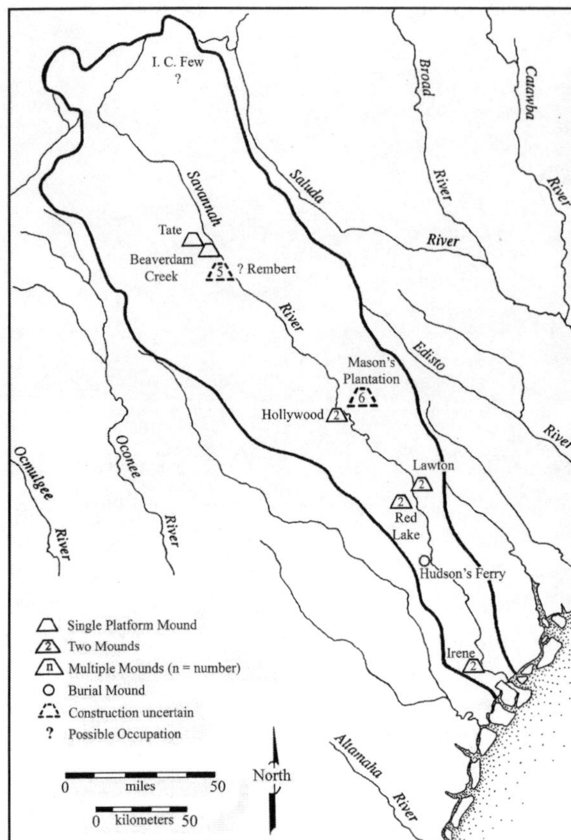

Figure 3.1. Location of the Irene site at A.D. 1250, the height of Mississippian expansion in the Savannah River Valley (Anderson 1994: Figure 42; courtesy of the University of Alabama Press).

of involvement with Mississippian elite-dominated lifeways, a chiefly regime was overturned in an evident example of a late prehistoric revitalization movement.

In this chapter, I review aspects of waxing and waning Mississippian influence in the late prehistoric Southeast, first with a broad brush, and then through the lens of activities at the Irene site.[1] Waselkov and Dumas (2009) make the case for a protohistoric revitalization movement at the turn of the seventeenth century that materialized on pottery by the use of a subset of "root cosmological symbols," which had originally appeared on Ramey Incised pottery in the Cahokia area centuries before. The root cosmological symbols, or cosmograms,[2] represented The Upper World, The Middle World, and The Lower World. Seen from above, the design layout around the circular vessel mouth references the quadripartite world symbol (Figure 3.2)—the cross-in-circle motif that represented the ordered cosmos. Ramey Incised jars were "quasi-sacred" wares produced for ritual use by a few pot-

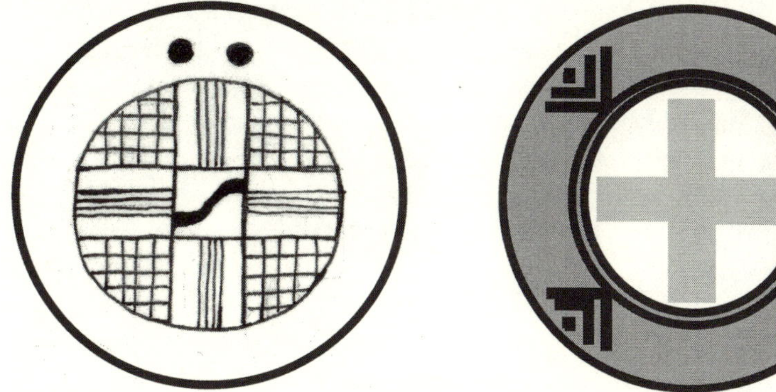

Figure 3.2. (Left) shell gorget with cross-in-circle design (after Holmes 1883: Plate LII; drawing by Sydney Szot McGraw). (Right) Ramey incised vessel as cross-in-circle (Pauketat and Emerson 1991: Figure 10F; reproduced by permission of the American Anthropological Association from *American Anthropologist* 93[4 December 1991]:919–941; not for sale or further reproduction).

ters in the American Bottom. When wielded by the elite during rituals, artifacts bearing root cosmological symbols (including the world symbol) simultaneously demonstrated elite identity and legitimated the authority of elites (Pauketat and Emerson 1991). Ramey Incised pottery was used as an elite ware in early and middle Mississippian societies of the eleventh and twelfth centuries. After that, the symbolism evidently changed in form and meaning—through time and from society to society—in complex ways we are only beginning to understand. It seems clear, however, that pottery bearing these designs was no longer restricted to the elite. While the details need to be worked out, a widespread resurgence in the use of these cosmograms apparently took place during the terminal or post-Mississippian period. Waselkov and Dumas note (2009:7) that "their use during the protohistoric is remarkably far flung, and apparently began abruptly at some point between the Spanish intrusions of the mid-sixteenth century and the mid-seventeenth."

Waselkov and Dumas (2009) theorize that the communalization of these symbols by the turn of the seventeenth century was brought about by social collapses in the protohistoric period. Along with other evidence of widespread societal change—like the appearance of square grounds—the resurgence of these symbols indicated a revitalization movement: "The panregional protohistoric distribution of the pottery cosmograms, a stylistic horizon, as additions to traditional local ceramic complexes, reflects broad acceptance of the revitalization doctrine. This widely shared world view, reformulated to promote community integration, must also have aided in the coalescence of disparate peoples who created new societal identities that crosscut linguistic and established ethnic lines" (Waselkov and Dumas 2009:13).

I reviewed the case of the Irene site, where a seven-stage, Savannah-period (Middle Mississippian) platform mound was abandoned around A.D. 1300 and then buried by subsequent Irene-period (Late Mississippian) peoples. The burial and reshaping of the mound required a volume of earth equal to or greater than the first seven stages of mound construction combined (Anderson 1994:180). In addition to eradicating the platform mound, the layout of the ceremonial center was completely reconfigured, apparently to provide more access to the refurbished mound. In addition, Savannah pottery was abruptly replaced with Irene pottery, which, at the Irene site, bore a single design motif (Caldwell and McCann 1941:47)—the filfot cross, another specific representation of the quadripartite world symbol (cross in circle) representing the cosmos. Changes in stable isotope values determined for different burial populations at the site indicate a considerable reduction in maize consumption during the Irene period, and changes in skeletal attributes suggesting alterations in postmarital residence practices. Indeed, in their initial site reports, Caldwell and McCann (1941) and Hulse (1941) recognized that the reorganization of the site reflected major changes in social structure, and they presented their respective analyses with this reorganization as the fulcrum. However, they lacked the vocabulary that would emerge with Anthony Wallace's (1956) formal definition of revitalization movements.

Despite the relatively abundant documentation of social changes at Irene (Anderson 1994; Crook 1986), new data and new theoretical approaches provide the basis for a reappraisal, and the ability to make an even stronger case for a revitalization movement at the site. For instance, agency theory is particularly appropriate to the study of revitalization movements, considering both the agency of people and the agency, or materiality, of things (Liebmann 2008). This case study joins only a few identifications of revitalization movements in the archaeological literature, and even fewer in the prehistoric record. The Irene people were successful in their revitalization, which is important in its own right because the most famous Native American revitalization movements are notable for their failures.

Before examining this case study, we should consider what constitutes a revitalization movement. Although other authors, such as Linton (1943), had previously discussed nativistic movements, Wallace (1956) was the first to bring nativism into a broader theoretical concern with revitalization in general. In his 1956 summary of the concept, Wallace states: "The revitalization movement as a general type of event occurs under two conditions:

high stress for individual members of the society, and disillusionment with a distorted cultural *Gestalt*. The movement follows a series of functional states: mazeway reformation, communication, organization, adaptation, cultural transformation, and routinization. Movements vary along several dimensions . . . [including] choice of identification, relative degree of religious and secular emphasis, nativism, and success or failure. . . . The movement is usually conceived in a prophet's revelatory visions, which provided for him a satisfying relationship to the supernatural and outline a new way of life under divine sanction" (Wallace 1956:279).

Wallace notes that revitalization movements are common; millenarian, nativistic, revivalistic, and messianic movements, along with cargo cults, can all be subsumed under the rubric. Critical to Wallace's concept (and presaging agency theory), in revitalization movements significant culture change is deliberate and abrupt, involving simultaneous shifts in many different aspects of a society. Wallace insisted that individuals in a society must be aware of the structural flaws in their system; individuals must be under stress for a revitalization movement to emerge; and individuals are responsible for the creation and maintenance of the movement. Stressors (clearly not mutually exclusive) include climate change, military takeover, political subordination, epidemics, and so forth; "The situation is often, but not necessarily, one of acculturation" (Wallace 1956:269). In addition, whereas nativism is often a part of revitalization movements, a return to a better past is often not in the original formulation of the movement and the degree of nativism in any particular movement varies considerably.

In a foreword to a volume edited by Harkin (2004a) on revitalization movements in North America and Micronesia, Wallace reflects that his early exposition of the theory was "rather abstract and perhaps fails to attend sufficiently to the unique texture of cultural and historical circumstances" (Wallace 2004:viii). His initial explication did incorporate the paradigmatic dogmas of the day—vacillation toward an equilibrium inherent in systems theory, incipient processualism in proscribing a specific set and series of stages, and abstractions from the school of culture and personality (Vokes 2007), to name a few. However, throughout the early work, Wallace insists that there is considerable variation in the expression of revitalization movements, and that "situational factors" must be taken into consideration (Wallace 1956:278). One could easily remove the dated dogma and the residual would be on the road to Historical Processualism, with a considerable dose of agency theory.

In any event, Wallace (2004) recognizes the need for an update of the concept, but he leaves that task for others. Harkin's volume contains many critiques of Wallace's concept (most of which focuses on its outdated paradigms and its conflict with the antigeneralizing spirit of late twentieth-century anthropology) and offers many different modern approaches to the study of revitalization movements. In two widely separated ethnographic examples, Henry (2004, Tahiti) and McMullen (2004, southeastern New England) reference the concept of "invented tradition" as inherent in revitalization movements as defined by Wallace. Invented, "reinvented" (Henry 2004), "created" (Liebmann 2008), or "negotiated" (Saunders 2001) traditions are particularly useful concepts for archaeologists, who can view long-term changes in material culture to analyze not only causes of revitalization movements, but also their long-term effects (Liebmann 2008). Indeed, in his study of the 1680 Pueblo Revolt as a revitalization movement, Liebmann delves considerably further into agency theory than did either Henry or McMullen. Liebmann emphasizes the agency of material culture in revitalization movements, whereby material culture proves crucial in "effecting and mediating revitalization" and creating traditions.[3] Further, "a focus on materiality suggests that the distinctive types of artifacts produced by revitalization movements are not secondary to these processes but, rather, are crucially constitutive of revitalizing phenomena, playing essential roles in their organization, legitimation, and performance. This forces us to consider why revitalization is expressed through a particular medium" (Liebmann 2008:361).

Liebmann offers solid documentary evidence for a revitalization movement and was able to tie the documentary evidence to archaeological materializations: construction of new villages with novel intrasite settlement patterns and the replacement of Jemez Black and White pottery, an ethnic marker, with a new type, Historic Red. Other postrevolt Pueblo peoples also produced Historic Red pottery, creating a "region-wide stylistic horizon" and "a unity that cross-cuts language groups and other important social differences among the Pueblos" (Mills 2002:95)—exactly what Waselkov and Dumas (2009) describe for their protohistoric Southeastern wares.

The long-term study of the Pueblo Revolt (Preucel 2002) is an excellent example of the value of Historical Archaeology to studies of the precolonial past. The documentary evidence provides indisputable evidence of a revitalization movement and the archaeological evidence provides us with patterns—in this case dramatic and abrupt changes in site layout and pottery styles—that can be used with other lines of evidence to suggest the presence of revitalization movements in the absence of the documentary record. As will be seen, the Irene folk also built new spaces and created new pottery types to forge new communities of practice—and possibly new social identities—after the overthrow of an overbearing elite.

Mississipianisms

In the context of this chapter, it is a bit ironic to note that the Southeastern Ceremonial Complex (SECC) was once considered a revitalization movement (Fairbanks 1981; Harkin 2004b:xvii also refers to the Mississippian "death cult" as a revitalization movement). However, neither the SECC in general nor the iconography of warfare that marks a certain period in its development (A.D. 1150–1300) meets the definition of revitalization movements. Most fundamentally, the SECC was an elite-driven phenomenon, not a rebellion of a subordinate class. The Mississippian way of life emerged in and around Cahokia between A.D. 1100 and 1150. Population at Cahokia and surrounding sites increased dramatically, probably by in-migration, and heretofore unseen levels of hierarchy emerged. Hierarchies were materialized in huge earthworks and the ritual display of exotic artifacts of exquisite manufacture. Intensive maize agriculture replaced a mixed hunting, gathering, and fishing subsistence economy. As noted, access to SECC objects was restricted to the elite and, although some of the subject matter concerns mythical beings, "references are primarily to the celestial realm of a layered cosmos" (Knight et al. 2001:129). The aforementioned Ramey pottery allowed the elite to wield cosmological symbols at ritual feasts, but it appears that ultimately the pots were redistributed to commoners, because shell-tempered Ramey Incised is a low-frequency but ubiquitous find in early farmstead and hamlet sites (Pauketat and Emerson 1991). Ultimately, the most widespread trait of Mississippian society for archaeologists to follow is shell-tempered pottery, an innovation that had practical implications but also may have functioned as a cultural identifier.

Aspects of Mississippian culture spread, either by colonization or emulation, throughout the Southeast, where local cultures adopted and reinterpreted what was useful. Throughout the Southeast, this expansion and reinterpretation continued until it reached a maximum penetration around A.D. 1250. Shortly after, whether because of drought, deforestation, disillusionment, or—more likely—a complex brew of factors, Cahokia was abandoned. A single primary center was replaced with numerous regional centers, all remarkable in their own right, but each significantly smaller than Cahokia. At this point, the "communalization" of SECC symbolism becomes apparent, when icons assignable to what Knight (1986, 1997:246) calls the "cosmogony complex" appeared "in the very commonplace medium of incised or engraved decoration on pottery" among cultures in Alabama. Parallels with the protohistoric case described by Waselkov and Dumas are clear.

In Georgia, as in many other areas of the Southeast, this communalization was coincident with a decline in two of the major symbols of elite

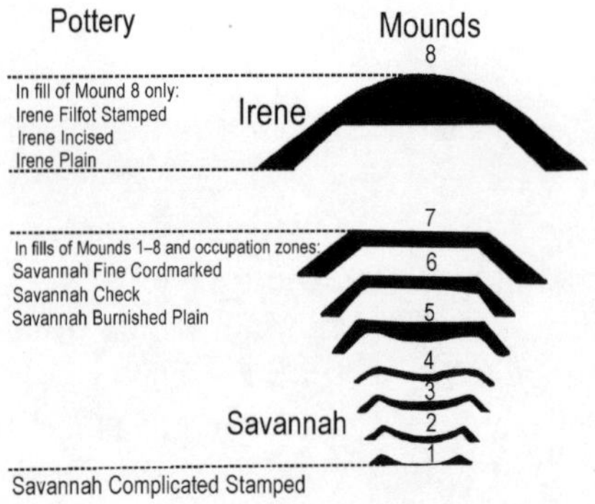

Figure 3.3. Savannah-phase mound stages (after Caldwell and McCann 1941: Figure 26, redrawn by Sydney Szot McGraw, courtesy of the University of Georgia Press). Note: Mound 3 was too disturbed for a reconstruction.

authority: platform mounds (Anderson 1994:27; cf. Knight 1986[4]) and the "warfare/cosmogony" symbols present on badges used to legitimize elite authority.[5] If revitalization movements represent, in Waselkov and Dumas's (2009) words, the "reimagining of the entire social structure . . . [allowing] for the possibility of a social system based on community input and consensus," then many Late Mississippian cultures shared in a revitalization movement (or movements) directed against the elaborate, costly, and rigid hierarchical social structures that existed in many areas of the Southeast between ca. 1050 and 1350. Along the Savannah River, the number of sites containing platform mounds decreased from a high of as many as eight by A.D. 1250 to four or five by A.D. 1350. By A.D. 1450, mound use had ended below the headwaters of the Savannah and only ephemeral hunting camps or other temporary settlements were present (Anderson 1994:326).[6]

The Irene Site Landscape

Developments at the Irene site exemplify the rapid reordering of late prehistoric social structures that occurred along the lower Atlantic coast around 1350. Irene lay at the margin of Mississippian expansion (Pluckhahn and McKivergan 2002), which was attenuated in many coastal areas in the Southeast. Savannah-period earthworks at Irene were limited to a low (2.5 ft, 0.76 m) burial mound and a single seven-stage platform mound, the only Mississippian platform mound on the Georgia coast (Figure 3.3, Table 3.1).[7] Burial mounds were built elsewhere along the Georgia coast, however, and there appears to be some hierarchical organization of sites containing burial mounds (Pearson 1977; Pluckhahn and McKivergan 2002).

The first reported excavations at the Irene site were by the ubiquitous Clarence B. Moore in 1897.[8] "It is only necessary to record that Moore was unfortunately somewhat more preoccupied with Irene, particularly the burial

Table 3.1. Sizes and Features of Savannah-Phase Mound Stages at the Irene Site

Mound Stage	Height (total in meters)	Base	Summit	Number of Structures	Size of Structures	Other
1	.38	18 × 12	n/a	1	7.6	
2	.51	18 × 12	n/a	1	7.6	elaborate seating
3	unknown	21.3 × 19.5	unknown	probably 1	unknown	palisade along most of mound perimeter; 9 possibly successive rectangular enclosures built around mound
4	1.07	21.3 × 21.3	13.1 × 13.1	1?	unknown	postholes are present
5	1.37	29.3 × 18.3	15.5 × 14.9	1	6.1 × 4.9	palisades on summit and slope; guttering system on hearth; log steps
6	1.5	32.6 × 25.9	18.9 × 14.9	2	19 × 22 ft unknown	summit palisade; more elaborate guttering on hearth; fragments of sheet copper w/repousse recovered on summit
7	2.9	25.9 m wide	19.8 m wide	2		eroded; summit palisade
8	4.7	48.8 m diameter	n/a			

Note: Measurements have been converted from English to metric.

mound, than he was with his more casual investigations on many southeastern sites" (Kelly 1941:vi). Other "complications" to site integrity involved modern borrowing from the "big" mound for fill; construction of a Moravian schoolhouse, complete with cellar (possibly the only cellar on the Georgia coast!), on the big mound; and use as a colonial-period cemetery. Major excavations were carried out continuously from September 1937 to January 1940, with as many as 50 field workers. Although Joseph Caldwell is generally credited with the excavations (because he and Catherine McCann wrote the report), there were four successive "archaeologists-in-charge" (Kelly 1941:vi), including Preston Holder, Vladimir Fewkes, Claude E. Schaeffer, and finally Caldwell. Caldwell and McCann note (1941:ix) that work at the site by Antonio J. Waring, Jr. and H. Thomas Cain provided some of the most valuable data. Skeletal analysis was accomplished by Frederick S. Hulse and Virginia Griffin (Hulse 1941). "The actual digging was done by Negro women and their work was eminently satisfactory" (Caldwell and McCann 1941:x).

The Irene site is located on a bluff on the south side of the Savannah River about five miles above the city of Savannah. When the site was inhabited, it was an "intermittent island": at high tides and during floods, water surrounded the site. While the topography of the site is flat, there are currently ten- to sixteen-foot bluffs on the south side of the river. Although reduced by erosion, the area of the "island" and of the site is about six acres (Caldwell and McCann 1941).

At the conclusion of the Savannah period, the Irene site appeared, as depicted in figure 3.4. The earliest construction was probably the burial mound (Caldwell and McCann 1941:69). As with most coastal Savannah-period burial mounds, the initial deposit was a central shell feature, and, also like many other mounds along the coast, in all initial burials (n = 7) the bodies were cremated[9] (Caldwell and McCann 1941:24). In addition, this initial deposit had a higher percentage of grave goods than did subsequent sets of burials. Caldwell and McCann note that "the high proportion of burial offerings in this deposit and in the subsoil below (with 57 percent of burials) and the fact that most of them consisted of pottery vessels (43 percent of offerings) was extraordinary" (Caldwell and McCann 1941:69).

Additional grave goods in this initial interment included a pottery elbow pipe and a large cut "conch" (probably *Busycon*) shell. The distinctive nature of this early, central deposit suggests the presence of a founding elite (as does the difference in some cranial traits for early Savannah men; see below). The fact that these central deposits appear at many coastal Savannah sites suggests a shared ritual tradition for the initiation of a site.

Subsequent burials (n = 106), most of which date to the Savannah period (Caldwell and McCann 1941:22), were placed in a series of shell lobes

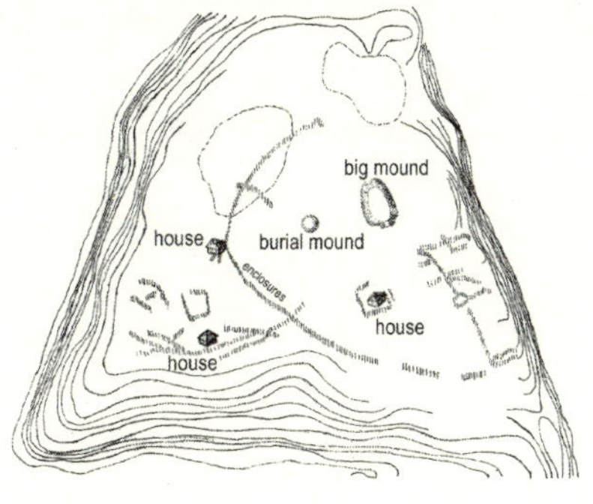

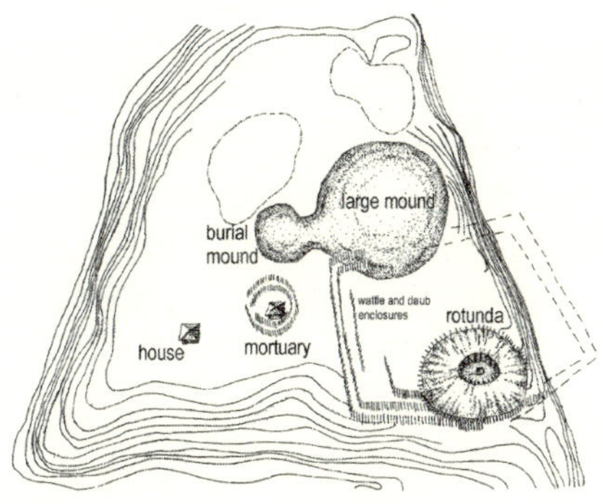

Figure 3.4. Savannah-period (top) and Irene-period (bottom) intrasite settlement patterning at the Irene site (after Caldwell and McCann 1941: Figures 28, 29; redrawn by Sydney Szot McGraw, courtesy of the University of Georgia Press).

flanking the central deposit. Not all of these lobes were well defined, but the grouping of burials in distinct lobes (six were identified) may reflect social houses, as described by King (2010) for late burials in Etowah Mound C. These later Savannah-period burials along with some Irene-period interments were primarily flexed and only five had grave goods.

In addition to the mounds, the built environment included extensive enclosures. Caldwell and McCann (1941:69) suggest there were at least two successive layouts of enclosures during the Savannah period. The large western wall may have served as a stockade, but it also segregated the mound precinct from the rest of the site to the west, where two houses and several smaller enclosures were built. Another enclosed house, possibly that of the chief, was within the stockade. Another house that Caldwell and McCann believed was built in the "transitional period" between Savannah and Irene is not plotted on the individual period maps but is shown on the overall map (Caldwell and McCann 1941: Figure 13) as Feature 61, northwest of the big mound. Lack of evidence for additional housing led Caldwell and McCann to conclude that the site had few permanent residents. They suggested that the substantial midden deposits at the site indicated periodic influxes of visitors, and that unpatterned postholes might be the remains of temporary shelters for these guests.

Caldwell and McCann (1941:33) believed that the unusual fencing along the eastern side of the site was associated with Stage 3 (see below) and that it was not built at the same time as the perimeter fencing. As Bigman et al. (2011:48) note, walls within communities are "a means of delineating space and defining different kinds of space." Details are unclear, but it appears that social space was carefully delimited and there were several realignments of space during the Savannah period. The seven stages of the platform mound,[10] as reconstructed by Caldwell and McCann, are shown in figure 3.5. (Stage 3 is not depicted in Figure 3.5 because more than half of the mound was destroyed; however, enough remained to trace the palisade and walls around the mound, as shown in figure 3.4.) The first four stages were not platform mounds at all, but what Caldwell and McCann refer to as saucer-shaped embankments. The addition of ramps created a pentagonal outline that was maintained throughout the Savannah period. In Stages 1–3, the embankments surrounded the rectangular structures. Caldwell and McCann (1941:33) believed that the unusual fencing along the eastern side of the site was associated with Stage 3, the first stage to be palisaded. A distinctly different set of enclosures walled off a ca. 50- x 50-ft (15.2 m) space in front of the ramp. There were at least three, and possibly as many as nine, of these walls. Stage 4 appeared to be a filling and leveling episode that transformed the earthwork into a platform mound. None of these stages is massive, although interior features in the structure in Stage 2 appear elaborate.

Stages 5 and 6 also did not increase mound height much, but effort was expended in extending the area of the platforms. In addition, there was at least one rectangular structure on the summit of Mound 5, and two were built on the summit of Mound 6. Both summits were palisaded. Both stages also underwent additional construction during use, apparently for erosion control. Still, the labor involved in constructing the first six stages was probably not onerous. Stage 7, however, was much higher and the sides were much steeper than the underlying mounds; construction would have required considerably more effort than any of the previous stages. Unfortunately, erosion on this stage was "considerable" on the northwestern side, and measurements for mound size and structure size are problematic. Nevertheless, Caldwell and McCann estimated an unprecedented increase of 1.4 m to a total height of 2.9 m.

Because platform mound construction ceased sometime after the completion of Stage 7, it is tempting to consider this massive construction as the proverbial straw that broke the chiefly camel's back. Unfortunately, it is

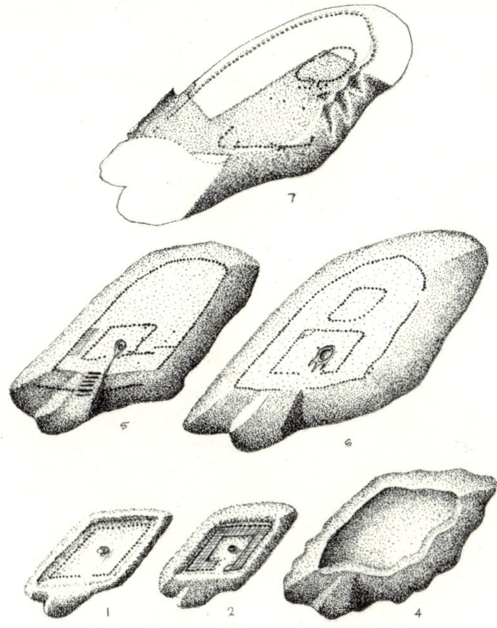

Figure 3.5. Relative mound stage heights, to scale, with mound stages numbered (after Caldwell and McCann 1941: Figure 1, redrawn by Sydney Szot McGraw and Rebecca Saunders, courtesy of the University of Georgia Press).

unclear how long this stage was actively used. Wherever possible, Caldwell and McCann carefully noted the depth and composition of occupational debris on the surface of each mound stage. No information is given for the first stage, but the second-stage surface "was covered by a thin cultural deposit of fine ash, charred wood, some shell, animal bones, and fragments of two large pottery vessels" (Caldwell and McCann 1941:11).

Occupational debris was not noted for the disturbed Stage 3. Stage 4, the transitional stage, had no definite cultural deposits, although an incomplete post mold pattern was found. Large portions of the summit and slopes of Stage 5 were covered by dark-gray, ashy sand "and other organic deposits" from 0.6 to 5 cm deep. Areas of fired sand also were encountered. A similar lens occurred at the top of Stage 6, but was more continuous and varied from 0.6 to 15 cm deep. Unfortunately, discussion of midden associated with Stage 7 is limited to the characteristics of the floors in the interior of the structures (also discussed for structures on Stages 5 and 6). There is no mention of a lens of occupational debris on the summit of the mound but no statement that debris was absent or discontinuous either. A comparison of the configuration of the structures on the summits of Stages 5 and 6 with that of Stage 7 might suggest that the southeastern structure was unfinished.[11] In addition, where preservation was adequate, all stages except for Stage 7 had a hearth. Hearths were in the center of the structures in the early stages, and central to the rectangular structures on the platform mound summits. However, Caldwell and McCann do not consider the possibility that the southeast structure was unfinished, perhaps because of the ash and organically stained sand within the walls.

Despite the shift from saucer-shaped embankment to platform mound, Caldwell and McCann considered all of the first seven stages similar. Ramps were maintained in approximately the same positions (although a second ramp was added to the southwestern side of Stage 7), preserving the pentagonal shape throughout the Savannah-period occupation. Although there were some differences, basic construction techniques and the use of the buildings and summits appeared similar.

Stage 8 was completely different. It was circular, as opposed to pentagonal, and an unprecedented volume of fill overlay the earlier stages, completely obscuring the pentagonal shape. As noted, Mississippian platform mounds are symbols of elite authority (Anderson 1994:27). Thus, with the burial of the platform mound, the configurations of power—the ascending ramp, the summit structures, the pentagonal shape—were "obliterated" (Caldwell and McCann's word) and replaced by with a dome-shaped, circular mantle wider and higher than all of the previous stages combined.

This burial was a provocative act. Reoccupation of mound sites (even vacant ceremonial centers) after abandonment is uncommon in the Southeast (Anderson 1994:81). Collapse of a chiefdom generally led to an exodus of the resident population. But the volume of Stage 8 indicates that labor was available at Irene. Indeed, other work included enlarging the original burial mound and the construction of two new structures, a rotunda (council house) 125 ft (7.6 m) in diameter and a 24 ft (7.3 m) square mortuary structure. The latter reflects significant changes in burial practices at the site that coincided with this reorganization of public space. The mortuary structure was built sometime after the completion of Stage 8. It was a semi-subterraneous wattle and daub structure that contained only four burials. In contrast to the burial mound, no mortuary items accompanied those burials. The structure was burned, possibly intentionally. After the burning, the mortuary was covered with a sand fill, which contained 13 burials. Subsequently, the area was used as a cemetery. Eighty burials were interred in two distinct episodes demarcated by palisades. A number of these were urn burials containing children. Mortuary items were found with 8 percent of the burials in the fill, 32 percent of the burials in the inner enclosure, and 17 percent in the outer enclosure.

The only other major enclosure, one that might be analogous to the Savannah "stockade," surrounded the plaza. That enclosure ties the council house into the large mound. The general configuration was similar to historic

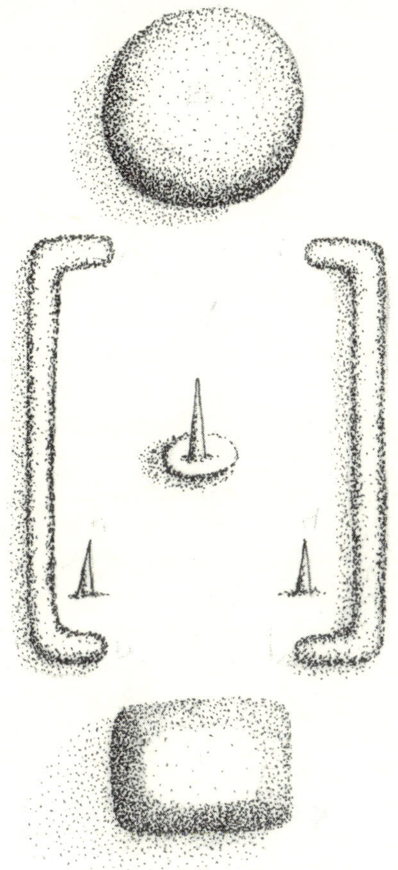

Figure 3.6. Bartram's sketch of mounds (after Caldwell and McCann 1941: Figure 30, redrawn by Sydney Szot McGraw, courtesy of the University of Georgia Press).

Creek ceremonial grounds, as depicted by William Bartram (Figure 3.6). Taken together, these changes reflect a more egalitarian ethos. Southeastern council houses (embodiments of the world symbol) are generally considered to represent more egalitarian sociopolitical structures than those associated with Mississippian platform mounds (Anderson 1994; DePratter 1991). Council houses provided a cohesive space for groups to discuss and form a consensus instead of receiving decisions from on-high—that is, from the lofty heights of a chief's platform mound. Some continuity in spatial concepts is apparent, however. The pentagonal shape of the first seven mound stages was recreated in the pentagonal shape of the plaza. "This suggests that the activities once carried out on the summits of the mounds were later transferred to the enclosure area" (Caldwell and McCann 1941:72). Activities once restricted to the elite were brought down from the summit and communalized in a capacious plaza area presumably capable of accommodating a large number of participants. Unlike in the Savannah period, there are no "houses" or specialized enclosures in the plaza that might have restricted participation.

Additional Aspects of Revitalization at Irene

As noted, the revitalization at Irene involved more than changes in the physical landscape. There is some indication of population change. Unfortunately, we cannot explore the biological identity of the initial, cremated Savannah-period burials, but Hulse (1941) did explore differences in metric and non-metric traits between subsequent Savannah- and Irene-period individuals. Whereas all other metric attributes were similar, Hulse (1941:67) found more heterogeneity in cranial length and a lower mean cranial breadth in Savannah-period men's burials than in Irene men's burials. He also isolated a set of early Savannah-period men with longer cranial lengths and bun-shaped occiputs. Hulse (1941:68) hypothesized that low population size in the earlier period led "local girls to marry men from some other place" where narrow craniums and bun-shaped occiputs were common. Hulse states that "the available evidence points to the conclusion that, while women often married outsiders of a diverse physical type during the earlier generations at the site, in the very latest generations they almost never did so, having enough potential mates in the locality" (Hulse 1941:68). Viewed in a slightly different way, it may be that "local girls" buried at the ceremonial site married into a founding population of males from a Savannah-period chiefdom or chiefdoms to the north, whereas Irene people cut ties with the Mississippian cultures to the north and married locally.

In addition to changes in physical attributes, there were dietary changes—a rejection of the subsistence system that fueled the labor projects that elevated, literally and figuratively, the elite. According to research by Larsen et al. (1992), Savannah-period folk ate fewer marine resources and more maize than their Woodland-period predecessors on the Georgia coast. However, there was a significant decrease in maize consumption in the later Irene sample, and an increase in the use of local (C3) resources. This is "a dietary shift markedly unlike that observed in most other late Mississippian populations from the region" (Anderson 1994:186). Anderson commented on the fact "that agricultural food production decreased appreciably in the period following the collapse of chiefly organization structures suggests intensive cultivation strategies may have been dictated by the elite, both to maintain the political economy and to further their own personal agendas" (Anderson 1994:293).

Figure 3.7. Pottery types (after Caldwell and McCann 1941: Figures 17, 18, 20, 21, redrawn by Sydney Szot McGraw, courtesy of the University of Georgia Press).

Finally, there is that communalization of iconography on a medium that has always been evocative in the Southeast: pottery. Let us consider in more detail the replacement of Savannah pottery with Irene.

Despite the fact that its definition (Caldwell and McCann 1941; Caldwell and Waring 1939) was based on sites around the city of Savannah, the Savannah period (A.D. 1000–1300) remains poorly understood on the Georgia coastal plain. It follows the Late Woodland Wilmington period, in which cord marking, fabric marking, and brushing were the decorative types. Savannah-period decorated pottery assemblages are primarily composed of cord marking, check stamping, and complicated stamping (Figure 3.7).[12] The complex as a whole was considered "a development of the immediate area," connected to northern and central Georgia by the presence of complicated stamping and the similarity of complicated stamped designs to designs from Etowah (Caldwell and McCann 1941:43; Crook 1986:43). Thus, the only Mississippian-influenced pottery type along the coast at this time is Savannah Complicated Stamped. Like other coastal pottery types during the Mississippi period, Savannah Complicated Stamped is not shell tempered.

Distribution of Savannah Complicated Stamped is very limited on the coast and the type appears to have been produced for only a short while. Although Anderson (1994) contests the idea, DePratter (1979; Thomas 2008:389) suggests Savannah Complicated Stamped was produced for only 50 years, from 1250 to 1300, or during the Savannah III phase (the last phase in the period). This restricted range is difficult to reconcile with its distribution at the Irene site, where it is present in the earliest contexts (see figure 3.3; Caldwell and McCann 1941), and in mound fills through Stage 6 but is absent from fill and occupational debris of Stages 7 and 8 (Caldwell and McCann 1943:78, Table II). Because of the decline in the uniformity of lands and grooves (interpreted as a decline in "the quality of the execution") from Savannah to Irene, it is tempting to suggest that Savannah pottery making paddles were imported along with a founding population.

It is unclear how long the site was abandoned before peoples making Irene pottery effected all the dramatic physical changes at the site. Caldwell and McCann believed the hiatus in occupation was prolonged, based on the extent of erosion on the Stage 7 surface and on the belief that, because there were no transitional types between Savannah and Irene, enough time must have passed for an entirely new type to develop. This last assumption—that a transition between types (in the absence of population replacement) necessarily involved a lengthy evolution—is a relic of the gradualism of the time. More recent authors (e.g., Crook 1986:41) suggest rapid replacement, even without recourse to the idea that style has function and that material culture can be used actively to promote change. While gradualism is clearly the case in some sequences, much pottery change is punctuated; styles can appear abruptly and in their final form. Ramey Incised comes to mind. One thing is clear from Caldwell and McCann's discussion: with a few exceptions, Savannah was completely replaced by Irene. There was almost no overlap in the use of these types at Irene. The Irene complex "was made to the exclusion of all others during the building of the last mound and later" (Caldwell and McCann 1941:19).

The few instances of overlap are significant, because the overlaps occur in special circumstances. In a "very small" structure (the aforementioned Feature 61, 3 x 3 m) on the extreme north edge of the site, next to the borrow pit and seemingly outside of the protective palisades, Caldwell and McCann recovered two vessels, large fragments of a Savannah Check Stamped vessel and an Irene Filfot Stamped vessel of unique shape. Other Savannah and Irene sherds were present on the floor, and there were another two Savannah Check Stamped vessels outside the structure. In another instance, a small Savannah Check Stamped vessel was found lying on its side in the sand fill of Mound 8; "It appeared to have been carelessly covered during the construction of the mound" (Caldwell and McCann 1941:20). These two instances may be a reflection of the variability of responses to revitalization movements within a single society, as discussed by Liebmann (2008). In particular, the latter instance appears to be hedging a bet. In the first case, the location of the structure suggests something more complicated might have been going on.

The replacement of Savannah types involved a rejection of check stamping and cord marking and, apparently, a co-opting of complicated stamping. In addition, after an absence of some 2,000 years, incising reappeared on the coast, no doubt derived from slightly earlier incising in the interior. While Savannah Complicated Stamped had a somewhat limited repertoire in terms of motifs (compared to, say, Swift Creek), at the Irene site Irene Complicated Stamped was limited to a single motif (albeit executed in a variety of ways)—the filfot cross. The filfot cross is a representation of the world symbol; the four arms of the cross represent the cords (and the four cardinal directions) from which This World is suspended from the Upper World. At the center is the sun, the principal deity, or (in some explanations) the people. Although this motif was not absent in Savannah assemblages, its dominance in the Irene-period assemblages suggests an emphasis on concerns with This World, not with the Upper World that so preoccupied the elite. In addition, the pervasiveness of the design on utilitarian pottery suggests a communalization of the design, similar to that described by Knight (1986, 1997:246). In addition, incised designs on Irene pottery, although not generally as well executed as examples from the interior, are the same set of designs that refer to the three worlds that were revived in the Protohistoric.

"Irene" became a recognizable culture on the coast that endured until contact. Archaeologically at least, the historic Guale coalesced on the coast, where Irene pottery and Altamaha, its Mission-period successor, probably did define an ethnic boundary (although this boundary is fuzzier on the northern edge than on the southern). As the Guale were forced south by European conflict, they brought Altamaha pottery with them. Called San Marcos in Florida, by the mid-seventeenth century, many Native groups around St. Augustine began to make San Marcos pottery (see Worth, this volume). Indeed, I have explored the possibility that Altamaha-San Marcos, with its broader lands and grooves (better designed to visually signal information on identity), might indicate some kind of revitalization or pan-Indian movement using a symbol widely understood by all Southeastern tribes. Thus, the world symbol that still figured prominently in the surface decoration of the historic types might explain the widespread use of Altamaha/San Marcos by Native Americans of many different tribes around St. Augustine (Saunders 2000, 2012). In the end, I could not separate the widespread use of San Marcos due to a possible pan-Indian affiliation (similar in distribution to Liebmann and Mills's Pueblo Historic Red ware) from the possibility of market influences of Spanish colonialism (Saunders 2012; see also Waters 2009). Nevertheless, in the development of Irene, Altamaha, and San Marcos potteries, we may see an instance of Henry's (2004) "on-going" revitalization. In the lower Southeast, surface decoration on pottery was long used to signal social information. The ongoing redefinition of pottery design and use by late prehistoric and historic Native Americans of the lower Atlantic coast is consistent with its use in earlier prehistory. Perhaps these "created traditions"—revised and revitalized social identities—were successful because they were so deeply rooted in the past.

Conclusion

After ca. A.D. 1350, in many areas of the Southeast, Mississippian lifeways were rejected and the material symbols of an elitist social system were transmogrified to represent a more inclusive society. At the Irene site, a revitalization movement occurred, as evidenced in the obliteration of platform mounds, a major reorganization of the internal site structure, different burial modes, different marital modes, different subsistence regimes, and a new pottery type that bore the icons of a more inclusive, egalitarian ethos. To the best of our ability to demonstrate through archaeology, these changes occurred simultaneously and abruptly at the Irene site, and well represent the characteristics of a revitalization movement. Many of the changes at Irene correspond closely to those inherent in the original definition of revitalization movements and in current uses, such as that documented recently for the Pueblo revolt. Significantly, the Irene revitalization movement succeeded. A "created tradition" installed during the early Irene period was present at contact, when the Irene/Guale were confronted with another set of elite mandates, this time more intractable that those of the Mississippian chiefly lineages.

Notes

1. The outlines of my argument were developed for a 2009 Southeastern Archaeological Conference symposium, organized by Greg Waselkov and Ashley Dumas, in which participants were asked to look for evidence of revitalization movements in their respective areas of expertise.

2. For more on Mississippian cosmograms, see, e.g., King 2010.

3. Liebmann substitutes "creation of tradition" for "invention" to emphasize that his traditions have antecedents—that they are not created out of whole cloth, as some of Hobsbawm's (1983) were.

4. Knight (1986) argues that platform mounds were *sacra* and platform mound construction was a communal rite. That platform mounds were also symbols of elite authority is not inconsistent with Knight's recognition of dialectical relationships between various cults associated with specific sacra.

5. Such badges were only prevalent for about 150 years. As Knight (1986:683) notes, the "zenith of chiefly co-opting of warfare/cosmogony symbolism seems to have occurred only briefly during A.D. 1200–1350."

6. Except in the extreme western part of the basin near the Oconee River.

7. There is some suggestion of a low platform mound at the Kenan Fields site on Sapelo Island. Crook (1986) was unsure and stated that, if present, the platform mound must have functioned differently from true Mississippian platform mounds.

8. Moore (1898:168) noted that there was already a large excavation in the Large Mound when he arrived.

9. There is only one other cremation on the site.

10. Mound C at Etowah also had seven stages. Coincidence?

11. Frankly, with structures off center and out of alignment with the orientation of the summit, Stage 7 looks seriously askew. If the eastern side actually extended farther east, the buildings might be brought back into alignment.

12. Complicated stamping was part of coastal assemblages in the area until around A.D. 600, when it disappeared. Some 600 years would pass before complicated stamping reappeared in the Savannah period. At Irene, Savannah Complicated Stamped was a minority ware, at least in the large mound (Caldwell and McCann 1941:78, Table II).

4

NAVIGATING THE MISSISSIPPIAN WORLD

Infrastructure in the Sixteenth-Century Native South

Robbie Ethridge

Scholars examining the Mississippi period of Southeastern pre-Columbian North America (ca. 900 to 1600 C.E.) have long understood that during that time numerous hierarchically organized, independent polities, or chiefdoms, rose and fell. More recently, archaeologists have come to agree that Mississippian chiefdoms were bound together in what could be called the "Mississippian world." Generally, one could define a "world" as the various polities within a defined time and geographic space, and the network of political, economic, cultural, and social relationships that exist between these polities. Such a "world" is not a discrete unit; its borders are porous, and it is often connected to distant places. However, it would be erroneous to assume that the people living in this world perceived of themselves as "Mississippians" or understood that such of a world existed. People from that time and place most likely identified with their towns and their polities (relational identities) and sometimes with larger regional political or ideological circuits (categorical identities). It is only in historical hindsight that we can discern that the Mississippian way of life had boundaries, within which people and polities functioned and interacted, that formed a "world." Today many archaeologists are working to decipher the multiple relationships that existed between chiefdoms and the multiple identities that defined the Mississippian world, an identity writ large.

The first step in reconstructing the Mississippian world involves establishing details of the infrastructure that supported and made possible the social, political, economic, and ideological relationships between chiefdoms. By infrastructure, I mean the roads, pathways, and navigable streams that enabled the movement of goods, services, people, and ideas within and between polities, as well as impediments to travel and movement, the resources necessary to support traffic such as accessible foodstuffs, and the human resources such as guides, carriers, and interpreters that were necessary components of the sixteenth-century infrastructure of the Native South (Hassig

1991:19). One avenue of inquiry that can provide insights into the Mississippian infrastructure is the written accounts of early Spanish expeditions that navigated much of the Mississippian world while it still functioned, led by men such as Hernando de Soto, Tristán de Luna, and Juan Pardo. Here I present a detailed analysis of the infrastructure that Soto and his army exploited in their trek through the Mississippian world between 1540 and 1543.

Knowledge of Hernando de Soto's expedition comes to us through four chroniclers. Hernandez Luys de Biedma (1993) was the expedition's factor, or royally appointed record-keeper. Another was Rodrigo Rangel (1993), Soto's personal secretary, and a third was a Portuguese man known only as the Gentleman of Elvas (1993). Finally, the Incan writer Garcilaso de la Vega (1993) was not on the expedition, but he interviewed three of the expedition's surviving soldiers and penned an account intended as a popular adventure tale. Of these, the Biedma, Elvas, and Rangel chronicles are the most reliable, although each has its own set of historiographical concerns (Galloway 2005 [1997]; Hudson 1997:441–455; Lankford 2009).[1] What I present here is a sort of snapshot of Mississippian infrastructure in the mid-sixteenth century as taken from the Biedma, Elvas, and Rangel accounts. However, one should not infer this snapshot to represent a generalized Mississippian infrastructure. For one, this is the infrastructure as experienced by a large, invading force, and the Spaniards certainly had transportation concerns particular to their goals. Also, infrastructures are unstable, they are built as geopolitical tools, and they respond to geopolitical fluctuations and changes (Dubcovsky 2016:4; Hassig 1991:25).

To understand Mississippian infrastructure circa 1540 C.E., we must reconstruct the geopolitical landscape. Most, if not all, Mississippian polities were made from the same building block—the simple chiefdom. Simple chiefdoms were characterized by two-tiered social ranking of elites and commoners, a civic and religious capital where the elite lineage lived and which was the capital town of a chiefdom, and five to ten affiliated farming towns strung up and down a river valley. In some cases, leaders elaborated on the simple chiefdom by establishing secondary mound centers a few miles away from the capital and instituting a second tier of control; archaeologists refer to this more elaborate polity as a complex chiefdom. Simple chiefdoms were fairly small, usually encompassing about 25 km (16 miles) of a river valley, and were separated from other chiefdoms by about 35 km (22 miles) of uninhabited space, what archaeologists call "buffer zones" (Hally 1993; Steponaitis 1978, 1991).

However, simple and complex chiefdoms sometimes merged to form larger political units that archaeologists call paramount chiefdoms, which

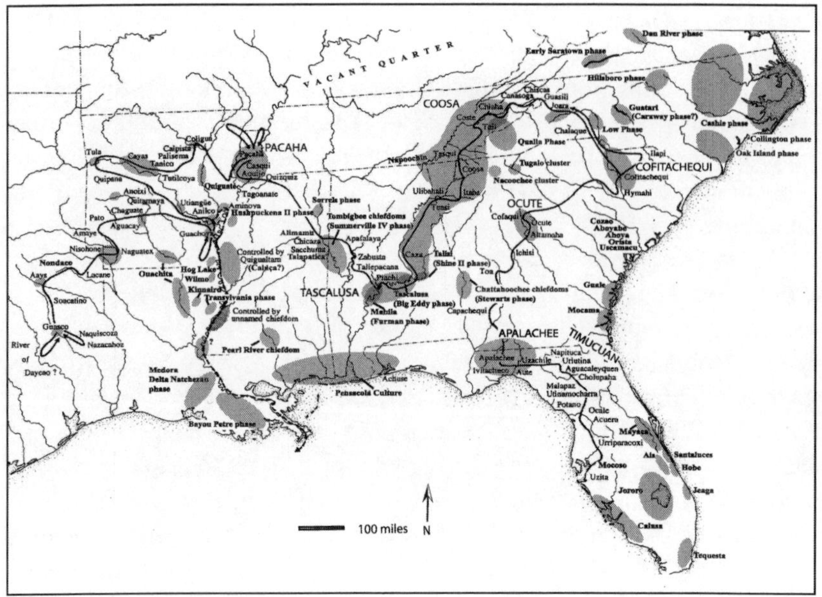

Figure 4.1. Mississippian World, ca. 1540 C.E., showing the route of Hernando de Soto.

could incorporate many small and complex chiefdoms. Paramount chiefdoms, in some cases, could span several hundred miles. Over the 700-year history of the Mississippian way of life, many simple, complex, and paramount chiefdoms rose and fell. This rising and falling, or cycling, was an internal dynamic common to Mississippian chiefdoms, and the life span of a typical chiefdom was about 150 to 200 years. Figure 4.1 shows the multiple polities that made up the Mississippian world at the time of the Hernando de Soto expedition, along with the expedition's route.

Shared structural elements aside, all Mississippian chiefdoms were not alike. On the contrary, we now know that Mississippian chiefdoms were quite variable. There were polities of various complexity, ideological convictions, centralized governance, and cultural expressions, although archaeologists have yet to map out each of these expressions. Such variation, however, did not lead to insular, inward-looking polities.[2] In fact, one archaeologist states that "linking and integrating different groups through contact, coalescence, and population movements . . . constitutes the Mississippian" (Blitz 2010:14 [quote]; Hally 2006; Jenkins 2009; Regnier 2014). Mississippian infrastructure—the ways in which chiefdoms connected—would have been integral to this linking, this "cultural pluralism."

Some of the most productive archaeological research on the relationships between chiefdoms has involved the study of high-prestige trade objects made of extralocal materials (such as shell, copper, and high-grade flints), reconstructions of the flow of these trade goods, and determining the sources of them or the raw materials from which they were made (Anderson and Sassaman 2012:167; Blitz 2010:13, 18). Archaeological investigations into the Mississippian trade system demonstrate that Mississippian chiefdoms, throughout their 700-year existence, were enmeshed in large trade networks with people from not only across the Southeast, but as far north as the Great Lakes, as far west as the Great Plains, and even into Mesoamerica. Elites of Mississippian chiefdoms usually controlled the manufacture and exchange of exotic trade items, and their access and control underwrote, to some extent, their authority and power (Blitz 2010:12, 18). They used these items to validate their authority, garner allies, soothe tensions, and ensure the loyalty of other elites. Even so, nonelites also participated in long-distance trade. There is evidence of "down-the-line" exchanges of everyday necessities, such as stone hoes and salt, wherein material goods moved from nonelites to nonelites sometimes over long distances (Blitz 2010:18; Cobb 2000:75–76; Early 1993; Muller 1984).[3] The assumption here, of course, is that an exchange of material objects, whether through elite-sponsored craftsmen and traders or down-the-line exchanges, usually also included sharing ideas, knowledge, information, and sometimes even people. It also assumes an infrastructure through which such items, people, and information could move.

That a large infrastructure connected sixteenth-century Mississippian polities also is evidenced simply by the fact that Soto and his army of more than 650 soldiers, horses, dogs, and pigs trekked through much of the heart of the Mississippian world using this infrastructure. When the Spaniards reached the edges of the Mississippian world, they were forced to turn back toward the heartland because thinly dispersed populations and local food stores could not feed the army. Soto reached the edges of the Mississippian world when his army ventured into the southern Appalachians, the plains of present-day eastern Texas and western Arkansas, and north of present-day Memphis where they entered an expansive, sparsely inhabited region that stretched to the Ohio Valley (called the Vacant Quarter by archaeologists; Cobb and Butler 2002; Elvas 1993:120; Williams 1990).

In addition to the Vacant Quarter, the Mississippian world had other large expanses of uninhabited territory that proved difficult for Soto. These were in the Savannah River valley (between Ocute and Cofitachequi), in present-day northern Mississippi (between Chicaza and Quizquiz), and in present-day north-central Arkansas (between Quiguate and Coligua). Whereas the typical buffer zone between chiefdoms usually took the expedition three to five days to cross, these larger expanses could take 10 to 12 days to traverse. Roads and paths through these larger expanses were poor to nonexistent, making the Spaniards especially wary of getting lost. The uninhabited areas in present-day Arkansas and on the Savannah River had been abandoned since at least 1400 C.E. In present-day northern Mississippi the vacant area had been last inhabited around 1200 C.E. (Anderson 1994; Hudson 1997:314; Jay K. Johnson, personal communication, 2015).

Granted, Soto's army was an exceptionally large group of travelers for the Mississippian world. Mississippian commoners probably did not travel much beyond their towns and fields, except for visits at certain times of the year to the capitals of their chiefdom. Elites, on the other hand, were more experienced travelers. Scholars believe that Mississippian chiefs conducted royal progresses, visiting the towns throughout their realm on a regular basis (Lankford 2008:99; Smith and Hally 1992:105–107). In these cases, chiefs would have traveled with a retinue of other elites, principal men, ladies in waiting, servants, burden bearers, and others. When Chief Tascaluza traveled to Mabila with Soto, for example, he had in attendance several principal men and two attendants (Rangel 1993:291). In addition, since leaders did not view Soto's entry into their chiefdom as unusual, we can infer that visits between chiefdom leaders also were not unusual. We have no documentary evidence describing such visits, but one can assume that, hostile encounters apart, they involved the usual pomp and circumstance that Soto encountered, such as gift giving, oaths of fealty and subservience, displays of power, and so on (Lankford 2008; Smith and Hally 1992).

Not all travelers came in peace, though. Hostility underlay the Mississippian world and underwrote masculine ideals, as well as chiefly authority. In short, chronic warfare characterized the Mississippian world. Warriors, then, were perhaps the best-traveled people in the Mississippian world, and they would have ventured far outside of their own polities. As best we can decipher, Mississippian warfare was conducted either by small, guerilla raiding parties or through large numbers of organized troops such as an army (Dye 1991, 2002; Ethridge 2010:50–52). A Mississippian army could number in the hundreds, perhaps thousands. In the lower Mississippi Valley, for example, the Spaniards encountered large naval forces that maneuvered flotillas of dugout war canoes with agility. Large numbers of foot troops, however, would have been cumbersome in travel and exposed to guerilla attacks along the roadways. From the Soto chronicles, it appears that, when a large force was needed, leaders sent word throughout their towns for men to assemble at a certain location (Biedma 1993:232–233, 236–237; Elvas 1993:96–101, 106–107; Ethridge et al. 2009:169–175; Rangel 1993:291–294, 297–298). Assembling forces near a designated attack point would alleviate the problems of moving an army long distances, because small groups of men could travel independently and more stealthily to the rendezvous point. In addition, the burden of feeding a large force would have been lessened because small swift ensembles would have been largely self-sufficient.

In the sixteenth-century Mississippian world, roads and navigable streams were the main conduits along which people, goods, and information traveled. (In one unusual instance, Soto's men witnessed the use of Indian smoke signals on the Gulf Coast of present-day Florida; Elvas 1993:57). The Soto documents indicate that the Southeast was well served with roadways and paths. In only a few cases did Soto find himself lost, with no known road, and these cases were usually when crossing large vacant areas (Biedma 1993: 230, 241; Elvas 1993:80–81, 122; Rangel 1992:304). The chroniclers never offer detailed descriptions of the roadways; still, there is much we can say about them from what they did report. Roads within a chiefdom were clearly defined, easy to follow, apparently maintained, and passed through and connected the towns of a polity. Within a chiefdom, there were many roads, but the main thoroughfares appear to have led to the capital and home of the chief and his or her lineage, thus connecting the town and its leaders to the entire chiefdom. In fact, most capitals likely had several roads connecting them. After taking a capital town, for example, Soto would post sentries at the roadways leading into the town, and they usually had to guard multiple entryways (Elvas 1993:58, 109).

Roads varied in that some were broad and open, and others were narrow, hemmed in by forest or mountainous terrain. As would be expected, the roadways conformed to the topography. In the relatively flat and sandy Coastal Plain, roads were wide and easily traveled, except where they crossed swamps and rivers (Elvas 1993:65, 72–73, 74; Rangel 1993:255, 259, 260, 268). Roads through the populous and rolling Piedmont were relatively easy, although the Piedmont, too, has the occasional steep slope (Elvas 1993:93–96; Rangel 1993:284–288). Roads through the Appalachian and Ouachita Mountains were steep, rugged, difficult, and tiring to travel (Biedma 1993: 231, 241, 243; Elvas 1993:86, 88; Rangel 1993:281, 282). In fact, Soto declined to take the army deep into the Appalachians to look for rumored gold because the roads passed through such rough terrain and "lofty mountains" (Elvas 1993:91). Also, there was a dearth of corn this far north (Elvas 1993:91).

In 1997, the scholar Jack Elliott (1997:254) lamented that we would likely never be able to map pre-Columbian roadways with precision. However, advances in geophysical techniques and Geographic Information Systems (GIS) computing software have belied his prediction. A recent study by Kathryn Sampeck, Jonathan Thayn, and Howard H. Earnest, Jr. (2015) used GIS modeling and archaeological data to determine the least-cost, or easiest, road that Soto and later Pardo may have taken from Joara to Chiaha. Their mapping of the two possible roadways is a marvel in the synthesis of technology, archaeology, and scholarship. This region is in the foothills of the Appalachians and has some steep slopes, which definitely would have been a consideration for the Spaniards. However, in their analysis, the size or width of the roadway and the number of people traveling were also important variables, and, in fact, were likely important factors in the ascendency of polities in the chronic geopolitical shuffling that was typical of the Mississippian world.

The chroniclers describe the lower Mississippi Valley as the most populous region in all of La Florida, as they called the Southeast. Roads in this area were well known and well traveled by the locals. Even so, they proved the most difficult for Soto because of the morass of wetlands that characterized the pre-levee river system there (Biedma 1993:239; Elvas 193:111, 114, 150; Rangel 1993:300, 304). Apparently many of the roads here did not always take the high ground, with many passing directly through swamps. In one case, in the chiefdom of Casqui (centered at the Parkin archaeological site) on the St. Francis River in northeastern Arkansas (Hudson 1997:289), Indians built a foot bridge "of ingenious construction" across a bayou for a road that led to the capital of their arch enemy, Pacaha (Elvas 1993:116, 121; Hudson 1997:293; Rangel 1993:301).

This bridge, however, was unusual. Most roads led straight into and across wetlands, where the water was often knee high, if not higher (Elvas 1993:114). These wetlands could be quite expansive and covered with dense canebrakes and forests, and the Spaniards feared getting lost while crossing them. None of the chroniclers describe exactly how roads through swamps were marked, but local Indians knew the roads and paths well, even across wetlands where the pathway was not obvious (Elvas 1993:114, 131, 134, 145). In three cases west of the Mississippi River, Soto's army lost sight of a road when it crossed a stream, lake, or swamp. In each case, Soto depended on local Indians to point the way through (Biedma 1993:241; Elvas 1993:143, 131). In fact, Biedma (1993:241) was dumbfounded when, after leaving Quiguate and crossing swamps, prairies, and mountains with no apparent road, their Indian guide "struck pointblank" at the town for which they had been headed, Coligua, on the White River in present-day Arkansas (Hudson 1997:314).

In addition, during the flood season low-lying areas flooded and left small, isolated islands of high ground. Most towns were located on elevated ground, so during flood season many towns would have been cut off from their connecting roads (Elvas 1993:152). Archaeologist Jay Johnson and colleagues, studying a Mississippi River tributary, the Yazoo River, propose that flooding defined a chiefdom's spatial extent in the Yazoo Basin. In particular, they note that the chiefdoms defined by Hushpuckna-Oliver- and Quitman-phase ceramics are both clustered on high elevations that would have been surrounded by water during the flood season (Johnson et al. 2014). How isolated such polities would have been, however, is less clear. Elvas states that at Aminoya, near the Mississippi River in present-day central Arkansas, during flood season the capital "became isolated and surrounded by water, so that it was impossible to go more than a league or a league and a half by land" (Elvas 1993:151; Hudson 1997:381). However, people then "came and went in canoes," indicating less isolation than one might suppose (Elvas 1993:152).

Canoe travel on the lower Mississippi Valley was commonplace, although overland travel seems to have been quite routine as well. The lower Mississippi Valley, obviously, is dominated by the Mississippi River, but it is also crosscut by numerous secondary and tertiary streams that flow into the Mississippi River. In the pre-levee past, swamps, back channels, oxbow lakes, and other wetlands dominated the region, making canoe travel not only preferred, but also necessary during flood season. The lower Mississippi River valley had a grand canoe tradition. Mississippians throughout the Southeast used canoes for mundane, daily affairs, but polities along the Mississippi River also had stupendous riverine navies comprised of hundreds of war canoes.

For example, when the Spaniards reached the Mississippi River, somewhere around present-day Memphis, Tennessee (Hudson 1997:278, 286), Soto immediately set his men to building canoes for crossing the mighty river. At one point, the chief of Aquixo arrived at the crossing point with 200 large war canoes carrying Indian warriors "painted with red ocher and having great plumes of white and many colored feathers on either side [of the canoes] and holding shields in their hands with which they covered the paddlers, while the warriors were standing from prow to stern with their bows and arrows in their hands" (Biedma 1993:238; Elvas 1993:112; Rangel 1993:300 [quote]).

In the chief's canoe, the chief sat under an awning in the stern. Other canoes bore his principal men, who also sat under colorful canopies and issued commands to paddlers in the canoes that followed "in splendid order" (Elvas 1993:112). According to Biedma (1993:238), the navy of Aquixo repeated the same display daily at 3:00 p.m. for the entire 28 days it took Soto's army to build four large canoes. When Soto's men finally made the crossing, the navy disappeared. A year later, the survivors of the Soto expedition were not so lucky. When they were navigating down the Mississippi River in watercraft they made during the preceding winter, they were attacked by the large navy of Quigualtam, which chased them out of Quigualtam territory, only to be attacked by a second and then a third navy of other polities (both unnamed) as they drifted down the river (Biedma 1993:245; Elvas 1993:156–158).[4]

Soto encountered canoe travel in other regions but not as frequently as in the lower Mississippi Valley. In present-day north Florida, part of the Coastal Plain physiographic province, the chroniclers only mention canoes once. Soto sent a contingent of soldiers to the Gulf Coast to wait for Spanish ships exploring the coastline. These soldiers built a large canoe in which they coasted off shore looking for the brigantines. While doing so, "several times they fought with Indians who were going along the keys in canoes" (Elvas 1993:72–73).

Otherwise, in the Coastal Plain, as well as in the Piedmont and Appalachians, the documents largely mention canoes only in the context of the army's efforts to cross streams (Biedma 1993:230, 238; Elvas 1993:118, 120, 131; Rangel 1993:271, 272, 278, 283, 296, 304). As the army moved into the interior, the first mention of canoes occurs at Ichisi, probably located on the Ocmulgee River near present-day Macon, Georgia (Hudson 1997:160), where the chief provided several for Soto's use in crossing the river (Rangel 1993:271). In another case, elites in sumptuously outfitted canoes greeted Soto. When Soto reached Cofitachequi, the chieftainess, known only as the "Lady of Cofitachequi," sent her niece to greet the Spaniards at a river crossing. Here several principal men and the royal niece boarded four canoes outfitted with woven cane mats, cushions, and canopies and crossed the river to welcome the Spaniards. The niece presented Soto with gifts and ordered canoes to aid them in crossing the stream (Biedma 1993:230; Elvas 1993:82–83; Hudson 1997:174–175; Rangel 1993:278).

Soto used offers of canoes to transport across deep streams the goods, people, and perhaps even the horses and pigs with which he traveled. In only one instance do the chroniclers mention using canoes for travel other than stream crossings. This occurred at Coste, where four ill Spaniards were transported downstream from Chiaha. One should keep in mind, however, that Soto's large army of soldiers, captives, horses, and pigs would have required hundreds of canoes for water travel. Overland travel was obviously the better choice for the Spaniards and, except in the lower Mississippi Valley, seems to have been the preferred mode of transportation for Indians as well. Canoe travel, then, was mostly local, largely for crossing streams and transporting goods, rather than across long distances.

Overland travel posed its own set of difficulties for the Spaniards. For one, Indian warriors oftentimes shadowed the army, hiding in adjacent forests and periodically sending volleys of arrows toward the Spaniards, sometimes forcing the army off the road (Elvas 1993:70, 72–73, 74, 78; Rangel 1993:260). Stream crossings proved especially problematic, in part, because of the sheer size of Soto's army. Soto's problems, however, provide some insight into how stream crossings figured into the Late Mississippian infrastructure. Except for some mountain rivers and at the topographical feature known as the Fall Line (where the Piedmont meets the Coastal Plain), Southern rivers are wide and deep. Crossings at the Fall Line were relatively easy because the streams break into wide, shallow shoals. Crossing above or below the Fall Line, however, meant crossing deep, wide, and swift streams, and heavy rains upstream could lead to rapid and deadly swelling of rivers downstream (Rangel 1993:271, 275; Elvas 1993:94, 144).

Roads typically led across rivers. Small streams posed little obstacle and most had fords, but the larger streams proved difficult, and Southeastern Indians did not build bridges across them. Rather, it appears that most people crossed large streams via canoes kept at crossing points. Although Soto never found any such stash of canoes at a crossing, later ethnographic evidence indicates that local Indians often hid canoes in plain sight at river crossings by keeping the bark on the underside of the canoe and turning it over so it looked like an old log (Ethridge 2003:124). Sometimes Soto's men fashioned canoes at particularly wide and deep stream crossings, which could take several days. At Capachequi, for example, it took the army six days to make a piragua, or large canoe (Biedma 1993:227; Elvas 1993:74, 112; Rangel 1993:268, 300). As noted, when crossing the Mississippi River, Soto's men took 28 days to make four large canoes. Elvas estimated the Mississippi River at the crossing to be a half-league wide (about one and three quarters of a mile), very deep, and with a strong current (Elvas 1993:113). He continues, "Its water was always turgid and continually many trees and wood came on it borne along by the force of the water and current" (Elvas 1993:113). Although they were harassed the whole time while making the canoes by the navy of Aquixo, it was worth the effort because, once made, the whole army crossed the Mississippi in two hours, albeit with some difficulty (Elvas 1993:113; Rangel 1993:300). Usually, though, as Soto moved from one polity to the next, leaders offered him assistance in crossing rivers by providing numerous canoes; others, however, suspecting ill intent on Soto's part, refused (Biedma 1993:230, 236, 238; Elvas 1993:81, 83, 98, 118, 121, 131, 133, 153; Rangel 1993:270, 271, 272, 278, 279, 284, 296, 304). In either case, evidence indicates that interior Indians kept a plentiful supply of canoes on hand for river crossings and transport.

In addition, the Soto accounts testify that Southeastern men and women were able and strong swimmers who could simply swim across many streams. Oftentimes when Soto was in pursuit of Indians, both Indian men and women eluded the Spaniards by easily swimming across river crossings, lakes, and into swamps, places where Soto's horses and men could not go without difficulty (Elvas 1993:68, 76, 121, 123, 131; Rangel 1993:265, 282). They also swam for recreation. At Chiaha, Spaniards and local Indians played together in the waters of the French Broad River (Hudson 1997:199; Rangel 1993:282).

There is some indication that Indian people may have built expedient, temporary bridges to cross streams and swamps. As we saw at Casqui, where Indians built an impressive footbridge across a large swamp, they apparently were experienced bridge builders. Elvas (1993:116) describes this bridge. It was constructed of wooden beams "extending from tree to tree, and at one of the sides a line of wood higher than the bridge in order to support those who should cross." In other words, it was a footbridge constructed of parallel logs laid from one tree to the next, with a hand rail. Accounts from later centuries describe bridges built by Southeastern Indians as pine logs laid across a stream, from bank to bank (Ethridge 2003:124). Still, if Indians built bridges other than at Casqui, Soto never had access to them. Soto deployed his army on numerous occasions to build bridges (Biedma 1993:227, 228; Elvas 1993:64, 67, 76, 114; Rangel 1993:259, 263, 264, 266, 269). Indians may have dismantled temporary bridges to thwart potential enemies from using them, or bridges simply may have had short lives (Hudson 1997:310).

Building bridges large enough to span major rivers was out of the question, given Soto's and the Mississippian Indians' limited technology. But they could build bridges to span small, secondary streams too wide and deep to swim or wade across (Biedma 1993:228). In these cases, Soto's men lashed together pine saplings and trees to fashion narrow footbridges (Biedma 1993:227, 228; Elvas 1993:64, 67, 76, 114; Rangel 1993:259, 263, 264, 266). Sometimes though, due to strong currents, it would take several tries to successfully span a stream (Rangel 1993:269). When bridges were not feasible, Soto's men strung ropes across a stream and, holding the rope, waded or swam themselves and their livestock across—a difficult endeavor to say the least and one in which both men and horses often drowned (Elvas 1993:76; Rangel 1993:260–261, 270, 279). In one instance, near Chiaha at a "hard river crossing," the Spaniards built a "bridge" by lining up horses across the river, head to tail. The riders kept them still while foot soldiers passed from one horse to the next "holding on to the tail, stirrup, cuirass [breastplate], and mane of one after another." They all crossed successfully (Rangel 1993:282).

Whatever the method used, stream crossings inevitably caused delays for travelers, especially for large parties such as Soto's. Delays were dangerous because they provided opportunities for enemy attacks, and cane brakes along rivers offered ample cover for warriors. In fact, Indians often ambushed Soto's army while it was most vulnerable, at river crossings, and the Spaniards encountered strenuous defensive measures by local Indians guarding the entrances to their chiefdoms at river crossings (Biedma 1993:236, 238; Elvas 1993:70, 98, 105, 143; Rangel 1993:267, 291–292, 297, 300).

All travelers need access to food. The support for travelers along Mississippian roads, paths, and waterways was provided at the towns through which the thoroughfares passed, and townspeople offered friendly travelers food and shelter. Alternately, travelers, especially warriors on the warpath, could rely on their own fortitude in withstanding privation and their abilities to hunt and gather wild foodstuffs while en route. When warring against Cofitachequi, for example, the warriors of Ocute managed by foraging and eating a little roasted corn they brought with them (Biedma 1993:229). During peaceful visits between towns and polities, Mississippians offered their guests gifts of food and other items from the communal stock (Smith and Hally 1992:102).

Soto depended on local food supplies, which explains why he was so concerned with locating populous towns and polities and why he traveled with a stock of pigs, which he reserved for starvation food. In fact, many of Soto's movements were guided as much by his need for food as for his search for precious metals (Hudson et al. 1987:19). Mississippians had a mixed economy of hunting, fishing, foraging, and agriculture, with corn being their primary crop. They also grew enough corn and other foodstuffs to provide a surplus for each town as well as stocking a communal granary in the capital that the chief oversaw. Soto's large army, restricted in hunting or foraging because of the constant worry of Indian attacks (Elvas 1993:77), usually depleted the surpluses of the towns through which they passed.

In addition to roads, pathways, stream crossings, food supplies, and so on, part of the Mississippian infrastructure included humans through the use of burden bearers, guides, and interpreters, all of which were necessary for a functioning infrastructure. As seen, travel through the Mississippian world was exclusively pedestrian or by watercraft, usually canoes, because the Southeastern Indians had no horses or draft animals. Without wheeled conveyances, Indians had to either carry goods on their person or pack them into canoes. Soto and his army had horses, but most of the army walked (Smith and Hally 1992:103). The Spaniards used their horses for travel and as packhorses, but given that Soto demanded throughout his march that local elites provide people as burden bearers to carry the army's supplies, the Spaniards, too, depended largely on humans to carry goods.

Later ethnographic accounts indicate that Southeastern Indians typically carried goods on their backs in baskets with straps that resembled modern backpacks, or by use of a tumpline for large baskets (Hudson 1976:284–285). Such transport limits the kinds and amounts of goods that can be carried. Large, unwieldy, and heavy objects (such as large logs) could not be transported long distances, whereas small portable objects (such as flint nodules, salt, or stone hoes) were easily carried. The kinds of things burden bearers could carry may have been limited, but collectively they could carry a substantial amount of easily portable items (such as foodstuffs and gifts for feasting events) over relatively long distances.

There is every indication in the Soto documents that elites could command burden bearers at a moment's notice and that this method of transport was indigenous to the Native South (Smith and Hally 1992:103). Upon entering a polity, Soto typically asked the chief and his leaders for two things: women and burden bearers. Whereas Soto's requests for women were oftentimes met with contempt and resistance, his requests for burden bearers were usually fulfilled (Biedma 1993:229, 232; Elvas 1993:69, 77, 80, 85, 86, 89, 91, 93, 95, 99; Rangel 1993:273, 279, 284, 285, 289). The number of burden bearers (*tamemes*) Soto received at a polity ranged from five to several hundred (Elvas 1993:77, 80, 85, 89, 91, 93, 95, 99, 121; Rangel 1993:280, 285; Smith and Hally 1992:103). Smith and Hally (1992:103) note that as a typical capital town had a population of about one thousand inhabitants, providing hundreds of burden bearers to the Spaniards meant a chief had to assemble them from several towns under his or her control. This also indicates that the elites could amass a large number of bearers when needed.

We have a poor reckoning of who served as burden bearers. Soto sometimes released bearers when the army passed out of their polity, suggesting that, in some cases, they were likely local citizens called to duty by the chief (Elvas 1993:69, 93; Smith and Hally 1992:103). However, when the Spaniards were finally leaving La Florida, they left more than 500 burden bearers on the banks of the Mississippi River, including some who had been with the army since Cofitachequi, in present-day South Carolina, indicating that the bulk of burden bearers were not released before departing their chiefdoms. The burden bearers left on the Mississippi River were distraught at being abandoned so far from their homes, many were seriously ill with dysentery, and, most likely, they knew their fate with the local Indians would end in slavery or death (Elvas 1993:150, 153, 216 note 287).

Those burden bearers taken by Soto, in fact, may already have been enslaved before the conquistador received them. In Cofitachequi, for example, the chieftainess, while traveling involuntarily with Soto, was carried on a litter by female slaves, suggesting that slaves made up a portion of the population of burden bearers. As Mississippian slaves were former war captives, the number of slaves in a community or polity was dependent on the military successes of that chiefdom. The larger, paramount chiefdoms obviously could command more slaves as burden bearers than could smaller, simple chiefdoms. In fact, this is what we see in the Soto documents. The larger polities for which we have estimates gave Soto hundreds of burden bearers each, such as Ocute (400 burden bearers), Toa (700), Chiaha (which was part of Coosa, 500), and Tascaluza (400) (Biedma 1993:229; Elvas 1993:77, 80, 91, 93, 121; Rangel 1993:283, 291). Other large polities, such as Coosa and Casqui, where we know leaders supplied burden bearers, though not how many, most likely provided comparable numbers (Elvas 1993:93, 121; Rangel 1993:285). Smaller polities, such as Ichisi (15 burden bearers), Gualquili, Xuala, Guasili, Coste (2), and Talise (40), could muster little more than a few dozen, at most (Elvas 1993:91, 95; Rangel 1993:272, 280, 281, 282).

Soto treated burden bearers in his custody deplorably. They were divided among the Spaniards, according to rank, and put into chains with collars about their necks. Bearers were responsible for not only carrying baggage, but also for grinding corn, gathering firewood, and completing any other chores they could undertake in chains. Burden bearers consistently tried to escape. Some, while gathering firewood or corn, would kill the soldier sent to guard them, then flee in their chains. Others managed to file off their chains during the night with pieces of stone, and some simply wandered away from the road, still in chains and still carrying their loads. To thwart such attempts to escape, Soto usually kept them in chains until they were 100 leagues (about 350 miles) from their homeland, at which point he would unchain the women and children (Elvas 1993:70, 93).[5] At the battle of Mabila, when the Spaniards endured a surprise attack by chief Tascaluza's forces, burden bearers took advantage of the chaos of battle to defect en masse. Most joined Tascaluza's army in the fight against the Spaniards (Elvas 1993:99).

In addition to burden bearers, another category of travel specialist most likely indigenous to the Native South was the guide. As a foreigner in an unfamiliar land, Soto obviously needed Native guides to help him navigate the many roads and pathways through the Mississippian world and to lead him to major population centers where he could replenish his stocks of food. In some cases, people volunteered to lead the army to its next destination; in others, chiefs offered guides to the Spaniards. Soto also coerced local Indians to act as guides and informants. In either case, the conquistador could not always rely on their guidance or on the information they offered. There are numerous examples of guides misleading the Spaniards, sometimes intentionally.

It appears that many of the captive guides were commoners, while the guides offered by the chiefs came from the ranks of the elites. Therefore, examining Soto's use of guides gives some clues into the territorial and geographic knowledge of commoners and elites, as well as differences in their ability to move between chiefdoms. In the case of captives, these Indians were most likely commoners captured when the Spanish army, on the march, happened upon a group of people away from their communities. When Soto departed a chiefdom, he also oftentimes forced local Indians to accompany him as guides. In many cases, the coerced guides clearly were "wandering and confused," and simply did not know the landscape well enough to steer the Spaniards to their desired destination. Or they managed to escape, forcing the Spaniards to find other guides (Biedma 1993:226, 229, 244; Elvas 1993:72–73; Rangel 1993:254, 255 [quote], 257, 267, 278). It is difficult to evaluate these incidents. On the one hand, perhaps these commoners "did not know two leagues farther" from their towns, as Biedma remarks about some captured Apalachee guides (Biedma 1993:226). On the other hand, though, Soto typically forced guides into service under pain of death. If they "guided poorly," he had them thrown to the war dogs he brought with him expressly for such purposes (Elvas 1993:80; Rangel 1993:237, 257 [quote]). Given the dire consequences of misleading Soto, one would assume that coerced guides would divulge the correct directions if they knew them. There are plenty of examples of apparent commoners who knew the landscape well, at least within their own chiefdoms. Coerced guides, for the most part, could not guide the army once out of their polity. In other words, commoners could navigate the roads and paths within their chiefdoms but not between chiefdoms.

There are also examples of coerced guides intentionally misleading the Spaniards or withholding information (Elvas 1993:82; Rangel 1993:276, 280). Moving from Ocute to Cofitachequi, the army took 12 days to cross the large uninhabited region along the Savannah River (Hudson 1997:167–169). Since Soto depended on local food stores to feed his army, 12 days without replenishing their supplies could have spelled doom for the Spaniards. During this trek, the army got into serious trouble when their guide, a young man by the name of Perico, lost his bearings and could not guide them out of this "wilderness." After much searching, a contingent of soldiers came across a small town of the paramount chiefdom of Cofitachequi, Aymay, from which they captured four Indians who they hoped would guide them to the capital town. But, according to Rangel (1993:276), "Not one would make known the town of their lord nor disclose its location, although they burned one of them alive in front of the others, and all suffered that martyrdom, in order not to disclose it." The next day, soldiers captured an Indian woman who had "news of a settlement," presumably the capital town, although Rangel is unclear whether she in fact knew the way there (Rangel 1993:276).

Perico is the best known of Soto's Native guides. He was a young man, around 17 years-of-age, whom Soto captured at Napituca, in present-day Florida. Perico relayed to Soto that he came from a distant land to the east, Yupaha, ruled by a woman (Elvas 1993:74). Scholars understand this to have been a reference to one of the towns of the paramount chiefdom of Cofitachequi in present-day South Carolina (Hudson 1997:130). Perico explained that "some time ago he had come in order to visit [other] lands," apparently as a trader, which took him far from his homeland, all the way to Napituca (Elvas 1993:74; Hudson 1997:130). He also told Soto about earlier Spaniards on the coast, presumably a reference to the short-lived Lucas de Ayllón colony of 1526 on the southern Atlantic coast, and he told of "riches" that Soto would find by traveling northeast. Soto determined to find these riches, using Perico as his guide into the interior. Thus began a long journey for the Spaniards under Perico's guidance (Biedma 1993:229–230; Hudson 1997:165–168; Elvas 1993:80–81, 83–84; Rangel 1993:259, 268–274).[6]

Perico first led them from Apalachee to Toa, then Ichisi, then to the main towns of the paramount chiefdom of Ocute (Altamaha, Ocute, and Cofaqui). At the River of Altamaha, most likely the Oconee River, local Indians reiterated what Perico had relayed about earlier Spaniards on the coast, which Soto took to mean at the mouth of the Oconee (Biedma 1993:229; Hudson et al. 1987:21). More importantly, this gave more credence to Perico as a guide. At Cofaqui, Perico told Soto that Cofitachequi was a mere four-day march away. The locals, however, warned that they knew of no towns in that direction and that Cofitachequi, which they knew about, was much farther than Perico's estimate. In fact, the people of Ocute told Soto they had little intercourse with Cofitachequi because they were at war with them. They warned that when warriors from both provinces struck out to make war they passed through much uninhabited lands by way of "hidden and secret places where they would not be detected and they spent twenty or twenty-two days on the road and ate only herbs and some roasted corn" (Biedma 1993:229 [quote]; Elvas 1993:80–81; Hudson 1997:166; Rangel 1993:273).

Although always cautious with guides, Soto had some confidence in Perico, plus the prospect of finding gold and silver led Soto to discount the people of Ocute's warnings, and he decided to follow Perico's route. After departing from Cofaqui for Cofitachequi, Soto's army soon entered the uninhabited zone around the Savannah River, and, as noted, the Spaniards became lost. The roads narrowed to nothing, the food they had with them was soon depleted, and Soto had to ration some of the precious pigs. Soto, enraged beyond words, threatened to throw Perico to the dogs and relented only because Perico was a necessary link in a chain of translators. The army eventually made its way to Cofitachequi (Biedma 1993:224, 230; Elvas 1993:80–83; Rangel 1993:274–275).[7]

What can Perico tell us about the Mississippian infrastructure? For one, certain categories of people, such as traders, could traverse long distances, apparently safely and without fear of being accosted by warriors from enemy chiefdoms. These people knew the landscape fairly well. Perico, after all, successfully guided Soto all the way from Apalachee to Cofaqui. Perico, who probably never actually visited the capital of Cofitachequi, may have come from a chiefdom on the coast of present-day Georgia that was under the rule of Cofitachequi (Hudson et al. 1987:19). So Perico, coming from the coast, would have followed certain trails in his travels. In fact, from Ichisi to Altamaha, Perico most likely led the army along a famous eighteenth- and nineteenth-century trail known as the Lower Trading Path that followed the Fall Line. At Altamaha, though, Soto left the Lower Trading Path when he turned north, up the Oconee River valley, toward Ocute (Hudson et al. 1997:21). This is where Perico began to lose his bearing, and once they ventured into the uninhabited area, which people traversed via "hidden and secret places," Perico got completely disoriented. If they had stayed on the Lower Trading Path, chances are good that Perico could have led them to Cofitachequi, or at least to some polities subject to the paramount (Marvin T. Smith, personal communication, 2015).

There are other hints at a category of professional guides in the Soto documents—evidence that certain men and women had considerable knowledge of the landscape over long distances, both within and between chiefdoms, and who served as guides when called upon by their chiefly elite.[8] There are numerous examples in the Soto documents of chiefs offering guides to Soto. Sometimes chiefs freely offered the use of their guides; sometimes Soto forced chiefs to comply with his demands (Biedma 1993:244; Elvas 1993:64, 77, 80, 91, 93, 123, 125, 126, 131, 139, 144–145; Rangel 1993:263, 273, 276, 297). In addition, Soto habitually put chiefs into captivity in order to move safely through their territories. Although the chroniclers only occasionally state that these chiefs acted as guides, one can presume that chiefs would have had intimate knowledge of their territories and could have served in this capacity.

As with all the guides, Soto could not depend on the truthfulness of guides a chief provided. Generally, local commoners who were captured and forced to act as guides had limited knowledge about roads, paths, and geography beyond their own chiefdom's boundaries. However, when chiefs offered guides to Soto, these men and women were able to navigate not only within a chiefdom, but also between chiefdoms, reflecting a broader network of geographical and geopolitical information than the rank and file. Given this, the guides offered to Soto, unlike the burden bearers, were not likely to have been slaves. In this regard, Juan Ortiz is an instructive special case. A young man from the Pánfilo de Narváez expedition, Ortiz had been captured by the Indians of Uzita and then Mocoso, near present-day Tampa Bay, put into slavery, and later rescued by Soto. Ortiz proved to be an invaluable translator, because he knew two local languages, but he was a dismal failure as a guide (Biedma 1993:225; Elvas 1993:62; Hudson 1997:83; Rangel 1993:254–256). As he told Soto, "He knew little of the land and had neither seen nor heard of things only twenty leagues [70 miles] away" from the town where he lived (Biedma 1993:225), indicating, of course, that this sort of knowledge would not have been accessible to slaves, whose every move was under surveillance by their owners.[9]

Unlike slaves, chief's guides knew how to cross long distances. For example, at Aguacaleyquen, in present-day Florida, Soto captured the chief, his daughter, and "a principal Indian named Guatutima," whom Soto used as a guide "because he said that he knew much of what was farther on and gave very great news about it" (Rangel 1993:263). This passage suggests that Guatutima was an elite and a knowledgeable and well-known guide, who perhaps served his chief in this capacity. At Ichisi, the chief provided a guide to direct Soto to Ocute, a neighboring paramount chiefdom to the northeast (Elvas 1993:77; Rangel 1993:273). At Toa, one of the towns of Ocute, the chief offered guides who could take the Spaniards to either Cofitachequi, which he recommended against, or to Coosa, which he recommended to Soto. As we have seen, Soto opted for Cofitachequi, even though it involved a dangerous march through expansive uninhabited territory. In this case, though, the Toa guides did not know the way through the Savannah wilderness, and Soto sent them home because he could not feed them (Elvas 1993:81; Rangel 1993:275). At Chiaha, in present-day northeast Tennessee, Soto sent some Spaniards to look for the chiefdom of Chisca, where Soto had heard there was a foundry for copper (which Soto thought could be gold). The chief of Chiaha sent some of his people who knew the land and language of Chisca with the troops (Elvas 1993:90). At Chicaza, in present-day northeast Mississippi, the chief offered guides and interpreters to Soto to take the army to the renowned province of Caluça (Rangel 1993:297). Soto declined to go there, so scholars are unsure where Caluça was located; however, it most likely was some distance from Chicaza (Ethridge 2010:37–38; Hudson 1997:265). Recall that the chroniclers expressed surprise when a guide from Quiguate led the army across dense swamps with no roads, only to emerge at Coligua, the exact town they had set out to find (Biedma 1993:241; Elvas 1993:122).

Guides dispatched by chiefs were also known to mislead the Spaniards. For example, after Soto's death in 1542, Luis de Moscoso took command of the army and, after consultation with the officers, decided to attempt an overland march to New Spain (Biedma 1993:243; Elvas 1993:139). This maneuver proved especially treacherous because the army pushed past the edge of the Mississippian world. Pedestrian and nomadic hunters and foragers lived to the west, so there were no towns with large food surpluses that could feed the 300 or so survivors and 500 captives of the expedition. Moscoso had numerous difficulties finding his way along this frontier. At Naguatex, in present-day western Arkansas, the chief refused to provide guides and burden bearers. In response, Moscoso ordered his soldiers to burn the town. Afterward, the chief sent six principal men and three guides to accompany Moscoso, but a few days later these guides began "wandering off the road" and taking circuitous routes. Moscoso "ordered them hanged from a tree," after which a captive woman from Nisohone was pressed into guiding the army to the next province of Lacane (Elvas 1993:145).

Moscoso eventually arrived at the province of Nondacao, in present-day east Texas, where locals informed him they had heard that the people of Soacatino, a province south of there, had seen other Christians.[10] The Nondacao chief also offered Moscoso a guide to take them to Soacatino, the largest province in the area where, he assured the commander, they also would find plenty of food. The guide instead led the army across "much rugged land and off road, until finally he told us that he no longer knew where he was leading us" (Biedma 1993: 244 [quote]; Elvas 1993:145–146). Under torture, the guide confessed that his chief had instructed him to take the Spaniards to where they would "die of hunger" (Biedma 1993:244 [quote]; Elvas 1993:146). Moscoso had him thrown to the dogs, and another captive guided them through the small province of Ays to their destination, Soacatino (Elvas 1993:146).

While in present-day east Texas, Moscoso also was misled when guides gave conflicting and faulty information. At Soacatino, Moscoso heard rumors that the people there had seen other Christians, which convinced him that New Spain was not far off. When queried more closely, locals informed Moscoso they had not actually seen the Christians, but they had heard Christians "were traveling about near there to the southward" (Elvas 1993:146). Soacatino proved to have little food, so Moscoso, hoping to find the rumored Christians, set out for the province of Guasco, marching for twenty days through a thinly populated region where local Indians hid what little maize they had (Biedma 1993:244; Elvas 1993:146). The Spaniards plundered Guasco for maize and continued to Naquiscoza. Here they captured some locals who informed Moscoso that they had never heard of other Christians. Later, under torture, the captives revealed that some Christians were known to be in the neighboring province of Nazacahoz (Biedma 1993:244; Elvas 1993:246). Pushing on to Nazacahoz, Moscoso captured some local women, one of whom told the Spaniard she had been captured by other Christians, but had escaped. She then led a reconnaissance group to the place where she claimed to have been with the Christians. Once there, though, she admitted it was all a lie. This convinced Moscoso that tales of other Christians were merely rumors or lies (Biedma 1993:244; Elvas 1993:246–247). Fearing either getting hopelessly lost or starving, Moscoso decided to return to the more populous polities along the Mississippi River.

The Mississippian world was also a place of great linguistic diversity and included about 20 or so known languages from five language families—Algonquian, Muskogean, Iroquoian, Siouan, and Caddoan (Hudson 1976: 22–25). Languages within a family were not necessarily mutually intelligible, but Southeastern Indians were superb linguists, and people could oftentimes speak several languages. However, there were also linguistic limitations. Perico, for example, spoke a Muskogean language, but he could not understand all of the Muskogean languages, despite his long journey to Napituca (Elvas 1993:76; Hudson 1997:174). Obviously, Soto, traveling the breadth and width of the Mississippian world, had need of interpreters from the moment his army stepped off the boats in Tampa Bay. In fact, Soto's first attempt to communicate with local Indians through "signs"—meaning hand gestures—was a complete failure (Rangel 1993:255). Then, as mentioned, by an unfathomable stroke of luck, Soto soon found Juan Ortiz, who, during his 12 years in captivity, had learned two of the local Timucuan languages (Uzita and Mocoso), which he could translate into Spanish (Biedma 1993:225; Elvas 1993:59–61; Hudson 1997:83; Rangel 1993:255).

As the army progressed in their march, Soto, then, needed to find Indians who could speak the Indian languages known by Ortiz, as well as any new local languages. Although the documents do not specify, one can imagine an increasingly cumbersome process wherein a chain of translators was necessary to translate from one language to another until finally arriving at the Timucuan languages of Ortiz, who then made the final translations into Spanish, and vice versa. Remember that Perico, the guide, was a vital link in this chain of translators and that it saved his life.

Ortiz died at the chiefdom of Utiangüe, in present-day eastern Arkansas. Although several of the young boys and girls captured along the way had learned some Spanish, and one particular youth captured at Cofitachequi knew it well enough to serve in Ortiz's stead, the death of Ortiz distressed Soto and the others (Elvas 1993:130, 154). For one, the Cofitachequi youth's command of Spanish was poor, and according to Elvas (1993:130) what would take Ortiz "four words" to translate would take the youth a whole day. More importantly, without Ortiz, the Spaniards more often than not received faulty intelligence due to inaccurate translations, which increased the risk of falling into enemy hands or, worse, getting lost and starving (Elvas 1993:170; Hudson 1997:334).

Like guides and burden bearers, there appears to have been a category of specialists in languages that was indigenous to the Mississippian world. In fact, one of the chroniclers on the 1566–1567 Juan Pardo expeditions into present-day South Carolina recorded the Muskogean names of several political positions, including *yatika*, the office of interpreter and spokesperson (Hudson 2005 [1990]:64–67). Soto rarely faced difficulties finding translators, except on the western fringes of the Mississippian world in present-day western Arkansas and eastern Texas. Similar to the guides and burden bearers, some of these translators fell into Spanish hands when Soto happened upon them while crossing a border; others were offered by local chiefs either voluntarily or under duress (Biedma 1993:226, 229; Elvas 1993:77, 125, 145; Rangel 1993:255, 274, 296, 297).

Interpreters and guides were vital to the expedition, and the Spaniards fretted much when they lacked them. This was especially true in western Arkansas and eastern Texas, where the Spaniards faced many difficulties, but none as dire as the lack of interpreters. Ortiz died on this leg of the journey, at the point when the expedition reached the western frontiers of the Mississippian world. Not only was this a geographic and cultural boundary between the Eastern Woodlands and the Great Plains, but there were social and linguistic boundaries as well. On several occasions, chiefs were unable to provide interpreters. For example, at the chiefdom of Cayas, on the central Arkansas River, Soto demanded a guide and interpreter to lead them to the next province, Tula (Elvas 1993:125; Hudson 1997:318). The Indians of Tula were different from the Mississippians, more affiliated with the western bison hunters (Hudson 1997:322). The Cayas chief provided guides to Tula, but he could not provide interpreters, because "he and his forebears had always been at war with the lords of that province, they had no converse, nor did they understand each other" (Elvas 1993:125–126). Once in Tula, Tula warriors attacked Soto, and the army retreated to Cayas, where they had been more welcomed. Of the Tula captives Soto managed to take, none could understand the language of Cayas (Biedma 1993:242; Elvas 1993:126; Hudson 1997:320–322; Rangel 1993:305). After a subsequent altercation with Tula warriors, the chief of Tula appeased Soto with a visit, gifts, and an interpreter who understood the language of Cayas. As Elvas relates, "The governor and all the men were very glad, for they could in no wise travel without an interpreter" (Elvas 1993:126).

In present-day east Texas, Moscoso faced serious difficulties in finding interpreters. Here, too, the army had crossed out of the Mississippian world and encountered hunters and fisher people (Hudson 1997:370–371). Once across the "River of Daycao" (most likely either the Brazos or Navasota), none of the Indians with the Spaniards could understand the local Indians (Biedma 1993:244; Elvas 1993:147; Hudson 1997:371). At this point, Moscoso, knowing that going further without interpreters courted disaster, and realizing that local Indian food reserves could not support the army, decided to return to the Mississippi River and attempt to sail to New Spain (Elvas 1993:147).

Moscoso, in fact, was not only entering a new geographic, cultural, and linguistic zone, but also entering into a new Native infrastructure, one that looked much more difficult for the Spaniards to co-opt than the one he was using. Despite some difficulties, the sixteenth-century Mississippian infrastructure, indeed, could support a large, foreign expedition marching through its entire extent. We should not be surprised. The Mississippian world was composed of sophisticated polities connected by friendship or enmity, organized around a stable infrastructure through which goods, people, information, and services flowed. Many of the polities, as Dubcovsky notes (2016:20), were small and competing, which could disrupt these flows. Yet I maintain that competition and hostility, as well as cooperation and amity, served as binding agents in the Mississippian world. The sixteenth-century Mississippian world was not fractured, but rather, like stained-glass, a mosaic of varied, brilliant pieces soldered together with an intricate infrastructure.

Notes

1. For this analysis, I have opted to not use Garcilaso because of imprecisions in that account.

2. One exception to this may have been the Plaquemine polities, which were a Mississippian variant on the lower Mississippi Valley and Gulf Coast. Livingood (2009) argues that these chiefdoms, unlike much of the rest of the Mississippian chiefdoms, were xenophobic and inward looking.

3. Archaeologists disagree whether salt was part of an elite trade network or down-the-line trade by commoners (Maureen Meyers, 2015, personal communication).

4. Soto also saw a fleet of war canoes at both Guachoya and Anilco; see Elvas 1993:131, 132, 133, 153.

5. A Spanish league was equal to 3.45 miles (Hudson 1997:469).

6. Hudson (1997:130, 165) names two young traders who went on to act as Soto's guides, Marcos and Perico. However, Hudson used Garcilaso as his exclusive source for Marcos. I rely solely on the Rangel, Elvas, and Biedma accounts, none of which mention Marcos, only Perico.

7. We do not know the fate of Perico. In Cofitachequi, he asked the Spanish friars to baptize him, which they did, christening him "Pedro." Soto then ordered him released from the chains with which he had been restrained (Elvas 1993:84). The chroniclers do not mention Perico or Pedro again, so one can presume that Soto allowed the young man to remain in his homeland of Cofitachequi.

8. Smith and Hally maintain that whether the use of guides was common during the Late Mississippian cannot be determined because of the "infrequency with which guides are mentioned" in the Soto chronicles (Smith and Hally 1992:104). However, Smith and Hally stopped their reading of the documents when Soto and the army passed through Coosa, and they only note that guides were mentioned at Ichisi, Patofa, and Cofitachequi (Smith and Hally 1992:104).

9. Elvas (1993:62) states that Ortiz claimed he had never gone more than 10 leagues from the town, but that he had heard about a chief named Paracoxi who lived about thirty leagues away.

10. This may have been a reference to the Coronado expedition, which took place in 1540–1542 (Elvas 1993:213, n270). Coronado marched as far east as present-day Kansas.

5

MARINE SHELL TRADE IN THE POST-MISSISSIPPIAN SOUTHEAST

Marvin T. Smith

While working on a protohistoric site sequence for the Coosa River valley of Alabama and Georgia years ago, I noted that marine shell artifacts disappeared from the area in the early seventeenth century. I wrote off this event as a consequence of the availability of comparable new materials from Europe, such as glass beads replacing shell beads and brass gorgets replacing shell gorgets (Smith 1987). However, over the years, it has become clear that marine shell continued to be used in many parts of the Southeast well into the eighteenth century. Could shell artifact distributions through time perhaps lead to an understanding of trade routes? Why do some areas have shell artifacts, while others, apparently occupied contemporaneously, lack them? With the collapse of the Spanish mission system in 1704 and the subsequent enslavement or relocation of most of Florida's Native inhabitants, who was left to relay marine shell, either as finished artifacts or raw material, into the interior? Could there have been production of marine shell artifacts by Europeans in the Southeast, as documented by Esarey (2013) for the seventeenth-century Northeast?

Evidence for Shell Trade in the Post-Mississippian Southeast

In this chapter, I focus on marine shell from sites with datable European trade materials. Although it would be preferable to have shell artifacts found in direct association with European trade goods, such excavation contexts are actually quite rare. I have applied dates to the sites in this study based on criteria in Smith (1987, 2000) and Waselkov (1989), but not all scholars agree on this dating of European artifacts (Little 2010). Unfortunately, the dating debate cannot be settled here, but I can confidently date these sites to within a half century—to the last half of the sixteenth century, the first half of the seventeenth century, or the second half of the seventeenth century—although, in a few instances, I can narrow the resolution to a third of a century. This study is limited to sites east of the Mississippi River.

Many species of marine shells were used as raw materials for ornaments by prehistoric and protohistoric Southeastern Native Americans. Most artifacts reported in the archaeological literature have not been identified to the genus or species level, but commonly utilized shells include members of the genera *Busycon*, *Strombus*, *Marginella*, and *Oliva*. These shellfish have a wide range along the Atlantic coast, around the Florida Peninsula, and into the Gulf of Mexico, which unfortunately obscures an individual shell's origin and complicates efforts to recognize trade networks (Claassen 1989; Emerson and Jacobson 1976; Ottesen 1979). Sourcing shells through trace element studies may be possible (Claassen 1989), but few such analyses have been attempted. Therefore, at this time we do not know the origin point(s) of marine shells entering the interior Southeast.

There are also problems with shell artifact typology. For example, terms applied to shell ear ornaments include pins, plugs, bracket-pins, mushroom-headed pins, spools, and so forth. It is not always clear what is being described when illustrations are lacking. Differentiating large columella beads, which are usually somewhat spherical, from flat disc beads cut from a shell wall would be helpful, but often the only description in an archaeological report is a vague "shell beads." Therefore, in this preliminary study I have had to consider *Strombus* and *Busycon* shell beads of various styles as a single category.

Marine shell artifacts clearly were in common use on archaeological sites of the sixteenth century that show evidence of contact (direct or otherwise) with Europeans. Engraved shell gorgets of the Rattlesnake type (Figure 5.1a and d, especially the Citico- and Carters Quarter-styles, as defined by Brain and Phillips 1996) and Mask types (Figure 5.1b and e, especially the Buffalo- and Chickamauga-styles of Brain and Phillips 1996) are found in Alabama, Georgia, Tennessee, North Carolina (Figure 5.2), and points farther north, even in Ontario, on sites that have produced European artifacts. Shell ear pins of the bracket- and knobbed-styles (see figures 5.1g and i), conch beads manufactured from the central columella, smaller beads made from the shell wall, and ear spools are also found. Beads manufactured from *Marginella* shells are present. Perhaps the best-documented assemblage, which includes examples of the aforementioned types, comes from the King site in northwest Georgia (Hally 2008), where marine shell artifacts accompanied 18 percent of the 249 burials. King is believed to have been occupied for a short time in the mid-sixteenth century. At the Citico site in Hamilton County, Tennessee, 34.9 percent of the 106 burials reported by C. B. Moore (1915) had marine shell in virtually all of the forms present at King. The higher frequency of marine shell in graves at Citico might have resulted from the fact that Citico was probably a chiefly capital, whereas King was

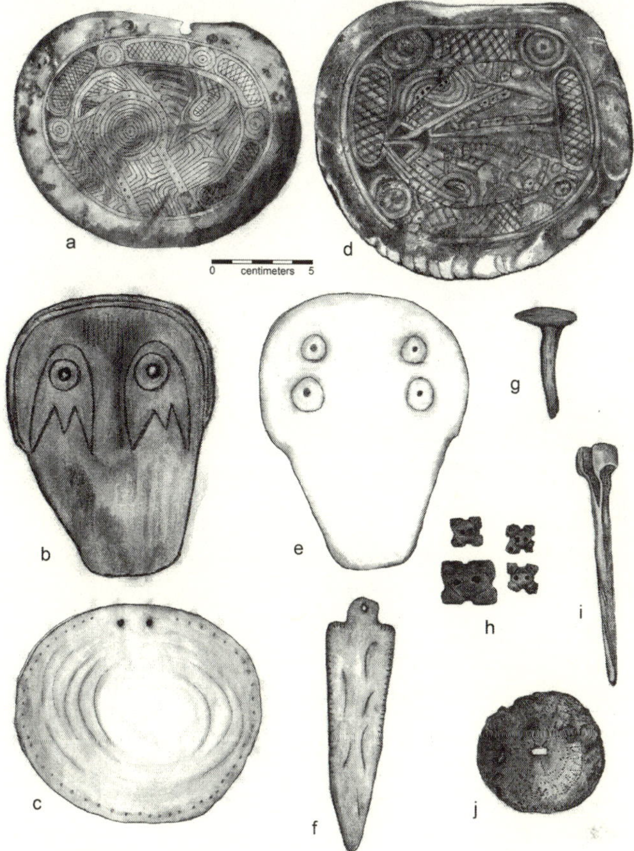

Figure 5.1. Marine shell artifacts in common use on archaeological sites of the Protohistoric Southeast. (a) and (d): rattlesnake-type gorget; (b) and (e): mask-type gorget; (c): Taskigi-style gorget; (f): "spearhead-" or "arrowhead"-shaped pendant; (g) and (i): bracket and knobbed styles of ear pins; (h): "buttons"; (j): gorget from Fredericks site (drawings by Julie Barnes Smith).

a small village. Ottesen (1979:20–21) noted long ago that major Mississippian centers tend to have more exotic materials than smaller sites. Also, because evidence suggests that Mississippian shell networks were disrupted following contact with Europeans, lesser quantities of new shell may have been entering the interior in the late sixteenth century. Consequently, the site of Citico, which spans the fifteenth and sixteenth centuries, might have more shell than a site such as King, occupied solely in the mid- to late sixteenth century.

The Brakebill Mound in Tennessee (Brain and Phillips 1996:209) has

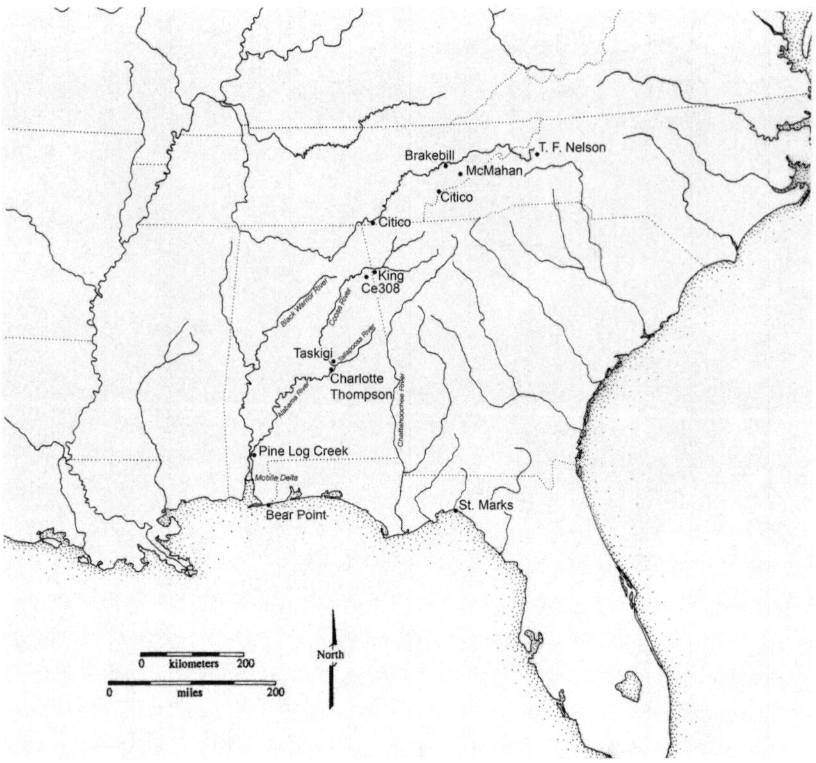

Figure 5.2. Sixteenth-century sites in the Southeast with marine shell artifacts (map by Julie Barnes Smith).

Rattlesnake- and Mask gorgets, knobbed- and bracket-style ear pins, and shell beads, an assemblage virtually duplicated at the McMahan Mound and at the Settico site, both in eastern Tennessee (Brain and Phillips 1996:210–211, 226–228; Smith 1987:92). These sites produced European artifacts of the sixteenth century, although Settico was also occupied in the seventeenth century, based on types of brass ornaments (Lewis 1960:101, 103). Rattlesnake and Mask gorgets are found down the Coosa River to the Taskigi site (Brannon 1931, 1935) but are not found immediately west of Taskigi on the Alabama River, at sites such as Charlotte Thompson or Thirty Acre Field (Moore 1899; see also Brain and Phillips 1996). As noted by Brain and Phillips, this abrupt end to their geographic distribution clearly indicates a cultural boundary, a border between Moundville-related cultures to the west and Lamar-related cultures to the east. Linguistically, this boundary probably separates proto-Choctaw from proto-Upper Creek Muskogee speakers (see Booker et al., 1992; Galloway 1995). Shell ornaments served as cultural markers and had sociopolitical meaning to their wearers.

In his study of shell gorgets in the Southeast, Hally (2007) suggests that gorget manufacture ended by roughly A.D. 1600. From the perspective of dating sites with European artifacts, my research largely supports this thesis with the exception of gorgets without engraved decoration, which continued to be made in much later times. Burial M at site 1CE308 (Little and Curren 1981:130) contains a shell gorget decorated on the convex side with dots drilled around the edge. This burial contained a necklace of shell and glass beads, including tumbled turquoise blue (Kidd type 11a40) and a faceted, seven-layer chevron bead. Deagan (1987) dates the turquoise blue beads post-1580 based on shipping lists, so this burial probably dates to the terminal sixteenth century. Other European items from 1CE308, including iron chisels and a brass cup weight, suggest a date closer to the middle of the sixteenth century, more in line with the Citico-style Rattlesnake and Mask gorgets also found there.

During the early seventeenth century, marine shell disappeared from the upper Coosa River valley of Alabama. The Bradford Ferry site provides the largest sample of burials from sites of the Weiss Phase, yet none of the 47 burials recorded from Bradford Ferry have marine shell. European objects are found in 66 percent of these graves (Smith 2000:106), suggesting that marine shell may have simply gone out of style once European objects were acquired through Native trade with coastal European settlements. Clearly, Native trade networks from the coast were still intact, as European artifacts are common. According to the historical record, no Europeans entered the interior at this time so the only mechanism of European artifact distribution was via Native networks, yet marine shell was not being imported from the coast. Interestingly, marine shell use also declined dramatically on Seneca Iroquois sites of the early seventeenth- century Northeast (Sempowski 1988).

In contrast, marine shell continues to be found at many other early seventeenth-century sites in the Southeast, suggesting that trade networks and Native demand were still intact in other areas (Figure 5.3). For example, from west to east, shell is found at the Rolling Hills complex in Mississippi (Atkinson 1979); many burial urn sites in Alabama (Curren 1984; Moore 1899); Patale Mission in Florida (Jones et al. 1991); Nacoochee (Heye et al. 1918) and 9HK33 (*aka* 9HK08) in Georgia (Blanton 1986), Hampton Place (McCollough and Bass 1983), Carter House, Williams Island, and Great Tellico in east Tennessee (Polhemus 1982); and Lower Saratown in North Carolina (Ward and Davis 1993). The most popular forms at this time include shell beads, shell ear pins, and unengraved shell gorgets, some of which have drilled dot decoration. Brain and Phillips (1996) refer to these dot-decorated gorgets as the Taskigi-style (see figure 5.1c). *Marginella* shell beads are still found at a few sites, such as Rolling Hills in Mississippi (Atkinson 1979) and Nacoochee in Georgia (Heye et al. 1918), but the contexts

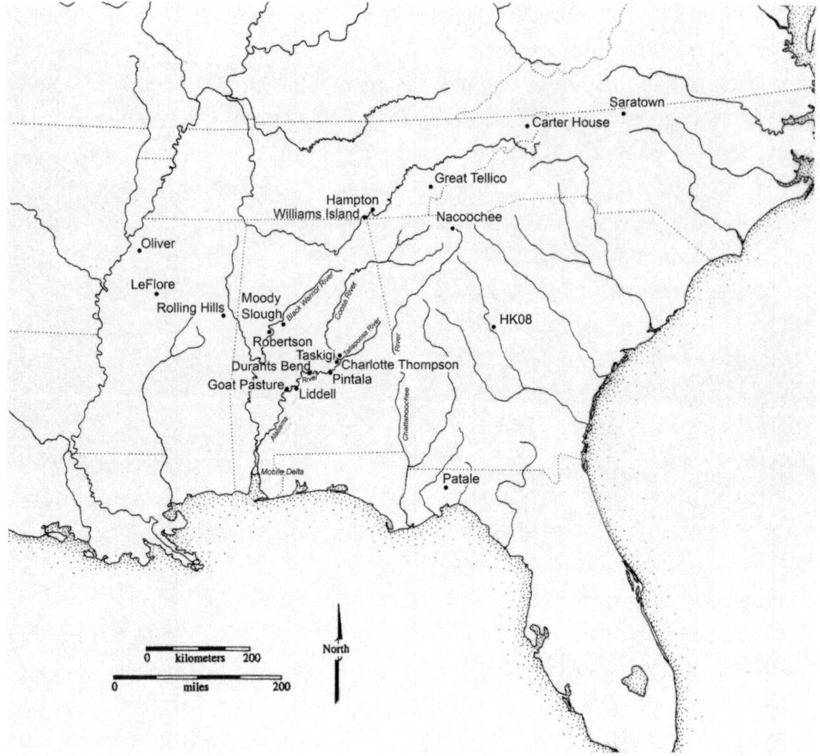

Figure 5.3. Early seventeenth-century sites in the Southeast with marine shell artifacts (map by Julie Barnes Smith).

at these sites are hard to date. Engraved shell gorgets are largely absent from early seventeenth-century sites, although a unique specimen comes from the poorly dated Rolling Hills complex in Mississippi, and a fragmentary engraved gorget was found at the Patale Mission site in Florida (Jones et al. 1991:96). A unique version of the Citico-style Rattlesnake gorget was reported from the Williams Island site in Tennessee in association with glass beads, including eye beads, and brass conical bangles suggesting an early seventeenth-century date (Smith 1976:37; Smith 1987:111). A Carters Quarter–style Rattlesnake gorget found at the Santa Catalina de Guale Mission in coastal Georgia could date to the late sixteenth or seventeenth century (Blair et al. 2009:151). These examples are probably the last remnants of the engraved shell gorget tradition in the Southeast.

The Taskigi site in Alabama provides much marine shell, but dating is problematical. Here members of the Alabama Anthropological Society (AAS) excavated "two thousand evidences of Urn-Burial" (Brannon 1935) and an unknown number of burials of other forms early in the twentieth century. Brain and Phillips (1996:293–295) quote another Brannon estimate of approximately 1,500 burials. Waselkov believes that Brannon was prone to exaggeration but notes that there are some 300 grave lots derived from AAS-donated collections that could be reconstructed in the Alabama Department of Archives and History curated collection (Waselkov and Sheldon 1987:315–411). The 300 lots at Archives and History definitely do not represent all the graves "investigated" at this important site, as only a few AAS members donated their collections. I believe that the site's occupation spans the second half of the sixteenth century and the first half of the seventeenth century. The forms of shell found here include Rattlesnake gorgets, several engraved Mask gorgets (see figure 5.1d), plain shell gorgets, beads, ear pins of the knobbed and bracket styles, and some unusual "spearhead" or "arrowhead" shaped pendants (Brain and Phillips 1996; Brannon 1935) (see figure 5.1f). This last form has also been called a "feather" pendant (Waselkov, personal communication) and appears to be restricted to the area of the junction of the Coosa and Tallapoosa Rivers. Brannon (1935:34) notes that these pendants were the central ornament on "several necklaces" excavated at Taskigi, although he only illustrates two specimens as line drawings. One example from a Taskigi grave lot in the Alabama Department of Archives and History collection donated by H. H. "Yank" Paulin includes a large-hole variety brass gorget, a type dated to ca. 1580–1650 (Waselkov 1989). Given its restricted distribution, I suggest that the extant examples may be the work of one craftsman.

Another interesting new form of shell bead, made from a long columella with a perforation that starts at the end of the bead but cuts diagonally through to a side, is reported from Early Upper Saratown (pre-1620) in North Carolina (Hammett and Sizemore 1988: Figure 5). The presence of an undrilled blank for a bead of this type suggests the beads were produced at the site (Hammett and Sizemore 1988). This type of bead does not appear to have been popular in the Southeast, although beads drilled in a similar fashion were recovered from a historic burial at Hiwassee Island in Tennessee, where they were believed to have been recycled from an earlier prehistoric Woodland-Period Hamilton burial (Lewis and Kneberg 1946:151). Given their larger diameter, compared with the Saratown examples, the recycling interpretation seems reasonable. The Hiwassee Island burial probably postdates the Upper Saratown context but still dates to the seventeenth century.

Potential seventeenth-century examples of bracket-style ear pins (see figure 5.1g) are found at Taskigi in Alabama (Brannon 1935) and at Great Tellico (Rice 1977) and Hampton Place in Tennessee (McCollough and

Bass 1983). All three of these sites may have had sixteenth-century occupations, and thus the later dating of the bracket-style pins is not secure, as we lack complete data on individual grave lots. However, bracket-style pins have not been reported from sites in the Southeast that I would postdate 1650. Penelope Drooker (1997:301) discusses the distribution of this form of ear pin in the Midwest and Northeast, where they are found on several Fort Ancient sites and the Neutral Grimsby site in Ontario, all of which probably predate the mid-seventeenth century. They are also found at the Powerhouse and Dann sites in the Seneca Iroquois sequence (Powerhouse dates ca. 1640–1655 and Dann dates ca. 1655–1675; Sempowski and Saunders 2001:6). Only the latter occurrence suggests use past ca. 1650.

Square shell "buttons" (see figure 5.1h; Moore 1899:139) are characteristic of the Markala Horizon defined by Steve Williams (1980), which he dates to "probably 1540–1650." They appear on sites that I date to the early to mid-seventeenth century in the present study area. They are found in Mississippi at the Oliver site, which has European trade material from the first third of the seventeenth century (author's notes); at LeFlore, which probably dates around the middle of the seventeenth century; and in Alabama at Charlotte Thompson, with trade material from the middle of the sixteenth to early seventeenth century, and Durants Bend, which was probably occupied from the sixteenth to seventeenth centuries (Drooker 1997; Williams 1980). The latest examples come from a Chickasaw site, MLe 18, which probably dates 1680 to 1730, according to John O'Hear (personal communication, 2015). Outside of the study area, this form has also been found at Madisonville, in Ohio, in what is probably a terminal sixteenth- or early seventeenth-century context (Drooker 1997:301). These "buttons" are a complex form with limited temporal distribution. Assuming a short manufacturing span, I suspect that they were made between 1625 and 1650, within the overlap of estimated occupation periods for most of these sites.

From this survey of shell artifacts from protohistoric sites in the Southeast, we know that marine shell continued to be introduced and utilized in the early seventeenth century over a large part of the interior. Why then did the Coosa River groups discontinue its use? As discussed below, marine shell made a return there in the mid-seventeenth century, although in limited quantities. What disrupted trade in raw material from the coast? Or was there simply a regional cultural preference to replace shell with glass beads and brass ornaments for their novelty? While marine shell was missing from the Coosa Valley, there appears to have been a greater frequency of European items placed into graves in this area than in other contemporary areas of the Southeast. The Coosa people had lengthy contact with the Soto and Luna expeditions and brief contact with the Pardo expedition, experiences that may have heightened their desire to obtain European items,

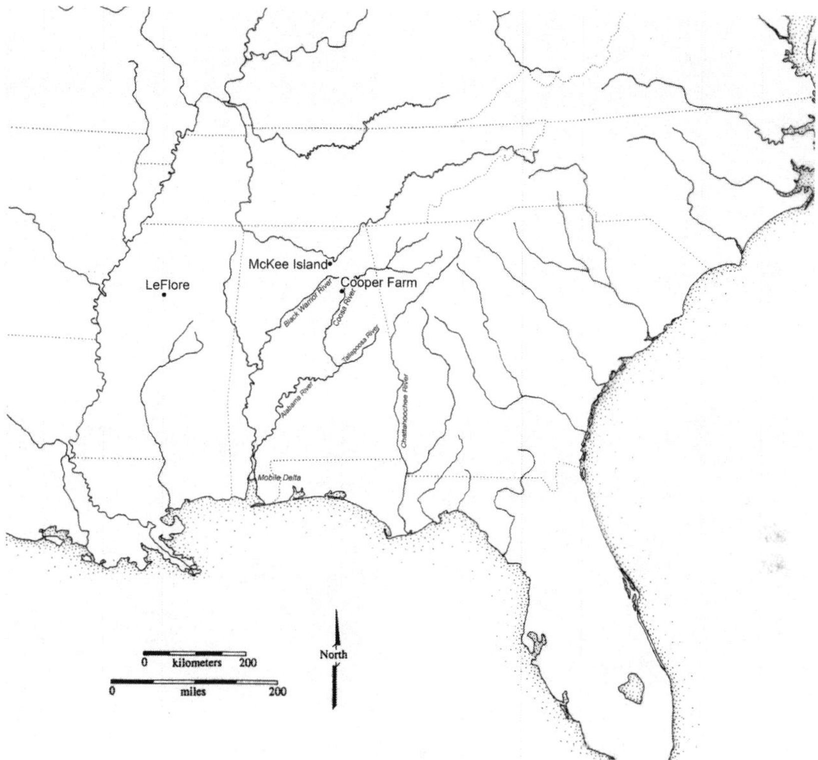

Figure 5.4. Mid-seventeenth-century sites in the Southeast with marine shell artifacts (map by Julie Barnes Smith).

apparently at the expense of traditional shell. Farther west on the Alabama River, where Native peoples had particularly bad experiences with Europeans, including the battle of Mabila, seventeenth-century burial urn sites have very few European artifacts, although marine shell continued to accompany the deceased.

By the middle of the seventeenth century, small amounts of marine shell are again found on the Upper Coosa Valley in Alabama (Figure 5.4). Shell beads, an ear pin, and an undescribed shell gorget are reported at the Cooper Farm site (Lindsey 1964; Battles 1969, 1972), whereas no marine shell is present at the nearby contemporary Milner Village site (Smith et al 1993), although we have data on fewer than 10 burials from Milner. Other mid-seventeenth century sites, such as LeFlore in Mississippi (Johnson n.d.) and McKee Island in Alabama (Webb and Wilder 1951), produce conch and *Marginella* beads, shell ear pins, and, at McKee Island, a badly decayed shell gorget.

In the late seventeenth century, shell again disappeared from the Coosa

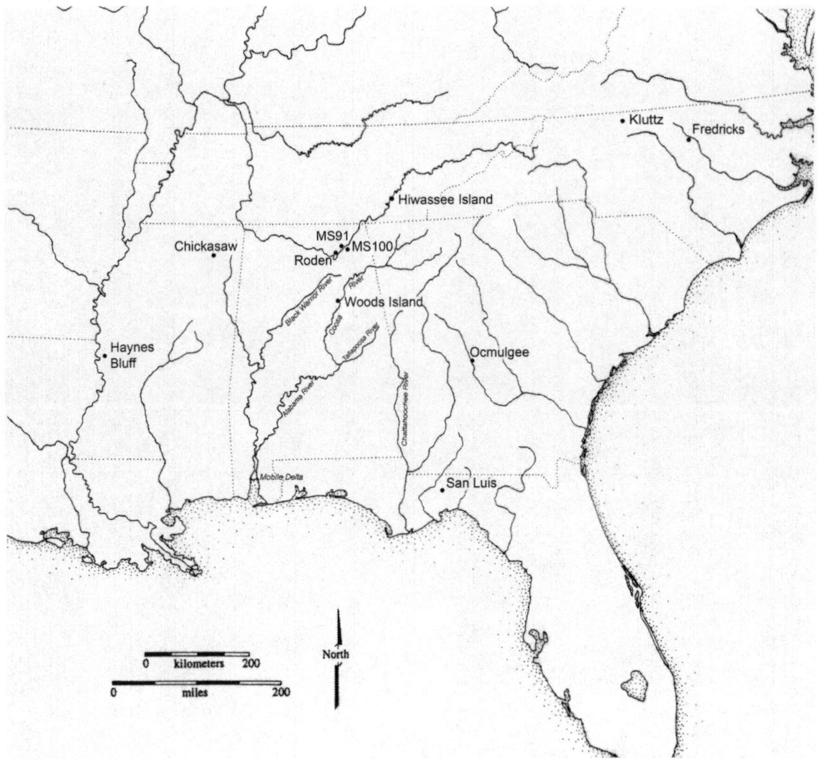

Figure 5.5. Late seventeenth-century sites in the Southeast with marine shell artifacts (map by Julie Barnes Smith).

Valley in Alabama. Just one of the 48 burials documented from the Woods Island site contained shell ornaments, the exception being an extended burial with three shell beads believed to date from an earlier component (Smith 1995). By way of contrast, conch shell beads are found across other areas of the Southeast in the late seventeenth century (Figure 5.5). They are known from Mission San Luis, 1656–1704, in Florida (Mitchem 1993); several sites in Marshall County, Alabama, on the Tennessee River (Webb and Wilder 1951); Ocmulgee (Mason 2005); Hiwassee Island (Lewis and Kneberg 1946); and the Fredericks and Kluttz sites in North Carolina (Hammet and Sizemore 1989; Ward and Davis 1993:308). Most sites produce roughly spherical columella beads, but long columella beads also appear in the Southeast, such as at 1MS100 in Alabama (Webb and Wilder 1951), Ocmulgee (Mason 2005), Hiwassee Island (Lewis and Kneberg 1946), Fredericks site (noted as metal-drilled by Hammett and Sizemore 1989:128), and the Haynes Bluff site in Mississippi (pre-1706) (Brain 1988). These beads seem to be more common in the eastern portion of the study area. Columella pendants were also found at 1MS91 in Alabama (Webb and Wilder 1951) and at Ocmulgee (Mason 2005). Tapering long tubular hair pipe-like beads have been found on Chickasaw sites in Mississippi (John O'Hear, personal communication, 2015), but these may date to the eighteenth century.

Late seventeenth-century/early eighteenth-century knobbed shell ear pins (see figure 5.1i) are found at Haynes Bluff (Brain 1988), Fatherland (Neitzel 1965), and Chickasaw sites in Mississippi (Jennings 1941), and they are known from 1MS91 and 1MS100 on the Tennessee River in Alabama (Webb and Wilder 1951), but have not been documented at sites farther east, such as Ocmulgee, Hiwassee Island (in historic contexts), or the Fredericks or Kluttz sites. The Mississippi Valley seems to be the last place this artifact style was used, well into the middle of the eighteenth century, at such sites as Trudeau (Brain 1979). Bracket-style ear pins and pulley-shaped ear spools are not found in late seventeenth-century contexts in the Southeast.

Late seventeenth-/early eighteenth-century shell gorgets are known from Chickasaw sites (Jennings 1941); Roden (Moore 1915), 1MS91, and 1MS100 in Alabama (Webb and Wilder 1951); Ocmulgee (Mason 2005); Hiwassee Island (Lewis and Kneberg 1946); and the Fredericks site (Hammett and Sizemore 1988). Most are plain discs, but the examples from Fredericks have complex drilled pit decorations and clearly relate to a different cultural tradition (see figure 5.1j; Hammett and Sizemore 1988: Figure 2f, g). With the exception of Ocmulgee, the other sites were occupied by Chickasaws and probable proto-Koasati peoples, in other words, all Western Muskogean speakers (see Booker et al. 1992).

The Question of European Manufacture of Shell Artifacts for Trade

Esarey (2013) has recently documented European manufacture of marine shell ornaments for trade in northeastern North American beginning as early as ca. 1630 and continuing well past the period under consideration in this study. His "Standardized Marine Shell" industry consists of ornaments and does not include wampum, whose production began even earlier. Some of these artifacts are made from marine shell imported from the West Indies. Esarey makes a compelling case that Europeans recognized the value of marine shell ornaments to Native Americans in the Northeast and organized production to meet that demand.

Did a similar process occur in the Southeast? We know Juan Pardo presented a large marine shell as a gift at Tocae, in modern-day North Carolina, in 1567 (DePratter and Smith 1980:71; Hudson 1990:266), so he clearly understood the value of marine shell to Southeastern Indians. Unfortunately, we do not know whether he brought the shell along as a gift item, or perhaps picked it up from Native Americans during his travels. An intriguing archaeological find of cowrie shells was made by C. B. Moore (1915:293–294) in Burial 44 at the Roden Mounds, on the Tennessee River. This otherwise Middle Woodland Copena burial mound contains no European trade material, yet nearby Burial 47 from the nonmound portion of the site yielded an "oblong looking glass, glass beads, shell beads, discoidal stone, and an undecorated shell gorget," which suggests a seventeenth-century date. Roden is located a short distance from other documented seventeenth-century sites in the Guntersville Basin in Marshall County, Alabama. These two cases hint that Europeans imported some marine shell into the Southeast.

This study of marine shell distribution establishes that marine shell continued to be utilized by Southeastern Native Americans well into the eighteenth century, yet the means by which shell made its way to the interior Southeast at that late date remains uncertain. Florida was largely depopulated of Natives between the massive slave raids of 1704–1705 and the gradual migration of proto-Seminole Creeks into that area in the mid-eighteenth century. So who made or traded the shell found on eighteenth-century Southeastern archaeological sites? Shell pins continued to be used in the Mississippi Valley but disappeared in the east, while conch shell beads are found throughout the Southeast. Perhaps Natives in Mississippi and Louisiana continued to produce shell artifacts, but it seems reasonable to suggest that Europeans took up production and supply of shell artifacts following the destruction of the Spanish Mission system and the subsequent collapse of Native population in what is now Florida and coastal Georgia.

However, I have been unable to find any documentation of significant marine shell artifact production by European colonists in the Southeast. If anything, the historical sources suggest the opposite: that Europeans did not manufacture shell artifacts in this region. John Lawson reported in 1709 that shell beads and gorgets were used in Carolina. According to Lawson, "Some English Smiths have try'd to drill this sort of Shell-Money, and thereby thought to get an Advantage; but it prov'd so hard, that nothing could be gain'd" (Lefler 1967:203). Lawson's account goes on to describe Native manufacture of shell beads. Evidently at least a few English colonists in the Carolinas tried to make shell beads, but they quickly abandoned the effort. Fleming and Walthall (1978:32) argue that shell beads found at the Guntersville Reservoir sites in Marshall County, Alabama, were likely made by Europeans based on tool marks and uniform sizes of holes, which suggested to them the use of steel drills. Of course it is also possible that Native craftsmen obtained metal tools for bead production. Evidence of metal drills certainly does not necessarily indicate European manufacture of shell beads.

In the eighteenth-century French colony Louisiane, Le Page du Pratz described shell ear pins in use by Native peoples in the lower Mississippi Valley. His contemporary, Dumont de Montigny, described ear pins and gorgets and specifically mentioned their manufacture by Native Americans (Swanton 1946:486). Unfortunately, I am not aware of any mention of shell artifact manufacture in Spanish sources. Archaeological evidence of shell bead manufacture is rare, but Mason (2005:123) notes unfinished conch columella beads from Ocmulgee (1690–1715) in central Georgia. From these historical and archaeological clues, it appears that Native Americans in the interior Southeast continued to obtain marine shell from coastal sources and manufacture ornaments well into the eighteenth century. Judging from their distribution, the latest manufacture likely occurred in the lower Mississippi Valley/Gulf Coast area. Although rare, some of Esarey's Standardized Marine Shell industry products did reach the Southeast. In particular, he documents examples from Chickasaw sites in Mississippi and sites in North Carolina (Esarey 2013:21, 177, 182). All of these sites postdate A.D. 1670, and this material arrived with English trade.

Discussion

Although it is clear from distinctive cultural borders, such as the one at the head of the Alabama River, that engraved marine shell appears to have signaled ethnicity or some other social factor during the sixteenth century, the reason for the sudden disappearance of the engraved shell tradition is less understood. Perhaps the collapse of Mississippian chiefdoms ended possible elite support of the craftspeople (Smith 1987) who made these intricate artworks; or perhaps collapsing populations and subsequent reformulations of societies made old symbols less important in the new coalescent societies. Old identities were lost as new identities were forged. Clearly, engraved marine shells quickly disappeared across the Southeast. In some areas, like the Coosa River valley, marine shell ceased to be used in any form during the early seventeenth century, but in other areas shell beads and ear pins continued to be used well into the eighteenth century. In contrast to the situation proposed for the Northeast by Duane Esarey, there is no archaeological evidence of European manufacture of marine shell ornaments for the Native trade in the Southeast.

Future Research

Although we know something about the forms of shell used at various times and in various places in the post-Mississippian Southeast, we still know little to nothing about shell sources, manufacturing centers, or trade routes.

Sourcing marine shell artifacts by analyses of trace elements and stable isotopes might add greatly to our understanding of the use of marine shell by Native peoples of the region.

Acknowledgments

Greg Waselkov has been most helpful in my study of the protohistoric period for decades. John O'Hear provided information on Chickasaw sites in Mississippi. Duane Esarey's research on the European shell industry in the Northeast made me think in new directions.

6

JOARA, CUENCA, AND FORT SAN JUAN

The Construction of Colonial Identities at the Berry Site

David G. Moore, Christopher B. Rodning, and Robin A. Beck

Until very recently, archaeologists have often had to rely on distributions of European artifacts on Native American sites to address questions of sixteenth-century colonial and Native interactions. The discovery of the sixteenth-century Spanish colonial outpost of Fort San Juan and Cuenca, at the principal town in the Native polity of Joara in western North Carolina, allows us to take an alternate perspective and attempt to better understand such issues as the creation and maintenance of social identities proposed in the introduction of this volume. In this chapter, we discuss the historical context of Fort San Juan and the archaeology that allows us to view this site as the location of a series of sixteenth-century events in which Native hosts and colonial intruders negotiated and maintained their identities.

For a brief time, from 1567 to 1568, the principal Spanish outpost along the northern frontier of the colonial province of La Florida consisted of Fort San Juan and the associated settlement of Cuenca, located at the Native American town of Joara, in what is now western North Carolina. Captain Juan Pardo and his men, acting on orders from Governor Menéndez at Santa Elena, established their outpost at Joara in early 1567. Initially peaceful, diplomatic relations between Pardo's colonizing garrison and the people of Joara deteriorated by the spring of 1568, when Juan Martín de Badajoz arrived in Santa Elena with news that warriors had attacked and destroyed Fort San Juan. In fact, all six of Pardo's outposts established at Native American towns in the interior had been lost. Following the abandonment of Fort San Juan and Pardo's other forts, the focus of Spanish colonialism in Southeastern North America shifted from exploration and military installation to missionization and trade. As the first interior colonial settlements within the modern-day United States, these forts established the landscapes of colonial interaction and identity in the sixteenth-century Southeast.

There are some written descriptions of events that took place at Fort San Juan and in surrounding areas in the 1560s, but there are no detailed descriptions or drawings of the fort itself, and there is some uncertainty

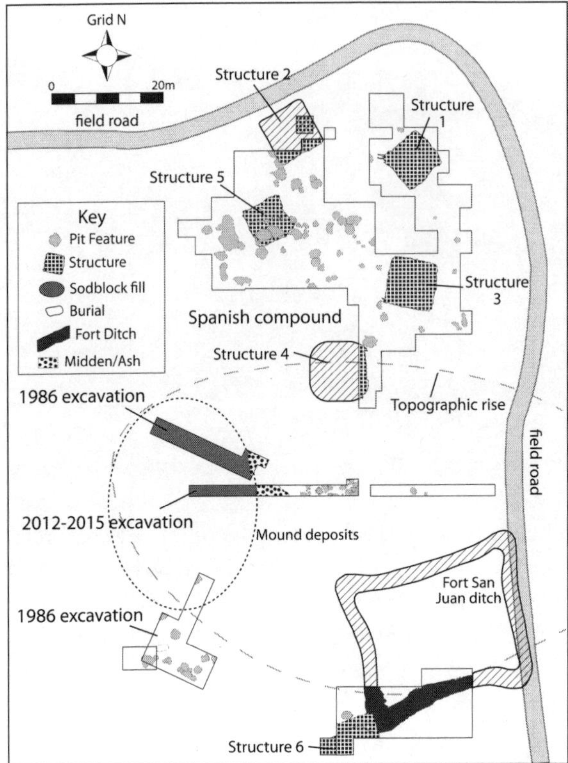

Figure 6.1. Berry site excavations, 1986–2015 (plan view) (drawing by Abra Joghart).

as to exactly what transpired during the 1568 attack. Given the incomplete and one-sided nature of the historical records of this important episode of American history, archaeological research has fortunately shed much-needed light on the subject. This chapter summarizes 14 years of archaeological investigations at the Berry site, the location of the remnants of Joara, Cuenca, and Fort San Juan (Figure 6.1). During that long-term effort, the goals and nature of our research have evolved, as we discuss below. Throughout this chapter, and in publications elsewhere (Beck 1997; Beck and Moore 2002; Beck et al. 2006, 2011; Moore 2002; Moore et al. 2005), we have depended heavily on the archival research and interpretations of Charles Hudson (1990, 2005) and his colleagues (e.g., DePratter and Smith 1980) on Pardo's expeditions and the forts built by Pardo's troops.

Juan Pardo's Expeditions

During the first half of the sixteenth century, numerous Spanish expeditions explored and mapped the Atlantic and Gulf coasts of North America, a land they referred to as La Florida. Period maps show remarkably detailed coastlines, but the interior of La Florida remained poorly understood. During this period several Spanish efforts to settle the coast and interior of La Florida ended in failure. Despite these failures, increasing French pressures to colonize the region spurred Spain's colonial ambitions. By the 1550s, French privateers were attacking Spanish ships as well as Spanish settlements in the Caribbean. King Phillip II of Spain was determined to block French access to the Southern coast and to prevent their ability to intercept the fleets of galleons carrying New World riches to Spain. By June 1559, Spaniards had identified the Point of Santa Elena (on today's Parris Island, South Carolina) in Port Royal Sound as a likely location for a potential settlement. In April 1562, Jean Ribault actually established a French settlement, Charlesfort, at that location, only to have it fail within the first year. In March 1565, Phillip II, already aware of Charlesfort, received news of a second French settlement, Fort Caroline, located farther south on the Atlantic coast. In response to these French intrusions on Spanish claims, Phillip II sent Pedro Menéndez de Avilés to found a Spanish colony in La Florida. In September 1565, Menéndez located Fort Caroline, defeated the small French force there, and established St. Augustine, his first colonial settlement, not far away. After securing the Southern coast, he moved north with most of his men to the Point of Santa Elena, where he planned to build his colonial capital. He arrived there in April 1566, laid out the city plan, directed construction of Fort San Salvador, and after leaving a detachment of soldiers at the fort returned to St. Augustine for additional provisions. The Spanish fort at Santa Elena was built on the same site as the preceding French outpost of Charlesfort, and, similarly, the town of St. Augustine effectively erased the presence of the French settlement at Fort Caroline. In these ways, Menéndez created a Spanish colonial imprint on the landscape of the Southeast, in part by displacing the French footprint that had been taking shape.

During the summer of 1566, a fleet of Spanish vessels arrived in St. Augustine with supplies and soldiers, among whom were Captain Juan Pardo and 250 men. Menéndez immediately dispatched Pardo and his troops north to resupply Santa Elena. When Pardo reached Santa Elena in July 1566, he found Fort San Salvador in very poor shape, and most of the garrison lost to a mutiny. Pardo and his men helped to rebuild the town, and they erected Fort San Felipe to replace Fort San Salvador. Menéndez returned to Santa Elena in August 1566. While Pardo had helped restore order, there were few provisions to support his large force. Therefore, Menéndez ordered Pardo immediately to execute his original colonial plan. Menéndez tasked Pardo with exploring the interior of La Florida, claiming the territory for Spain while pacifying and evangelizing Native American groups, and establishing an overland route connecting Santa Elena with the Spanish silver mines near Zacatecas, Mexico. The Zacatecas mines, which produced vast amounts of wealth for the Spanish colonial empire, were erroneously thought to lie within easy march of the La Florida coast. Because he could not spare provisions from the town's storehouses, Menéndez instructed Pardo to feed his men by extracting tribute from the Indians he encountered. Thus, Pardo began his first expedition with a monumental task. Not only was he to extend the colony across La Florida, but also he would have to rely on Native Americans to host and provision his men. As a result, although Pardo did command an army, he placed greater emphasis on diplomacy than had his conquistador predecessors, such as Hernando de Soto, who briefly traversed the province of "Xuala" in 1540, some 26 years before Pardo arrived at the principal town of Joara.

On December 1, 1566, Pardo departed Santa Elena with a company of 125 men. They marched on foot and carried their possessions, moving from one Native American town to the next, including several visited by the Soto expedition years before. At many such places, Pardo gave formal diplomatic talks to Native American community leaders, and he gave them gifts, while also asking that they become allies of the Spanish colonial province of La Florida. At certain towns he demanded that they build houses and set aside food for their Spanish visitors.

Pardo's small army arrived at the town of Joara several weeks after departing Santa Elena. With abundant farmland and other resources near this prosperous and powerful town, and with snowcapped peaks visible to the west, Joara was chosen by Pardo as the location for a Spanish fort and settlement. He presented gifts to the chief of Joara, and he renamed the place Cuenca, after his hometown near Madrid, Spain (Hudson 2005:153). Pardo spent two weeks at Joara. Fort San Juan was completed in January 1567, although little was written by the expedition's chroniclers about the dimensions or other characteristics of the fort. Before departing, Pardo placed Sergeant Hernando Moyano in charge of approximately 30 men stationed at the fort. Pardo provisioned these troops with match cord, gunpowder, and other supplies and set out on his return to Santa Elena. Heading east, he visited other Native towns in the surrounding area. At the town of Guatari, Pardo received instructions summoning him quickly to Santa Elena to help protect the capital from a feared attack by the French. Without time to build another fort, Pardo assigned the expedition's priest, Sebastian Montero, along with several soldiers to remain at Guatari while he and the balance of the force returned to Santa Elena.

On September 1, 1567, Pardo led a second expedition of 120 men with extra provisions from Santa Elena into the interior. Without authorization from Pardo and in his absence, Sergeant Moyano engaged in minerals prospecting and had participated in raids on Native American villages to the north and west of Joara. When Pardo reached Joara in September 1567, he learned that Moyano and several of his men were surrounded by Indians at the town of Chiaha (in eastern Tennessee). Pardo rescued Moyano, built a fort at Chiaha, marched southwest toward the powerful chiefdom of Coosa but turned back east to cross the mountains en route to Joara. Pardo and his men built forts at the town of Cauchi, then returned to Joara, where Pardo met in November with many Native American community leaders from surrounding areas. He dispatched several people on prospecting trips during this period, and he did some prospecting himself in the area around Joara. The Spaniards found corundum, quartz crystal, and other gemstones, perhaps contributing to Spanish legends that later circulated about "Los Diamantes," mountains made of crystal or diamonds (Hudson 2005:189–195). Pardo visited several more Native American towns in the Carolinas and established three more forts before arriving at Santa Elena in early March 1568. In June 1568, news reached Santa Elena that Fort San Juan and Pardo's other outposts had been attacked by Native American warriors. It is uncertain how many of the soldiers died in the uprising, but only one is known to have made it back to Santa Elena alive (Hudson 2005:175). Pardo's second expedition to the interior marked the last attempt by Menéndez to extend Spain's reach across the interior of La Florida. Fort San Juan and Cuenca, the first of the six Spanish interior settlements, were occupied for only 18 months.

Juan Pardo's Forts

Archaeologists know relatively little about sixteenth-century Spanish forts in La Florida, but archival research suggests considerable variability in the shapes, dimensions, and other characteristics of Spanish colonial forts. Generally, forts consisted of ditches or moats, log stockades, and earthen embankments enclosing spaces where wells, pit features, and structures such as *casas fuertes* were present. Entryways to Spanish colonial forts and churches were sometimes paved with pebbles and crushed oyster shell. Archaeological excavations have uncovered evidence of all these features in Fort San Felipe, at Santa Elena, point of departure for the Pardo expeditions (South et al. 1988).

Pardo's men built six forts during his two expeditions (Hudson 2005). Fort San Juan was constructed first, at Joara early in 1567, when Pardo also renamed the Native town "Ciudad de Cuenca" (Hudson 2005:153). The fort was named Fort San Juan to mark the army's arrival at Joara on the Day of San Juan, December 27 (Hudson 2005:147). There are no known written descriptions or visual depictions of the fort. Hudson (2005:147) suggests that Pardo justified building this fort "to prevent the land from remaining a wilderness (*disierto*)," perhaps implying that Indian towns were considered less than civilized, parts of "a wilderness." However, we think it more likely that Pardo was following a well-established convention of Spanish colony-building. Rather than merely applying a Spanish name to the Indian town, Pardo was intentionally giving a name to the new Spanish colonial town, the built environment of which encompassed a fort and a domestic compound (Beck et al. 2016). This convention was followed at all but one of the towns in which Pardo's men built a fort. Fort San Juan was the only fort built during Pardo's initial advance into the interior, and although there were approximately 30 men garrisoned at Fort San Juan, there were as many as 125, and perhaps as few as 10, of Pardo's men at the fort and its associated domestic compound at any given time.

The remaining five forts were built during the second expedition. Hudson (2005:148) suggests that they were built as defensive responses to the hostilities Pardo faced in the mountains on the second expedition. Following Pardo's rescue of Moyano and his men from the Chiaha threat in eastern Tennessee, the army moved briefly west to the town of Satapo before being warned of a planned ambush by warriors from Satapo, Coosa, and other towns. As Pardo and his small army retreated from Satapo, they built their second fort, Fort San Pedro, at the town of Olamico (or Chiaha) (Hudson 2005:40). No details of its construction are known, but Bandera reported that the men spent four days laying out the town and building the fort. Interestingly, this is the single location for which Pardo provided no Spanish name for the settlement, save that of the fort. This might support the idea that Pardo was not renaming the Indian towns but providing names for intentional Spanish colonial settlement. Fort San Pedro may have been seen as a more temporary fort holding the western flank of his conquered territories.

Turning east from Olamico to Joara, Pardo paused to build Fort San Pablo in Cauchi, where a house had previously been built for the Spaniards. The fort was constructed in three or three and a half days (Hudson 2005:40), but nothing is known about the relationship between the fort and the house. Fort San Pablo was garrisoned with 11 men, before Pardo and the rest of his detachment marched from Cauchi to Tocae, then through the Swannanoa River valley to the trail leading from the mountains to the province of Joara.

Reaching Joara, Pardo reprovisioned Fort San Juan with the largest quantity of supplies at any of the forts, including additional gunpowder, match cord, and lead balls. Interestingly, he also left the majority of iron shovels, socketed axes, and mattocks as well as the only nails recorded for any of the forts. Hudson (2005:41) suggested that the fort was again garrisoned with 30 men, and the large quantity of supplies supports his notion that

Fort San Juan was intended as the central outpost of the Spanish colonial frontier. Finally, Pardo issued 42 chisel-like tools (*azolejas*) to Fort San Juan, an item left at none of the other forts. In all, Pardo gave chiefs at many of the villages a total of 126 chisels and wedges of various types and names. Though azolejas do not appear on lists of traded chisels and wedges, their large number suggests they are included in the total or were otherwise intended for trade. Regardless, the scale of munitions, supplies, and possible trade tools left at Fort San Juan speaks to its intended role as the central Spanish interior settlement.

Pardo's men built their fourth fort, Fort Santiago, at the town of Guatari, in the Yadkin River valley, and Pardo named the settlement "Ciudad de Salamanca." Twenty-two days were spent building Fort Santiago, which consisted of two bastions built of logs and earth, "four tall 'cavaliers' of thick wood and dirt and a wall of high poles and dirt" (Hudson 2005:151). The people of Guatari helped in the construction of Fort Santiago, and Pardo supplied them with two socketed axes to cut wood for the fort. Because this is also the town at which Pardo had previously installed his chaplain, Sebastian Montero, it is possible that the details of this construction (none of which were noted for the other forts) were meant to leave a record of protection for the mission that Montero planned to build. Fort Santiago was garrisoned with 17 men.

Neither Pardo nor Bandera described the next fort, built at Cofitachequi, which Pardo later referred to as Fort San Tomás. Pardo named the settlement "Ciudad de Toledo," and he stayed there for 18 days but left no men or munitions upon his departure (Hudson 2005:151)

Pardo's sixth and final fort was "Fuerte de Nuestra Señora," built at the Native town of Orista located on the coast a short distance from Santa Elena. Apparently construction here differed from the other forts, being described as "a strong house (*casa fuerte*) built out of sawn lumber" (Hudson 2005: 152). Pardo renamed the settlement "Villa de Buena Esperança." Little else is recorded about this casa fuerte or the surrounding settlement, but the reference to "sawn lumber" suggests that Pardo's men did carry with them one or more saws during the expeditions.

Pardo clearly built these forts with every intention of supporting future permanent Spanish colonial settlements. Hudson suggested that the presence of *micos* (principal chiefs) at Joara and Guatari persuaded him to construct larger forts there than at other sites. Pardo intended for Cuenca and Fort San Juan to be the major metropolis of the interior settlements on the northern frontier of La Florida. It may have been important to him to establish a colonial presence visible both to Native peoples and to any French interlopers who threatened Spanish claims to the interior. Hudson (2005:152) suggests that the forts not only served a defensive military purpose, but were also intended as a means by which the Spaniards could exploit interior Native towns for food (principally corn) for Santa Elena.

Unfortunately, there is almost no information about the size or design of any of the forts, merely a few hints gleaned from the Spanish documents including an occasional report of the length of time spent on fort construction. Hudson (2005:152) thinks that the forts "resembled the small, hastily constructed fortifications that Europeans built in other parts of the world." Perhaps they were smaller versions of the first forts that were built at Santa Elena, but we can have no sure knowledge until one of these forts is located—if we can be so lucky—and excavated by archaeologists" (Hudson 2005:166). Our discovery of Fort San Juan at last provides definitive evidence for the most important of the interior forts. Fort San Juan furnishes a baseline, with details on a substantial construction for permanent occupation. Bandera's lists of munitions and supplies indicate it was the most heavily provisioned, and it may also have been the largest fort.

Archaeological Investigations at the Berry Site

When Hudson (1990) first published his book about the Pardo expeditions, the location of Fort San Juan was unknown. But archaeological investigations at the Berry site (Moore 2002) and reconstructions of the Soto and Pardo routes across western North Carolina (Beck 1997) persuaded him that the Berry site is the location of Joara, Cuenca, and Fort San Juan (Hudson 2005:ix–x). Our research at the Berry site, located in the upper Catawba River valley of western North Carolina, has now spanned nearly three decades (Beck and Moore 2002; Beck et al. 2006, 2011; Moore 2002). We have been extremely fortunate that the Berry site has been available for extensive long-term excavation, as it is unlikely that the fort would have been identified otherwise. The following section briefly describes the evolution of the research designs that have guided our excavation strategies since 1986. The site covers some five hectares in a bottomland along Upper Creek, which meets Irish Creek nearby to form Warrior Fork, which then flows to the Catawba River some 12 kilometers to the south. Berry and other sites in the upper Catawba Valley are attributed to the Burke phase, an archaeological manifestation of Mississippian culture dating from A.D. 1400 to 1600 (Beck and Moore 2002; Moore 2002). Archaeological surveys (Beck 1997; Moore 2002) indicate that the Burke-phase settlement pattern includes a range of sites, from dispersed farmsteads to nucleated villages of various size, integrated at a multicommunity level. The Berry site probably functioned as a regional central place (Beck 1997:55; Beck and Moore 2002). On this landscape, the Spaniards attempted to transplant a Spanish colonial identity on the frontier of La Florida.

The Berry site was first described in the 1880s as the location of an earthen mound, "about 15 feet high and unexplored," on the west bank of Upper Creek (Thomas 1891:151). There are no known photographs of the mound, but James Berry, 80 years old in 2015, remembers riding a tractor across the steep slope of the mound when he was young, and he also reports that the mound was bulldozed in the past to fill erosional damage in the surrounding fields. All local informants associate the mound location with a small rise about one meter tall (indicated by dashed line on figure 6.1). It is possible that the mound was destroyed around 1940 following one of the most damaging floods in the region's history (Geiger et al. 2012; Moore 2002). The Berry site is by far the largest of more than 26 Burke-phase sites in the Upper Creek drainage. On the basis of its size and the presence of the earthen mound, Beck (1997) proposes that the Berry site was the major settlement within a regional settlement hierarchy.

Modern systematic study of the Berry site began in response to renewed interest in the sixteenth-century routes of the Soto and Pardo expeditions (DePratter 1994; Hally 1994b; Hally et al. 1990; Hudson 1997, 2005; Hudson et al. 1985, 2008; Levy et al. 1990). David Moore's 1986 survey of South Appalachian Mississippian sites and ceramics in the Catawba and upper Yadkin River valleys demonstrated that a relatively large number of Indians lived in these areas during the fifteenth and sixteenth centuries. Based on ceramics, this population is believed to have been directly related to other Lamar cultural groups located in the Carolinas and Georgia (Moore 2002). Moore also conducted excavations at three of the largest sites in the region, including the McDowell site (31MC41) in McDowell County, the Shuford site (31CT115) in Catawba County, and the Berry site (31BK22) in Burke County. The Berry site investigations were the most extensive and included excavation blocks and trenches on and adjacent to the presumed mound. Moore reported intact postholes and numerous features beneath the plowzone along the southwest edge of the mound. He also observed "sod-block" deposits in excavation units (see figure 6.1) across the top of the remnant mound feature (compare with Sherwood and Kidder 2011).

In 1994, Robin Beck contacted David Moore to report that he had found several sherds of Iberian olive jar vessels on the surface at the Berry site. Moore had a small number of historic potsherds in his 1986 collection but they had been identified fragments of eighteenth-century Moravian vessels. Upon comparison, they appeared to be identical to Beck's potsherds. Beck and Moore took these artifacts (along with a nail found by Beck) to Santa Elena, where Stanley South and Chester DePratter confirmed their identification as sixteenth-century Iberian olive jar. They also found the nail to be consistent with the nails from the Santa Elena excavations. Following this development, Moore and Beck decided to pursue additional fieldwork at Berry to try to determine the source of the sixteenth-century Spanish artifacts. Later that summer, Beck carried out geophysical surveys (performed by Thomas Hargrove) and soil coring at the north end of the site, where most Spanish artifacts had been collected, which revealed the presence of several burned structures and large pit features in an area of some two hectares, north of the mound remnant. The identification of mid-sixteenth-century Spanish artifacts and the presence of a small compound of burned buildings provided the first evidence that the Berry site might represent an early Spanish contact site. On this basis, Moore and Beck (1994, 1997) proposed that the Berry site represented the location of the Native American town of Joara, where Juan Pardo built Fort San Juan.

In 2001, we all investigated the Berry site, and especially the compound of burned structures, to determine whether this could indeed be the location of Joara and Fort San Juan. In addition, the project team (Rodning, Moore, and Beck) wanted to understand better the Native American occupation of the larger encompassing site, and the nature of encounters and entanglements among the Native people of Joara and the Spanish colonists at Cuenca and Fort San Juan. Our excavations from 2001 to 2005 identified foundations of at least five burned structures. Interestingly, we found no evidence that any of the buildings had been rebuilt after their destruction. We also excavated numerous related pit features around the structures. Feature fill included relatively large quantities of Native American ceramics, along with archaeobotanical and zooarchaeological remains, as well as numerous Spanish artifacts including Iberian olive jar sherds, nails, lead balls, and rolled copper aglets. It became clear that the area adjacent to and just north of the mound constituted an unusual domestic compound of less than one-half acre consisting of five buildings loosely arranged around a small "plaza."

During this period of our investigations, we were unable to locate any features or structures that could be interpreted as part of a formal defensive "fort," despite carefully examining every line of postholes that we uncovered. We came to interpret the five buildings as a domestic compound for Spanish soldiers stationed at Fort San Juan, and we began to wonder whether the structures themselves constituted the "fort." The structures were probably burnt by the Joarans when they destroyed Fort San Juan. Following this interpretation, we focused our efforts from 2006 through 2009 on excavations to expose more of the burned structures and surrounding areas, including, with the help of a National Science Foundation grant in 2007 and 2008, intensive excavations of Structures 1 and 5 (Beck et al. 2016).

Structures

Only two of the five burned structures have been excavated and the details described here are more fully discussed in Beck et al. (2016:85–149). Structure 1, measuring slightly more than 8 by 8 meters square with rounded corners, was built in a shallow semisubterranean basin with entryway trenches on the southeast corner. Upright log posts formed the framework for earthen walls, and four large posts placed around the central hearth supported a roof made of log poles, earth, bark, and thatch. The dirt dug from the ground to create the structure basin was presumably the source of earthen material incorporated in the walls and roof of the structure. In all of these respects, Structure 1 reflects many common Mississippi-period Native American architectural practices. In other respects, Structure 1 reflects Spanish colonial practices and Spanish material culture. Lee Ann Newsom's (2016) analysis of wood samples from Structure 1 indicates that many post and timber elements were harvested, prepared, and shaped with metal tools, such as axes, adzes, chisels, and saws—tools noted in lists of items carried by Pardo and his men. Some wooden elements have saw marks; at least one chestnut plank from Structure 1 demonstrates quarter-sawing, which is only possible with metal-edged tools; and some wooden elements have holes that may have been created by iron nails. Structure 1 appears to have been built by people with intimate knowledge of Native American architectural design and materials. However, it also appears that many of the posts were cut or shaped with metal axes, possibly wielded by the Spanish soldiers. We suggest that the people of Joara built Structure 1, but Pardo's men actively assisted in the construction.

Structure 5, located southwest of Structure 1, resembles Structure 1 in its general configuration and dimensions, but there are considerable differences in construction details. Most notably, Structure 5 lacks the foundational shallow basin and, based on posthole evidence, has no discernibly clear entrance. In addition, the central roof support posts in Structure 5 were placed more shallowly than those in Structure 1, and they are shallower than many wall posts in Structure 5. Several wall posts in Structure 5 were placed in postholes much larger than the posts themselves, perhaps because the holes were dug with a metal shovel. By contrast, postholes in Structure 1 were the same diameters as the posts themselves. Finally, the posts used in Structure 5 are younger and smaller in diameter than those of Structure 1. Even more significantly, many of the structural elements of Structure 5 appear to be split or sawn to double or triple their effective length, perhaps saving time in procurement but possibly resulting in a less durable structure (Newsom 2016:199). These construction details along with many other examples of metal tool use within Structure 5 lead us to suggest that Structure 5 was built by people who knew what Native American structures looked like but did not follow standard practices for constructing a more durable building. We think that Structure 5 was built by Pardo's men.

Aside from the architectural aspects of the structures, we are also interested in understanding how they were used. Unfortunately, the structures appear to have been cleaned and most evidence of activities removed before their destruction. Despite the relative paucity of material remains on the structure floors, both Native and Spanish artifacts were recovered from the floors of Structure 1 and Structure 5.

Several sixteenth-century Spanish artifacts have been found on the ground surface and in the plow zone in this area of the site, including Iberian olive jar fragments and other Spanish pottery, lead shot, wrought iron nails, chain mail, brass aglets, rolled brass beads, brass or copper scrap, and glass beads. These and other types of sixteenth-century Spanish artifacts—including chain mail links and other metal items—have also been found in intact deposits, including several of the large pit features present in this area of the site, as well as in the burned structures themselves. Finding a concentration of sixteenth-century Spanish artifacts in and around the burned buildings, along with our emerging understanding of construction details for the two structures, continued to support a compelling argument for our interpretation of this compound as a part of Cuenca and Fort San Juan, if not the fort itself (Beck et al. 2006, 2011).

Even more interesting are the results of the paleoethnobotanical (Fritz 2016) and zooarchaeological (Lapham 2016) analyses conducted on the structures and other Spanish compound features. Taken as a whole, the distribution of Spanish artifacts and the ethnobotanical and zooarchaeological analyses suggest there may have been evolving patterns of activity within the compound. It appears that at least one structure was built cooperatively by Natives and Spaniards, whereas a second was primarily the result of Spanish labor. Native men may have at times helped the soldiers procure meat while Native women very likely procured food for the soldiers and cooked within the compound. Even over the short 18-month occupancy of Cuenca, interactions between the soldiers and Native women and men were likely to have been continually negotiated with respect to social boundaries and identity (Fritz 2016:268–270; Lapham 2016:300).

Fort San Juan Revealed

Although we continued to explore the structures and activity areas in the Spanish compound at Berry, we also remained interested in clarifying the spatial and temporal relationship between the earthen mound and the Spanish compound itself. As seen in figure 6.1, we originally understood the topographic rise to correspond generally to the location of the earthen mound. Over the years of investigation, we considered various excavation strategies to learn more about the mound itself. We thought that basic information, including the actual mound footprint, could help us understand the timing of mound construction, as well as give us a more accurate picture of the built environment at Joara at the time of Spanish contact. We also hoped to resolve questions about the northern edge of this topographic rise, where complicated stratigraphy suggested that mound deposits may even sit atop the burned remnants of Structure 4.

Determining the footprint of the mound seemed a relatively simple task. We began in 2007 with several excavation units at the southeastern edge of the topographic rise associated with the mound. These units revealed a new pattern of horizontal stratigraphy that appeared to follow the edge of the rise and that we thought had resulted from plowing across several layers of mound deposits. This seemed consistent with Moore's 1986 excavation results across the western summit and at the southwestern margins of the rise and appeared to confirm the original supposition that this rise was the bulldozed and plowed remnant of the earthen mound reported to be 15 feet tall in the late nineteenth century (Thomas 1891).

We continued this task in 2011 with a mound-coring regimen (Geiger et al. 2011) designed to define the mound footprint and possibly determine stages of mound construction. Systematic 1-meter-interval soil coring, bisecting the rise north to south and east to west, revealed a wide variety of soil profiles that included ashy and burned soils in some locations, mixed and complex layers in others, and potential deep pit features. Although this information was useful, it was also difficult to interpret. At the very least the data suggested the mound had a slightly smaller footprint (see solid line in figure 6.1) that did not exactly coincide with the existing topographic rise. To obtain better clarity of mound stratigraphy, we returned in 2012 to the 2007 test excavations on the southeast mound edge and expanded those units to the west. Once again, as we moved to the west, the horizontal stratigraphy seemed to correspond to the southern edge of the mound.

However, our interpretation changed drastically as we continued to expand these units westward in 2013. As we moved west, it became clear that the horizontal stratigraphy did not curve to the northwest as expected to conform to the mound edge, but instead continued in a straight southwesterly direction. In addition, we began to recognize similar stratigraphy heading north at a right angle to our original southwest trending linear bands of fill. Suddenly, it was obvious that we were not following the edge of the mound, but had instead encountered a very large feature, larger than any feature or structure seen to this point at the Berry site. Several days of conjecture led to the stunning conclusion that we had exposed a corner and a portion of one side of the moat or ditch around Fort San Juan. Nearing the end of the 2013 field school, we bisected the ditch feature with an 80-cm-wide trench, revealing a deep V-shaped ditch nearly three meters across and over two meters deep. We found very few artifacts within a complex stratigraphy. After consultation with numerous colleagues, including Chester DePratter, Sarah Sherwood, David Anderson, Jeffrey Mitchem, Kathleen Deagan, David Thomas, and Charles Ewen, we determined that this feature did not resemble known Native American moats around sites like Etowah or Parkin, but that it was nearly identical in cross section to the moat associated with Fort San Felipe at Santa Elena (Chester DePratter, personal communication 2013). After 14 years of exploration, we had rediscovered Fort San Juan.

This discovery significantly altered our planning and, indeed, the entire frame of reference for our research design heading into the future. In 2014, we expanded the excavation of the southwestern corner of the ditch and continued northward, toward the edge of the "mound." Numerous features were revealed in the southwest corner area including a large intrusive structure (see figure 6.1), not unlike the burned structures in the Spanish compound, several possible pit features, and a single row of well-defined postholes. The intrusive structure must postdate the destruction of Fort San Juan and the filling of the ditch, but the potential association of the other features and the fort is unclear. Following the 2014 field season, another systematic soil-coring regime (Kipfer 2014), along with additional remote sensing studies (Timothy Horsley, personal communication 2014), appeared to have confirmed nearly 90 percent of the ditch outline. Details of these studies are forthcoming, but the apparent footprint of the ditch surrounding Fort San Juan has a trapezoidal shape, about 23 by 30 meters, smaller than but comparable to the shape and size of Fort San Felipe, at Santa Elena, which Pardo and his men built before marching inland to Joara in 1566.

Understanding the Berry Mound

As described, the discovery of the Fort San Juan moat clarified the nature of the overall Spanish compound. It is clear that the fort was a distinct entity, separate from the five buildings located north of the fort; the fort and the five buildings constitute Cuenca, the Spanish settlement at Joara. What remains unclear is the relationship of the fort to the indigenous settlement of Joara and especially to the Berry mound. We have always considered the proximity of the Spanish compound to the mound remnant to be surprising. It seemed unlikely that the Joarans would have tolerated the construction of the Spanish compound in such close proximity to the mound, and a mound reportedly 15 feet tall next to the Spanish compound would seem to confer to the Joarans a strategic advantage over the compound. In fact, there are no written references in primary documentary sources from the sixteenth century of an earthen mound at the principal town of Joara. We have therefore wondered whether the Berry site mound was built or enlarged over the fort after it was attacked and destroyed. This question demands further consideration and investigation.

However, as we have further explored the area of the presumed mound base, we find the life history of the mound, like that of the ditch and fort, to be increasingly complex. At the west edge of Moore's 1986 excavation (see figure 6.1), and in our current excavation across the topographic "rise" in the field, we see significant horizontal stratigraphy within the presumed mound base. In 1986, Moore (2002:214–218) identified significant deposits of sod blocks as well as large ash deposits, presumably the remnants of Native American mound building. To the east in our current trench crossing the rise, we have exposed an ashy midden that corresponds to similar deposits identified by Moore in 1986. As we continued east across the highest elevation of the presumed mound remnant in 2015, we identified more ash deposits and several hearths that may be associated with additional structures located between the fort and the burned buildings. However, no further sod-block deposits have been identified.

What remains to be answered is whether the sod-block deposits actually represent Native American mound building and, if so, does mound construction predate or postdate fort construction and destruction? Figure 6.1 shows the relationship between the sod-block (presumed to be mound) deposits and the existing topographic rise. As of the end of the 2015 field season, it remained unclear whether mound deposits covered any portion of the footprint of the fort. We are still investigating the spatial and temporal relationship between fort and mound. However, there are suggestions in the profiles of Ditch Trenches 1 and 2 that, when the fort ditch was dug, diggers sliced through an existing earthwork of some kind at its northern edge. That is, when Pardo and his men cut this part of Fort San Juan's dry moat, they may have sliced through the toe slope of the Berry mound or, alternatively, there may have been an earlier construction stage or embankment of the fort. If it was an existing mound, it was probably a very low feature at the time of the Spanish occupation, similar perhaps to the low mounds described by Cyrus Thomas (1891:152) along the Yadkin River, in Caldwell County, just northeast of the Berry site. In either case, it remains possible that the greatest period of mound construction (to the reported height of

15 feet) occurred after the destruction of Fort San Juan. Such a sequence of events would indicate a complete reassertion of Joaran identity within the landscape of the Spanish colonial encounter.

Fort San Juan, Joara, and the Berry Mound: A Landscape of Interaction and Identity

Before the arrival of the Spanish armies in the mid-sixteenth century, Joara probably functioned as a regional central place (Beck and Moore 2002). The Pardo documents clearly demonstrate that Native peoples regularly traveled between towns, and Joara likely constituted a native landscape of interaction in which Joara social identity was maintained within regional political and economic interactions. Maintenance of Joaran social identity may have been greatly challenged when Pardo arrived and the Spaniards attempted to transplant a Spanish colonial identity on the frontier of La Florida.

The activities briefly described above reveal a host of intriguing possibilities for further understanding of social identity on the colonial frontier. In fact, the juxtaposition of Fort San Juan, the Cuenca domestic compound, the Berry mound, and the rest of the town of Joara may be seen as mapping the social landscape of an early colonial event. Indeed, we may eventually be able to understand it as a complex mid-sixteenth-century physical and figurative landscape of interaction and identity. After 14 years of investigations, we are convinced that we have identified the basic footprint of Fort San Juan and the adjacent domestic compound constructed to house the Spanish soldiers who manned the fort. We believe that a wide variety of activities took place within the domestic compound, perhaps involving the presence of Native women on a daily or a semipermanent basis. We also suggest that the domestic compound and the fort represent private and public dimensions of the colonial enterprise and encounter.

Given our present understanding of the Spanish colonial fort at the Berry site, it looks broadly comparable to Fort San Felipe, the fort constructed at Santa Elena by members of the Pardo expedition before they marched inland and built Fort San Juan. At several European colonial settlements in eastern North America, there were spatial distinctions between public and private sectors.

In 1588, John White reported discovering Ralph Lane's settlement on Roanoke Island some three years after its abandonment; its fort, he wrote, had "sundry necessary and decent dwelling houses made by his men about it the yeere before" (Quinn 1985:280). Also, French Fort Caroline, founded in 1564 at the site where St. Augustine was established in 1565, was depicted as having houses outside the fort itself (Bennett 2001:19). There were spatial distinctions between forts and residential areas at the Spanish colonial capital of Santa Elena, in coastal South Carolina (Lyon 1976, 1988, 1990; South et al. 1988). Similarly, there seems to have been a spatial separation at the Berry site between the setting of Spanish domestic life at Cuenca, in the Spanish compound at the northern end of the site, and a more public space represented by Fort San Juan.

Our finds at the Berry site shed light on the landscape of interaction and identity at Joara and Fort San Juan. The ditch itself is perhaps the most powerful symbol of this changing landscape. Recall that the preliminary analysis of the life of the ditch suggests that, when the ditch was cut, it sliced through an earthwork of some kind along its northern edge. It is possible that the ditch around the fort cut through a small mound that was present at the site when Fort San Juan was built, in which case the fort would have encompassed and appropriated that mound, making a powerful statement about the colonial presence in a Native town. Alternatively, the ditch may have cut through an earthen parapet or rampart that was part of an earlier construction stage of the fort. In either case, it looks increasingly likely that the earthen mound at the Berry site was either built or significantly enlarged on top of the remnants of the fort, becoming itself a monumental statement about the conquest of Fort San Juan. The rediscovery of Fort San Juan in 2013, after its abandonment in 1568, presents us with the unique opportunity to explore the myriad ways in which both Spanish colonists and Native Americans from Joara attempted to orchestrate—to control—the public face of this important colonial encounter, and this decisive episode in American history. Fort San Juan seems to have separated the Spanish domestic compound of Cuenca from the Native American town of Joara, a clear separation and change in the new colonial social and political landscape. Yet, following the destruction of Fort San Juan and the conquest of the northernmost outpost of Spanish colonial La Florida, that separation may have been obliterated while being marked in Native monumental form by construction or enlargement of the Berry site mound. The mound construction itself may have represented a reassertion of Joaran identity and authority.

Acknowledgments

We first wish to thank the Berry family for their continued stewardship of the Berry site and for their interest and support of our project. Our research has been supported by the National Science Foundation, the National Geographic Society, Certified Local Government grants to the city of Morganton from the Department of the Interior administered by the State Historic Preservation Office and the North Carolina Department of Cultural Resources, the Western Piedmont Community College Foundation, the Woodbury Family Foundation, Warren Wilson College, Tulane University, the University of Michigan, the University of Oklahoma, and the Exploring Joara Foundation. Thanks to our field crew supervisors and all of the field school students and volunteers who have participated in our project and to the many people from Morganton and Burke County, North Carolina, who have contributed to this project.

Thanks to Greg Waselkov and Marvin Smith for inviting us to contribute to this volume in honor of Judith Knight. We appreciate their editorial comments as well as those of the anonymous reviewers. Any errors remain our responsibility. Finally, it is an honor to participate in this volume and we thank Judith Knight for her friendship and for her significant service to Southeastern archaeology.

7

WHAT'S IN A PHASE?

Disentangling Communities of Practice from Communities of Identity in Southeastern North America

John E. Worth

The study of human social organization in the past is always a daunting challenge, but especially so in the absence of textual or other documentary sources of evidence. Lacking written records for most of human history, archaeologists rely on material culture and other preserved traces of human activity as a basis for understanding the complex webs of social interaction that shaped the daily lives of people in the past. Whereas the social landscape of the historic era appears populated by comparatively straightforward sociopolitical units identified as tribes, chiefdoms, kingdoms, empires, and nation-states, the archaeological landscape of the prehistoric era is populated only by a dizzying array of artifacts and other material traces that display a range of spatial and temporal variation that generally ranges from continuous to somewhat less continuous. It has always been the task of the archaeologist to impose order on that variation, using the geographic distribution of preserved material culture to infer units of social integration at various scales, from households to regional culture areas. Sometimes there is relatively strong empirical correspondence between archaeological material distribution and historically documented social groups; many times, however, the situation is far more complex.

In North America, the earliest widespread systematic attempt to organize archaeological data in a consistent and uniform fashion was that of the early twentieth-century culture historians (Lyman et al. 1997). Their dependence on using the spatial and temporal distribution of material culture (particularly ceramics) as the basis for a strongly normative model of culture was later decried and nominally rejected by processualist archaeologists, who focused instead on the systemic dynamics of culture process itself (e.g., Binford 1962, 1965, 1968; Flannery 1967). However, although many facets of the taxonomic framework originally developed and employed by culture-historical archaeologists have subsequently fallen out of use, several important conceptual units have survived the test of time to remain part of current usage among contemporary archaeologists. The hierarchy of spatial and temporal units has included W. C. McKern's *component, focus, aspect, phase,* and *pattern,* and Gordon Willey and Phillip Phillips's more simplified *component* and *phase* coupled with the broader *horizon* and *tradition* (McKern 1939, 1943; Phillips and Willey 1953; Willey and Phillips 1958:11–43). Two unit concepts still in widespread usage today are the relatively uncomplicated *component,* as well as the somewhat more ambiguously conceived *phase,* which remains a foundational concept framing many archaeological interpretations, irrespective of theoretical orientation.

Following critiques of their original scheme and subsequent revisions (e.g., Rouse 1955; Willey and Phillips 1958), Willey and Phillips defined the *phase* as "an archaeological unit possessing traits sufficiently characteristic to distinguish it from all other units similarly conceived, whether of the same or other cultures or civilizations, spatially limited to the order of magnitude of a locality or region and chronologically limited to a relatively brief period of time" (Willey and Phillips 1958:22). They furthermore asserted that the phase is "the basic space-time-culture concept in all that follows" and "the practicable and intelligible unit of archeological study" (Phillips and Willey 1953:620). Both of these propositions seem to have been accepted widely in the archaeological community, probably in part explaining the persistence of the phase concept even today.

As a cluster of archaeological sites characterized by a similar assemblage of ceramic types and other material culture within a bounded geographic space for a limited span of time, just what exactly does an archaeological phase represent in terms of the living human society to which it bears mute witness? Directly addressing this question in their initial proposal, Phillips and Willey go to great lengths to caution practitioners against presumptions of one-to-one correspondence between archaeological and "sociological" units: "For the purpose of this discussion, however, let us think of society in the terms most often implied in the older ethnographic studies, i.e., a relatively small aggregate comprising a number of closely integrated communities. How does this correspond to the concept of phase? Logically, the correspondence is perfect. The society consists of a number of communities; the phase consists of a number of components; component equals community; therefore phase equals society—QED. Unfortunately in practice it doesn't work" (Phillips and Willey 1953:622). They go on to state flatly that "ethnography offers abundant examples of different societies sharing a material culture that would be impossible to differentiate archeologically" and that "probably it would be only slightly more difficult to find examples in which the culture of individual communities within a society diverged sufficiently to cause them to be classified archeologically in separate phases" (Phillips and Willey 1953:622). In addition, they point out that "within the time span of a phase, determined by material traits which can, under certain circumstances, be remarkably stable, it is conceivable that sociological changes might be sufficient to enable our hypothetical ethnographer to speak of several societies. Conversely, under special conditions, even a primitive population may exhibit revolutionary changes in material culture without losing its identity as a society. We have abundant examples of this in recent history" (Phillips and Willey 1953:622).

In the light of these clarifications, Phillips and Willey (1953:623) provide extraordinarily sage advice: "We do not maintain that any specific archeological phase corresponds to a former society. We simply call attention to the fact that there is a certain conceptual agreement between phase and society . . . this congruence, which can as yet be demonstrated only on the theoretical level, offers the best hope of incorporating archeology into general anthropological science." I contend in this chapter that although the existence of this theoretical "congruence" has provided implicit justification for the "phase equals society" assumption for many decades, its implications have yet to be fully explored and explained directly using empirical data. To a large extent, this task still remains to us today. Here I offer an avenue for reconciling these concepts.

For most of the Southeastern United States, and likewise for other regions of North America, what might be described as an enhanced culture-historical framework is still commonly used by archaeologists to generate the geographical-chronological units called *phases* that are employed in the primary analysis of Native American social structure, even in their most sophisticated and modern analyses of prehistoric sites. Moreover, this foundational framework, and the principal assumptions that underlie it, is so pervasive as to influence most recent archaeological work on historic-era Native American groups, even when contemporaneous documentary evidence can readily dispute many important aspects of this perspective.

In the Southeast, household production by female potters seems to have been the dominant mode of utilitarian ceramic production among indigenous groups across the late prehistoric and early historic periods (e.g., Bartram 1792:511; Holmes 1886:371–372; Hudson 1976:264; Le Page du Pratz 1758:178–179; Romans 1776:96; Sassaman and Rudolphi 2001:408, 420; Swanton 1946:549–555, 710; Thomas 2001:33), making ceramic assemblages particularly well suited for archaeological analyses of the spatial distribution of material culture at all scales of social integration, from households to communities to polities to regions. When Southeastern archaeologists speak of archaeological phases with relatively discrete spatial distributions during later prehistory, they commonly conceive of them as roughly equivalent to familiar social groups such as chiefdoms or tribes, either singly or as components of broader regional polities. This is perhaps most notably the case where there is clear evidence for multiphase longevity in these discrete areas, especially when such phases are geographically bounded by relatively unambiguous unoccupied zones, and even more so when they include one or more platform mounds with construction episodes contemporaneous with the phase (e.g., Hally 1993, 1996:116–118). Indeed, the "patchy" nature of the social geography of this broad region during the late prehistoric and early historic eras has perhaps served to reify the "congruence" between phases and societies that Phillips and Willey (1953:623) warned about more than half a century ago.

It is unlikely that any modern archaeologist would dispute the fact that there are always "formidable difficulties" in "finding social equivalents for archaeological units" (Willey and Phillips 1958:48), but I would argue that, at least in the Southeast, and certainly elsewhere as well, this has nonetheless become somewhat entrenched in implicit practice, as evidenced by many examples in the literature of direct correspondences between specifically named archaeological phases and historically documented polities at various scales. Examples of such proposals include a number of phases thought to correspond to polities documented during sixteenth-century Spanish exploration of the interior Southeast, and particularly during the Hernando de Soto expedition. These identifications include the Parkin phase as Casqui (Hudson 1985; Hudson et al. 1987:853; Jeter 2009:369, 371; Mainfort 1999:146; Morse and Morse 1983), the Nodena phase as Pacaha (Hudson et al. 1987:853; Jeter 2009:369, 371; Mainfort 1999:146; Morse and Morse 1983), the Mulberry phase as Cofitachequi (Ethridge 2010:104), the Caraway phase as Guatari (Ethridge 2010:104), the Walls phase as Quizquiz (Mainfort 1999:146), the Dyar phase as Ocute (Kowalewski and Hatch 1991:10), the Cowart's phase as Ichisi (Hudson 1994), the Lockett phase as Toa (Worth 1988), the Lake Jackson and Velda phases as Apalachee (Ewen 1996; Scarry 1990, 1996; Scarry and McEwen 1995:484–485), the Alachua "tradition" as the Potanos (Milanich 1972a:35, 1978:76; Rolland 2012:126), the Suwannee Valley culture as the Timucuas (Worth 2012:171), the Safety Harbor phase as the Tocobagas (Bullen 1978:50), the Irene and Altamaha phases as Guale (Pearson 1977:128; Saunders 1992:140–142, 2000:1, 15), the Kymulga or Shine II phases as Talisi (Ethridge 2010:70; Hudson et al. 1985:731, 735; Jenkins 2009:220; Smith 2000:100), the Big Eddy phase as Tascalusa (Jenkins 2009:215, 221, 223), the Furman phase as Mabila (Jenkins 2009:216), the Blackmon phase as Apalachicola (Worth 2000), the Estatoe phase as the Lower Cherokees (Hally 1986:95–111), the Qualla phase as the Middle Cherokees (Dickens 1976:213; 1986:84), the Brewster phase as Itaba (King 1999:116), the Barnett phase as the "heartland" of Coosa (Hudson et al. 1985: 732; Hudson et al. 1987:850; Langford and Smith 1990), and portions of the Burke phase as Joara (Beck and Moore 2002:201; Ethridge 2010:104), among others. This expected correlation between archaeological phases and named polities is in fact so strong that when Charles Hudson and colleagues reconstructed the sixteenth-century Coosa paramountcy to encompass all or part of no fewer than five distinct phases, they were prompted to remark that "one would expect that the chiefdom of Coosa should coincide rather more neatly with the distribution of protohistoric archaeological phases" (Hudson et al. 1985:724).

From the relatively easy-to-digest expectation of a correlation between late prehistoric phases and named Native American polities on the comparatively stable social landscape of the early historic era, archaeologists have naturally been prone to make the leap between the material culture (generally ceramics) characteristic of those same phases and the ethnic identity of the groups and individuals who relocated so frequently across the sixteenth- to nineteenth-century Southeastern landscape in the widespread diaspora of indigenous polities that occurred in the context of European colonialism. Many examples can be found in the archaeological literature attributing specific ceramic assemblages or types to the members of named ethnic groups, or *ethnies* (sec. Smith 1986), whose members or ancestors once belonged to polities generally believed to be coterminous with phases characterized by the same or similar ceramics. To cite some examples, specifically named ceramic assemblages and types found in mixed or extralocal colonial contexts have been claimed to be diagnostic for a diversity of Native American ethnies, including the Guale (Deagan 1973:61; 1978a:31, 33; 1978b:115; 1990:304, 1993:95–101; Hoffman 1997:33; King 1984:79: Saunders 1992:143, 2000:1; Waters 2005:79, 103–121), the Mocama and Eastern Timucua (Deagan 1990:304, 1993:95–101; Hoffman 1993:76; 1997:33; King 1984:77–78; Milanich 1972b:290–291; Waters 2005:80, 135–147), the Yamasee (Deagan 1993:95–101; Milanich 1972b:290; Waselkov and Gums 2000: 126; Waters 2005:147–149), the Creek (Honerkamp and Harris 2005:108; Johnson et al. 2008:11; Sears 1955; Silvia 2000:46, 217; Waselkov and Gums 2000:124, 127) and their constituent ethno-linguistic groups such as the Hitchiti (Foster 2004), the Apalachee (Cordell 2002; Deagan 1990:304; Goggin 1951:171; Silvia 2000:26, 45, 122, 126, 217, 252, 305, 342–343; 2002:29–31; Waselkov and Gums 2000: 126, 127; Waters 2005:77–78, 95–103; Worth 1992:171–182), the Potano and Western Timucua (Slade 2006:97–101; Waters 2005:78–79, 121–135), the Chato/Chacato (Silvia 2002:27; Waselkov and Gums 2000: 124, 126–130), the Tomé (Silvia 2000:46–47, 217; 2002:29–31; Waselkov and Gums 2000:125), the Mobilians (Cordell 2002:51–52; Silvia 2000:46–47, 217; 2002:29–31; Waselkov and Gums 2000:125, 127), the Choctaw (Quimby 1942:265; 1957:127, 162; Silvia 2000: 217, 305; Waselkov and Gums 2000: 124, 128), the Natchez (Johnson et al. 2008:11; Quimby 1942:268; Silvia 2000:48, 148), the Taensa (Silvia 2000:48), the Cherokee (Caldwell 1955; Sears 1955), and the Caddo (Silvia 2000:46, 148). Clearly, there is a long and ongoing tradition of lending ethnicity to pottery, even if only on an informal basis.

Thus, Southeastern archaeologists have long been prone to connect assemblages of ceramic types both with the political identity of geographically stable polities, and also with the ethnic identity of geographically mobile groups and individuals. As one of my anthropology professors (who shall remain nameless) once commented ironically regarding archaeologists' typical view of the relationship between pots and people, for most archaeologists, "the pots *are* the people." Despite protestations to the contrary, and routine clarifications and caveats, there seems to be a generally accepted underlying consensus that pottery, as measured through assemblages of archaeological ceramic types, represents a reasonably good indicator of political affiliation and ethnic identity. Pottery, in other words, can almost be viewed to *possess* ethnicity, insofar as it is generally viewed as a relatively conservative dimension of everyday culture that persists alongside political and ethnic identification.

In recent decades, with the florescence of various strains of postprocessual theoretical approaches to the archaeological analysis of material culture, there have been several attempts in the Southeast to conceptualize this longstanding assumption within the framework of more contemporary theories of agency, practice, and materiality, positing an active role for ceramics in constituting and communicating what is characterized as social identity. For the region under consideration here, for example, Rebecca Saunders (1992:139, 2000:49–51, 169–170, 180–181) conducted extensive and detailed ceramic analysis to propose that the presence of the "world symbol" in stamped pottery decorations among the Guale Indians represented a conscious communication of a distinctive Guale identity, and that the persistence of this style on documented Guale sites from both their homeland in the northern Georgia coast and at relocated settlements in northeastern Florida reflected the maintenance of this Guale identity throughout much of the mission period in Spanish Florida. In the same general region, Gifford Waters (2005, 2009) has more recently drawn on the tenets of practice theory (discussed further below) to examine the consolidation of mission populations around eighteenth-century St. Augustine by using archaeological ceramics in "an examination of how . . . consolidated multi-ethnic contact situations affected patterned material expressions thought to reflect cultural or ethnic identity among the Indians of the southeastern United States" (Waters 2005:xiv). Explicitly connecting specific ceramic assemblages to the Bourdieuian *habitus* of documented Native American ethnic groups originally located across Spanish Florida (Waters 2005:72–73, 76–80, 95–149), Waters used observed changes in ceramic decoration and technology based on the relative proportions of archaeological ceramic types in St. Augustine-area sites to infer varying degrees of identity maintenance or change among specific groups (Waters 2005:150–175). The increased percentage of check stamped St. Johns pottery, for example, is suggested possibly to represent a "revitalization movement among Eastern Timucua identity" (Waters 2005:168), whereas the increase in plain pottery at the expense of increasingly degraded stamped motifs is hypothesized to reflect "stresses in Guale society" associated with the collapse of the mission system, even if only indirectly reflecting shifts in identity that are "embedded in the more technological stylistic production aspects of pottery" (Waters 2005:167).

The lynchpin of these and many other recent studies in the Southeast and beyond is the connection of archaeological ceramics to what I would argue is the very hazy but now almost ubiquitously employed concept of identity, which could be characterized in this context as the postprocessualist explanation for and justification of what is essentially still the old culture-historical tendency to equate pots with people, or more specifically to define political and ethnic groups by their ceramic assemblage. Though the current focus on materialized social identity clearly provides archaeologists with a far more sophisticated and analytically robust mechanism to explain the social context of technological and stylistic aspects of ceramic production, my impression is that more often than not it simply reifies the same old equation of pottery with social identity. The effect is to lend postprocessual legitimacy to what I argue is essentially a culture-historical assumption, one that has not been thoroughly examined for empirical validity, and thus still a "theoretical" congruence, as originally asserted by Phillips and Willey (1953:623). Archaeological phases have long been entangled with political and ethnic identity in the minds of most researchers, but with little more than a token acknowledgment of the potential difficulties of this widespread assumption.

Comparing the Archaeological and Documentary Record

My research over the past few decades has led me to examine the question of equating ceramics with political and ethnic identity from a variety of perspectives and in a variety of circumstances. As both an archaeologist and ethnohistorian, I have focused efforts in particular on making concurrent and direct use of dual sources of evidence—documentary and archaeological—to evaluate the extent to which archaeological ceramic assemblages corresponded either to well-documented polities or to specific named ethnies (e.g., Worth 1997a, 1997b, 1998a, 1998b, 2009a, 2009b, 2010). A detailed review of the totality of this research is beyond the scope of this chapter, but it is instructive to point out several very clear examples as illustrations of my fundamental conclusion that ceramic variability as measured by archaeologists does not appear to be coterminous at any level or scale of social integration as traditionally conceived, and that archaeologically derived units of material culture distribution (such as phases) are therefore not equivalent to historically derived units based on political or ethnic identity. Furthermore, archaeological assemblages of ceramic types do not appear to be derivative or directly reflective of ethnicity, inasmuch as specific ethnic groups can be documented to have changed their ceramic styles in the context of new social interaction patterns both *in situ* and as a result of migration. I elaborate on these conclusions below.

The European colonial era in Southeastern North America provides a uniquely suitable laboratory for comparing documentary and archaeological evidence regarding indigenous social groups and material culture variability across a broad region over the course of several centuries. Ethnohistorical evidence pertaining to the social geography of the Southeastern landscape begins to appear during the first half of the sixteenth century, exploding spectacularly for the interior regions with the Spanish expeditions of Hernando de Soto (1539–1543), Tristán de Luna (1559–1561), and Juan Pardo (1566–1568), all of which have been meticulously traced by modern scholars in recent decades (e.g., Hudson 1997, 1990; Hudson et al. 1989). The Atlantic coastal regions around and between Pedro Menéndez's twin colonies established at St. Augustine (1565) and Santa Elena (1566) witnessed far more intensive and lengthy colonial interactions between Spaniards and Native Americans during the last third of the sixteenth century. Rapid expansion of the Franciscan mission system after 1587 ultimately assimilated not only these coastal groups but also Florida's transpeninsular interior peoples by the 1630s, ultimately encompassing dozens of indigenous chiefdoms within several broad language groups, all of which are documented by a voluminous ethnohistorical and archaeological record for greater Spanish Florida (e.g., Bushnell 1994; Hann 1988, 1996; McEwan 1993; Milanich 1999; Thomas 1990; Worth 1998a, 1998b, 2007, 2013a, 2013b). Moreover, the expansion and eventual collapse of this immense multiethnic colonial system across the Southeastern landscape were also accompanied and ultimately overwhelmed by the extension of both English and French colonial interests from the north and west during the seventeenth and eighteenth centuries, considerably augmenting the available documentary record for a diverse range of Native American groups across the region beyond Spanish Florida (e.g., Ethridge and Hudson 2002; Ethridge and Shuck-Hall 2009; Pluckhahn and Ethridge 2006). Between Contact and Removal in the sixteenth and nineteenth centuries, Southeastern North America represents an almost unparalleled laboratory for the comparative study of both documentary and archaeological evidence for Native American polities and ethnies undergoing dynamic and turbulent processes of colonial assimilation and transformation. Here we have many different circumstances and situations available for detailed examination. My research summarized below represents a mere fraction of the potential embodied by this region and time period, when prehistory and history effectively overlapped for indigenous groups in the eye of the colonial maelstrom.

With respect to the specific topic under consideration here, the mission system of Spanish Florida presents perhaps the best opportunity for a particularly robust case study, as it ultimately encompassed a broad region characterized by considerable cultural diversity before the colonial era and possesses a comparatively detailed documentary record spanning well over a century in duration, as well as a still-growing body of modern archaeological data. Tens of thousands of Native Americans organized into dozens of small-scale chiefdoms within several regional polities, and broader linguistic zones were assimilated into the expanding colonial system of Spanish Florida between the 1580s and 1650. Despite epidemic depopulation and English-sponsored slave raiding during the late seventeenth century that ultimately resulted in the contraction and withdrawal of only a few hundred surviving Mission Indians to St. Augustine by 1706, Native American ceramic production remained robust even until their 1763 evacuation to Cuba and Mexico. As a result, archaeologists can potentially track change and continuity in ceramics produced by individual households and communities with documented political, ethnic, and linguistic identity, even as such groups consolidated and relocated across the landscape during specific documented periods of this turbulent era.

Native-style ceramics represent the vast majority of all ceramics present at predominantly Native American missions and contemporaneous satellite communities in Spanish Florida, and indeed form a substantial portion of ceramics found at the handful of predominantly Spanish colonial communities (St. Augustine and Pensacola) as well. Easily a third to half or more of the ceramics at Spanish presidios in Florida are fully Native in both form and manufacture (e.g., Bense 1999:215; 2004:59; Deagan 1983:233–234; Harris and Eschbach 2006:109–110), despite solid documentary evidence for only minimal resident Indian presence on these sites. That the Florida Mission Indians sometimes made pottery for Spanish consumption is indeed documented in the historic record, as is the fact that Indian pots were used and sometimes exchanged among Spaniards in Florida (e.g., León 1745:223v; Leturiondo 1685:102v; Menéndez Márquez 1714:306r; Wenhold 1957:252; Worth 2007:114, 125). Moreover, the archaeological record quite clearly demonstrates that in addition to ceramics of indigenous style and form, native potters made an extremely limited (less than 3 percent) but nonetheless recognizable amount of Spanish-style tableware and other ceramic items generally called Colono Wares by Florida archaeologists (e.g., Cordell 2001; Rolland and Ashley 2000; Vernon 1988; Vernon and Cordell 1993), and their distribution generally seems to conform to their principal use as substitutes purchased by or provided to Spaniards (particularly military) for their own use (Melcher 2010:116–125). A weekly dole of ollas, caçuelas, and jarros, for example, was to be provided by Mission Indians among other items for the small resident garrison at Mission Santa María on Amelia Island in 1685 (Leturiondo 1685:102v), and pottery was evidently exchanged to Spanish soldiers by an entrepreneurial family of Lower Creeks living adjacent to fort San Marcos de Apalache in 1745, as described by its Captain Juan Isidoro de León: "Here I found a family of mother, daughter, and son, with another Indian woman named Agustina, whose husband was killed by the Indians. These maintain themselves here without wanting to separate themselves from the Spaniards. . . . It has seemed in the service of the King to give these women two arrobas of flour monthly, since the month of February. These Indians serve as great relief here, because they are continually crafting pots, bowls, jars, and other necessary things of clay, easy things with which they maintain themselves with the help of potatoes and oysters that they go out to search for" (León 1745:223v). The fact that the captain went out of his way to allocate them rations, and make specific note of this in his letter to the Florida governor, suggests that such craft specialists were somewhat out of the ordinary by that time, but the fact that they existed suggests one mechanism by which Native Americans were able to fulfill the ceramic needs of their colonial Spanish neighbors. Furthermore, the fact that these female potters were said to "maintain themselves" by potting, supplementing their subsistence needs with tubers and shellfish (and the Spanish flour added upon León's arrival), simultaneously indicates not just that their ceramics were likely bartered on an individual level to garrison soldiers in exchange for foodstuffs and other goods, but also that this craft production was insufficient to allow full-time specialization.

In this connection, there is no evidence for anything other than household-level ceramic production and consumption among Florida's Mission Indians themselves. The entire new Spanish colonial market for both Native-style and Colono Ware ceramics actually consumed only the tiniest fraction of overall indigenous ceramic production in the region. During the first half of the seventeenth century, the demographic balance in greater Spanish Florida was overwhelmingly weighted in favor of indigenous populations, with perhaps 500 to 1,000 Spaniards living amid 20,000 to 30,000 Mission Indians (Dunkle 1958:3–10; Worth 1998b:8–10), translating to a total population that was between 95 and 98 percent Native American. If the 2 to 5 percent of the population that was immigrant (Spanish, African, and other nationalities) consumed Native-made ceramics for about half their ceramic needs (as demonstrated archaeologically), that amounts to only 1 to 2.5 percent of the total consumption of all ceramics produced by Mission Indians as a group. Minor surplus household production by any or all Native potters with access to colonial markets can easily account for the archaeological signature observed on Spanish presidio sites as well as missions and frontier garrisons located amid predominantly indigenous populations.

In the context of this model of predominantly household ceramic production and consumption, the spatial distribution of archaeological ceramics at mission-era Native American sites of documented political and ethnic affiliation provides an excellent measure of the degree of congruence between utilitarian ceramics on the one hand, and political and ethnic identity on the other. The best starting point for such comparative analyses in Spanish Florida is probably the year 1650, which I would argue was near the zenith of the colonial system's combined geographic extent, resident population, and systemic functionality as regards the region-wide interplay of land and labor to produce staple foods (Worth 1998a:126–214). Moreover, an extensive body of available documentary and archaeological evidence from this period provides an extremely robust regional dataset from which to push our analyses forward and backward in time from this point. To this end, detailed analyses of these data provide what I believe is firm and unequivocal evidence that the regional ceramic style zones that crystallized across Spanish Florida by 1650 were equivalent neither to well-documented Native American political or linguistic groupings at the same time, nor to overarching Spanish-imposed provincial groupings, nor even to the region of Spanish Florida as a whole (Figure 7.1).

Before the sixteenth century, this same region had been characterized

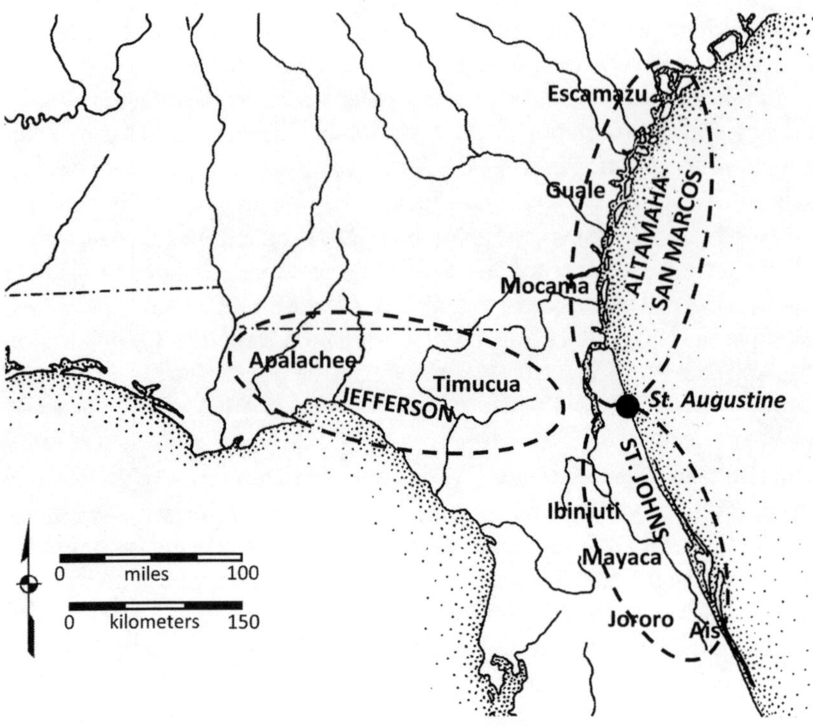

Figure 7.1. Ceramic style zones and political groupings of Spanish Florida, c. 1650.

by at least six distinct ceramic style zones that might easily be conceived of as phases (although they generally are not), but by the mid-seventeenth century only three style zones remained across the same region (Table 7.1). Documentary records do confirm localized intraprovincial settlement aggregation and consolidation in response to ongoing demographic collapse (Worth 1998b:27–29), and very occasional longer-distance interprovincial resettlement of Native towns overseen by Spanish authorities during the early seventeenth century (Worth 1998b:30–32). The vast bulk of this evidence nonetheless demonstrates substantial locational stability for the politico-linguistic units inhabiting this region during the precise era of this ceramic transformation. In other words, despite my early attempts to explain the apparent "homogenization" of six style zones or phases into only three as a product of interprovincial migration before 1650 (Worth 1992:171–182; Worth 1998b:36–37), over decades of research I have been forced to conclude that the weight of evidence is clearly against such an explanation. The unconnected but well-documented later population movements in many of these same regions during the latter half of the seventeenth century unquestionably postdate the ceramic transformation that happened before 1650 (Worth 2009a, 2009b). Whatever happened within and beyond the expanding mission system to homogenize previously disparate archaeological phases into three broad style zones by the mid-seventeenth century, it happened *in situ* to locationally stable (if declining) populations interacting with one another.

Setting aside for now an explanation of the origins of the three ceramic style zones that are known to have characterized mid-seventeenth-century Spanish Florida, what is nonetheless extremely clear (in the context of a comparatively rich and detailed documentary record) is the fact that they correspond to no social group as traditionally conceived at any scale of analysis. More specifically, as noted in table 7.2, the three regional ceramic style zones that characterized the Florida mission system by 1650—Altamaha-San Marcos, Jefferson, and St. Johns—are characterized by markedly different assemblages of archaeological ceramic types, as distinguished from one another primarily on the basis of paste and surface treatment recorded from sherds. By about 1650, the Altamaha-San Marcos regional style zone, extending along the northern axis of Spanish Florida bordering the Atlantic coastline, encompassed at least three distinct Native American political units (Mocama, Guale, and Escamazu) and crossed not only a major indigenous linguistic boundary, but also the very borders of Spanish missionization and direct political control (Worth 1997a, 2009a). The Jefferson-style zone along the western axis of Spanish Florida, extending across the peninsula to the Gulf of Mexico, encompassed two major political units (Timucua and Apalachee), again crossing a major linguistic boundary (Worth 1998a, 2009a, 2009b). To the south, a third ceramic style zone—St. Johns—extended along the Atlantic coast and inland waterways and lake districts to encompass a number of distinct political units (including the "Freshwater" Timucua and the provinces of Acuera, Mayaca, Surruque, and Ais), crossing yet another major linguistic boundary and extending well beyond the realm of direct Spanish control. The nexus of these new ceramic style zones seems to have been the colonial capital of Spanish Florida, St. Augustine itself, which on a local level appears to have maintained a blend of both the northern (Altamaha-San Marcos) and southern (St. Johns) coastal style zones that intersected there (Waters 2008, 2009:167–169). In colonial Spanish Florida, therefore, Mission Indians were participants in three broad ceramic style zones, each of which comprised potters from multiple political and linguistic affiliations. A Christian Mocama potter living in a mission in northeastern Florida made the same general suite of ceramic types as a non-Christian Escamazu potter living outside the mission system in southeastern South Carolina, and neither spoke the other's language. Similarly, Apalachee and

Table 7.1. Regional Ceramic-Style Evolution in and around Spanish Florida, c. 1500–1650

Groups c. 1650	Escamazu	Guale	Mocama	Apalachee	Timucua	Potano	Acuera	Ais
Language c. 1650	(Cusabo)	(Guale)	Timucuan	Muskogean	Timucuan	Timucuan	Timucuan	(Ais)
Affiliation/ Religion c. 1650	autonomous/ indigenous	Spanish/ Catholic	Spanish/ Catholic	Spanish/ Catholic	Spanish/ Catholic	Spanish/ Catholic	Spanish/ Catholic	autonomous/ indigenous
Style Zone c. 1650	Altamaha-San Marcos	Altamaha-San Marcos	Altamaha-San Marcos	Jefferson	Jefferson	Jefferson	St. Johns	St. Johns (Malabar)
Style Zone c. 1500	Irene	Irene	San Pedro	Fort Walton	Suwannee Valley	Alachua	St. Johns	St. Johns (Malabar)

Table 7.2. Characteristics of Ceramic Assemblages Comprising Style Zones Discussed

Ceramic Assemblage	Primary Paste	Primary Decoration	Secondary Decorations
Altamaha-San Marcos	sand/grit	rectilinear complicated stamped/ cross-simple stamped	incised, red filmed, check stamped
Jefferson	grog	curvilinear complicated stamped	incised, red filmed, check stamped
St. Johns	sponge spicules	check stamped	incised, red filmed
Lawson Field	sand/grit	roughened (brushed, cob marked)	incised, red filmed, check stamped

Timucuan potters living on opposite ends of the interior western mission chain also shared a single ceramic assemblage (although not a language) that was nonetheless substantially different from those of the Mocama and Escamazu. And all of these potters made ceramics that were substantially different from Christian Acuera and Mayaca and unmissionized Surruque and Ais potters to the south, all of whom spoke languages unintelligible to the previous hypothetical potters. There is simply no level of sociopolitical integration as traditionally defined that is coterminous with the ceramic style zones that developed by 1650 across and beyond the margins of greater Spanish Florida.

Importantly, even beyond mid-seventeenth-century Spanish Florida, this same clear lack of correspondence between archaeologically defined phases and historically described polities and ethnies is also evidenced among Native American groups in other regions and times during the historic era (Figure 7.2). One case in point is the Yuchi Indians, who incorporated themselves into the Creek confederacy during the eighteenth century (e.g., Jackson 2012). They were reported by many contemporary authors to have been fiercely independent from their new neighbors in terms of their language and ethnic identity, but by the end of the eighteenth century the assemblage of ceramic types on well-documented Yuchi sites along the Chattahoochee and Flint Rivers was identical to that of their Creek contemporaries, making it impossible to distinguish the assemblages of pottery types made by Yuchi and Creek potters, who would never have considered themselves to be the same people (Braley 1998; Worth 1988, 1997b, 2009b). Even though Creek Agent Benjamin Hawkins (1848:62) claimed of the Yuchi that "they retain all their original customs and laws, and have adopted none of the Creeks," the archaeological sites of documented Yuchi villages are characterized by the same sand-tempered assemblage of brushed, red filmed, and plain pottery that all their contemporary Creek neighbors also used (the Lawson Field Phase; Knight and Mistovich 1984:226–228), providing clear evidence that the conscious cultural independence of the Yuchi, which was so patently obvious to Hawkins, did not extend to the realm of utilitarian household pottery. Yuchi ethnic identity has been preserved from the moment of their incorporation into the Creek confederacy to the present day, but their pottery reflected the exact opposite: effectively complete assimilation into the local traditions of their Creek neighbors, the very people from whom they otherwise distinguished themselves.

This same phenomenon applies to the hundreds of Yamasee immigrants into the Florida missions during the late seventeenth century, whose ceramic assemblages quickly adapted to match those of their new neighbors in both Mocama and Apalachee (Worth 1997, 2004, 2009). The Atlantic

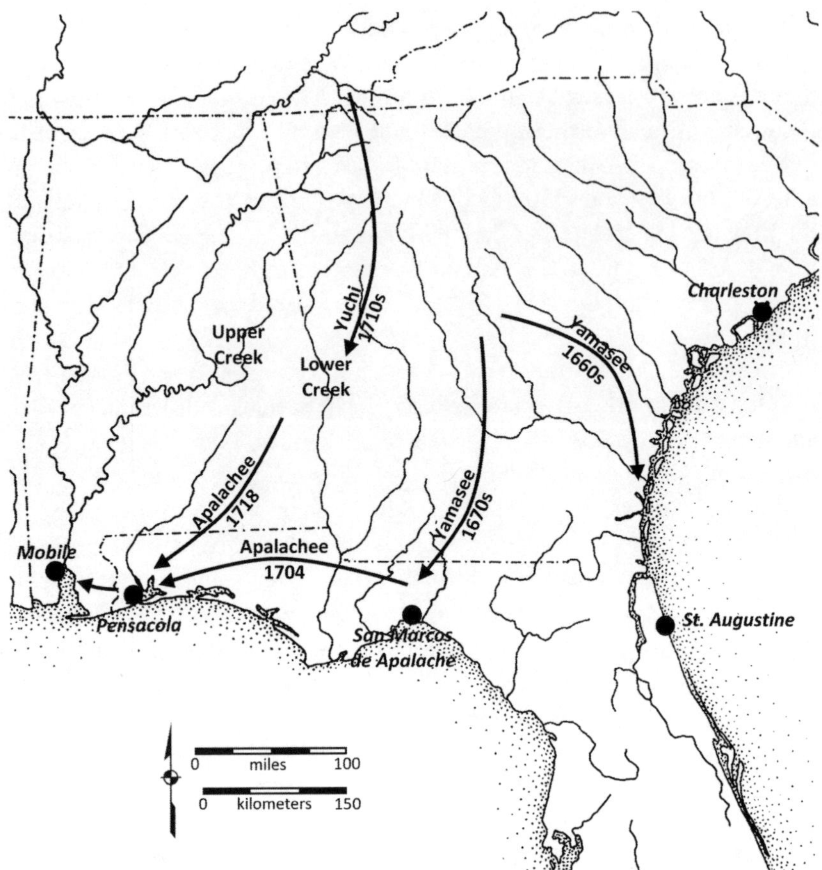

Figure 7.2. Selected colonial migrations in and around Spanish Florida.

coastal Yamasee were explicitly exempted from the requirement to convert to Christianity in exchange for their contribution to the annual Florida labor draft known as the *repartimiento* (Worth 1995:35; 2004:249), and maintained a distinct political and ethnic identity throughout their stay in the missions from the 1660s through the early 1680s. Yet, their archaeological sites display the same Altamaha-San Marcos ceramics then in use by their predominantly Mocama neighbors, who of course had adopted this ceramic tradition from the Guale just a few decades earlier, as noted above. Moreover, after these Yamasee fled the missions en masse following a 1683 pirate raid along the coast, and eventually coalesced by the end of 1684 on the margin of English territory just outside the mission system in the old Escamazu province bordering the then-abandoned Guale mission province, they subsequently continued to produce this same Altamaha-San Marcos ceramic assemblage during the next three decades operating as slave raiders for Carolina traders (e.g., Green and DePratter 2000; Sweeney 2005, 2009; Worth 2009b:199–200). They even continued to produce these same types upon their return to the vicinity of St. Augustine after the 1715 Yamasee War, when they lived near other refugee missions whose inhabitants were also characterized by Altamaha-San Marcos ceramics (e.g., Boyer 2005:81–82; Waters 2008:150–154; White 2002:71–82). Just as was the case for the Yuchi, the Yamasee preserved a distinctive ethnic identity for decades after they settled among the Mission Indians of Florida, but nonetheless seem quickly to have adopted the ceramic practices of their new neighbors.

Details of a similar pattern are now also emerging among the eighteenth-century Apalachee immigrants to the Franco-Spanish borderlands in the far western Florida Panhandle and coastal Alabama. By the end of the seventeenth century, this region seems to have been severely depopulated, except for the Mobile-Tensaw River Delta region, where several communities of Mobila (French Mobilian) and Tomé Indians continued to reside through 1763 (Waselkov and Gums 2000:6–21). The few remnant settlements of Panzacola and Chacato (French Chato) Indians on Pensacola Bay seem to have disappeared not long after the 1698 arrival of the Spanish (Harris 1999:45–49, 2003:265–269; Waselkov and Gums 2000:21–23), but both areas were soon bolstered by an influx of Apalachee Indians from the east. Two major episodes of immigration are documented, including an initial influx of Apalachee refugees into both Spanish Pensacola and French Mobile after the 1704 destruction of the Apalachee mission province by allied English and Creek Indian forces, and the 1718 immigration of Apalachees returning to Spanish territory from exile in Creek territory after the 1715 Yamasee War against English Carolina (Clune et al. 2003: 28–29; Covington 1964; Hann 1988: 305–308; Harris 1999:49–53, 58–62, 2003:269–272; Worth 2008; Worth et al. 2011, 2012). The earliest years of the first Apalachee immigration are captured in archaeological collections from Old Mobile (1702–1711) and Presidio Santa María de Galve (1698–1719) and imply substantial persistence of Jefferson ceramics similar to the San Luís phase in the Apalachee homeland in Tallahassee (Cordell 2001; Harris 1999, 2003:277–292; Silvia 2000:98–148). In contrast, the archaeological signature of local Apalachee ceramics following the second wave of immigration by the northern band of Apalachee refugees is best represented in archaeological collections from Presidio Isla de Santa Rosa (1722–1756) and Mission San Joseph de Escambe (1741–1761) and shows strong affinities to Creek ceramic traditions (particularly the Lower Creek Blackmon phase), although clearly bearing unmistakable traces of their Apalachee heritage as well (Harris 2007; Harris and Eschbach 2006:109–113; Johnson 2012:89–90; Worth et al. 2011,

2012). Beyond this, the contemporary mid-eighteenth-century French-allied Apalachee village site at Blakeley Park on the Tensaw River displays the results of several decades of ceramic change after the initial 1704 migration into the Mobile Bay region (which also sustained indigenous Mobila and Tomé populations throughout the period) and shows both divergence and similarity to the contemporaneous Spanish-allied Apalachee at Mission Escambe not 37 miles away (Melcher 2012; Pigott 2013, 2015). Although the historical scenario is complex, and the archaeological analysis is still ongoing, this case study of the results of the Apalachee diaspora unquestionably provides even further evidence that assemblages of archaeological ceramic types do not correspond neatly to the documented ethnic identity of their makers, but instead seem to vary more directly with geographic proximity within the current social landscape at any given time.

Immigration, however, was not the only catalyst for wholesale stylistic change of utilitarian household ceramics among Southeastern Indians. Returning to my original example above, the *in situ* transformation of the Mocama ceramic style (San Pedro) into that of their Guale neighbors to the north (Altamaha-San Marcos) by 1650, and the contemporaneous transformation of both the Potano and Timucua ceramic styles (Alachua and Suwannee Valleys, respectively) into that of their Apalachee neighbors to the west (the Velda phase, or Jefferson), also provide clear evidence that new patterns of social interaction between polities could also result in ceramic transformation among locationally stable populations (Figure 7.3). In this case, the integration of two or more ceramic style zones, or phases, into a single corridor of transport and interaction under the overarching politico-economic system administered by the Spanish appears to have resulted in homogenization of household ceramics within each of these branches. However, it did not result in a unified ceramic style throughout the entire Florida colonial system, indicating that such transformations were probably more influenced by geographic proximity than political affiliation. The pre-Spanish landscape of warring chiefdoms and long-term social and linguistic boundaries between regional provinces gave way to a sort of pan-Florida *pax hispanum* during the early seventeenth century. Even though both Spanish and Native leaders are documented to have taken great care to recognize and maintain traditional provincial and ethnic distinctions within the northern and western mission chains, by 1650 the previously disparate ceramic style zones along these corridors coalesced into just two styles (Altamaha-San Marcos and Jefferson), not counting the continued persistence of a third style zone (St. Johns) along the short-lived southern mission chain along the St. Johns River drainage (Worth 2009a, 2009b:199, 201–207).

A fuller explanation of this broader phenomenon awaits additional tar-

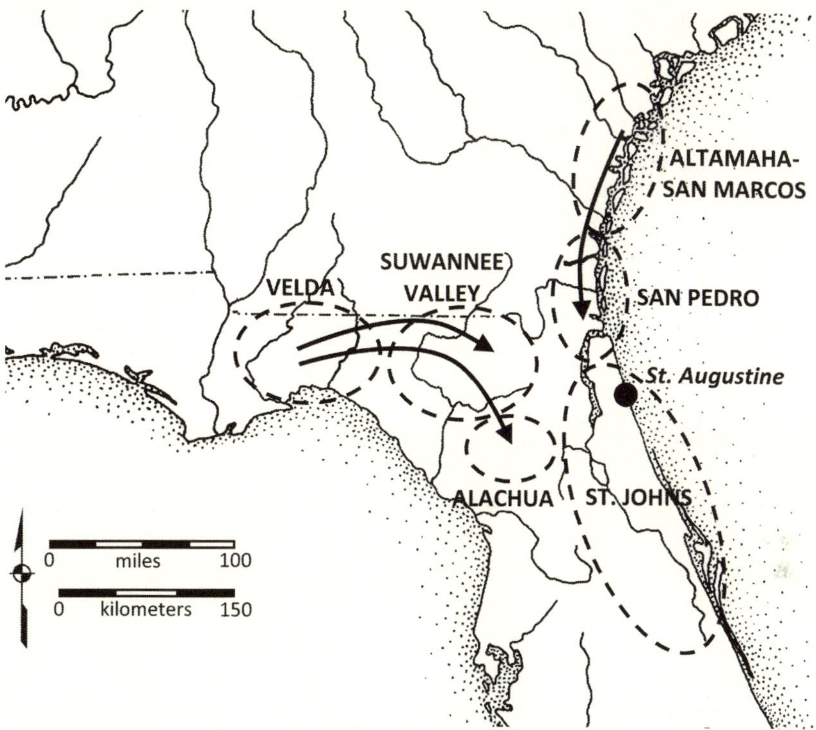

Figure 7.3. In situ ceramic transformations in early seventeenth-century Spanish Florida.

geted research, but it is perhaps telling that the homogenization of ceramics along the northern and western mission chains seems to have followed a pattern where the provinces nearest to St. Augustine, and thus the earliest-assimilated and most severely depopulated due to the effect of epidemics and the Spanish labor system, adopted the ceramic style of the most distant provinces, which were not coincidentally more populous and, at least in the case of Apalachee, most recently assimilated. Moreover, this apparent "backflow" of ceramic homogenization literally followed the path of the annual *repartimiento* labor draft, which brought scores of unmarried male workers from the far ends of the mission chain through the most depopulated provinces to St. Augustine for seasonal farm work (Bushnell 1994: 121–123; Worth 1998a:187–197). There is also no documentary evidence for the kind of widespread interprovincial population movements that might otherwise account for this ceramic transformation, and indeed good evidence for its explicit prohibition, at least for men, as recorded in several visitations and other official documents (Hann 1993:119, 214–215; Worth

1998b:22–26). This may in part have been a response to complaints that single women were often unable to find marriage partners and married women were often living without their husbands because of the absence of men working as Spanish laborers, contributing to reduced population growth in already-devastated villages (Menéndez et al. 1657; Worth 1998b: 21–22). As discussed, there is no evidence for a widespread shift to marketplace ceramic production and consumption among Mission Indians, despite recent suggestions by Saunders (2001, 2009, 2012) and Waters (2005:170–175; 2009:176) that the prevalence of Altamaha-San Marcos wares can be explained as a sort of "negotiated tradition" incorporating Spanish consumer preferences into a new marketplace model. Whatever the exact mechanism for the *in situ* ceramic transformations during the early seventeenth century, what seems quite clear is that the assimilation of previously antagonistic groups with different languages into a new overarching colonial system resulted in the homogenization of ceramic styles along each corridor of regional interaction extending away from the colonial hub at St. Augustine.

In all the cases described, increased social interaction between previously separate indigenous groups brought together either by immigration or by *in situ* assimilation into a single society resulted in the adaptation of the ceramic style of the immigrant or least populous group to match that of their proximal neighbors within the same society, even while nonetheless continuing to maintain independent ethnic and political identities as a matter of public knowledge. How quickly such transformations occurred is an empirical question that has yet to be explored in depth, although the temporal scale seems to be one of years rather than decades in several cases. Ongoing and future research using collections from unambiguously identified, well-dated, short-lived, and spatially segregated sites and proveniences holds considerable promise in this regard. Nonetheless, sufficient data are available now to state unequivocally that for Southeastern North America, and likely elsewhere as well, the equivalency of archaeological phases with polities or ethnies is clearly a proposition that must be demonstrated, not assumed. As archaeological phases represent the material manifestation of patterned human behavior, and the explanation of these patterns of behavior remains only an object of study rather than a predrawn conclusion, it seems only logical that we should initially focus our efforts on the behaviors themselves and how those individual behaviors were situated in a broader social context. More specifically, we need to focus on the actual practice of ceramic production and how such practices came into being and were transmitted both spatially and temporally to create and maintain the patterns that we witness in the archaeological record. In short, we need to turn our attention to the social context of learning and practice for the individual household potters who made the pots from which phases are indirectly constructed.

Landscapes of Practice

The concept of practice employed here corresponds to that embraced by adherents of broader practice theory, which explores the relationships between individual agency and collective structure, between intentionality and habit, and between tradition and change (e.g., Bourdieu 1977; Dobres and Hoffman 1994; Dobres and Robb 2000; Dornan 2002; Giddens 1984; Joyce and Lopiparo 2005; Lightfoot et al. 1998; Ortner 1984:144–160, 1992:11–18; Pauketat 2001; Silliman 2001). As elaborated from foundational concepts proposed by Pierre Bourdieu (1977) and Anthony Giddens (1984), practice theory posits that individual practice generates collective structure while that same structure reflexively influences and shapes individual practice, and situates human actions within the framework of habitual dispositions, or *habitus*, that governs the conscious and unconscious production and reproduction of these structures through daily practice. Much of this literature focuses on the power relationships viewed as implicit in the concepts of agency and structure, particularly as regards the relative degrees of freedom and autonomy exercised by individual agents within a collective structure, and often implicitly presuming or inferring that this relationship is contested or political at some level, even in the arena of mundane daily activities. Even more importantly, practice theorists commonly seem to explore structure and agency in a more generic and universal sense, without explicitly distinguishing fundamentally different types of social structures beyond the obvious "society" and "individual," even when examined at different scales. As my intention is to examine the exact nature of the social entity that might be responsible for the spatial patterns of human behavior that we see reflected in the archaeological record of ceramic assemblages, especially given that these patterns do not appear to be equivalent to polities or ethnies, I have expanded my view to incorporate useful insights from social learning theory regarding the specific nature of social structures that derive from routinized individual practice, and how such structures may differ from those principally based on explicit social identity.

Social learning theory, which is grounded in a range of disciplines from anthropology and sociology to psychology and education, provides a useful framework for approaching the relationship between individual practice and its social context. In particular, the concept of community of practice would seem to be especially applicable to the phenomenon of household ceramic production and its relationship to social organization and social identity. Archaeological applications of this concept have been explored by several authors in recent years (e.g., Minar 2001; Minar and Crown 2001), including prehistoric and historic ceramics in the Southeast and elsewhere (Crown 2001; Michelaki 2007; Sassaman and Rudolphi 2001), but the concept nonetheless remains to be operationalized effectively or extensively in archaeological application. A community of practice is defined by Etienne Wenger (1998:72–85) as a special type of community united by three dimensions of coherence: mutual engagement, a joint enterprise, and shared repertoires. As "an aggregate of people who come together around a mutual engagement in an endeavor . . . defined simultaneously by its membership and by the practice in which that membership engages" (Eckert and McConnell-Ginnet 1992:464), it represents "a locus of engagement in action, interpersonal relations, shared knowledge, and negotiation of enterprises" (Wenger 1998: 85) and "a historically constructed, ongoing, conflicting, synergistic structuring of activity and relations among practitioners" (Lave and Wenger 1991:56). Moreover, because communities of practice are maintained and reproduced by patterns of learning, they can also be conceptualized as "shared histories of learning" (Wenger 1998:86).

From a spatial perspective, communities of practice can also be conceptualized as forming part of a broader "landscape of practice" on which "the texture of continuities and discontinuities . . . is defined by practice, not by institutional affiliation" (Wenger 1998:118). Indeed, such communities are qualitatively distinct from formal sociopolitical institutions as traditionally defined: "since the life of a community as it unfolds is, in essence, produced by its members through their mutual engagement, it evolves in organic ways that tend to escape formal descriptions and control. The landscape of practice is therefore not congruent with the reified structures of institutional affiliations, divisions, and boundaries. It is not independent of these institutional structures, but neither is it reducible to them" (Wenger 1998:118–119). Not only are communities of practice often discontinuous with traditional sociopolitical units, but they also display dynamic qualities based on the very nature of learning in practice; "the geography of practice reflects histories of learning, but learning continues to reconfigure relations of proximity and distance . . . the landscape of practice is an emergent structure in which learning constantly creates localities that reconfigure the geography" (Wenger 1998:130–131).

In this vein, I propose that archaeological phases or other equivalent "style zones" based on material culture (particularly ceramics) should not be thought of as behavioral byproducts of polities or ethnies for which ceramic style is seen as a natural outgrowth of ethno-political identity, but should instead be conceptualized as the material and spatial trace of past communities of practice that were fundamentally based on the routine practices of and interactions between the very craftspeople whose behaviors generated the patterned distribution of material culture that archaeologists study. Seen in this light, archaeological phases would be linked first and foremost to the practices of the individuals responsible for the material manifestation of phases, and only secondarily and indirectly to the ethno-political units that framed the social landscape within which such practices took place. Instead of viewing material practice as a unidirectional outgrowth of ethno-political identity, practice and identity are perceived to be independent dimensions of variability, recursively related but each capable of producing distinct material manifestations on the archaeological landscape.

Building upon this proposal, it is useful to highlight Suzanne Eckert's (2008:2–3, 57–58) recent delineation of the difference between what she calls "communities of practice" and "communities of identity." Although not explicitly based on the social learning theory concepts outlined above (Eckert and McConnell-Ginnet 1992; Lave and Wenger 1991; Wenger 1998), Eckert's conceptual framework provides an important discrimination between two broad categories of community that may influence the practice of potters, coinciding quite nicely with the distinction I have alluded to regarding identification based on membership in polities and ethnies, and identification based on shared practice. In her analysis of prehistoric Pueblo pottery in the American Southwest, Eckert defines communities of practice as "social networks in which Pueblo potters learn their craft from other women in the community . . . defined by a shared history of practice and not by spatial constraints" (Eckert 2008:2). She contrasts these with communities of identity, which are "social networks in which potters share a group identity . . . based in a shared language, migration history, religion, kinship, or some other social process" (Eckert 2008:3). She furthermore observes that "as communities of identity are based on social perception, they may or may not correspond to communities of practice" (Eckert 2008:3). Indeed, a major part of her analysis is based on empirically determining which dimensions of ceramic variability may correspond to either or both types of communities.

Incorporating these concepts into my evaluation of the relationship between archaeological phases and historically documented polities and ethnies, I suggest that the most useful approach is to classify archaeologically defined phases as communities of practice, and to classify historically documented polities and ethnies as communities of identity. This is not to say that practice and identity have nothing to do with one another, but rather that each type of community is principally defined by different dimensions of human culture, and that only by disentangling these units and analyzing

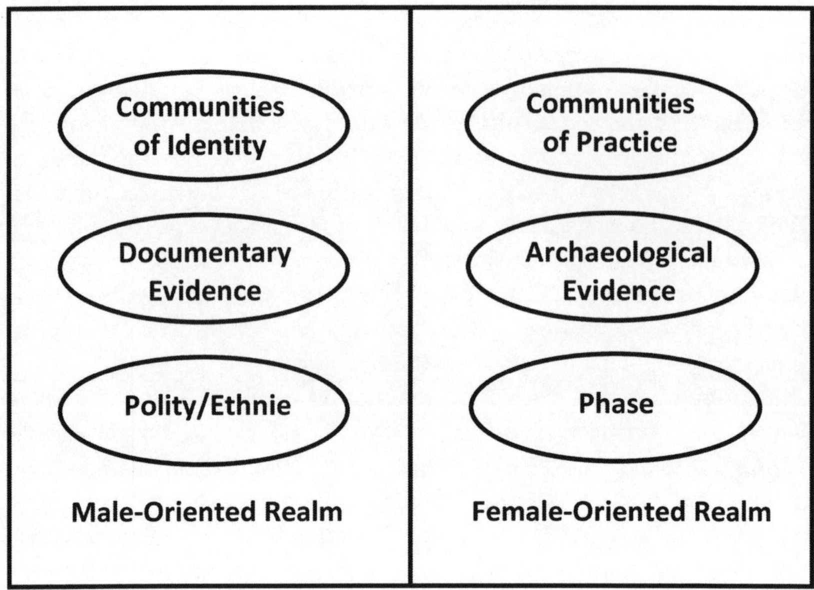

Figure 7.4. Identity vs. ceramic practice for southeastern Indians.

them by separate and appropriate criteria can any correspondence, or lack of correspondence, between the two types of community be demonstrated empirically. Members of a community of identity definitely conceived of themselves (or were identified by others) as belonging to the same social unit but might not necessarily have shared a bond of common practice in all areas of material culture. In contrast, members of a community of practice definitely shared a bond of common practice but might never have conceived of themselves (or have been identified by others) as belonging to the same social unit. Perhaps most importantly from a methodological standpoint, polities and ethnies, as communities of identity, are most readily defined by the belief of membership, whether internal or external, and are therefore most readily observable through the documentary record, which is directly derived from the mental dimension of culture, and which only provides indirect access to the behavioral dimension (Figure 7.4). In direct contrast, phases and other archaeological style zones, as communities of practice, are most readily defined by spatially and temporally distinguishable patterns of routinized behavior, as shaped by learning and interaction, and are therefore most readily observable through the archaeological record, which is directly derived from the behavioral dimension of culture, and which only provides indirect access to the mental dimension.

In detaching social entities based on practice from those based on identity, researchers will be more effective in their ability to analyze the precise relationship between material practice and ethno-political identity under a variety of different circumstances. Ceramics in particular will no longer be automatically or necessarily linked with political or ethnic identity, but instead with the practices of individual potters whose collective behaviors and interaction made up a different kind of social entity: a community of practice. By no means does this imply that ethno-political identity was never materialized through ceramic practice, or that communities of identity cannot be discovered or reconstructed using archaeological data alone, but rather that the spatial distribution of archaeological ceramics is first and always a function of the landscape of practice, and only when specific practices can reasonably be inferred to have communicated or corresponded to ethno-political identity can those communities of practice be concluded to reflect or equate with corresponding communities of identity. In other words, archaeological materials represent materialized practice, so communities of identity can only be reconstructed indirectly through equivalent communities of practice, and such equivalence must be demonstrated, not assumed.

Worth reiterating here is the fact that in Southeastern North America these communities of ceramic practice were almost certainly made up of women, whereas the more familiar communities of ethno-political identity were traditionally dominated by men, making this distinction between types of communities particularly relevant to archaeological studies of gender. Moreover, in this context, we can actually explore the specific conditions under which ceramic style zones either corresponded to or crosscut political or linguistic boundaries, or under which immigrants or refugees either maintained, modified, or abandoned their ceramic traditions while nonetheless maintaining their distinctive ethnic identities. We can furthermore tease apart those elements, scales, and dimensions of ceramic learning and practice that may have reflected different degrees of correspondence to, or difference from, the ethno-political landscape within which potters found themselves. This includes breaking down the exact operational sequences, or *chaînes opératoires* (Dietler and Herbich 1989, 1998; Gosselain 1998, 2000; Lemonnier 1986; Stark 1998), involved in ceramic production, and the social context of each step, as has been done fruitfully by archaeologists in other areas of North America (e.g., Crown 2007; Michelaki 2007). What this approach really means is that we will be examining archaeological material culture as a result of practice, and separately addressing the extent to which these practices may or may not have been coterminous with political or ethnic categories so familiar to us from the documentary record. Admittedly, the bulk of this research remains to be carried out and will undoubtedly require substantial revisitation of older conclusions and reanalysis of existing collections and databases in a new framework. Nevertheless, the disentanglement of ceramic practice from ethno-political identity will allow us to make more effective and reliable interpretations based on empirical evidence drawn variously from either the archaeological or the documentary realm, or both simultaneously. Given the undeniable importance to archaeologists of ceramic analysis in reconstructing the social geography of both the prehistoric and historic past, the reconceptualization of archaeological phases as communities of practice instead of communities of identity may provide us with an important tool in bridging the ontological and methodological gap between prehistory and history. To this end, I offer some preliminary proposals toward operationalizing this concept in specifically archaeological analyses.

Operationalizing the Landscape of Practice Concept

Pivotal to any definition of archaeological phases as communities of practice is an acknowledgment of both the geographic and chronological dimensions inherent to their definition. Specifically, communities of practice always exist within a broader landscape of practice, and these landscapes have histories. As practice is ultimately manifested through the actions of individual agents, each with their own histories but acting within a current social context, communities of practice are dynamic entities in daily reinvention by their constituent members interacting with one another. They therefore evolve over time in response to the constant push-and-pull interplay between continuity and change. Simply put, local and regional phase chronologies originally formulated by culture historians are nothing more than the material manifestations of historical landscapes of practice. The socially and historically contextualized practices of individual potters manifested themselves as more or less distinctive communities of practice in a broader landscape of practice, and as those practices and contexts evolved over time, so too did the landscape itself. Practices may have changed yet the community itself may have remained constant, or practices may have remained the same while the community grew or diminished within the broader social landscape.

It is furthermore important to emphasize that defining a community of practice based on surviving archaeological traces of the end-product of that shared practice necessitates a sufficiently detailed and nuanced understanding of what that practice actually entailed. The *chaîne opératoire* involved in producing a finished ceramic vessel encompassed a series of choices and actions in four major domains of practice, including selection and preparation of raw materials for the clay paste, fabrication of the vessel itself, application of decorations or other surface treatments on the surface of the vessel, and its firing (*sensu* Tite 1999:182, 184–191). Even within a model of local-scale household ceramic production under consideration here, the individual practices within each of these four domains may have been performed in a slightly different social context, or even by different individuals within a household. Moreover, not all of these practices had equal relevance in the context of day-to-day social interactions between the potters who made up the broader community of ceramic practice (see discussion by Carr 1995:185–215 on the "visibility hierarchy" of artifact design). Highlighting this, Gosselain (2000:191–193) categorizes stages in the manufacturing process "according to salience, technical malleability, and the social context in which the techniques are learned and conducted," breaking ceramic production practices down into three broad categories: (1) "techniques that leave visible evidence on the finished products" and that are technically malleable because their "motifs and tools" may readily be changed, (2) techniques that "cannot be 'read' on the finished product" but that are nonetheless still malleable, and (3) techniques that "leave no apparent traces on the finished product" and that are more resistant to change because they rely on "specialized gestures" or "motor habits" internalized through early learning and repeated practice.

The importance of these distinctions lies in the relationship between individual practice and its broader social context and more specifically highlights those specific practices that have the greatest likelihood of being altered by postlearning social interaction. This is the foundation of the community of practice concept, which I suggest provides a mechanism to operationalize both the Bourdieuian concept of *habitus* and the Giddensian concept of structuration using archaeological data. In Gosselain's formulation, techniques in the first category allow "a wide range of people to be aware of potters' behavior and, consequently, to influence potters' choices of techniques," resulting in visual qualities that "render them especially likely to be ascribed aesthetic, economic, or symbolic values and thus consciously borrowed or manipulated" (Gosselain 2000:191). The techniques in the second category are generally only recognized by "a limited category of people—fellow potters and their assistants," meaning "the adoption of new techniques occurs infrequently, primarily when artisans relocate their homes or clay sources or both, or seek to produce a new type of pottery artifact" (Gosselain 2000:192). The third category involves techniques that are "especially resistant to change" because they are acquired "during early socialization involving deep and formal relationships with a limited set of people, usually close relatives" (Gosselain 2000:192–193).

Elaborating on this point, table 7.3 presents a simplified matrix of rele-

Table 7.3. Ceramic Practice Domains

Domain	Overt/Malleable	Obscure/Malleable	Obscure/ Resistant
Paste Preparation	(some) Clay Selection (some) Tempering Agent(s)*	(most) Clay Selection (some) Tempering Agent(s)* Clay-processing Technique	—
Vessel Fabrication	Vessel Form Secondary Forming of Decorative Features*	Vessel-forming Technique	Motor Habits of Vessel Formation
Surface Treatment	Surface Treatment Technique* Decorative Style (Gross Scale)*	Decorative Style (Fine Scale)*	Motor Habits of Surface Treatment
Firing	Firing Atmosphere	Firing Temperature	—

*Readily observable from sherds

vant practices grouped by domains (Tite 1999) and degrees of visibility and malleability (Gosselain 1999). Within the four domains of ceramic practice, specific practices are grouped as to the relative degree of social visibility (whether more overt or obscure) and the extent to which they were prone to being adopted or manipulated consciously (whether more malleable or resistant to change). Beyond this, I have also highlighted those practices that are more readily observable from sherds alone and thus better suited for routine archaeological analysis. This table illustrates the fact that some practices within the *chaîne opératoire* are more likely than others to be picked up and spread among potters, although only some of these practices are susceptible to identification by analysis of archaeological sherds alone.

A thorough analysis of the entire suite of socially contextualized practices comprising ceramic production would, in theory, permit the comprehensive reconstruction of a "living community of ceramic practice" among the Southeastern Indian groups under consideration here. But archaeologists are necessarily limited to those practices that left material traces readily observed in archaeological assemblages and must therefore rely on a somewhat narrow subset of the original totality of ceramic practice. As archaeologists normally classify ceramics into typologies based on macroscopic attributes observable in broken vessel fragments (potsherds), those domains of the ceramic *chaîne opératoire* that are readily observable in sherds (such as temper and surface treatment) tend to take priority over those (especially vessel form) that do not in definitions of archaeological ceramic types (e.g., Colton and Hargrave 1937:2–3; Krieger 1940:9; Phillips 1958:119, 123; Scarry 1985:199–210; Wheat et al. 1958; Willey 1949:5–6). Furthermore, as archaeological phases have historically been defined based on the relative proportions of types created in this manner, it naturally follows that if we are to define archaeological phases as communities of practice, we must explicitly acknowledge the specific domains of ceramic practice drawn upon to create these archaeological ceramic types. Consequently, when we speak of an archaeologically defined community of specifically ceramic practice, we are actually referring to an interacting community of potters who can be demonstrated through sherd analysis to have shared a similar set of practices with regard to the domains of paste preparation (particularly tempering agents, or aplastics) and surface treatment (both decorative and otherwise), including not just the techniques (tools and execution of designs), but their stylistic content as well. Practices associated with the vessel form domain, although clearly less evident in assemblages of sherds, nonetheless can still form part of the observed set of practices, especially with secondary decorative features commonly associated with vessel rims.

I suggest that the concept of a community of practice must necessarily remain somewhat flexible in terms of both scale and composition, to allow it to be adapted to particular cases and circumstances where appropriate. Nevertheless, the term "community" must imply something more specific than simply a collection of craftspeople at any scale who happen to share one or two practices in common, which I would relegate to a "horizon of practice" (defined below; see also Carr 1995:236–246 for a broader discussion of what he calls the "geographic distribution hierarchy"). If we accept the documentary evidence that utilitarian household ceramics were indeed normally produced by female potters among the late prehistoric and early historic Southeastern Indians, and furthermore that ceramic production and consumption took place predominantly in the household context , then a community of ceramic practice may be defined as that group of female potters whose individual ceramic *chaînes opératoires* had come to resemble one another as a result of the mutual and reflexive influence of other potters from whom and with whom they learned, with whom they practiced, or whose crafts were routinely available for firsthand inspection. In this context, the empirical evidence reviewed in this chapter supports the following inferences for the region and time periods under consideration:

1. Greater social interaction tended to result in greater similarity of ceramic practice.
2. The current social and material environment of a potter tended to exert a greater influence on her ceramic practice than her past social and material environment.

3. Physical proximity (geography) tended to play a more important role than social proximity (political/ethnic identity) with respect to social interactions within the broader landscape of practice.

These inferences can be summed up by stating that communities of ceramic practice seem to reflect an underlying tendency of household potters to conform to the existing practices of the neighboring potters with whom they interacted most regularly, or whose pots they saw or used routinely. Utilitarian household ceramics therefore may be interpreted to reflect an ethic of conformity and social unity rather than distinctiveness and social division. Consequently, the landscape of practice within which individual communities of practice may be mapped is in actuality a reflection of the landscape of social interaction among female potters, with degrees of similarity or difference in local or regional ceramic practice reflecting the extent of such interaction. Empirical data already reviewed in this chapter make it clear that even profound linguistic differences between neighboring polities, villages, or families did not necessarily hinder the kinds of interaction that led to increasing similarity of ceramic practice.

More specifically to the point of this chapter, if we take archaeological assemblages of potsherds as the material manifestation of *chaînes opératoires* of the female potters who produced them, and the geographical distribution of these assemblages as a reasonably accurate reflection of not just their final location of discard, but also their original production and use in household context, then by evaluating the degrees of geographic variation between these assemblages (continuous vs. discontinuous, homogeneous vs. heterogeneous), archaeologists are actually mapping past landscapes of ceramic practice, corresponding to past landscapes of interaction between female potters. Consequently, to the extent that archaeologists have developed typologies that allow them to define archaeological phases based on the presence/absence and relative percentages of named ceramic types, these phases may be considered the geographically bounded material manifestations of past communities of ceramic practice.

It is important to recognize that archaeological phases have historically been defined and subsequently reified using widely variable standards with more or less rigorous measures of empirical sufficiency, at least as regards the extent to which intraphase assemblage variation is (or is not) demonstrably less than interphase variation and what amount of data is minimally sufficient to make such assertions. One could easily argue, for example, that the many late prehistoric and early historic phases defined for northern Georgia and Alabama (among many other examples across the Southeastern United States) are more a reflection of the geographically discontinuous distribution of settlement across the broader landscape (e.g., "site clusters" located along productive floodplains within major river valleys) than they are a rigorously tested collection of comparably robust site-level datasets demonstrating statistical clustering of ceramic assemblages within each phase (but see Foster 2004). Nevertheless, even though additional research is clearly needed to evaluate the level of ceramic variation both within and between such phases, available literature indicates that archaeological phases are generally distinguished from one another principally using the relative proportion of ceramic types (commonly percentages by count) within sherd assemblages from archaeological proveniences identified as belonging to the appropriate time period (e.g., Blitz and Lorenz 2006:62–73; Hally 1970: 13–22, 1986, 1994a:149–152; Hally and Langford 1988:47, 59, 71; Hally and Rudolph 1986:41, 56, 67–68; Knight 1985:9–13, 1994:186–189; Knight and Mistovich 1984:222–228; Moore 2002:174–184; Williams and Shapiro 1990: 39–80). Even though many researchers have incorporated additional subtypological stylistic variables in their characterizations of and comparisons between phases, the fundamental definitions of phases seem to rely principally on the ceramic types themselves.

If we examine these ceramic types through the lens of the landscapes of practice framework outlined above, then archaeological phases as traditionally defined represent more or less geographically bounded clusters of contemporaneous archaeological sites bearing evidence for a common set of practices within two primary domains of the overall *chaîne opératoire*, namely clay paste preparation (temper selection) and surface treatment (techniques and decorative styles), as supplemented by limited sherd-based evidence from the vessel fabrication domain (primary vessel form and secondary decorative features). The choice of specific practices employed within each of these domains were rarely if ever completely uniform, and thus the common ceramic *chaîne opératoire* that would be considered definitional for an archaeological phase would normally include a suite of several different practices employed in roughly the same relative proportions by all potters living within the area encompassed by the phase. It is important to emphasize here that whole-site archaeological assemblages commonly comprise the sum total of all discarded sherds from broken vessels of all different types, sizes, and functions, each of which may have been produced, used, broken, and discarded in different relative proportions, meaning that just because two alternative decorative techniques appear in equal proportions in the final archaeological assemblage does not necessarily mean that every vessel had an equal chance of being decorated with either technique. Equally plausible is the explanation that each decoration belonged exclusively to a different vessel form or size category, or perhaps even that the decorations were applied to different areas of the same vessels. As archaeologists are commonly obligated to work from aggregate data based on shattered ceramic vessels, the proportionality reflected in ceramic type counts also reflects the aggregate of all practices employed by all potters who made many different vessel forms and sizes over the course of their residence at a given archaeological site.

Because archaeological phases have normally been defined by archaeologists based on a common set of choices by female potters with regard to which tempers would be added to their utilitarian household vessels and in what relative proportions, and which surface treatment techniques and decorative styles would be applied to these vessels and in what proportions, and to some extent also by aspects of the shape of some of their vessels, as well as some decorative secondary features, then here we have an operational definition of a ceramic community of practice that can be employed for archaeological assemblages of sherds. Specifically, a ceramic community of practice represents a geographic area within which female potters interacted frequently enough with one another through initial learning or ongoing ceramic practice, or saw enough of each others' finished pottery, to adapt several fundamental aspects of their own individual ceramic *chaînes opératoires* to match that of the rest of the potters in that same geographic area. This included not just the most overt and malleable practices of surface treatment and decoration, which could presumably be perceived and copied individually based solely on the finished vessels in their neighbors' households, but also some of the more obscure practices that seem most likely to have been picked up through the shared collecting and processing of clays and tempers, or through more in-depth conversations with other potters. Nevertheless, the end result of such a community of ceramic practice was a geographic area within which utilitarian household pottery assemblages (analyzed as aggregate collections of sherds) evidenced substantial similarity in both the overt characteristics of surface treatment, vessel form, and temper, as well as more visually obscure characteristics of both temper and decorative style.

Taking this a step further, individual communities of practice are best defined with reference to the broader landscape of practice of which they formed a part. In an effort to map out these landscapes applying the same criteria used to define communities, if we break down each of these readily observable ceramic practice domains into a series of major and readily distinguishable practices (such as brushed vs. stamped vs. incised vs. plain surface treatment), or simply axes of variation along a continuum of practice (such as thick to thin incised lines), it naturally follows that each specific practice, while linked to the *chaîne opératoire* of which it formed a step or stage, may have been characterized by its own distinct distribution in both time and space, as framed of course within the spatial distribution of inhabited sites on the physical landscape. Experience shows that in Southeastern North America, for example, the geographic distribution of Native American ceramic tempers during the early historic era differed from the contemporaneous distribution of surface decorations, overlapping in some areas and not in others. Furthermore, these geographic distributions changed over time, such that for example one may speak of the "spread" of shell-tempered ceramics over the course of several centuries during the late prehistoric era (e.g., Feathers 2006; Feathers and Peacock 2008; Weinstein and Dumas 2008), or the emergence of a completely new "brushed pottery horizon" during the historic era within the historically documented territory of the Creek Indians (Cantley and Joseph 1991:205; Knight 1985:188). As it happened, during the late seventeenth and early eighteenth centuries, these two specific horizons overlapped for a time, but this, too, was only temporary, and shell-tempered brushed ceramics (the type Walnut Roughened) were eventually replaced by sand-tempered brushed ceramics (Chattahoochee Roughened), leaving the distribution of shell tempering and brushing largely separate from one another by the end of the eighteenth century (e.g., Foster 2007:90–94; Knight 1994).

Although each of these "horizons of practice" represents the physical manifestation of a geographically extensive group of contemporaneous potters who employed the same specific practice as part of their own individual *chaînes opératoires*, such horizons are not equivalent to communities of practice, but instead form part of the broader landscape of practice within which such communities existed. A single decorative technique forms only one of several ceramic practices in multiple domains used to define an archaeological ceramic type, and a single ceramic type forms only one part of an assemblage of types employed to define an archaeological phase. Furthermore, phases are not defined solely by the presence or absence of types, but rather by their relative proportions among sherd assemblages within each phase. Horizons of practice, therefore, are not simply two-dimensional plots of the simple existence of a particular practice, but should instead be viewed as three-dimensional contour maps showing both the spatial bounds of a practice as well as its proportional frequency with respect to other practice choices within the same domain (see Foster 2004 for one approach). In this context, then, a community of ceramic practice might be mapped out as the spatially bounded locus of overlap between all the various three-dimensional horizons of ceramic practice that formed part of the *chaîne opératoire* used in household pottery production within each community of practice. The geographic configuration of the loci formed by these overlap-

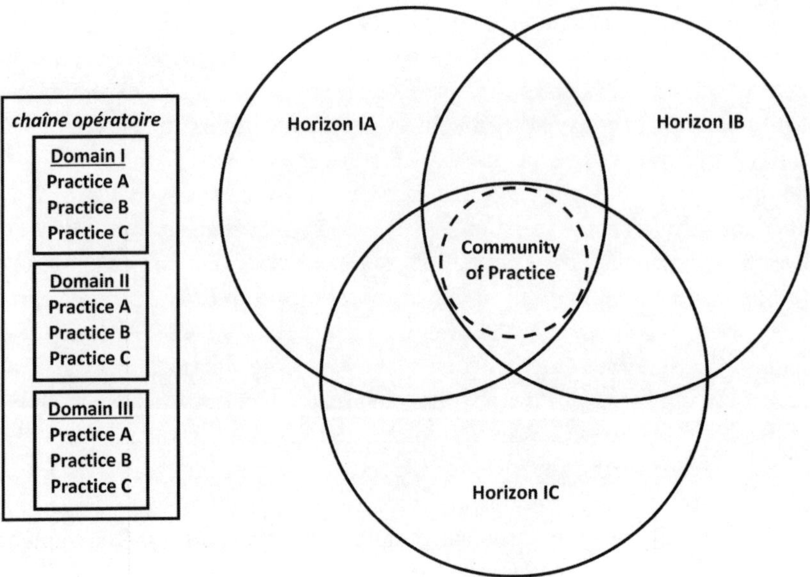

Figure 7.5. Partial schematic of a landscape of practice.

ping horizons of practice would effectively map out the broader landscape of practice which evolved historically as a continually "emergent structure" (Wenger 1998:130). Not only could these horizons expand and contract spatially across the inhabited portions of the physical landscape over the course of time as the pattern of social interaction between potters changed, but also within each horizon the contours of its proportional density changed over time, reflecting the rise and fall of the relative abundance of that particular practice within its domain (Figure 7.5).

For the sake of clarity, a few operational definitions are warranted here, specifically focusing on the operationalization of the landscape of practice theory for studying household ceramic production:

1. *Practice*: A specific technique or technical choice employed as a part of a particular domain in a *chaîne opératoire* (e.g., shell tempering, coil construction, incising); the term also refers in a general sense to the routine habitual behaviors of individual craftspeople in the past.
2. *Domain of Practice*: A category of functionally related practices within a *chaîne opératoire* (e.g., paste preparation, vessel fabrication, surface treatment).
3. *Chaîne Opératoire*: The operational sequence of practices (broken

down into several functional domains) associated with the production of a specific class of material culture, in this case ceramics; this can refer to the specific sequence used to produce one ceramic type or vessel type, or to the aggregate set of practices employed by a potter to produce an entire suite of vessel types.

4. *Horizon of Practice*: A geographically bounded area encompassing the contemporaneous spatial distribution of a single practice, incorporating both the presence and relative frequency of that practice in comparison to alternative practices within a particular domain.

5. *Community of Practice*: The geographically bounded aggregate of craftspeople with a common *chaîne opératoire* resulting from shared histories of learning and practice, as manifested materially as a locus formed by the intersection of multiple horizons of practice reflected in the spatial distribution of material culture produced by this process.

6. *Landscape of Practice*: The geographic space within which communities of practice exist as loci of overlap between the horizons of practices associated with a specific *chaîne opératoire*.

7. *Ceramic Type*: An analytical unit of archaeological potsherd classification characterized by a defined set of practices from multiple domains in a ceramic *chaîne opératoire* that consistently co-occur on individual sherds; as it is based on sherds, two or more ceramic types may be associated with any given ceramic vessel, and each ceramic type may occur independently on multiple vessel types.

8. *Vessel Type*: An ethnographic unit of whole-vessel classification characterized by a defined set of practices from multiple domains in a ceramic *chaîne opératoire* that consistently co-occur on individual vessels; each vessel type may encompass multiple sherd-based ceramic types.

Although several of these definitions clearly correspond to roughly equivalent units employed by culture historians decades ago (e.g., phases as communities of practice, or traits as practices), this is no mere rebranding of antiquated concepts with new terminology or redefinition of old terms (such as ceramic types). Instead, my intent is to shift the focus away from the static, normative culture historical units constructed using the material end results of ceramic practice and redirect our attention toward the underlying practices of individual potters, teasing apart the exact social context of both learning and practice for each step within the entire ceramic *chaîne opératoire*, and weaving these contextualized practices into the fabric of an evolving landscape of practice.

Reconciling Landscapes of Practice and Identity

To bring this chapter full circle, my conclusion that geographic variability in archaeological ceramics is best viewed through the lens of practice, and that archaeological phases correspond better to communities of practice than communities of identity, is only one step in exploring the fundamental and complex relationship between practice and identity and material culture. In this particular adaptation of practice theory, the task of the archaeologist is not just to identify and distinguish the suite of choices that each potter practiced in producing their pottery within their own community of practice, but also to harness empirical data regarding the geographic distribution (horizon) of each practice over time. This should be part of an effort to reconstruct more precisely the social context of learning and practice involved in its origination, spread, reproduction, and eventual replacement or disappearance, all within the operational context of the broader ceramic *chaîne opératoire* that produced the assemblages of vessel types (and subordinate archaeological ceramic types which crosscut vessel types). Moreover, detailed analysis of these contextualized practices may provide insights that will help explain why certain practices persisted longer than others under specific circumstances, such as migration or *in situ* shifts in social interaction networks among potters. Finally, only by examining individual practices within the various practice domains making up such an operational sequence will it be possible to clarify which, if any, of these practices have been connected directly to the communication of social identity at any scale of social integration, from families to communities to polities. As I have emphasized, the coexistence of both communities of practice and communities of identity within the same social landscape does not guarantee automatic correspondence between the two realms, nor even does any demonstrated correspondence necessarily prove a causal link between a community of practice and a community of identity that happen to be coterminous. Each type of community must be studied independently using appropriate and available data, and only by first disentangling the two can any demonstrable connection between communities of practice (such as archaeological phases) and communities of identity (such as polities or ethnies) be established empirically. Only then can the exact reasons for any congruence (or lack thereof) be explored in a systematic and rigorous manner.

Paradoxically, the "norms" of practice shared by potters within each community of practice were in fact produced by the individual agency of female potters, each of whom effectively chose to conform (or was unconsciously habituated to conformity) to a shared *chaîne opératoire* that reproduced itself through the practices of community members. In fact, the relationship described here between individual potters and the community of practice that emerged organically from their collective practice bears very obvious parallels to the Bourdieuian concept of *habitus* and Giddensian concept of structuration, as noted above (Bourdieu 1977; Giddens 1984). It is important to highlight, however, that in this instance a ceramic community of practice is actually an aggregate unit comprised solely of female potters practicing their craft within a broader social landscape made up of many other members of the society or societies in which the potters lived. As I have detailed, this more comprehensive social landscape is perhaps best characterized as a landscape of identity, the spatial configuration of which, while obviously shaped and constrained by the natural environment, was likely also dominated by geopolitical concerns of warring chiefdoms and chiefly confederations at different scales and levels of complexity. These two landscapes coexisted and overlapped one another, and while the landscape of ceramic practice (comprising female household potters) may be seen as a subset of the landscape of sociopolitical identity (encompassing everyone inhabiting a given region), this does not necessarily mean that the membership and geographic distribution of communities of practice corresponded directly to that of the communities of identity within which they were situated. In other words, although the constituent members of communities of ceramic practice necessarily lived within communities of sociopolitical identity, the geographic distribution of their interactions was not necessarily constrained by boundaries between communities in the broader landscape of identity. As discussed, the configuration of these two landscapes was based on fundamentally different dimensions of culture; communities of practice were defined by mutually shared histories of learning and practice as opposed to conscious belief in or awareness of membership. Communities of practice and identity interpenetrated one another at various levels, and the complex relationship between both landscapes must be viewed as an object of empirical study rather than a theoretical assumption.

As a final comment, I have identified one approach to this type of research, namely the evaluation of familiar archaeological phases defined by the relative proportions of archaeological ceramic types to determine if they actually correspond to the historically documented polities and ethnies of their makers. But exploring landscapes of practice can and should examine similar questions at both large and small scales of analysis, including dimensions of ceramic variability at the subtypological level. By embracing the perspective of landscapes of practice, however, I am by no means advocating the abandonment of traditional ceramic typological analysis. Instead, I suggest that we must both acknowledge and make use of the fact that existing archaeological ceramic types are the material manifestation of those ceramic production practices that left the traces most readily observed in the analysis of potsherds. Each of those practices formed part of a specific practice domain within the *chaîne opératoire* followed by each potter in practicing her craft, and each practice was learned and practiced in its own social context, potentially resulting in a distinctive social and resulting spatial horizon for that practice. Even though the best way to recognize communities of practice (phases) may well be the tried-and-true method employing the relative percentages of ceramic types in archaeological assemblages, the most effective way to evaluate the reasons for their geographic distribution (and whether such communities of practice correspond to other social entities such as polities or ethnies) is to break each ceramic type down into the specific practices that it manifested and explore their individual distributions within the broader landscape of practice.

To this end, in an effort to examine stylistic variability within a single ceramic type in a single archaeological phase, more than two decades ago I conducted a study of incised design motifs excavated from households within the well-studied sixteenth-century Coosa chiefdom in northwest Georgia (Worth 2010; n.d.). The ceramic type Lamar Bold Incised was chosen for stylistic analysis principally because the designs seemed to possess characteristics that would make them likely candidates to communicate social identity. They were created freehand for each new vessel, represented a limited range of simple geometric figures, and were crafted on the most visible upper surfaces of vessels commonly employed in serving food. After breaking the designs down into hierarchical design configurations based on primary motifs and secondary (or filler and border) elements, and isolating a series of discrete "design types" generated empirically, I was able to compare the roster of design types present on vessels recovered from 10 individual households in two communities within two distinct archaeological site clusters in the same historically documented chiefdom (Hally 2008; Hudson et al. 1985; Smith 2000). Just as was the case for ceramic assemblages defined by types, there was no level of social integration, from the household to the chiefdom, displaying the kind of ceramic homogeneity that would imply the use of ceramic decorative motifs to signal group identity. Instead, the continuum of stylistic variability observed seemed a much better match for a model of interacting potters drawing upon a small suite of motifs decreasing in similarity with social distance between potters.

Viewed from the perspective of ceramic practice, household potters living near one another in the same community clearly shared a common suite of readily visible design choices for their incised decorations, and although the number of designs was similar for each household, the exact roster of choices decreased in similarity with social and geographic distance. The potters in each household made use of no more than about 10 design types, slight variability between households increased that number to roughly 15 design types for the community, and additional variability between communities in different site clusters broadened the variation to some 21 design types. Overall, however, similarities seemed to outweigh differences in terms of how members of these communities incised decorations on their pots, which of course accounts for the fact that all of them fall within the same archaeological phase (Barnett), and all the sherds bearing such decorations fall within the same archaeological ceramic type (Lamar Bold Incised). This type has a huge geographic extent, but the individual horizons of practice for each specific design motif are far more limited, although similar stylistic analysis has yet to be conducted in rigorous detail for other Lamar assemblages elsewhere in the Southeastern United States (but see Hally 1994a:151, 153–154). In my view, however, such analyses hold considerable promise for elucidating the landscape of ceramic practice at both the micro- and macroscale, providing an empirical base from which to reconstruct the social landscape of those potters, including the communities of practice and identity to which they belonged simultaneously.

In conclusion, applying the tenets of practice theory and social learning theory to the culture-historical concept of archaeological phases engenders a useful and instructive balance between individual agency and collective social structure within a broader landscape of practice and gives archaeologists a practical mechanism for linking preserved material culture directly to both. For ceramic analysis, each individual potsherd is seen as the material product of routinized practices of individual potters situated in a complex social web comprising not just the community of ceramic practice in which they learned and practiced their craft, but also other communities defined more by perceived identity than shared practice. Ontologically, all of these communities truly existed only in the socially contextualized behaviors and thoughts of the individuals that comprised them (in effect, their *habitus*), and it was precisely this recursive relationship between multiple communities of individuals acting and thinking in relationship to one another, as both individuals and as a collective whole, within interpenetrating landscapes of both practice and identity, that simultaneously imparted both stability and dynamism to the entire cultural system. It should therefore come as no surprise that assemblages of archaeological ceramic types defined using observed traces of these practices can be empirically demonstrated to form the archaeological phases and phase chronologies on which culture historians relied so heavily, any more than it should surprise us that those phases are not directly equivalent to the polities and ethnies portrayed in contemporaneous documentary texts and maps. Practice and identity are inextricably related to one another in every realm of material culture, and it is in these relationships that individual social identities are formed and reproduced. But defining the nature of that relationship using archaeological materials requires a detailed reconstruction of the historical landscapes of practice that coexisted and overlapped with the landscapes of identity that are much more familiar to the ethnohistorical record. This is one area where a truly historical archaeology, drawing simultaneously on material and textual traces of past cultures in any time or place, can provide an empirical testing ground for robust methodological and theoretical insights that will not only strengthen the practice of archaeology in general, but also contribute to the broader anthropological understanding of the fundamental relationship between practice, identity, and materiality at all scales of social integration.

Acknowledgments

This chapter is the culmination of more than two decades of musing about the nature of ceramics and ethnicity, and I am grateful to many colleagues and students who have encouraged me and given me input and feedback as I developed the concepts expressed herein. Although it would be excessive to attempt to list them all here, Norma Harris deserves singling out because of our many conversations on the subject over the course of many years, as does Becky Saunders, whose extensive work in this arena has continuously spurred me to develop my own sometimes divergent ideas, and with whom I have also had many fruitful and pleasant discussions. For this chapter, I am particularly thankful for valuable direct feedback by Ramie Gougeon, Jennifer Melcher, and Victor Thompson, and for productive in-depth discussions on the implications of the subject with Gregg Harding. I am also grateful for the editorial assistance provided by Greg Waselkov and Marvin Smith, as well as the anonymous reviewers of the manuscript.

8

PLANT USE AT A MISSISSIPPIAN AND CONTACT-PERIOD SITE IN THE SOUTH CAROLINA COASTAL PLAIN

Kandace D. Hollenbach

The concept of "foodways" refers to the ways in which people procure, produce, prepare, display, consume, store, and discard food (Johannessen 1993). These activities are tightly wound into culture and identity, both shaping and shaped by the individuals who perform and observe them. Food choices reflect and influence a person's identities: ethnicity, group, class, religion, family, gender, age, and more (e.g. Goody 1982; Mintz 1985; Twiss 2007). Following the familiar adage, the foods we eat (and how we procure, prepare, eat, and dispose of them) tell us something about who we are.

Fortunately, much of the archaeological record pertains to daily tasks associated with foodways. For instance, projectile points and knives reflect hunting and butchering activities. Ceramics inform us about cooking, display, and storage of food. Plant and animal remains derive from gathering, planting, harvesting, fishing, trapping, sharing, and sometimes feasting. The study of foodways thus provides a perspective for analyzing and interpreting artifacts and ecofacts, and ultimately an avenue for understanding the cultures and identities of the people who made, used, and consumed them.

Here I examine changes in plant use at a location in the South Carolina coastal plain over the course of some seven centuries, by reference to archaeological plant remains from three occupations of the Riverfront Village site (38AK933). From these data, we can see continuity in foodways from the Early Mississippian to the early Contact-period occupations of the site and distinct changes between the early and late Contact-period occupations. How Native people at Riverfront Village managed their local landscape and interacted with their own and European communities in the region changed substantially by the early eighteenth century. These changes in foodways and relationships would have affected their identity as a group, sometimes reinforcing differences between themselves and their neighbors, and other times blurring these lines.

The Occupants of Riverfront Village

Riverfront Village occupies a second terrace of the Savannah River, within the city limits of North Augusta, Aiken County, South Carolina. Situated in the Fall Line Hills district of the Southern Coastal Plain, the site lies within easy reach of river shoals and islands, flooded back channels and smaller tributaries, the Southern Outer Piedmont to the northwest, and the Floodplains and Low Terraces of the Coastal Plain to the southeast.

Due to impacts by the South Carolina Department of Transportation's Georgia Avenue Extension Project associated with riverfront revitalization, the archaeological site was mitigated by Brockington and Associates in 2005–2006 (Whitley 2013). These efforts revealed three major site occupations. The first was an Early Mississippian palisaded village of circular and rectangular houses, dating to approximately A.D. 1000–1250, associated with predominately sand-tempered Savannah I pottery types and Hamilton and Madison projectile points (Whitley 2013).

After an apparent abandonment of the middle Savannah Valley by roughly A.D. 1400, the site was reoccupied sometime after A.D. 1600 by a group whose identity is not entirely clear. Various Native peoples moved through the middle Savannah Valley during the seventeenth century, including the Savannahs (Shawnees) and Chiscas. This group made shell-tempered pottery similar to the Fort Ancient Madisonville series or Mississippian Dallas series and also had access to glass trade beads from Europeans (Whitley 2013).

In 1660 the Westo Indians swept into the middle Savannah Valley from the Lake Erie region (via Virginia), established their town of Hickahaugau some 15 to 20 miles upstream from the Riverfront Village site, and began raiding other Native towns to steal corn and take captives to sell in the booming Virginia slave trade (Bowne 2009; Meyers 2009; Whitley 2013). This period of endemic warfare and slave raiding marks another hiatus in site occupation at the site. It was reoccupied again, not long after the A.D. 1680 defeat of the Westos, probably by one of the Savannah towns formed by a coalition of Apalachees, Savannahs, and Yuchis. This latest component of Riverfront Village is associated with a smattering of European trade materials, including glass beads, tinkler cones made of sheet brass, kaolin pipes, and gun parts, signifying trade ties between site occupants and the Charles Town colony. Riverfront Village was finally abandoned around 1715, when the Yamasee War brought another wave of violence to the region (Whitley 2013).

The samples of plant remains analyzed here derive from thirty-three excavated features (Table 8.1). Seventeen features, including various pits, hearths, and a wall trench, are associated with the Early Mississippian occupation. The early Contact-period occupation is represented by twelve fea-

Table 8.1. Summary of Samples Analyzed from the Riverfront Village Site

Feature Type	Features	Sample Count	Plant Weight (g)	Wood Weight (g)
Mississippian (A.D. 1000–1250)				
Basin-shaped pit	860, 875, 1848, 2159, 2513, 2795, 3389, 4319	9	33.94	23.21
Bell-shaped pit	845, 1929, 2174, 2619, 4284	10	83.40	29.38
Hearth pit	1102	1	0.60	0.51
Post	4492	1	2.74	2.16
Wall trench	1337, 2538	2	2.36	1.17
Contact, A.D. 1600–1660				
Basin-shaped pit	720, 846, 1523, 1584, 1623, 1809, 2254, 2498, 3383, 4472, 4490	13	171.24	69.47
Hearth pit	1952	2	14.73	12.06
Contact, A.D. 1680-1715				
Basin-shaped pit	1591, 1958, 2320	7	73.03	35.80
Smudge pit	747	1	482.62	1.10

tures, including basin-shaped pits and one hearth. Three basin-shaped pit features and a smudge pit (Feature 747) filled with corncob fragments, which yielded an AMS radiocarbon date of A.D. 1680, are associated with the late Contact-period occupation (Whitley 2013).

Analytical Methods

Floatation soil samples were processed by Brockington and Associates staff using a Flote-tech machine. A 1-mm fiberglass mesh retained the heavy fraction, and the light fraction was captured using sheer, nylon-like fabric (Whitley 2013). At the Archaeological Research Laboratory (ARL), University of Tennessee, I analyzed both fractions using standard paleoethnobotanical procedures (Pearsall 2000). With the aid of a stereoscopic microscope at 10- to 40-power magnification, carbonized nonwood plant remains greater than 2.00 mm in size were identified to the lowest possible taxonomic level. Materials less than 2.00 mm in size were scanned for seeds and plant remains not represented in the larger-size fraction. When present, acorn remains were pulled from the 1.40-mm sieve, as well as the 2.00-mm sieve, to mitigate biases against their preservation. All taxa were then counted and weighed.

There were two exceptions to this standard protocol. A remarkable number of acorn shell fragments were recovered from the light and heavy fractions of Bag 355, Feature 1929. Those recovered from the heavy fraction were counted, with a total of over 3,000, but the daunting number of specimens in the light fraction led to an estimate of over 10,000 shell fragments for the entire sample. A similarly impressive number of acorn shell fragments were recovered from Bag 247, Feature 1809. In the interest of time, acorn shell was pulled from a one-quarter subsample of the 1.40-mm light fraction materials.

Due to the large amount of material smaller than 0.71 mm in the light fractions, this portion of most samples was subsampled by riffle splitting. These subsamples, and the proportion of the total they represent, are denoted by superscripts in table 8.1. In addition, due to the large quantity of carbonized plant remains in Bag 16 from Feature 747, only one-fourth of the sample smaller than 6.4 mm (0.25 in) was analyzed. No attempts were made to extrapolate counts or weights from these subsamples.

Identifications were made with reference to Martin and Barkley's (1961) *Seed Identification Manual* and the PLANTS Database (U.S. Department of Agriculture-Natural Resources Conservation Service 2014), as well as modern comparative specimens housed at ARL. Because uncarbonized plant materials are unlikely to be preserved in the moist, acidic soils of the Southeast, even from relatively recent historic contexts (Reitz and Scarry 1985:10; Yarnell 1982), only carbonized plant remains are considered here to be part of the archaeological record. Uncarbonized plant materials were assumed to be modern contaminants that reflect the present-day local habitat and are therefore not reported or discussed.

Discussion of Identified Taxa

Analysis of 39 floatation and 12 screen samples yielded 864.66 g of carbonized plant remains, 174.86 g (20%) of which is wood (see table 8.1). Nonwood plant categories include nuts, fruits, starchy/oily seeds, crops, and miscellaneous taxa (Table 8.2; see Hollenbach 2010, Whitley 2013 for details of sample contents).

Nuts

Of the nut taxa recovered, acorn stands apart for sheer quantity, with more than 16,000 shell fragments. As noted, this number is in part an estimate. In comparison, 4,724 fragments of hickory nutshell were recovered from the samples, roughly one-third the number of acorn shell fragments. Such a large quantity of acorn is exceptional. Hickory nutshell is both more durable and more likely to be carbonized, as it burns well and appears to have been purposefully used as fuel (Gardner 1997; Scarry 2003). Acorn shell,

Table 8.2. Plant Taxa Identified in the 38AK933 Samples

Common Name	Taxonomic Name	Seasonality	Count	Weight (g)
Nuts				
Acorn	*Quercus* sp.	fall	16098	33.89
Acorn cf.	*Quercus* sp. cf.	fall	35	0.05
Acorn meat	*Quercus* sp.	fall	74	5.23
Acorn meat cf.	*Quercus* sp. cf.	fall	39	0.87
Acorn meat/bark cf.	*Quercus* sp. cf.	fall	11	0.04
Acorn meat/bean/ persimmon	*Quercus/Phaseolus/ Diospyros*		26	0.18
Black walnut	*Juglans nigra*	fall	91	8.35
Black walnut cf.	*Juglans nigra* cf.	fall	8	0.04
Black walnut/peach	*Juglans/Prunus*		3	0.03
Hazel cf.	*Corylus* sp. cf.	late summer	3	0.01
Hickory	*Carya* sp.	fall	4727	104.96
Hickory cf.	*Carya* sp. cf.	fall	41	0.21
Hickory husk	*Carya* sp.	fall	35	6.60
Walnut family	Juglandaceae	fall	161	1.55
Fruits				
Black gum	*Nyssa sylvatica*		1	0.00
Black gum cf.	*Nyssa sylvatica* cf.		1	0.01
Blackberry/raspberry	*Rubus* sp.	summer	4	0.00
Blueberry	*Vaccinium* sp.	summer	1	0.00
Elderberry	*Sambucus* sp.		3	0.00
Elderberry cf.	*Sambucus* sp. cf.		10	0.01
Fruit cf.			17	0.46
Grape	*Vitis* sp.	summer	174	0.25
Grape cf.	*Vitis* sp. cf.	summer	49	0.01
Groundcherry	*Physalis* sp.	fall	1	0.00
Hawthorn cf.	*Crataegus* sp. cf.	summer/fall	13	0.08
Honeylocust cf.	*Gleditsia triacanthos* cf.		8	0.14
Maypop	*Passiflora incarnata*	summer	65	0.06
Maypop cf.	*Passiflora incarnata* cf.	summer	1	0.00
Peach	*Prunus persica*	summer	10	1.61
Peach cf.	*Prunus persica* cf.	summer	3	0.02
Persimmon	*Diospyros virginiana*	fall	36	0.55
Persimmon cf.	*Diospyros virginiana* cf.	fall	20	0.06
Persimmon seed coat	*Diospyros virginiana*	fall	8	0.01
Persimmon seed coat cf.	*Diospyros virginiana* cf.	fall	23	0.06
Plum/cherry cf.	*Prunus* sp. cf.	summer	1	0.00
Plum/cherry meat	*Prunus* sp.	summer	1	0.00
Strawberry cf.	*Fragaria* sp. cf.	summer	2	0.00
Sumac	*Rhus* sp.	fall	23	0.00
Sumac cf.	*Rhus* sp. cf.	fall	35	0.02
Sumac meat cf.	*Rhus* sp. cf.	fall	3	0.00

Continued on the next page

Table 8.2 *Continued*

Common Name	Taxonomic Name	Seasonality	Count	Weight (g)
Starchy/Oily Seeds				
Chenopod	*Chenopodium* sp.	late summer/fall	2	0.00
Chenopod cf.	*Chenopodium* sp. cf.	late summer/fall	9	0.00
Little barley cf.	*Hordeum pusillum* cf.	spring/early summer	1	0.00
Maygrass	*Phalaris caroliniana*	spring/early summer	445	0.11
Maygrass cf.	*Phalaris caroliniana* cf.	spring/early summer	14	0.00
Sumpweed cf.	*Iva annua* cf.	late summer/fall	1	0.00
Sunflower	*Helianthus annuus*	late summer/fall	1	0.00
Crops				
Bean	*Phaseolus vulgaris*	late summer/fall	9	0.04
Bean cf.	*Phaseolus vulgaris* cf.	late summer/fall	15	0.05
Bean/persimmon cf.	*Phaseolus/Diospyros* cf.		8	0.01
Corn cob	*Zea mays*	late summer/fall	470	389.34
Corn cob cf.	*Zea mays* cf.	late summer/fall	25	0.19
Corn cob/cupule cf.	*Zea mays* cf.	late summer/fall	13	0.03
Corn cupule/glume	*Zea mays*	late summer/fall	3997	94.43
Corn cupule/glume cf.	*Zea mays* cf.	late summer/fall	28	0.07
Corn embryo	*Zea mays*	late summer/fall	3	0.00
Corn kernel	*Zea mays*	late summer/fall	147	1.00
Corn kernel cf.	*Zea mays* cf.	late summer/fall	61	0.30
Cucurbit rind	Cucurbitaceae	late summer/fall	14	0.04
Cucurbit rind cf.	Cucurbitaceae	late summer/fall	2	0.00
Peduncle	Cucurbitaceae	late summer/fall	1	0.18
Squash	*Cucurbita pepo*	summer/fall	1	0.00
Squash cf.	*Cucurbita pepo* cf.	summer/fall	1	0.00
Tobacco	*Nicotiana* sp.		1	0.00
Tobacco cf.	*Nicotiana* sp. cf.		1	0.00
Miscellaneous				
Aster family	Asteraceae cf.		1	0.00
Aster family cf.	Asteraceae		1	0.00
Bark			283	2.58
Bark cf.			70	0.41
Bearsfoot	*Polymnia uvedalia*		224	0.19
Bedstraw	*Galium* sp.		2	0.00
Bedstraw cf.	*Galium* sp. cf.		6	0.01
Bud			127	0.31
Bud cf.			7	0.02
Bulrush	*Scirpus* sp.		2	0.00
Cane	*Arundinaria* sp.		2124	16.92
Cane cf.	*Arundinaria* sp. cf.		1	0.00
Carpetweed	*Mollugo* sp.		2	0.00
Catchfly	*Silene* sp.		1	0.00

Common Name	Taxonomic Name	Seasonality	Count	Weight (g)
Cheno/am	*Chenopodium/ Amaranthus*	late summer/fall	1	0.00
Copperleaf cf.	*Acalypha* sp. cf.		1	0.00
Dock	*Rumex* sp.		17	0.01
Dock cf.	*Rumex* sp. cf.		1	0.00
Dock/knotweed	*Rumex/Polygonum*		14	0.00
Goosegrass	*Eleusine indica*		6	0.00
Grass family	Poaceae		34	0.00
Grass family cf.	Poaceae cf.		7	0.00
Knotweed	*Polygonum* sp.		19	0.00
Legume	Fabaceae		1	0.00
Legume cf.	Fabaceae cf.		4	0.00
Mallow family cf.	Malvaceae cf.		1	0.00
Monocot stem	Poaceae		4	0.06
Morning-glory	*Ipomoea/Convolvulus*	summer/fall	140	0.24
Morning-glory cf.	*Ipomoea/Convolvulus* cf.	summer/fall	1	0.01
Mustard family cf.	Cruciferae		3	0.00
Nightshade family	Solanaceae		11	0.00
Pine cone	*Pinus* sp.		475	1.55
Pine cone cf.	*Pinus* sp. cf.		9	0.08
Pine cone core/stem	*Pinus* sp.		3	0.01
Pine needle	*Pinus* sp.		1	0.00
Pine needle fascicle cf.	*Pinus* sp. cf.		1	0.00
Pitch			1722	11.45
Pokeweed	*Phytolacca americana*	summer/fall	4	0.01
Pokeweed cf.	*Phytolacca americana* cf.	summer/fall	5	0.00
Purslane	*Portulaca* sp.	summer/fall	9	0.00
Sedge family	Cyperaceae		3	0.00
Sedge family cf.	Cyperaceae cf.		1	0.00
St. Johnswort cf.	*Hypericum* sp. cf.		1	0.00
Stem/peduncle			34	0.07
Stem/pine needle			2	0.00
Stem/twig			9	0.02
Thorn			3	0.00
Tuliptree	*Liriodendron tulipifera*		23	0.02
Unidentifiable			650	2.72
Unidentifiable seeds			728	0.24
Unidentified			21	0.16
Unidentified seeds			240	0.04
Weedy legume	Fabaceae	late summer/fall	1	0.00
Yellow star-grass	*Hypoxis* sp.		7	0.00
Wood, not carbonized			3	0.02
Wood, part carbonized				1.47

in contrast, is much thinner and less likely to survive carbonization and archaeological recovery, is not an efficient fuel, and is therefore generally underrepresented at archaeological sites. Yarnell and Black (1985:97–98), among others, have recommended multiplying the weight of acorn shell fragments by 50 to arrive at a better approximation of the importance of acorn relative to hickory nuts in prehistoric diets. Even without this multiplication, it is apparent from the raw number of nutshell fragments recovered that acorns in particular, but also hickory nuts, were important components of the diets of Riverfront Village occupants.

Acorn and hickory nuts were important subsistence items throughout prehistory in the Southeast (Gardner 1997; Scarry 2003; Yarnell and Black 1985). Hickory nuts are high in fat and protein (U.S. Department of Agriculture, Agricultural Research Service, Nutrient Data Laboratory [USDA NDL] 2004). Among historic Native American groups such as the Cherokees, hickory nuts were often crushed, shell and all, and formed into balls that could be readily stored. The balls were then dropped into boiling water, the shell pieces would sink and the nutmeats would float, and the meats could be skimmed off or further boiled to produce a milky beverage (Fritz et al. 2001; Gardner 1997; Talalay et al. 1984). In contrast, acorns are high in carbohydrates (USDA NDL 2004) and have large nutmeats that are easily extracted but contain tannins. These tannins must be removed by leaching or denatured by toasting to render most acorns palatable (Bettinger et al. 1997; Petruso and Wickens 1984; Scarry 2003:66). After being leached of tannins, the nutmeats were commonly ground into a meal and subsequently made into a mash or bread (Carr 1895:172; Densmore 1974:320; Kuhnlein and Turner 1991:200–201; Palmer 1871:409–410; Peterson 1977:204). Hickory nuts are easily stored in the shell, but acorns must first be processed immediately by parching to prevent them from sprouting and to ward off worms and molds (Petruso and Wickens 1984:362; Scarry 2003:66).

Additional nut taxa identified in the samples include black walnut and three possible hazelnut shell fragments. In contrast to acorn and hickory, only 91 definitive black walnut shell fragments were recovered in the samples, suggesting that they were used less frequently by site occupants. Black walnuts grow as solitary trees, rather than in stands like hickories and oaks, making collection of large numbers of walnuts more difficult. Because the bitter hull remains attached to the nutshell, black walnuts cannot be boiled like hickory nuts and therefore have higher processing costs, which probably discouraged greater use of these flavorful nuts (Gardner 1997; Talalay et al. 1984).

Hazelnuts grow on shrubs and must be picked, similar to berries, requiring more time to collect than other nuts (Gardner 1997; Talalay et al.

1984). They ripen as early as late summer, whereas the other nut taxa mature in autumn (Schopmeyer 1974). Furthermore, hazelnuts grow in thickets along forest margins, rather than in wooded stands like oaks, hickories, and walnuts (Radford et al. 1964). Use of hazelnuts thus requires gathering in slightly different settings and seasons than the other nuts. These differences may contribute to the low recovery of hazelnuts.

Fruits

Among the fruit taxa, grape seeds and fragments were most frequently recovered, with more than 170 specimens. Maypop is well represented, along with persimmon and sumac. Additional wild fruits include black gum, blackberry/raspberry, blueberry, elderberry, groundcherry, and plum/cherry. In addition, hawthorn, honey locust, and strawberry were tentatively identified.

Ten definitive fragments of peach pit were recovered, all from late Contact features. Peaches are not native to North America and may have been brought to the New World as early as Columbus's second voyage. Trees were propagated by the Spanish settlers of La Florida in the mid-sixteenth century and soon naturalized to the region. Well suited to the climate of the Southeast and likely encouraged by Native Americans, peaches spread relatively rapidly throughout the region (Gremillion 1993:16). As such, peach trees may have been tolerated as much as actively cultivated by the occupants of the site. The recovery of peach from all three late Contact features, and their absence in early Contact samples, provides a useful timeline for their introduction to the surrounding area, and speaks to the popularity of the fruit once it became established in the local habitat.

The various fruits may be eaten fresh or dried (Havard 1896; Kuhnlein and Turner 1991; Moerman 2004; Swanton 1946; Yanovsky 1936). Ripe persimmons were apparently consumed in "large quantities" by some historic Native groups (Palmer 1871:471). Persimmons were processed for winter use by fashioning the pulp into cakes that were then dried (Swanton 1946: 265, 285, 288, 291, 363, 373) or cooked into preserves (Palmer 1871:471). Dried cakes and preserves were also made from grapes, blackberries, raspberries, blueberries, elderberries, groundcherries, hawthorns, plums, cherries, and strawberries (Angier 1974; Fernald and Kinsey 1943; Medsger 1972; Moerman 2004; Peterson 1977; Yanovsky 1936). Maypops were generally used to make beverages. The pulp and seeds were scooped from the fruit and boiled to obtain a juice, which could be consumed or cooked with cornmeal (Ulmer and Beck 1951:48, 58; USDA-NCRS 2014). Sumac berries made a beverage similar to lemonade. The berries were crushed, bruised, or roasted, in part to abate tannins (Havard 1896:44–45; Kindscher 1987:191–

193; Peterson 1977:186; Yanovsky 1936:40–41). Similarly, the sweet pulp of honey locust pods were turned into a beverage, eaten raw, or used to sweeten medicines or children's dispositions (Moerman 2004; Ulmer and Beck 1951:58; Yanovsky 1936:36). Black gum fruits, as well as most of the other fruits listed here, were mixed into cornmeal, legumes, or stews as a flavoring agent (Angier 1974; Fernald and Kinsey 1943; Kindscher 1987; Kurz 1997; Medsger 1972; Peterson 1977; Swanton 1946).

The fruits recovered from Riverfront Village generally ripen in summer, with the exception of sumac, groundcherry, and persimmon (Radford et al. 1964; Schopmeyer 1974). The fleshy fruits of persimmon, in particular, are not palatable until the first frost of autumn. While grapes and black gums tend to prefer wooded habitats, most of the fruit taxa thrive in disturbed habitats, such as agricultural fields, including blackberry/raspberry, maypops, peaches, persimmons, and sumac (Radford et al. 1964). Yarnell (1993) argues that maypops were actively cultivated in prehistoric gardens and fields. At the very least, the presence of these tasty fruits, as well as the others, would certainly have been tolerated, if not encouraged.

Starchy/Oily Seeds

Several taxa with edible seeds were recovered from the Riverfront Village samples, including more than 400 maygrass seeds, two definitive and nine possible chenopod, one sunflower, one possible little barley, and one possible sumpweed. These starchy and oily seeds are associated with a complex of Native plants cultivated by peoples living in the Southeast beginning approximately 3,500 years ago (Smith and Cowan 2003; Yarnell 1993). In general, relatively few of the plants included in this suite of Native cultigens have seeds that display definitive morphological evidence of domestication, such as increasingly thin seed coats that appeared in chenopod, *Chenopodium berlandieri* ssp. *jonesianum*, or an increase in seed size that occurred in sunflower, *Helianthus annuus* var. *macrocarpus*. Although the other seeds, including maygrass and little barley, do not show morphological markers of domestication, they are regularly recovered from archaeological sites in association with these clearly domesticated species, often in quantity, suggesting cultivation and harvest alongside each other. Maygrass is often found at sites outside of its natural range, which includes the Coastal Plain and Lower Piedmont, further suggesting it was cultivated (Cowan 1994:283–284). The significant amount recovered from Riverfront Village, in the middle Savannah River valley, where maygrass is endemic, indicates use of this starchy seed by site occupants. Although domestication status of the chenopod and sunflower seeds recovered has not been determined, site occupants quite possibly cultivated them, along with maygrass and perhaps little barley and sumpweed, in garden plots or fields.

All of these various seeds can be eaten raw, toasted, or boiled into porridge. The starchy seeds, which include maygrass, chenopod, and little barley, can also be ground into flour to make bread or mush (Kuhnlein and Turner 1991; Moerman 2004; Palmer 1871; Yanovsky 1936). The spring leaves and shoots of chenopod can be eaten as greens (Kuhnlein and Turner 1991; Palmer 1871; Yanovsky 1936).

The edible seed taxa thrive in disturbed settings, such as human dwelling areas, garden plots, or agricultural fields. Sumpweed, however, requires a wet or marshy locale (Radford et al. 1964). Chenopod, sunflower, and sumpweed would have been planted in spring, with seeds ripening in late summer and early autumn (Radford et al. 1964; Scarry 2003). Maygrass and little barley, however, typically require planting in early winter for harvest in May or June (Cowan 1994:267; Scarry 2003:71). All would have been planted by broadcasting the seeds, in contrast to the deliberate planting of each corn kernel, bean, or squash seed (Smith and Cowan 2003). Alternatively, these taxa may simply have been tolerated as beneficial weeds within corn fields, rather than purposefully cultivated. Maygrass appears to be the exception, due to the quantity recovered.

Crops

Crop taxa recovered from Riverfront Village include corn, squash, and beans. Corn served as a dietary staple among late prehistoric and historic Native communities throughout most of the Eastern Woodlands (Smith and Cowan 2003). Corn is predominantly represented by corncob fragments, including cupules and glumes, which together number more than 4,000. The majority of these were recovered from Feature 747, a smudge pit that yielded an AMS radiocarbon date of A.D. 1680 (Table 8.3). In contrast, only 147 corn kernels were positively identified in the samples. This pattern is not surprising, because edible kernels are usually only carbonized by accident, whereas the inedible byproducts (cobs, cupules, and glumes) served as fuel, for example in smudge pits like Feature 747.

Similar to corn kernels, relatively few beans and squash seeds, rind fragments, and peduncles (stems) were recovered. The low numbers of these taxa are not surprising, as they lack the substantial but inedible byproducts (like corncobs) that were often burned as fuel and were thus preserved. Even if bean pods were not eaten, they have high water content and are unlikely to survive burning and therefore are unlikely to be recovered archaeologically. Instead, beans, squash seeds, and squash rinds are typically boiled,

Table 8.3. Plant Taxa Recovered from the Smudge Pit (Feature 747)

Common Name	Count	Weight (g)
Nuts		
Hickory	1	0.02
Crops		
Bean cf.	4	0.02
Bean/persimmon cf.	7	0.01
Corncob	261	124.03
Corn cupule/glume	3614	92.27
Corn kernel	43	0.21
Corn kernel cf.	7	0.01
Miscellaneous		
Bark	1	0.00
Cane	64	2.76
Pitch	5	0.02
Unidentifiable	5	0.02
Unidentifiable seeds	2	0.00

roasted or dried, and eaten (Moerman 2004; Ulmer and Beck 1951; Yanovsky 1936) and are therefore recovered relatively infrequently from archaeological contexts, which can belie their dietary importance.

Cultivation of corn, beans, and squash requires preparation of fields, sowing, weeding, protecting crops from predators such as deer and birds, and harvesting (Smith and Cowan 2003). These activities were performed from spring through late summer or early autumn. Historic accounts relate that Native Americans intercropped their fields, with corn stalks serving as supports for growing bean plants and leafy squash vines smothering weeds and keeping the ground moist and cool (Hudson 1976:292–294, 297; Wagner and Civitello 2000; Wilson 1917). It is likely that more than one variety of corn was grown and that plantings were staggered. These strategies would reduce the risk of losing crops to late spring or early autumn frosts, late spring floods, or droughts (Cutler and Blake 2001; Hudson 1976:297; Scarry 1993:178–180; Smith and Cowan 2003).

A single tobacco seed was identified in Feature 846 (Bag 41), an early Contact basin-shaped pit. A possible tobacco seed was recovered from Feature 2795 (Bag 499), an Early Mississippian basin-shaped pit feature. Rather than being planted among food crops, tobacco plants were often tended in separate garden plots, sometimes in relatively secluded areas (Hudson 1976:353; Wilson 1917). The leaves of tobacco may be applied to the skin as a poultice for a number of ailments, and, of course, the dried blossoms, leaves, and stems may be smoked for medicinal and ceremonial purposes (Hamel and Chiltoskey 1975; Knight 1975; Moerman 2004).

Miscellaneous Taxa

The miscellaneous plant remains recovered from Riverfront Village provide a general indication of local habitat. For example, recovery of numerous pinecone scales and pitch (among other vitrified materials) suggest the presence of pine trees in the local forests. Tulip tree seeds similarly indicate that these early successional trees grew in the site vicinity, further suggesting the presence of fallowed fields or disturbed areas in which these trees quickly establish themselves.

The various weedy taxa include bedstraw, bulrush, carpetweed, *Chenopodium/Amaranthus* (cheno/ams), dock, goosegrass, knotweed, morning glory, pokeweed, purslane, wild legumes, yellow star-grass, and members of the Aster, Grass, Nightshade, and Sedge families, among others. They also indicate the presence of disturbed ground, such as garden plots and domestic settings, in which these weedy species thrive. Bulrush serves as an indicator of local wetlands (Radford et al. 1964).

Many of these weedy plants have useful properties. For example, bedstraw has a variety of medicinal uses and its spring leaves can be eaten as greens (Gilmore 1932b; Moerman 2004; Powers 1873–1874). The spring leaves and shoots of purslane, bulrush, dock, knotweed, morning glory, and poke can be eaten as greens (Kavasch 1977; Kuhnlein and Turner 1991; Moerman 2004; Niethammer 1974; Palmer 1871; Yanovsky 1936). Bulrush, dock, and knotweed seeds may be eaten, and the stems of bulrush can be woven into mats. The leaves, bark, stems, and branches of many of the weedy seed plants have medicinal uses. Given their various useful properties, many of these weedy plants may have been encouraged rather than pulled from gardens. Carpetweed and goosegrass are the exceptions, with no known ethnohistoric uses (Moerman 2004). Goosegrass (*Eleusine indica*) is an introduced species native to Africa, recovered only from late Contact samples at Riverfront Village (Table 8.4). Naturally red-black in color, the seeds recovered here appear to be carbonized. This suggests that this noxious weed spread relatively quickly through the region, most likely as an incidental stowaway on European ships, perhaps among plantings that the British colonists at Charles Town brought to establish orchards on their new plantations.

Although listed here among miscellaneous taxa, bearsfoot had a number of uses. Scarry (2003:71) suggests that this member of the Aster family, which has edible oily seeds similar to sunflower, may have been actively cultivated, or certainly tolerated. VanDerwarker and Stanyard (2009) recovered

Table 8.4. Comparison of Plant Taxa from the Riverfront Village Site by Component

Common Name	Mississippian		Early Contact		Later Contact	
	Count	Weight (g)	Count	Weight (g)	Count	Weight (g)
Nuts						
Acorn	11429	24.13	4648	9.75	22	0.02
Acorn cf.	13	0.01	21	0.03		
Acorn meat	56	4.68	18	0.55		
Acorn meat cf.	15	0.05	14	0.31	10	0.51
Acorn meat/bark cf.			11	0.04		
Acorn meat/bean/ persimmon	1	0.00	25	0.18		
Black walnut	34	0.78	30	0.94	27	6.63
Black walnut cf.	1	0.00	4	0.01	3	0.03
Black walnut/peach					3	0.03
Hazel cf.	1	0.00	2	0.01		
Hickory	727	20.49	3657	71.45	342	13.00
Hickory cf.	10	0.06	25	0.11	6	0.04
Hickory husk					35	6.60
Walnut family	31	0.19	123	1.15	7	0.21
Fruits						
Black gum	1	0.00				
Black gum cf.			1	0.01		
Blackberry/raspberry	1	0.00			3	0.00
Blueberry	1	0.00				
Elderberry	3	0.00				
Elderberry cf.	9	0.01			1	0.00
Fruit cf.	17	0.46				
Grape	53	0.04	102	0.18	19	0.03
Grape cf.	9	0.00	38	0.01	2	0.00
Hawthorn cf.	1	0.00	10	0.08	2	0.00
Honeylocust cf.			8	0.14		
Maypop	28	0.01	33	0.05	4	0.00
Maypop cf.			1	0.00		
Peach					10	1.61
Peach cf.			1	0.01	2	0.01
Persimmon	12	0.11	20	0.20	4	0.24
Persimmon cf.	11	0.02	7	0.03	2	0.01
Persimmon seed coat	5	0.00	3	0.01		
Persimmon seed coat cf.	5	0.00	18	0.06		
Plum/cherry cf.			1	0.00		
Plum/cherry meat	1	0.00				
Strawberry cf.	2	0.00				
Sumac	9	0.00	12	0.00	2	0.00
Sumac cf.	2	0.00	33	0.02	3	0.00

Common Name	Mississippian Count	Mississippian Weight (g)	Early Contact Count	Early Contact Weight (g)	Later Contact Count	Later Contact Weight (g)
Starchy/Oily Seeds						
Chenopod	2	0.00				
Chenopod cf.	5	0.00	4	0.00		
Little barley cf.			1	0.00		
Maygrass	385	0.09	60	0.02		
Maygrass cf.	10	0.00	4	0.00		
Sumpweed cf.	1	0.00				
Sunflower			1	0.00		
Crops						
Bean			9	0.04		
Bean cf.	4	0.01	7	0.02		
Bean/persimmon cf.					1	0.00
Corncob			12	0.03	1	3.13
Corncob cf.	1	0.01	11	0.06	13	0.12
Corncob/cupule	1	0.01				
Corncob/cupule cf.			13	0.03		
Corn cupule/glume	239	0.91	46	0.25	98	1.00
Corn cupule/glume cf.	17	0.04	11	0.03	5	0.01
Corn embryo	2	0.00	1	0.00		
Corn kernel	49	0.36	52	0.41	3	0.02
Corn kernel cf.	33	0.13	15	0.13	6	0.03
Cucurbit rind	1	0.00	3	0.00	10	0.04
Cucurbit rind cf.	1	0.00			1	0.00
Peduncle					1	0.18
Squash			1	0.00		
Squash cf.			1	0.00		
Tobacco			1	0.00		
Tobacco cf.	1	0.00				
Miscellaneous						
Aster family	1	0.00				
Aster family cf.	1	0.00				
Bark	94	0.65	176	1.86	12	0.07
Bark cf.	17	0.08	41	0.21	12	0.12
Bearsfoot	27	0.02	159	0.15	38	0.02
Bedstraw			2	0.00		
Bedstraw cf.	5	0.01	1	0.00		
Bud	75	0.20	47	0.10	5	0.01
Bud cf.	3	0.01	2	0.01		
Bulrush	1	0.00			1	0.00
Cane	891	6.13	1131	7.86	38	0.17
Cane cf.			1	0.00		

Continued on the next page

Table 8.4. *Continued*

Common Name	Mississippian Count	Mississippian Weight (g)	Early Contact Count	Early Contact Weight (g)	Later Contact Count	Later Contact Weight (g)
Carpetweed			2	0.00		
Catchfly	1	0.00				
Cheno/am					1	0.00
Copperleaf cf.					1	0.00
Dock			17	0.01		
Dock cf.					1	0.00
Dock/knotweed			14	0.00		
Goosegrass					6	0.00
Grass family	12	0.00	5	0.00	17	0.00
Grass family cf.	1	0.00	1	0.00	5	0.00
Groundcherry	1	0.00				
Knotweed	11	0.00	6	0.00	2	0.00
Legume	2	0.00				
Legume cf.	1	0.00	3	0.00		
Mallow family cf.			1	0.00		
Monocot stem			4	0.06		
Morning-glory	98	0.19	42	0.05		
Morning-glory cf.	1	0.01				
Mustard family cf.			3	0.00		
Nightshade family	7	0.00	4	0.00		
Pine cone	137	0.37	273	1.04	65	0.14
Pine cone cf.	2	0.07	7	0.01		
Pine cone core/stem			3	0.01		
Pine needle			1	0.00		
Pine needle fascicle cf.			1	0.00		
Pitch	723	4.79	691	4.35	303	2.29
Pokeweed	4	0.01				
Pokeweed cf.	2	0.00	2	0.00	1	0.00
Purslane	2	0.00	3	0.00	4	0.00
Sedge family	2	0.00	1	0.00		
Sedge family cf.	1	0.00				
St. Johnswort cf.	1	0.00				
Stem/twig	23	0.03	20	0.06	4	0.00
Thorn	2	0.00	1	0.00		
Tuliptree	8	0.01	15	0.01		
Yellow star-grass	1	0.00	6	0.00		
Unidentifiable	237	0.89	366	1.66	42	0.15
Unidentifiable seeds	365	0.11	295	0.12	70	0.01
Unidentified			23	0.20		
Unidentified seeds	95	0.01	101	0.02	40	0.01
Wood, not carbonized					3	0.02
Wood, part carbonized		0.42		0.30		0.74

78 bearsfoot seed fragments from 22 samples at the Sandy site (44RN220), a Late Woodland (A.D. 1040–1220) campsite on the Roanoke River in Virginia. They listed the numerous medicinal qualities of bearsfoot, including poultice, laxative, stimulant, and emetic (VanDerwarker and Stanyard 2009:134; see also Moerman 2004) and argued that residents either brought bearsfoot with them as part of a first-aid kit of sorts, or more likely collected bearsfoot for future use while camping along the river (VanDerwarker and Stanyard 2009:145). The 224 fragments of bearsfoot seed recovered in this assemblage certainly indicate that the occupants of Riverfront Village similarly found the plant useful.

More than 2,000 fragments of cane and monocot stem were recovered from Riverfront Village samples. Both have a variety of uses. Fibers of monocot stems can be braided into cordage, as well as woven. Cane was used in wattle-and-daub construction as webbing between large posts, split and woven into baskets and mats, cut to make arrow shafts and blow guns, whittled into flutes, and burned as a fuel, notoriously in the form of torches (Moerman 2004; Watson and Yarnell 1966). Cane prefers to grow along riverbanks and in other wet grounds but can be found in a range of settings (Radford et al. 1964).

Comparisons of Plant Use by Site Component

The large number of samples analyzed here allows for several qualitative and quantitative comparisons. The simplest, and perhaps most useful, comparison is an evaluation of taxa by presence/absence in each of the three occupational components (see table 8.3). Not surprisingly, corn, acorns, and hickory nuts were recovered from each component. Interestingly, no definitive beans were recovered from the Mississippian samples. Bean does not appear in the Eastern Woodlands until approximately A.D. 1200 (Hart et al. 2002), around the end of the Early Mississippian occupation of Riverfront Village. Also noteworthy is the recovery of definitive specimens of peach only in the late Contact samples. As mentioned, peach is an Old World fruit that spread and became established throughout the Southeast after being introduced to the region by Spanish colonists (Gremillion 1993). The recovery of only one possible peach pit from the early Contact occupation of Riverfront Village suggests either that this occupation dates relatively early in the 1600s, or that peach arrived relatively late in the vicinity of this site.

Another immediately apparent trend is the lack of native cultigens, such as maygrass and chenopod, in late Contact samples. With just three contexts analyzed from this component, the data are not extremely robust. But this trend at least tentatively suggests that the foodways of post-1680 site

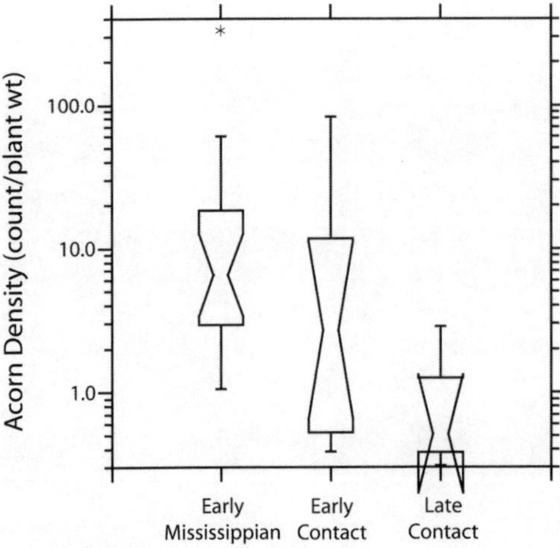

Figure 8.1. Comparison of acorn density (count/plant weight in grams) in floatation samples by component.

occupants, whether Apalachees, Savannahs, Yuchis, or another group all together, differed significantly from their predecessors.

Significant differences also exist in the recovery of acorn shell. A boxplot of acorn count divided by the total plant weight of each sample demonstrates a significantly lower recovery of acorn from late Contact samples (Figure 8.1). For centuries, Europeans had managed woodlands to produce acorns as fodder for livestock, particularly pigs (e.g., Jørgensen and Quelch 2014), in stark contrast to Native people's use of the nuts as a dietary staple. This, coupled with the removal of cultivated "weeds" such as maygrass from the plant assemblage, indicates that late Contact-period site occupants practiced foodways more similar to Europeans than did earlier Native peoples of the region.

Another trend revealed by boxplots is a marked decrease in the number of corn kernels relative to corn cupules recovered from late Contact samples (Figure 8.2). This suggests differences in disposal, and perhaps processing and storage, of corn and similarly points to differences in foodways from earlier occupations.

These findings dovetail well with an apparent shift in burial treatment. Of the 17 burials encountered during excavation of Riverfront Village, 14 interred in a flexed position were in poor condition, suggesting their older age. One in fair condition was a supine male interred in a shallow pit feature with his arms close to his body and legs bent behind him (perhaps suggesting his hands and feet were bound behind his back). Whitley (2009) wonders whether this man was killed just before the abandonment of the site in the 1660s, with the arrival of the Westos and rise of slave raiding in the region. The remaining two burials were extended, with heads to the west, and were

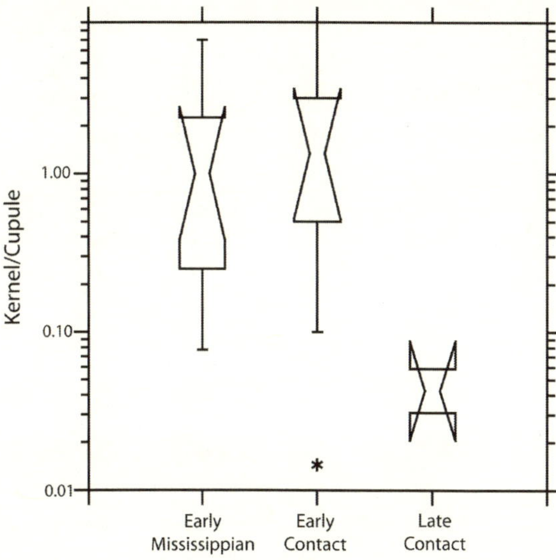

Figure 8.2. Comparison of corn kernel/cupule ratio in floatation samples by component. Note that Feature 747, a smudge pit full of corncobs, is not included.

in good condition. Considering their better preservation and Christianized burial style, Whitley (2009, 2013) suggests that these two interments are related to the post-1680 occupation and may have been Catholic Apalachee refugees from the missions of Spanish Florida (Whitley 2013:328).

When one also considers the European trade goods found in late Contact contexts at Riverfront Village along with these differences in foodways and burial practices, these later site occupants had strong ties—certainly economic but also social ties—with European colonists, whether Carolina traders or inhabitants of Spanish missions. Bowne (2009:107–108) describes "settlement Indians" who moved their communities adjacent to Charles Town and other Carolina settlements, often living and working closely with the colonists, for protection from the Westos. The disruptive actions of the Westos, whose slave raids had dispersed and fractured Native communities across the region, led groups like the Apalachees, Savannahs, and Yuchis to coalesce and form social amalgams with new social identities (Bowne 2009). In the late seventeenth century, many of these new groups forged ties with the recently established British colony. Indeed, the Westos were driven from the Savannah Valley largely by the efforts of South Carolina colonists eager to establish stable trade relationships with Native peoples in the interior (Meyers 2009). The late Contact residents of Riverfront Village, then, appear to have been a Native group, perhaps comprising an alliance of previously distinct communities, whose relationship with European settlers in the region had led them to abandon some of their traditional foodways and burial practices.

An examination of bearsfoot remains across the three occupations of Riverfront Village tells a more nuanced story. Although no significant differences in the recovery of bearsfoot were revealed by boxplots, there is an apparent increase in ubiquity of this seed through time. Only two of the 21 Early Mississippian floatation samples yielded bearsfoot, giving a ubiquity of 9.5 percent. In contrast, 42.9 percent of the early Contact samples and 100 percent of late Contact samples contained bearsfoot (although the number of late Contact samples is relatively small). As mentioned, bearsfoot seeds may have been eaten, similar to sunflower seeds, by Native peoples (Scarry 2003:71), but VanDerwarker and Stanyard (2009) make a compelling argument that bearsfoot was targeted, at least by some groups, for its medicinal uses.

Given the devaluation of acorn and maygrass by late Contact occupants of the site, it seems unlikely that a weedy seed like bearsfoot was considered an important foodstuff in the late 1600s. Maybe disposal practices or use of bearsfoot changed through time, leading to an increase in the burning of seeds and an increase in their recovery. Yet it is no more speculative to reason that late Contact site occupants had a great need for medicinal plants such as bearsfoot. As European illnesses and internecine raiding took significant tolls on local populations, Native groups may have turned to traditional remedies as a means of purging themselves of the bodily effects of destabilizing forces. VanDerwarker and colleagues (2007) suggest that a late Contact (1670–1710) feature from Upper Saratown, a Sara Indian village in the northern North Carolina Piedmont, held evidence of a ritual feast harkening back to traditional identities. Large quantities of corn kernels, beans, hickory nuts, and acorns were recovered from the feature, but notably few peach pit fragments compared with other contexts, leading those authors to suggest that the late Contact occupants of Upper Saratown, in response to population loss from disease and raiding, turned to traditional foods for purification and renewal (VanDerwarker et al. 2007). The late Contact residents of Riverfront Village may have similarly turned to traditional medicinal plants, such as bearsfoot and morning glory, for comfort or relief during this time of instability.

Aside from these broader trends, several specific archaeological features deserve additional mention. Among Early Mississippian contexts, Feature 1929 is notable for its impressive quantity of acorn shell. Too numerous to count individually, acorn shell is estimated to top 10,000 fragments from this bell-shaped pit feature, which was likely used to store acorns. At the very least, it served as a receptacle for debris from acorn processing. A large number of corn cupules and maygrass seeds were recovered from Feature 845, another Early Mississippian bell-shaped pit that certainly served for storage during its initial use, but ultimately contained refuse from food processing. Recovery of 97 morning glory seeds from Feature 2795, an Early Mississippian basin-shaped pit, also stands out.

Among early Contact features, Features 1809 and 2254 are both notable for large quantities of nutshell. More than 3,000 acorn shell fragments were recovered from Feature 1809, and a subsample from Feature 2254 yielded a similar proportion. Those feature samples produced the largest quantities of hickory nutshell in the assemblage, with more than 1,000 fragments each, outstripping other features by a factor of 10. Feature 1809 also contained over 800 fragments of cane and 50 maygrass seeds.

Feature 1952, an early Contact hearth pit, held more than 100 fragments of bearsfoot, 31 dock/knotweed, 35 morning glory, and more than 200 unidentifiable or unidentified seeds, along with a range of fruits, including grape, maypop, and sumac, as well as squash rind, bean, and corn. This hearth witnessed the preparation of many meals, tended by a particularly messy cook(!), who also appears to have concocted numerous medicinal remedies.

Discussion and Conclusions

The plant remains from Riverfront Village document how the site's various occupants tended a wide variety of plants, from native cultigens to useful weeds, in addition to their main staple of corn, and eventually corn, beans, and squash. These staples were supplemented by acorns and hickory nuts, as well as various wild and not-so-wild fruits. The broad range of plants recovered from the site certainly suggests it was occupied year-round during all three occupations. Fields and garden plots would have been prepared and planted in the spring and tended through summer, when occupants gathered fruits as various berries and fleshy fruits ripened, before turning their attention to harvesting beans, corn, and squash in late summer. In autumn they collected hickory nuts and acorns, as well as persimmons, groundcherries, and sumac. Early on they likely broadcast maygrass seeds in their fields, establishing this starchy seed crop for harvest in spring. Site occupants likely also collected roots and starchy tubers year-round, although these are poorly preserved in archaeological assemblages. Similarly, the site's occupants likely gathered various parts of plants for medicinal and ritual purposes, some of which, along with various foodstuffs, may have been dried for use throughout the year.

Significant changes appeared through time in the plant assemblages, particularly among the food plants, as contact with Europeans increased. We know from other archaeological studies of plant remains in the coastal

Southeast that Europeans introduced peaches by the sixteenth century. Yet, peach remains at Riverfront Village are limited to the late Contact occupation, suggesting either that the site's early Contact occupation dates very early in the seventeenth century, or that peaches were not commonly grown in the area until after A.D. 1680. Use of acorn dropped notably during the late Contact occupation, and native cultigens like maygrass disappeared completely. This pattern may be due in part to the relatively few samples analyzed from the late Contact occupation. Taken in total, however, the late Contact plant assemblage suggests that site occupants had abandoned some of the traditional foodways of the region by 1680, during the disruptive era of slave raiding by the Westos between 1660 and 1680. Given the recovery of significant numbers of bearsfoot seed fragments, though, late Contact residents continued to gather plants with traditional medicinal uses.

Contemporaneous sites in the region show a similar range of plant taxa (Table 8.5). Other Mississippian sites in the Savannah River valley demonstrate a similar reliance on corn, hickory nuts, acorns, and native cultigens such as chenopod and maygrass. Beans are notably absent, whereas maypops appear to have been highly encouraged, at least at the Beaverdam Creek site. Various weedy taxa certainly thrived in the disturbed grounds of villages and fields and were likely used for a variety of purposes.

Comparative data for the Contact period is available from the broader Southeast. Analyses of Cherokee contexts in northern Georgia, western North Carolina, and eastern Tennessee also indicate continued use of nuts, corn, beans, and squash, alongside adoptions of Old World crops like peach and cowpea (black-eyed pea, *Vigna unguiculata*). Both Old World taxa are present at Cherokee sites in the Tellico Reservoir (Chapman and Shea 1981), whereas only peach was recovered at Coweeta Creek, a late Qualla-phase site in western North Carolina. Additional taxa recovered at Coweeta Creek include little barley (*Hordeum pusilum*), another native cultigen, along with smartweed (*Polygonum* sp.), holly (*Ilex* sp.), seeds from the Spurge and Sedge families, and beechnut shell (VanDerwarker and Detwiler 2000). Peach was also recovered from Cherokee contexts at 9FN341 in northern Georgia (Hollenbach 2008).

Gremillion (1995) compares assemblages dating to the latter half of the seventeenth century from the Graham-White site in Roanoke, Virginia, the Fredericks site (31OR321) in the Piedmont of North Carolina, and Fusihatchee village (1EE191), an Upper Creek *talwa* in central Alabama. These various groups also kept fields of corn, beans, and squash, further evidenced by weedy taxa such as maypops and morning glory that thrive in tilled ground. Gremillion (1995:6) notes that these and other weedy taxa were likely tolerated for their medicinal and other uses. She further argues that mast resources, particularly hickory nuts, remained important to these Native

Table 8.5. Plant Taxa Recovered from Several Mississippian Sites in the Savannah River Valley

Taxon	Beaverdam Creek[a]	Clyde Gulley[b]	Simpson's Field[b]	Rucker's Bottom[c]
Nuts				
Acorn	6.055 g		X	X
Black walnut	0.13 g			
Hazelnut	0.26 g			
Hickory	26.84 g	X	X	X
Juglandaceae				X
Fruits				
Blackberry/raspberry	2		X	
Grape	48		X	X
Maypop	166	X	X	X
Persimmon	14		X	
Plum	1			
Strawberry	3		X	
Starchy/Oily Seeds				
Chenopod	48		X	X
Maygrass	68			
Sumpweed	3			
Crops				
Corn cupule	43.63 g	X	X	X
Corn kernel	96			
Cucurbit scars & seeds	1			
Gourd rind	0.03 g		X	
Squash rind	0.005 g			
Sunflower	1			
Miscellaneous				
Amaranth	1			
Carpetweed	3			
Doveweed (*Croton* sp.)				X
Grass family	6	X		
Legume	2			
Panic grass	1			
Pine cone		X		
Purslane	12			
Spurge (*Euphorbia* sp.)	1			

[a] Includes data from the village, pre-mound midden, earthlodge, and three overlying mound stages, all Mississippian in age (9EB85; Gardner 1985).

[b] Clyde Gulley (9EB387) is a small Early Mississippian village or several hamlets; Simpson's Field (38AN8) represents a small Middle Mississippian site with at least one structure (Anderson 1988).

[c] Includes Early and Late Mississippian components (Moore 1985).

communities, although use of native cultigens like chenopod and little barley seems to have waned. Gremillion (1995:7) points to the Mitchum site (31CH452) in the North Carolina Piedmont, where numerous maygrass seeds were recovered, as an example of a group who continued to use native seed crops. Adoptions of Old World crops are evidenced by the recovery of peach from both Fredericks and Fusihatchee, as well as cowpea at Fusihatchee and watermelon (*Citrullus lanatus*) at Fredericks.

Bonhage-Freund (2007) compiled plant data from five eighteenth-century Lower Creek sites along the Chattahoochee River, including Cusseteh Town site (9CE1), Buzzard Roost (9TR41 and 9TR54), Ochillee Creek (9CE379), and Yuchi Town (1RU63). Corn and peach were the only two taxa found at all five sites. Unidentified European cereal grains were identified at Cusseteh and Buzzard Roost, and cotton from one of the two Buzzard Roost sites (9TR54), but no other Old World crops were found. Interestingly, the Ochillee Creek site, the latest of the five with a late eighteenth- to early nineteenth-century occupation, is the only one that lacks both acorn and hickory nutshell. This site also lacked the range of useful taxa with edible seeds, leaves, and medicinal properties found at the other sites, including maygrass, sumpweed, chenopod, amaranth, smartweed, knotweed, wild bean (Fabaceae), pokeweed, purslane, copperleaf, doveweed, spurge, bedstraw, clover, and greenbriar. The only exception was nineteen dock (*Rumex* sp.) seeds. Maypops, blackberries/raspberries, and grapes were frequently recovered wild fruits (Bonhage-Freund 2007).

In sum, the plant remains from three occupations of Riverfront Village provide an invaluable view of changes in foodways through time in the middle Savannah River valley. The plant assemblages from these three components are broadly comparable to those from contemporaneous sites in the region but demonstrate interesting local trends. The earliest component indicates the site's Early Mississippian occupants practiced corn agriculture and grew squash, maygrass, and perhaps chenopod, but likely not beans, in their fields. They also collected significant quantities of acorns, and to some degree hickory nuts, along with a variety of wild fruits. Few changes are apparent between the Early Mississippian and early Contact occupants of the site, suggesting a large degree of continuity in foodways among these farming communities, although the latter group had added beans to their agricultural fields and may have gathered weedy plants such as bearsfoot and morning glory for medicinal or ritual purposes. The most significant shift in identity suggested by the plant remains, then, is that the early Contact occupants were farmers of the three sisters—corn, squash, and beans—and attendant to the myths, ideologies, and practices associated with cultivating the three crops.

By the late Contact period, the final occupants of Riverfront Village seem to have shunned traditional foods like acorns and native cultigens—viewed as fodder and weeds by Europeans—and adopted Old World foods like peaches. The recovery of numerous bearsfoot seed fragments, however, suggests that they continued to prepare traditional remedies. Whether these final residents were Apalachees, Savannahs, Yuchis, or other Native peoples, this displaced and likely coalescent group with strong trading ties to the Charles Town colonists seems to have established fields and perhaps orchards that in some ways resemble European farming practices. Yet they continued to seek out plants with which Southeastern Native peoples had long-standing relationships for use in medicines and rituals, perhaps as a source of comfort and relief in a time of upheaval and uncertainty. Their use of plant resources, then, suggests that the late Contact occupants sought to downplay the differences between themselves and their European neighbors. However, when facing illness and stress, they appear to have found some solace in their traditional recipes and practices, identifying with the customs of their elders and ancestors.

Viewed in concert with other elements of material culture, these plant remains tell us about the daily lives of the site's various occupants, how they managed their local landscape, and how they acted within their own communities and interacted with others in the region. They also give us glimpses of the occupants' identities as a group, as cultivators of corn and maygrass, to farmers of the triad of corns, beans, and squash, to eighteenth-century farmers with practices more similar to their European neighbors than their indigenous predecessors.

Acknowledgments

This project was funded by the city of North Augusta, the Leyland Alliance (a private development group), and the Federal Highways Administration. I am grateful to Greg Waselkov and Marvin Smith not only for their suggestions that have improved this chapter, but also for their invitation to participate in this volume to honor Judith Knight. Without her pragmatic encouragement, I might not have finished my book with two small children in tow. From her role behind the scenes, she has been both a strong proponent and role model for women in Southeastern archaeology.

9

THE GRAND VILLAGE OF THE NATCHEZ INDIANS WAS INDEED GRAND

A Reconsideration of the Fatherland Site Landscape

Ian W. Brown and Vincas P. Steponaitis

The Fatherland site, located near the city of Natchez, Mississippi, is one of the best-known archaeological sites in the American South (Figure 9.1). It was the Grand Village of the Natchez Indians, home to chiefs who held the titles Great Sun and Tattooed Serpent. Dramatic accounts of numerous French colonists brought these people to life for European readers, as they related the intricate story of French-Indian relations in colonial Louisiane. There never seems to have been a question as to where the Grand Village was located. As a consequence, it has been a prime source for understanding the relationship between the colonial-era and precolonial Indians, as archaeologists work from the known to the unknown in the region. As such, Fatherland played a major role in James Ford's *Analysis of Indian Village Site Collections from Louisiana and Mississippi* (1936:59–64). Moreau B. Chambers, Ford's partner in Mississippi archaeology, excavated a series of burials from the site that helped Ford formulate what historic Natchez Indian material culture looked like. George Quimby (1942) later drew heavily from findings at this site when he wrote his major study on Natchezan pottery.

Later still, Fatherland was the subject of two monographs by Robert S. Neitzel. His first book (1965) concentrates on exploring the three surviving mounds at Fatherland, two of which he dated to the eighteenth century, and his second (1983) deals mainly with the remains of wooden buildings in and around the plaza. The small number of buildings made sense, as this was a ritual and political center. One mound supported the residence of the chief, the other a temple, and between the two mounds was a plaza where ceremonies took place. History and archaeology were in agreement, so one might wonder just what use there may be in devoting further attention to Fatherland, especially as there have been no recent excavations there. Our purpose here is to bring attention to some early documents that merit further study. We examine a 1723 map drawn by Ignace-François Broutin and compare it with an anonymous 1730 map showing the

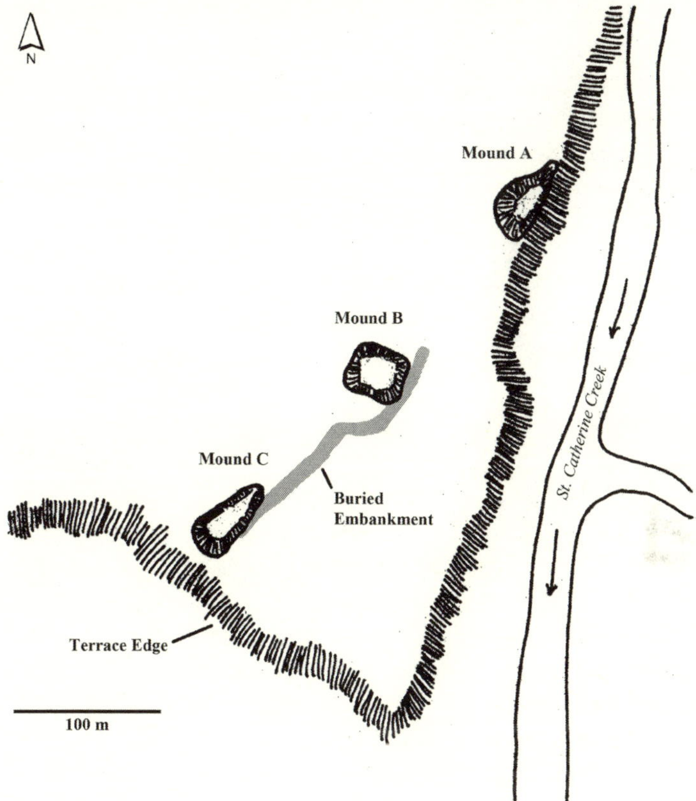

Figure 9.1. Modern map of the Fatherland site, showing the three surviving mounds and the approximate location of a buried feature, which Neitzel interpreted as an embankment associated with the French siege trench (adapted from Barnett 2007: Figure 6 and Neitzel 1978: Figure 1b).

French siege of the site following the Natchez Uprising. The Broutin map, in particular, indicates that the Grand Village landscape was far more complex than supposed by twentieth-century investigators. We also consider several nineteenth-century texts that refer to the Fatherland site, because they shed light on the number of mounds that existed there and on a feature of the landscape that puzzled Neitzel.

Background

Let us start with some background on the site itself and its importance in Southern Indian history. As stated, in the early eighteenth century Fatherland was the capital of the Natchez nation, and thus it received great attention in the writings of Le Page du Pratz (1758, 1972), Dumont de Montigny

(1753, 2012), and other French writers, most of whom are quoted in great detail in John R. Swanton's 1911 landmark study (see also Delanglez 1935; French 1869; Giraud 1974; McWilliams 1988; Miller Surrey 2006; Rowland and Sanders 1927, 1929; Rowland et al. 1984a, 1984b). The Natchez Indians were among the last manifestations of the Plaquemine culture in the lower Mississippi Valley (Barnett 1998, 2007; Brain 1978; Brown 1985, 1998b, 1998d, 2007; Oswalt and Neely 1996; Quimby 1942; Stern 1977). European explorers were fascinated by the complex social and political structure manifested by the inhabitants of the Natchez Bluffs, and their detailed descriptions of Natchez society provided considerable fodder for historians and anthropologists for many years to come (Albrecht 1946, 1948; Brain 1971; Brown 1982, 1989, 1990, 1992; Clayton et al. 1993; Fischer 1964; Hart 1943; Knight 1990; Loren 1995; Lorenz 1997; Quimby 1946; Steponaitis 1978:421–423; Tooker 1963; White et al. 1971).

The Grand Village of the Natchez, located on St. Catherine Creek, was situated midway between the French concessions of Terre Blanche to the west and St. Catherine to the east, the colony's two largest plantations in the 1720s. The location of the Grand Village may have been passed down in the lore of the region, never quite forgotten, but archaeologists were the ones to establish its pedigree beyond question. As a result of analysis done by Moreau B. Chambers, James A. Ford, Jesse D. Jennings, Robert S. Neitzel, George I. Quimby, and many others, we know that the Fatherland site was indeed the Grand Village (Albrecht 1944; Baca 1989:36–38; Barnett 1998: 4–8, 2007:45–48; I. Brown 1978:3; 1998a:175–176, 1998c; J. Brown 1990; Ford 1935, 1936:50–68; Green 1936; Jennings 1940; Lorenz 1997:106; Neitzel 1964, 1965, 1978, 1981, 1983; Phillips 1970a:948–949; Quimby 1942, 1953; Shafer 1972; Truett 1938; Williams 1962, 1966, 2003:xiii, xvii–xviii).

Early eighteenth-century French accounts seem to mention only two mounds at the site. One supported the Great Sun's house and the other supported the temple, with a plaza between them. Mound A showed no archaeological evidence of colonial-era occupation, so Neitzel (1965) reasoned that the Indians had abandoned it before the French arrived on the scene, perhaps because it had been partly eroded by St. Catherine Creek. He went on to argue that Mound B was the Great Sun's house and Mound C the temple, the repository for the many rich burials that were excavated by Chambers in the 1930s. The diminutive size of the plaza between Mounds B and C pales in comparison with its historic stature, as it was in this space that numerous momentous events occurred. For example, this was the scene of the 1725 funeral of Tattooed Serpent, war chief of the Natchez, brother of the Great Sun, and one of the most steadfast friends the French ever had in Louisiane. In Le Page du Pratz's well-known illustration of this ceremony, the temple is clearly shown atop a mound (Figure 9.2).

Figure 9.2. Funeral of the Tattooed Serpent in 1725 (Le Page du Pratz 1758:3: facing p. 55).

Neitzel's investigations of Mounds A, B, and C revealed that the Fatherland site had considerable time depth (1965). Although the site was the habitation of the Great Sun and his retainers in the late seventeenth and eighteenth centuries, it is doubtful that it had been the paramount Natchezan center for very long (Brain 1978:360–361; Brown 2007). Nevertheless, Fatherland seems to have been occupied to some extent, without any obvious breaks, for more than five centuries before its abandonment in 1730 (Brown 1998c). Although there was significant habitation at Fatherland during the Anna phase, between A.D. 1200 and 1350, mound construction does not appear to have begun until the following Foster phase, between A.D. 1350 and 1500. Additions continued to be made to the Fatherland mounds during the Emerald phase, between A.D. 1500 and 1650, and it is most likely during that time span that Fatherland attained its status as the capital. In earlier times the much larger Emerald and Anna sites were probably the paramount centers of the Natchez chiefdom (Beasley 2007; Brain 1978; Brown 2007; Cotter 1951).

In addition to social changes, the Natchez region experienced considerable physical changes over the years. For example, during his 1972 excava-

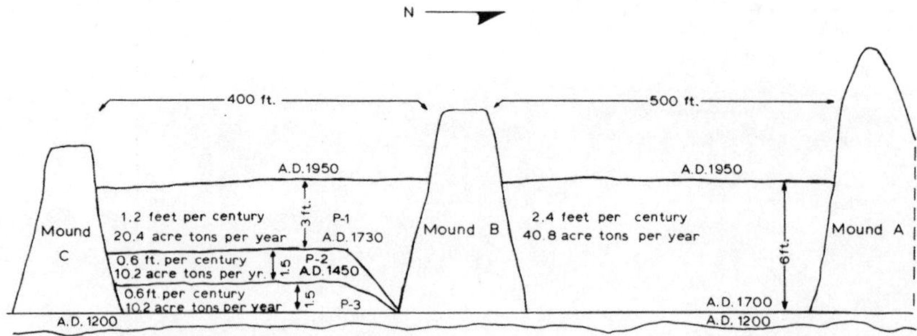

Figure 9.3. Idealized diagram of stratification in the plaza at Fatherland (Neitzel 1983: Figure 5; courtesy of Mississippi Department of Archives and History).

tions Neitzel was hard-pressed to find the 1730 surface at the Grand Village. He eventually found it, well into the season, almost 2 m below the present ground level (Figure 9.3). Neitzel (1978) attributes this great accumulation of soil deposition to nineteenth-century deforestation. As trees were felled, both for expansion of arable land and for stoking the furnaces of hundreds of steamboats, the land paid a horrible price. Year after year abundant rainfall eroded the loam, lowering bluffs and choking bayous in the process. When the course of St. Catherine Creek was purposefully shortened, causing it to flow west into the Mississippi River, the gradient of the stream greatly increased. St. Catherine Creek and its many tributaries cut deeply into the land, and a constant creep of soil covered evidence of earlier occupations along St. Catherine's banks, laying a thick mantle of sediment above early occupation zones at sites like Fatherland.

Neitzel also noticed something else while digging at the Grand Village in 1972. Between Mound B and C, he observed what appeared to be a buried ridge, the result of a great deal of earth movement (see figure 9.1). Neitzel (1978) interpreted this feature as part of a siege trench dug in February of 1730 by the French army, which had returned to punish the Natchez for the previous November's uprising. The basis for this interpretation was a French military map of the siege (see figure 9.5), which we will discuss in more detail presently. In trying to reconcile this map with the archaeological record at Fatherland, Neitzel was faced with a dilemma: rather than showing three mounds in a linear arrangement as in figure 9.1, the military map depicted four mounds in a diamond pattern. In an extended argument too long to recount here, Neitzel explained away this discrepancy by suggesting that the north arrow on the military map was off by 90 degrees, that is, that the map's north arrow actually pointed east. This change in orientation, he argued, together with some understandable confusion on the part of the cartographer in adding a fourth mound, was sufficient to account for the differences between the French map and Fatherland's modern appearance.

Our analysis of the French maps, including two that were not available to Neitzel at the time of his study, leads us to a different and more parsimonious explanation; to wit, that the Grand Village had more than three mounds, which obviates the need to invoke errors by the anonymous mapmaker. Furthermore, nineteenth-century descriptions of the Fatherland site indicate that the ridge between the mounds was actually an artificial levee built to prevent flooding, rather than a military fortification connected with the French siege. We now consider each line of evidence in turn.

Eighteenth-Century French Maps

Perhaps the best-known maps of French colonial Natchez are an engraving and four manuscripts by Jean-François-Benjamin Dumont de Montigny.[1] All are oblique views, drawn in Dumont's cartoonish style, and none depict any mounds at the Grand Village. Their general lack of detail, as well as a lack of consistency among his maps in the details they do show, clearly indicates they were impressionistic sketches, not measured drawings (see Litschi 2011 for a useful summary of the manuscripts). Dumont was never a stickler for precision, so his renderings of the Grand Village tell us little about what it may have looked like.[2]

A much better source of information for present purposes is the remarkable map of Natchez by Ignace-François Broutin, which was based on his detailed survey in 1723 and drafted by his assistant Gonichon in 1727 (Figure 9.4, inset).[3] Broutin was a French officer, a trained engineer, and an extraordinary cartographer (Wilson 1969). In contrast to Dumont's sketches, his map is a precise, carefully measured plan—so well done, in fact, that one can overlay this map on the modern topography of Natchez with a very close fit (Steponaitis et al. 2006).

Although Broutin's map is large and shows the entire French settlement, here we focus only on his depiction of the Grand Village. It is one of the very few contemporary maps, and the only accurate one, of an Indian capital in French Louisiane. Figure 9.4 shows six mounds, which for convenience we designate with the letters A–F. Mounds A, B, and C appear to correspond with the three mounds that survived into the twentieth century, identified by the same letters. The map also shows the locations of buildings (drawn as red dots), as well as trails that passed near the settlement.

The map depicts Mound A with four structures on the summit but is silent as to their function. Mound B has two structures on top and is labeled "*cabanne du grand chef*" (cabin of the great chief). Mound C has one building

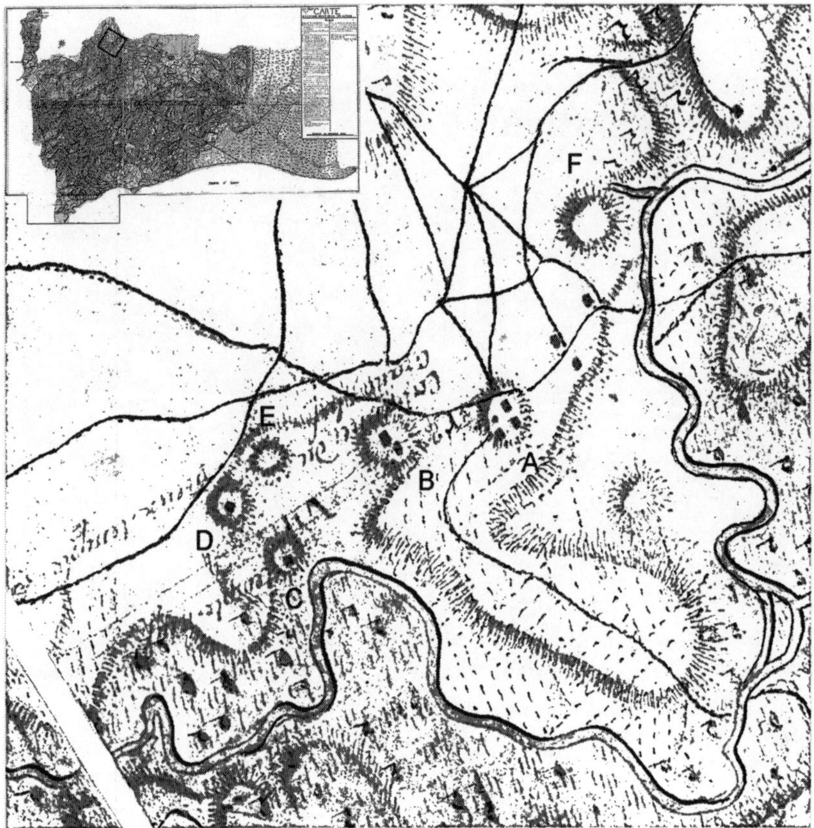

Figure 9.4. Detail from Broutin's 1723 map of the Natchez settlements, showing the Grand Village, rotated with north at the top. The mounds are labeled A–F. Mounds A, B, and C correspond to the modern mounds with the same designations. Mound descriptions as they appear on the map: Mound B, cabin of the great chief ("cabanne du grand chef"); Mound C, new temple ("temple neuf"); Mound D, old temple ("vieux temple"). Inset at upper left shows the full map with area of detail outlined, north at lower left (adapted from Bibliothèque nationale de France, Département des cartes et plans, Ge DD 2987–8834B).

called "*temple neuf*" (new temple), and Mound D also has one building with the caption "*vieux temple*" (old temple). The two remaining mounds, E and F, have no buildings. The map confirms contemporary descriptions of the Grand Village as having very few houses (e.g., Swanton 1911:158, 190–191).

In addition to these architectural details, Broutin provides valuable information on how the land in the immediate vicinity of the mounds was used. The open area bounded by Mounds B, C, D, and E—essentially the area between the chief's cabin and the two temples—has no trails running through it, consistent with the long-standing idea that it was a ceremonial

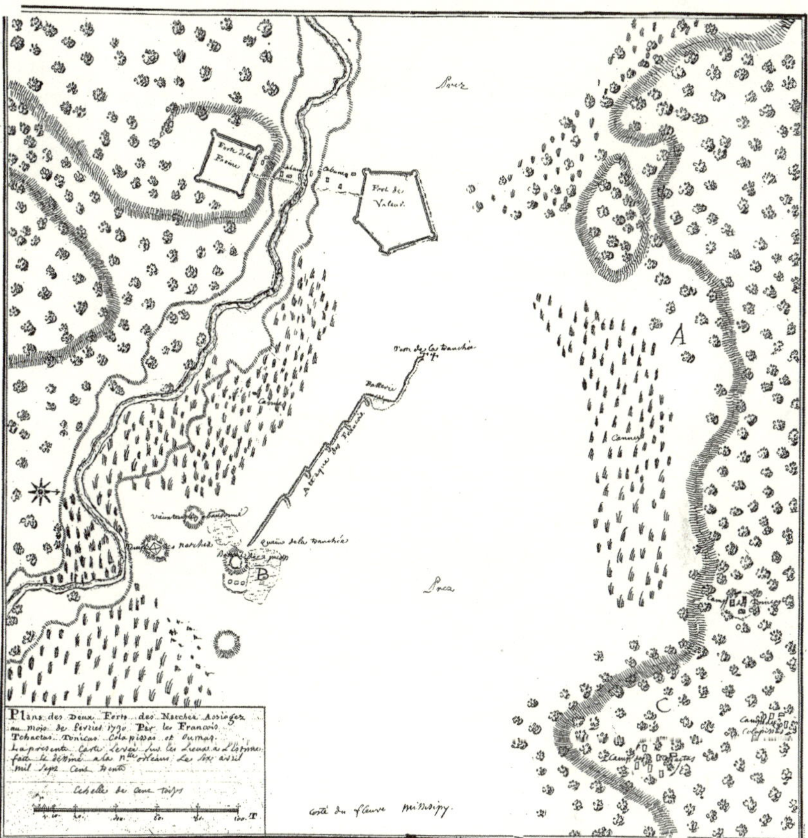

Figure 9.5. Anonymous 1730 map of the French siege at Natchez, showing four mounds along with the French and Indian fortifications. North arrow points right (adapted from Bibliothèque nationale de France, Estampes, Vd 21 [3] Fol.).

plaza. The area enclosed by Mounds A, B, and F, however, is crisscrossed with paths, suggesting that it lacked such a special function. Yet another interesting feature is the large cultivated area indicated by tiles of dashed parallel lines, located just southeast of Mounds A and B on the map.

Broutin's map not only gives us a fascinating glimpse of the Grand Village while still in use, but also provides the key to resolving Neitzel's conundrum in identifying the mounds mapped there during the 1730 siege (Neitzel 1978:29–33, 1983:46–50). Before we solve this mystery, we discuss in more detail the two existing maps that show the siege.

The better-known siege map, and the one Neitzel discussed at length, "Plans des Deux Forts Natchez," is currently housed in the Bibliothèque nationale de France.[4] It depicts four mounds, two Indian forts, and French batteries and siege works (Figure 9.5). The map is unsigned, but Neitzel

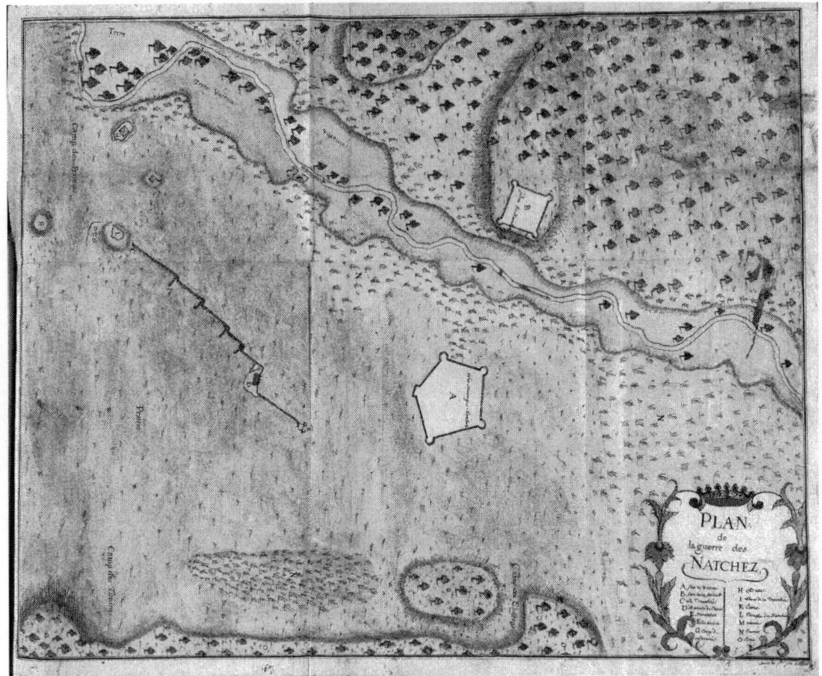

Figure 9.6. Caillot's 1730 map of the French siege at Natchez. North is toward the bottom (The Historic New Orleans Collection, acc. no. 2005.0011).

(1983:48) attributes it to a Lt. de Niné—a misreading of a poorly written portion of text, "*et dessiné*" (and drawn), in the cartouche. For now we simply refer to this manuscript as anonymous.[5]

The second manuscript map, "Plan de la Guerre des Natchez," now at The Historic New Orleans Collection, only recently came to light (Figure 9.6; Greenwald 2013: Plate 22).[6] It was drawn by Marc-Antoine Caillot, a clerk for the Company of the Indies who lived in New Orleans from July 1729 to April 1731 (Greenwald 2013:xxii–xxix). Although Caillot was in Louisiane during the 1730 siege at Natchez, he never left New Orleans, so there can be little doubt that the siege map he made to illustrate his memoir was a copy, presumably from an original document available to him in the capital.

Despite minor differences in the coverage and the labeling of features, the two siege maps are very similar, particularly in the layout of the mounds. This layout, when compared with that in Broutin's earlier map, provides the solution to Neitzel's dilemma. Figures 9.7 and 9.8 show the corresponding areas in the Broutin 1723 and the anonymous 1730 maps, resized to the same scale and rotated with north at the top. Note that the relative locations of Mounds B, C, D, and E are identical. On both maps, Mound D is labeled as the old temple ("vieux temple" in 1723 and "vieux temple abandonné" in 1730) and Mound C is marked as the current temple ("temple neuf" and "temple des Natchez," respectively), so the mound descriptions fit perfectly. The surrounding landscape features are also generally similar, particularly the lobe in the terrace edge north of Mound B. Mounds A and F are not depicted in the anonymous map, probably because neither was involved in the siege; the location of A is obscured by the cartouche, and F would have straddled the neatline along the eastern edge. The Caillot map also lacks Mounds A and F, as both fall outside its eastern boundary. This correlation among the maps, if it holds true, leads to several interesting implications.

First and foremost, there were more mounds at the Grand Village than currently meet the eye, or that were mentioned in the early accounts (Figure 9.9). As stated, the two mounds that supported the chief's cabin and the temple are consistently mentioned in the eighteenth-century narratives, and three mounds are visible today. Yet the cartographic evidence suggests six mounds existed in 1723, four of which had wooden buildings on their summits and two of which did not. Three of the mounds with buildings can be identified as to function. One supported the cabin of the chief (B), another the new temple (C), and a third the old temple (D). The presence of two temples at the Grand Village is interesting in light of a Natchez story recounted by Le Page du Pratz (Swanton 1911:170–171; see also Neitzel 1965:63), which makes reference to an old and a new temple and may have served as a charter myth for such an arrangement.

Second, the north arrow on the anonymous 1730 map is actually correct (cf. Neitzel 1978: Figure 1a). Neitzel was understandably led to argue otherwise because he lacked the information from the 1723 map and could not have known which mounds were depicted on the 1730 map—for example, that Mound A was missing and that two additional mounds were being shown.

Third, the French siege works and Indian forts can now be more accurately placed (see figure 9.9). The French approach trenches and batteries would have been located well north and west of Mounds B and C, not between these mounds as Neitzel argued (cf. 1978: Figure 1b, 1983:47–50). The two Natchez forts, which the trenches were designed to attack, were located west of the Grand Village, not to the south as previously believed (cf. Neitzel 1978: Figure 1a). Whether any portions of these forts have survived the erosion caused by St. Catherine Creek and twentieth-century development in the area remains to be seen.

Finally, the cartographic evidence confirms Neitzel's identifications of Mound B as the chief's residence and Mound C as a temple (1965:64–85). The suggestion that Mound A was abandoned by the 1720s, perhaps because it was eroding into the creek, no longer holds true (cf. Neitzel 1965:64). The

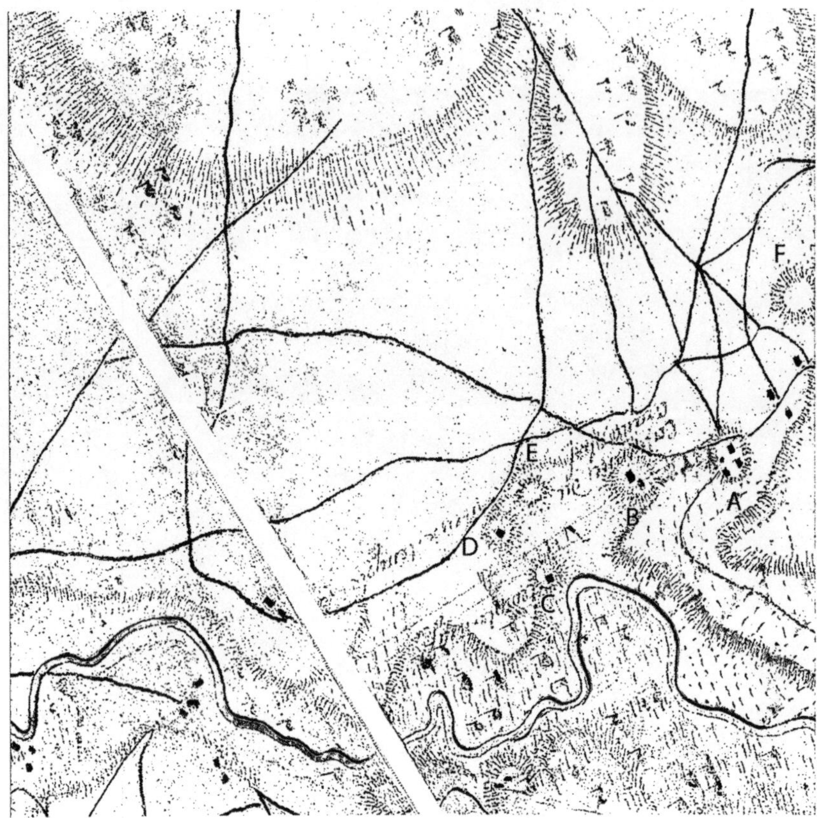

Figure 9.7. Detail from Broutin's 1723 map, oriented with north at the top and with the modern mound designations A to E added. The map is shown at the same scale as Figure 9.8 (adapted from the original).

1723 map shows this mound intact with four unidentified buildings on top and the creek rather far away.

A puzzle still remains, however. If the siege line was located north and west of the plaza marked by Mound B and C, what exactly did Neitzel discover in the plaza in his 1972 excavations? Clearly there was a ridge, but if it was not the French siege line, then what was it? For that, we must turn to a number of nineteenth-century scholars who left written descriptions of the ever-changing landscape of the Fatherland site.

Nineteenth-Century Descriptions

Montroville Dickeson was a colorful man by any definition—an antiquarian who loved to dig, to collect, and to speculate. He commissioned a renowned panorama, which he used to entertain the masses with the glories of prehis-

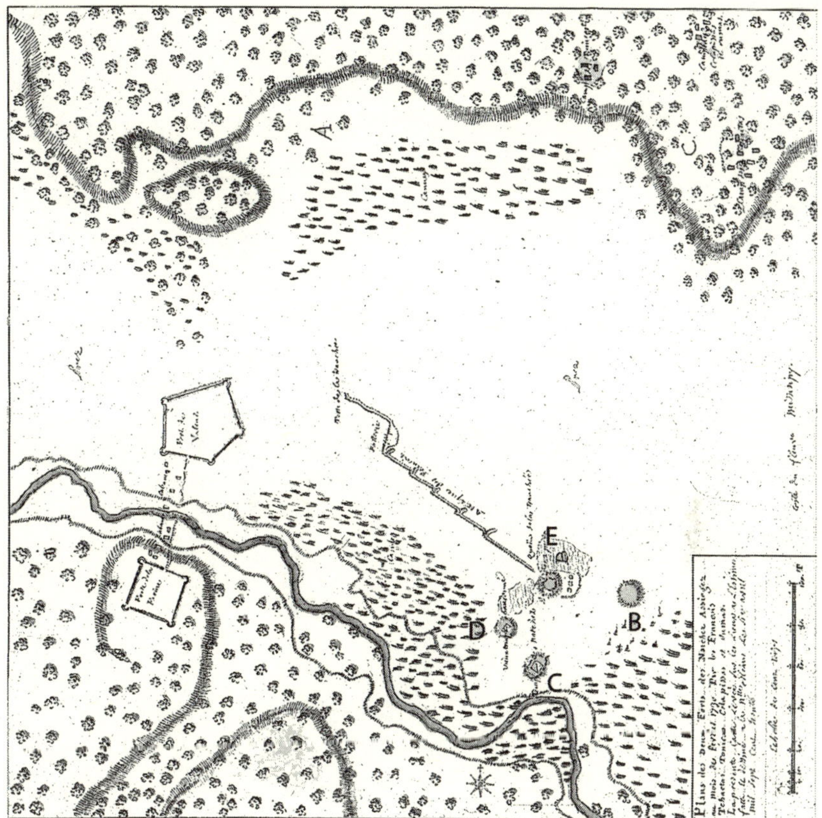

Figure 9.8. Detail from the anonymous 1730 map, oriented with north at the top and with the modern mound designations A to E added. The map is trimmed at its neatline and shown at the same scale as Figure 9.7 (adapted from the original).

tory (Culin 1900; McDermott 1958:170–172). Although he explored widely in the lower Mississippi Valley, Natchez was a constant draw for him, as he wrote many reports on its archaeological productivity in a magazine called *The Lotus*. In 1842, on one such exploration in Natchez, he spent a considerable amount of time digging mounds on Colonel Bingaman's plantation, which contained the Fatherland site. Dickeson's (1848) account of this work in *The Lotus* provides a fine description of what the site looked like a little more than 170 years ago.[7] Of interest to the present study is his reference to an embankment, more than 2 m high, which connected the mounds:

> In July, 1842, accompanied by a friend, I drove to the plantation of Col. A. L. Bingaman, situated two miles [3.2 km] east of the town of Natchez. . . . On the western bank of the St. Catharine stand three

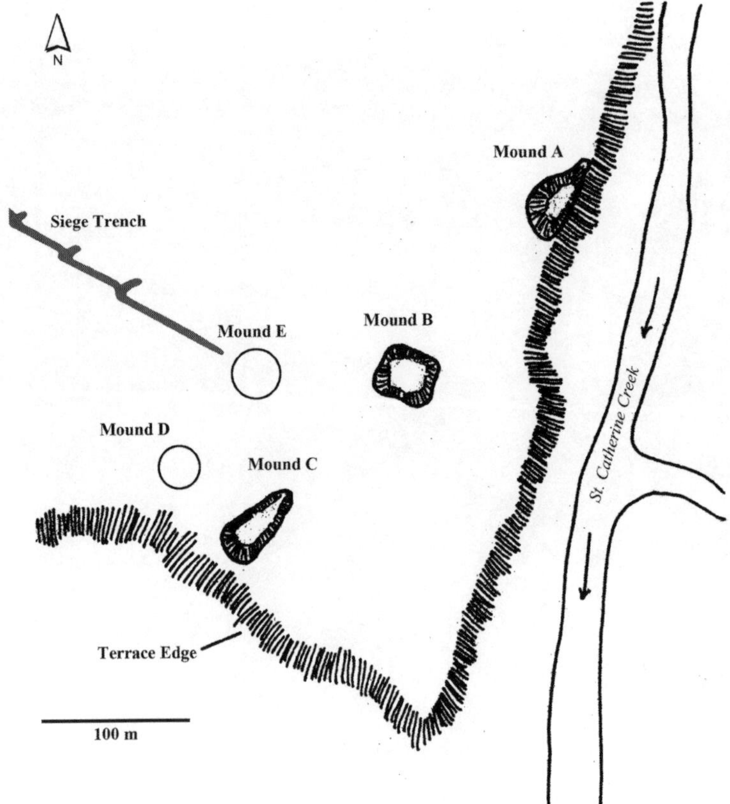

Figure 9.9. Map of the Fatherland site, showing the approximate locations of Mounds D and E, no longer visible, as well as the French siege trench.

Aboriginal tumuli; equi-distant from each other. The largest is twenty feet [7.6 m] in height and ninety feet [27.4 m] at base, and its form as nearly as we could determine, a rectangular pyramid. On the west side stand five large red elm trees, the largest upwards of three feet [.9 m] in diameter. The other two [mounds] being so much defaced by the sundry examinations, destroying entirely their original figure, but the Colonel informed me since, if his memory served him correctly, they were originally all of the same angles. The distance between each is fifty yards [45.7 m].

At present, they [the mounds] are united by a bank or line eight feet [2.4 m] high and twelve feet [3.7 m] at base, the soil of which has been chiefly taken from the north side of one of the small mounds, by the present proprietor, to protect the cotton crop from the destructive

> effects of an overflow from the St. Catherine, which runs in torrents shortly after an extensive rain. The west sides of the smaller mounds were covered with a small growth which deprived us, in a measure, of making a thorough examination. [Dickeson 1848:129–130]

This account makes clear that an artificial levee was raised between at least some of the surviving mounds at Fatherland, so as to keep St. Catherine Creek from flooding the cotton fields. To create this levee, the builders carved away portions of the mounds as sources of fill for construction.

The overseer for Bingaman's plantation provided Dickeson with both a work force and tools to dig the mounds: "We all repaired to the spot, and after taking their proper dimensions, and a sketch of the outlines of the group, we set our force to work. The overseer informed us, that in digging away the west side of one of the small mounds, to form the bank or levee, several fine terra cotta vases and jugs, highly ornamented, were found, and in every instance lying around the head and neck of the skeleton. Several of these were presented to the Rev. Mr. Chase, by the wife of the overseer, the others were in the possession of the blacks on the plantation, from whom we purchased them at their own price" [Dickeson 1848:130]. It is important to note in this passage that the "west side of one of the small mounds" was removed to form the levee, whereas in the previous quotation the "north side of one of the small mounds" was excavated. The first passage also mentioned that "the west sides of the smaller mounds were covered with a small growth which deprived us, in a measure, of making a thorough examination." Such dense vegetation is typical of recently disturbed ground and may have grown up after the earth removals he mentioned. In short, the edges of the mounds—perhaps all three that Dickeson saw—were already reduced by the early 1840s.

Dickeson also wrote of several mounds that stood apart from the three just described: "The open flank, to the west of the group, has been guarded by several smaller circular mounds, which has been cut down by a continued series of cultivation; but their outlines are readily seen after a recent ploughing. North of the main group stands a mound of considerable size, this contains a few bones, much decayed, and we thought of Choctaws from their burial. This was evidently used as an outpost" (Dickeson 1848:130). The two mounds "to the west of the group" were undoubtedly D and E. Although he said they were destroyed by cultivation, one cannot help but suspect that borrowing earth to construct the levee also played a role.

Dickeson's mention of a large mound to the north of the main group is of some interest, as it probably corresponds to Mound F. He continues: "A few years prior to my investigation, the extreme northern mound was partially examined by Dr. Powell, a distinguished phrenologist of the west, who obtained three crania. Two of the three were heads of Choctaws, a male and a female, which had been placed there within the remembrance of the proprietor, who informed me that the female head was that of a very beautiful Indian girl, not over twenty years old, who died while on a visit from her nation. Since the desertion of this part of the state by the Choctaws, it has been a custom for small tribes with their petty chiefs to visit annually Natchez, and barter their wares, skins, mocasins, &c., &c." (Dickeson 1848:130).[8] Whether or not these skulls were actually of people from Choctaw towns, it is fascinating that Indians may have been burying their dead in Natchez mounds as late as the first decades of the nineteenth century.[9] Dickeson says this mound was of considerable size, but no trace of it exists today. Its location on Broutin's map has long since been swallowed by St. Catherine Creek.

The Dr. Powell that Dickeson mentions is an interesting character—one William Byrd Powell, author of the 1856 book on *The Natural History of the Human Temperaments*. From the introduction to this volume, we learn that Powell was active in the South in 1835, when he gave a series of lectures at the Medical College of Louisiana. At one point he states, "During the course, we demonstrated the truth of our doctrines by crania furnished by the class" (Powell 1856:11). One wonders whether the Fatherland skulls were included among the instructional crania.

Before leaving the nineteenth century, it is worth considering the exploits of another local scholar—Benjamin L. C. Wailes, who served as Mississippi's first state geologist (Sydnor 1938). Wailes was very interested in the archaeology of Mississippi and recorded many sites during the years he was employed by the state (Brown 1998a; Wailes 1843–1862, 1852/1854). Following a visit made on March 2, 1853, he noted a number of mounds on Bingaman's plantation. The levee that Dickeson described 11 years earlier clearly had been breached by the time Wailes made his study:

> At St. Catherine, near the bridge, up the creek ¼ of a mile [.4 km], is the group of mounds, three in number, the site of an old indian village. The largest is highest up the creek and near the bank. They all seem to have been square or rectangular. The largest is some ten or 15 ft [4.6 m] high and seem to have been about one hundred ft [30.5 m] square on the top. All have been much modified and dug away, the earth taken to form a levee along the creek from mound to mound to protect the bottom fields from overflow of the creek, but without success; a recent freshet has covered a large portion of the flat and left large quantities of mud or silt spread over it. A few bones and a

> little pottery were seen on the sides of the mounds where the earth had been dug away . . . the larger mound with a group of large elm trees growing on the northern, the northern side remains of its original form and dimensions. The outline of the other sides can be recognized, but the earth has been removed considerably by the plow, the washing of the rains and the overflow of the creek. Mound B. shows also a part of one side in its original state, but more than half of it has been removed by digging down the sides. The small and lowest mound C. has already been entirely destroyed. [Wailes 1853, in Brown 1996:15–16]

It is clear that the number of mounds had diminished since Dickeson explored the site, as Wailes's description corresponds to the way the Fatherland site appeared throughout the following century. Of particular interest, however, is Wailes's comment with regard to soil movement, wherein he says, "A recent freshet has covered a large portion of the flat and left large quantities of mud or silt spread over it." We believe that event was not unique and explains why soil accumulated to such great depth at the site and why it proved so troublesome to Neitzel in his 1972 excavations. The levee that ran from mound to mound is undoubtedly the earthwork that Neitzel encountered (see figure 9.1), and the one that he mistakenly attributed to the French.

Summary and Conclusions

Based on a study of French colonial maps—some only recently discovered—and a fresh look at nineteenth-century texts, we have come up with a more accurate view of the early eighteenth-century landscape of the Grand Village. What the site looked like earlier is anyone's guess, but it is reasonably clear now that there were originally at least six mounds at the site and that half of them disappeared in the mid-nineteenth century as a result of levee building and erosion.

We can now describe and compare the mounds as they appear on the maps. Doing so yields insights on their functions both before and during the siege (Table 9.1; Figures 9.1, 9.10, 9.11). Some of the descriptive labels applied to the mounds refer to how they were used by the Indians, and others to how they were employed by the French. Let us consider each mound in turn.

Mound A only appears on the Broutin 1723 map and was not involved at all in the siege. However, we now know it was occupied historically, as it had three square buildings on its summit and one smaller round structure.

Table 9.1. Mounds Shown on French Maps

	Broutin 1723		Anonymous 1730		Caillot 1730	
	Buildings	Description	Buildings	Description	Buildings	Description
Mound A	4	(none)	—	—	—	—
Mound B	2	*cabanne du grand chef* (cabin of the great chief)	0	(none)	0	*butte* (mound)
Mound C	1	*temple neuf* (new temple)	1	*temple des Natchez* (Natchez temple)	1	*corps de l'armée* (headquarters)
Mound D	1	*vieux temple* (old temple)	1	*vieux temple abandonné* (old abandoned temple)	1	*les blessez* (the injured)
Mound E	0	(none)	0	*batterie de 2 pièces* (two-piece battery)	0	*temple des Natchez* (Natchez temple)
Mound F	0	(none)	—	—	—	—

Mound B is depicted in 1723 with two buildings on its summit, which Broutin called the cabin of the great chief ("cabanne du grand chef"). It is therefore interesting that both 1730 siege maps show nothing on top. Both are silent as to this earthwork's function, and Caillot's map simply labels it a mound ("butte"). Whether the chief's house had been dismantled before the siege, or the building was omitted because it played no role in the battle, we may never know.

Mound C is consistently topped by a building in all three maps. This structure is called the new temple ("temple neuf") by Broutin, the Natchez temple ("temple des Natchez") on the anonymous map, and the army's headquarters ("corps de l'armée") by Caillot. The clear implication is that the Natchez temple was repurposed as the French command post during the siege, a conclusion supported by historical accounts that state the French commander took up residence there (Charlevoix 1872:98; Claiborne 1880:46; Merveilleux 2003:17; Rowland and Sanders 1927:78; cf.). Both siege maps show the summit encircled by a parapet, undoubtedly built by the French.[10]

Mound D is also consistently shown with a building called the old temple by Broutin and the old abandoned temple by the anonymous cartographer. On Caillot's map, however, it is marked "*les blessez*" (the injured), which im-

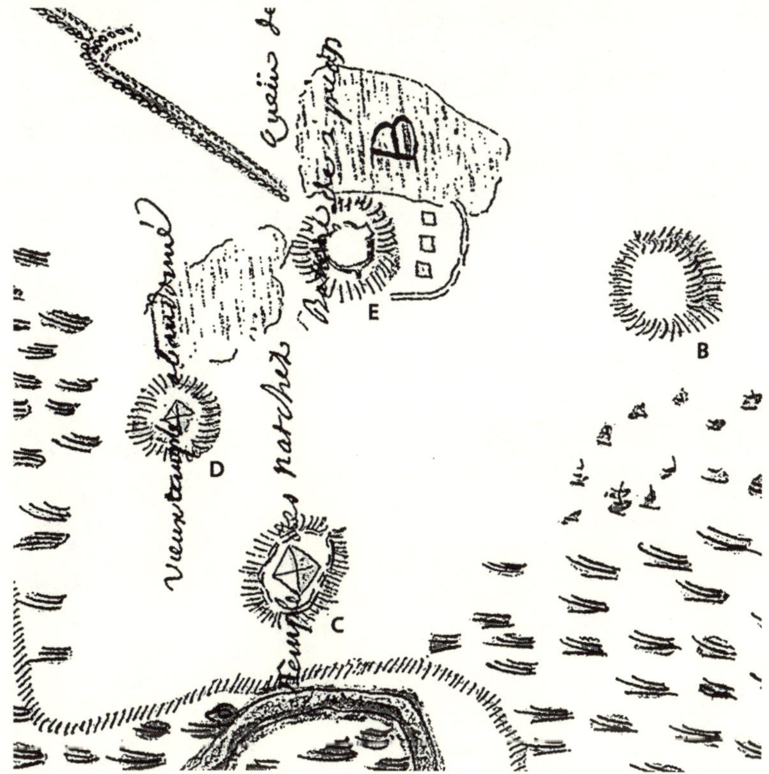

Figure 9.10. Detail from anonymous 1730 siege map, reoriented with north at the top. Mound descriptions as they appear on the map: Mound B, no description; Mound C, Natchez temple ("temple des Natchez"); Mound D, old abandoned temple ("vieux temple abandonné"); Mound E, two-piece battery ("batterie de 2 pièces") (adapted from the original).

plies the French converted it to a field hospital. If the structure was weather-tight enough to be used in this way, it clearly had not been abandoned by the Indians for very long, if at all.[11]

Mound E has no wooden building depicted on any of the maps, but both siege maps place a French parapet there. The anonymous cartographer explicitly identified this parapet as a "*batterie de 2 pièces*" (an artillery battery), while Caillot incongruously labeled it the "*temple des Natchez*" (the Natchez temple). The latter description makes no sense in the absence of a roofed structure. Perhaps Caillot's label was a mistake introduced when his map (or an earlier version of it) was copied. Then again, it may refer to the summit's previous use. A number of historical accounts allude to a battery on or near the Natchez temple, but all are either ambiguous (Clai-

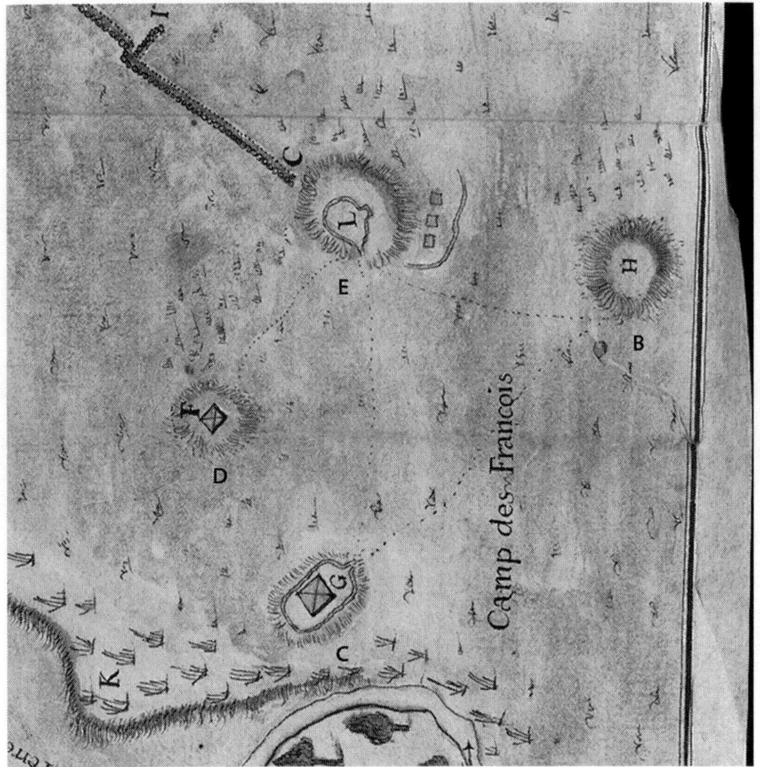

Figure 9.11. Detail from the Caillot 1730 siege map, re-oriented with north at the top. Mound descriptions as they appear in the map's legend: Mound B, mound ("butte"); Mound C, headquarters ("corps de l'armée"); Mound D, the injured ("les blessez"); Mound E, Natchez temple ("temple des Natchez") (The Historic New Orleans Collection, acc. no. 2005.0011).

borne 1880:46) or second hand (Gayarré 1854:429–430), leaving open the possibility that they conflated the French "post" established in the temple on Mound D with the battery on Mound E (cf. Swanton 1911:238). Whether or not Mound E ever supported an Indian temple, it was clearly used by the French during the siege.[12]

Mound F only appears on Broutin's 1723 map. It is clearly a mound, as it has the same identifying characteristics as the other mounds, but the lack of structures on its surface suggests it was no longer in use. Paths run by it but not up to it. It is perhaps the mound that Powell investigated, as discussed earlier, but we will never know for sure because it had disappeared by the early twentieth century.

In sum, the six mounds at the Grand Village supported a chief's residence, at least two temples, and several wooden structures of unknown functions. From maps generated in 1723 and 1730, we know that at least some of the mound summits were bare, and one (Mound B) may have lost its building in the interim. During the 1730 siege, three of the mounds were commandeered by the French for use as a headquarters, a field hospital, and an artillery emplacement, an act the Indians undoubtedly viewed as a desecration (Barnett 2007:116). At some time in the mid-nineteenth century these mounds fed into the economy of the region. Whereas the Indians valued them for their sanctity, the new inhabitants saw them merely as sources of soil and scientific amusement. Three of the mounds (D, E, and F) disappeared completely and the other three (A, B, and C) were badly damaged.[13] Earth borrowed from several contributed to a massive levee, the feature Neitzel detected in his excavations but did not quite understand. New data have helped solve the riddle and, at the same time, shed light on this amazingly complex and interesting site. The Grand Village itself truly was grand and around its periphery are stories yet to be told.

Acknowledgments

Our thanks go to James Barnett, James Brown, Kathleen DuVal, Erin Greenwald, Elizabeth Jones, David Morgan, and to the volume editors for their help and useful comments. In addition, we will always be grateful to Robert S. Neitzel, who was a great mentor and friend to both of us as we began our careers in archaeology. It feels good to finally solve a puzzle that so vexed him as he dug Fatherland in the summer of 1972, when we all shared a field house on the bluff in Natchez.

Notes

1. The engraving was published in Dumont's *Mémoires historiques sur la Louisiane* (1753, vol. 2: facing p. 94). The four manuscripts were drawn in Dumont's own hand, all in the 1740s: "Fort Rozalie des Natchez," Service historique de la Défense, Département de l'Armée de Terre, Etat-Major 7C 211 (Neitzel 1983: Plate Ia); "Carte du Fort Rozalie des Natchez François," Archives nationales, Paris, Cartes et Plans, N III Louisiane 1/2 (Neitzel 1983: Plate Ib); "Carte de la Disposition des Maisons des Habitants Francois des Natchez," from "*Poème en vers touchant l'établissement de la province de la Louisiane,*" 1744, Bibliothèque nationale de France, Arsenal, MS-3459 (Villiers 1931: Figure 43); and "Carte du Fort Rozalie des Natches Francois avec ses Dependances et Village des Sauvages," from "Memoire de Lxx Dxx Officiere Ingenieur," 1747, Newberry Library, vault oversize Ayer MS 257 map 9 (Dumont 2012: Plate 4). Detailed images of all are posted online at *Early Maps of the American South,* http://rla.unc.edu/emas/local-settl.html.

2. In addition to these holograph maps, there exists an unsigned manuscript that is often attributed to Dumont (Green 1936: Plate 1): "Carte Particulière des Natchez Établi par

les François et Détruit par les Sauvages du Dit Lieu en 1729," Service historique de la Défense, département Marine, Cartes et plans, recueil 68, no. 60, formerly in Bibliothèque de la Service hydrographique, 4044C-48. This map is drawn by a different hand and in a style somewhat different from Dumont's. Even so, this map so resembles Dumont's holograph maps in the content and layout that a relationship is undeniable. One possibility is that it was a copy made by (or for) the cartographer Phillipe Buache, with whom Dumont collaborated in the early 1750s (Sayre 2012:41). See *Early Maps of the American South*, http://rla.unc.edu/emas/local-settl.html.

3. The map is titled "Carte des Environs du Fort Rosalie aux Natchez" (Bibliothèque nationale de France, Département des cartes et plans, Ge DD 2987–8834B). Although long listed in a published finding aid (Leland 1932:228) and mentioned in an article by Samuel Wilson (1982:201), this map drew little attention from scholars until a detailed scan was posted online by the Bibliothèque nationale in 2007 (http://gallica.bnf.fr/ark:/12148/btv1b530530625). The map was then rediscovered by Joseph V. Frank, who brought it to our attention. We are also grateful to Elizabeth Jones for her help in translating portions of this map.

4. The full title is "Plans des Deux Forts des Natchez Assiégés au Mois de Février 1730 Par les Français / Tchactas Tonicas Colapissas et Oumas / La Présente Carte Levée sur les Lieux à L'Estime / Faite et Dessinée a la N.lle Orleans Le Six Avril / Mil Sept Cent Trente" (Bibliothèque nationale de France, Estampes, Vd 21 (3) Fol.). Neitzel (1983: Plate IIa) published an inverted photograph of this map, consistent with his idea that the north arrow was wrong (see also Neitzel 1978: Figure 1a).

5. We know that Broutin sent a map of the 1730 siege to Maurepas in Paris, as did Étienne de Périer, the governor of Louisiane (Rowland and Sanders 1927:72, 135). Of the two men, Broutin is the one who took part in the siege and was an excellent cartographer. Hence, it is plausible, indeed likely, that he made one or both of these maps. The anonymous map under consideration here was clearly not drafted by Broutin, as the handwriting in the cartouche does not match his neat and distinctive script. Of course, it was not at all unusual for manuscript maps to be copied, in which case the handwriting would match that of the draftsman rather than the cartographer. The designations of the temple buildings on the mounds in the anonymous 1730 map are similar to those on Broutin's 1723 map and imply that the cartographer knew of their use before the siege—a knowledge that Broutin certainly possessed. All in all, the evidence of Broutin's authorship is suggestive but not definitive. It is also worth noting that this map uses letter labels (A, B, and C) that are not explained in a legend, the kind of error one might expect in a hastily drawn copy.

6. Caillot's map is called "Plan de la Guerre des Natchez" and is bound as an illustration in his manuscript memoir titled "*Relation du Voyage de la Louisianne ou Nouvelle France fait par Sr. Caillot en l'Annee 1730*" (The Historic New Orleans Collection, MSS 596). This remarkable memoir surfaced about a decade ago and was acquired at auction by The Historic New Orleans Collection in 2005. It has recently been published in translation (Greenwald 2013; the map appears as Plate 22). A detailed comparison of Caillot's drawing with the anonymous siege map reveals some interesting differences. The anonymous map covers a much larger area than Caillot's, but the latter is not simply a subset of the former. Rather, each map includes some territory that the other lacks, with Caillot's drawing extending farther to the west, and the anonymous one farther to the north, east, and south. This pattern suggests that both maps are copies descended from a larger original. Although the general configuration of the two maps is very similar, they are

different in some details, including the labels applied to some of the mounds (see table 9.1) and the locations of some of the Indian camps. For example, the anonymous map places the "*camp des Chactas*" (Choctaw camp) to the northeast of the mounds, whereas Caillot's map places it to the northwest. Such differences raise the possibility that there may have been more than one original.

7. Curiously, Dickeson did not include a description of Fatherland in his manuscript, "Catalogue of the Stone and Terra Cotta Implements and Ornaments of the North American Mound Builders" (University of Pennsylvania Museum of Archaeology and Anthropology, Archives, American Section), even though the same document lists many artifacts from the site. An edited version of this manuscript was published by Culin (1900).

8. Joseph Holt Ingraham's 1835 book, *The South-west by a Yankee*, also contains a rambling description of Fatherland. At one point Ingraham states, "One of these [mounds] was recently excavated by Dr. Powell, a distinguished phrenologist of the west" (1835, vol. 2:217). It seems that Dickeson was familiar with Ingraham's description of Powell and had no qualms about using it verbatim.

9. There are many accounts of "Choctaws" in the Natchez district and throughout the southern lower Mississippi Valley in the 1820s through 1840s. One gets the impression that "Choctaw" was commonly used in that area as a synonym for Indian, in much the same way that the term "Cherokee" was used in the Carolinas. That said, Ingraham (1835, vol. 2:217), in his own account of Powell's finds, describes two of the skulls as "Choctaw" and one as "Natchez," further evidence that all such designations must be taken with a healthy dose of skepticism.

10. In addition to the well-known published accounts of the 1730 siege, a manuscript by Jean-Baptiste Delaye, a French *habitant* who participated in the battle, describes it in great detail ("*Relation du massacre des françois aux Natchez et de la guerre contre ces sauvages, 1er juin 1730*," Archives nationales d'Outre-Mer, 04DFC 38). A helpful English translation of this narrative was recently posted online by Gordon Sayre (http://darkwing.uoregon.edu/~gsayre/De Laye on Natchez massacre slation.htm). Delaye confirms that the French command post was the Natchez temple, which he alternately called "*maison de valleur*" or "*temple de valleur*" (pp. 32, 34, 35, 44). This suggests the term *valeur* was associated with the Grand Village—not surprising given that it can be taken as a loose synonym for *grand*, i.e., both words carry the connotation of "important." If this congruence holds, then it provides a valuable clue to the identity of the Indians involved in the battle, for "Valeur" was also the name the French used for one of the two Natchez forts under attack (see figure 9.5). The second Natchez fort, directly across St. Catherine Creek from Valeur, was called "*Farine*," also the name of a Natchez town. All in all, it appears that each fort was associated with a different town, which in turn suggests that the other Natchez towns (such as White Apple, Jenzenaque, and Grigra) may not have participated in this fight (cf. Barnett 2007:114). For more on Delaye, see Giraud (1991:178–180).

11. James Brown (1990:6–8) reviews the various written descriptions of "the Natchez temple" over the period from 1700 through the 1720s and notes their many inconsistencies (see also Swanton 1911:158–173). Given what we now know from the cartographic evidence, at least some of these apparent inconsistencies may be due to the fact that there were two temples, not one.

12. At the height of the battle, Delaye was stationed in the French emplacement atop Mound E, which he described as being protected by a "low wall," consistent with the parapet shown on both 1730 maps (op. cit., p. 45).

13. Although Mounds D and E are no longer visible, traces of them may still remain

in the earth. In 1984, a deep utility trench excavated just west of the former location of Mound E encountered archaeological deposits dating to the early eighteenth century, and perhaps a bit earlier (Barnett 1984). These deposits included at least two pit features, a line of postholes, and a thick, refuse-filled accumulation that may have been a midden or the edge of a low mound—perhaps a small earthwork not recorded by the French, as it seems a bit too far west to be part of Mound E. All of these remains were found below 1.6 m of sterile overburden, which covered the former Indian settlement during the nineteenth century and nowadays both hides and protects any portions of Mounds D and E that survive.

10

NUANCES OF MEMORY

Historical Legend vs. Legendary History

George E. Lankford

Oral narrative, commonly known as oral history, allows us to carry the story of Southeastern identities seamlessly across the largely artificial "prehistoric/historic" divide. With narratives drawn from the three principal segments of Southeastern society—Native Americans and peoples of European and African descent—I explore how legend has always helped build and express community identity while giving a public voice to issues of contention.

When asked to tell about something that happened in the past, most people respond with a story. If history teachers expect to keep students' attention, they tell stories. It's a human characteristic—history is remembered as stories. Historians tend to dismiss stories as inaccurate historical sources, while folklorists enthusiastically analyze them as historical insights. One kind of story identified by folklorists is called historical legend, but a much broader sweep of legends could be called legendary history. This chapter defines some folklore boundaries and rules for interpreting historical content, and, in the process, explores several bodies of legends.

Here are some brief propositions for consideration. First, legends are *oral* narratives. We humans spoke long before we wrote, and billions of people have been able to hear without being able to read or write. Legends are *living* forms of communication, and they are produced by most people to this very day, even in literate societies. Some of our legends may have an antiquity of millennia, whether we can prove it or not. That may make us a bit uncomfortable, because we are so accustomed to the unnatural habits of literacy that we readily think of legends as written texts. Those who study the historical dimension of legends are usually forced to deal with written texts—whether Indian myths, Biblical accounts, or Greek myths—and we have to remind ourselves constantly that these texts are not the original legends, which were oral in nature.

Second proposition: Legends are oral *narratives*. There are lots of verbal forms of folk narrative, such as jokes, proverbs, anecdotes, and so on. The two longer genres that concern us here, though, are folktales and legends. Let me try to contrast them, because that will give us some helpful demarcations. Both tell stories, which is why we call them narratives. Both usually presuppose a prior agreement between teller and hearer as to which genre they are indulging in. Folktales, or simply "tales," are fiction, and they frequently include markers to alert the listener to the genre, such as "once upon a time" or "it was a dark and stormy night." Or even "on a planet far, far away." When we hear the clue, we know to set our minds for a fictional story. That's important, because the way we listen, the way we understand, is determined by our assumption that we know the genre and therefore know the rules for listening. We know, for example, that for a tale we must be willing to suspend disbelief, that we should give the taleteller the latitude to change even the laws of physics as the plot develops. Most six year-olds are adept at recognizing the bedtime story genre, so they know not to ask whether horses can fly; of course they can, in tales.

The importance of genre leads us to a third proposition: The legend is not fictional. Just the opposite: Legends are about reality. More precisely, legends are about beliefs about reality. Reality is too big and too complex for us to understand, even if we focus on just what we can personally perceive and experience. Factoring in the aggregate perceptions and experiences of all of us is beyond possibility. So we make connections between those experiences that seem to "make sense." Then we agree to believe as a group in that way of making sense of the world. We call it culture. One of our strongest beliefs about our beliefs is that we are right. "Wrong thinking" is measured by the extent to which other people disagree with us.

Experiences of reality keep changing on us, though, and anthropologists have taught us that successful societies are those that can adapt the culture—the belief complex—to accommodate new experiences. Stories about new experiences—legends—cause speculation and doubt. Those two, doubt and speculation, are useful characteristics of human beings, because they are the mental tools that enable us to test whether our worldview still fits our experiences. Most of us are smart enough not to test our theories too directly. The man who tests the belief in gravity by jumping off a tall building we call demented—and deceased. Yet we might want to argue, at least, about whether all objects fall at the same rate, or whether a staircase from Pontius Pilate's palace in Jerusalem really flew through the air to Rome. In the latter case, whether or not we believe it, we call it a "saints' legend" and recognize it as an important subgenre of legend.

In fact, the word "legend" comes from the old church practice of reading the stories of the Christian saints on their assigned ecclesiastical calendar dates. By medieval times, most of the major saints had the stories of their deeds, including the required miracles, recorded in books that were used as the source for reading aloud to congregations and monastic orders at meals and in liturgies. One famous collection is Jacobus de Voragine's *Legenda Aurea* (Voragine 1941). The stories were the "golden readings"—*legenda*—for education and inspiration. To name oral narratives "readings" rather than "listenings" is a nice bit of literate irony.

One major function of the stories of the saints is to reinforce the Christian belief that the divine power must be part of everyone's worldview. Miracle stories are offered as evidence of the validity of that realm of belief. Those narratives are emphatically not for entertainment by fiction or fantasy, but truths buttressing belief. The legends are a vital part of an ongoing discussion of the nature of reality. Each one tacitly poses the question, "Is your ordinary worldview big enough to make sense of everything that happens?"

The fourth proposition about legends is this: At the heart of every legend, whether or not directly expressed, is one or more beliefs. That does not imply or require that the legend teller believe the story. It may be told as an invitation to rebuttal by a skeptic. The belief embedded in the legend is its heart and is independent of the beliefs of the narrator. A little probing of the content of the story will reveal some beliefs that are challenged or affirmed by this event that is claimed to have really happened.

This can be easily tested. Gather a few people around a campfire some night and ask them whether ghosts exist. The response will be a flood of both narrative performances and discussion, and the focal point will be the beliefs challenged by the claims of the stories about reality. This insight about the inherent relationship of legend and belief can be seen in most of the subcategories of legend, such as disaster legends (hurricanes, tornadoes, floods, fires), heroic legends (courage under fire, superhuman achievements), urban legends (organ theft, cobras in imported carpets, microwaved cats). Do you believe those things happened? Should you?

One more definitional nuance is needed. Folklorists are careful to separate personal experience narratives from legends. Some narrators insist that the story they wish to tell is derived from their own experience, and they are likely to insist that it is a historical account. Such narratives, frequently called *memorates*, claim the authority of personal knowledge and thus can readily slide into the category of oral history. Memorates need to be judged carefully by canons of evidence, evaluated in the light of what we know now about the untrustworthiness of eyewitness accounts and the dynamics of memory formation. Interpreting and evaluating memorates is a different process from trying to understand legends, and folklorists emphasize that legends must be recognized as second-hand stories at best. Years ago, when I first began reading the many volumes of ex-slave narratives compiled by the Works Progress Administration (WPA), I quickly saw the importance of determining whether the narrator was telling a memorate or passing on the stories of her parents, which are by definition legends, belief stories in the oral tradition. We think about the two genres differently.

This kind of struggle with definitions is tedious, but it highlights different kinds of questions about these narratives. Let me summarize a general definition of legend: Legends are oral traditional narratives that offer purportedly historical events as evidence of the correspondence of reality and worldview; they spring from articulated or tacit beliefs about reality, usually those that are contested or part of ongoing discussion. Beliefs and legend themes are developed from conversational origins into artful performances by outstanding narrators, at which point they take on some of the characteristics of tales. When they are written down, the stories then become the basis of literary treatments and achieve new patterns of diffusion, reaching wider audiences and taking on new meanings and functions, such as entertainment. Folklorists delight in spotting in movies and books narrative motifs and tale types (which have all been numbered and cataloged; Thompson 1956–1960).

Bert Wilson, one of the many folklorists who has wrestled with the relation between history and legend, offers a useful observation about the problem of obtaining a cultural understanding of historical events:

> Every individual view of events is just that, an individual view. Hence the need for broad sampling of opinion, something not always easy when many of the people from a period being studied are either dead or have lost from memory details of earlier years. Folklore, on the other hand, provides a sort of automatic random sampling. No matter what the origin of a folklore item, it will, if it is to survive, move from the individual expression of its originator to the communal expression of those who preserve it, sloughing off as it passes from person to person and through time and space the marks of individual invention, and in a short time reflecting quite accurately the consensus of the group (Wilson 1979:456).

Group consensus is not necessarily a path to revealing and documenting a specific set of details about an event, or even that it happened, but it does open the possibility of understanding the way the society has chosen to interpret and remember it. In short, there may be a different kind of understanding of the past that can be gleaned from "legendary history" in contrast to "historical legend." It can be a useful exercise to examine ways of interpreting legendary history, forcing legends to provide historical insights. It is this pursuit of the historical contributions of legend research that provides this chapter's title. One of the characteristics of legend is the tendency of tellers to disguise the genre as normal conversation (i.e., historical). This point will be made tacitly by examining specific legends from peoples of the American Southeast, including Native Americans, Europeans and European Americans, and African Americans. In every case the legends, even though they may be recognizable as general stories, are thoroughly linked to the particularities of those social groups.

Native American

Legends contain embedded beliefs that are part of the cultural discussion, and they serve as preservers and transmitters of worldview. They are clues to the beliefs, and the telling of legends within the society provides a teaching and reinforcing mechanism for passing on the cultural belief system. If the legends are focused on ultimate beliefs, those that today would be considered basic religious concepts, then we give this subgenre of legend the name "myth." Here is an example.

Antoine Le Page du Pratz, a French colonist, lived among the Natchez tribe from 1718 to 1734. (Nah-chay is the way it was said, but the English-speaking town uses Na-chez.) He kept a journal that provided the basis for a memoir that gives us a great deal of the surviving cultural information about that tribe. After war with the French in 1729 and the flight of Natchez survivors to the Creeks and Chickasaws, Le Page du Pratz returned to France, where in 1758 he published his book.

For brevity's sake, let me summarize a legend he recorded from the chief guardian of the Natchez temple. Their ancestors were taught their religion by a "brilliant" man and woman who came from the sky to enlighten them. They were taught how to build a temple where a flame brought from the sun was used to start a fire that was to be perpetually maintained by teams of holy men. Later on, after the couple had returned to the sky, one of the keepers stepped out of the temple for a while, and the other keeper inside dozed off and allowed the fire to go out. When he realized what he had done, he secured from a passerby an ordinary coal "to light his pipe," and the fire was restarted. Within days sickness broke out among the ruling family, the Suns, who were thought to be descended from the ancient couple. The Suns began to die, and in four years the tribe was badly reduced. The temple guardian who had committed the crime also fell terminally ill. Despairing, he confessed his crime to the new chief Sun. The polluted fire was extinguished and a coal brought from a sacred fire in another town. The sacred fire was restarted, and the people regained their health (Swanton 1911:171–172).

This is clearly a legend whose superficial purpose is a warning about preserving the sacred fire. There is more than that here, though. Here is a beginning list of what can be learned from this story. The Natchez believed their traditions were not indigenous but were brought to them by culture-bringers, a couple from the sky who was related to the Sun. In some way (progeny?), they left descendants who became the ruling family of the Natchez. A key symbol of the relationship with the sky people is the preservation of the fire from the sun in a special building, but the fire is more than a memorial recalling a primordial event. The original temple has been replicated in other locations as the tribe has grown and split, and the original fire has been extended to those places. Although multiplied, each fire remains the original because it is protected from ordinary use by religious specialists who guard the fire and preserve it from extinction. Although this myth does not mention it, there were probably specified ritual usages of the fire by the town leaders.

While the keepers of the fire were charged with its protection, the societal responsibility for maintaining the purity of the fire is emphasized in the taboos surrounding the fire. The ultimate protection of the fire's sacredness rests in the fire's special nature, for to break the taboos is to break the relationship between the tribe and the celestial source that originally gave them the solar fire. The result of the severed relationship with the Sun is not dependent on any human awareness of the break, for the sanction, in the form of sickness and death, follows in an impersonal, automatic way. In fact, the disaster that struck the society was the clue that the relationship had been broken.

There is good news in the story, though. The relationship can be restored by the extinction of the false fire and its replacement by solar fire from another temple. When that is done, the sickness and death drop to normal levels. The myth thus reinforces the importance of maintaining the fire by obeying the taboo rules. The fact that the irresponsible guardian of the fire also dies of disease bespeaks a sense of cosmic justice, and his fate gives successive generations an idea of the extraordinary disgrace he bears.

The myth does not have to be probed too deeply to reveal that it also implies a strong principle of societal organization: the ruling family, called Suns, have that role because they are related to the Sun, and therefore the fire. It seems right that they are the ones who suffer sickness and death, for they claim the special relationship to justify their political power. The fact that the sacred fire can be understood to maintain its connection to the Sun even when it is exported to other locations is also a way of saying that the ruling family can extend its hegemony to other towns, for the family and the fire are linked. We should not be surprised to learn from other sources that other peoples of the Southeast also maintained sacred fires, and that to "share fire," to "be of one fire" with another town, is a metaphor for political and cultural affiliation.

This myth can yield further insights when compared with equivalents from other tribes. The continuation of the illness and death among the Natchez for more than four years means that the sacred fire is understood to be permanent, without break. Examination of the concept of other peoples, such as the Muskogean-speaking Choctaw, Chickasaw, and Creek towns across the Southeast, reveals that they believed the sacred fire became weakened and polluted just by normal existence through time, and so it is ritually extinguished and restarted by priestly figures every year. The "new fire" ceremony of those peoples, although it rests on the same basic principles as the Natchez sacred fire, is in contrast to the insistence on perpetual, uninterrupted fire in the lower Mississippi Valley. The Natchez myth thus even offers a clue to drawing a cultural boundary line between groups of similar peoples. The Natchez, at least, were distanced from the others by their belief that under normal circumstances no weakening of the fire's power occurs. That was, in modern terms, a doctrinal difference.

That is a lot of information to glean from a brief account of a single event in Natchez traditional history, but that is one of the gifts provided by myths: they carry a lot of knowledge, thus serving as the libraries of nonliterate societies. This example underlines the principle that myth as a subgenre of legend is about reality and truth, the very opposite of the current popular usage of "myth" to mean "lie."

European and European American

In 1541, the world of the Natchez met the world of the Europeans in the form of 600 people encased in metal clothing who came by way of Tampa Bay to claim La Florida—the land north of Mexico—for the Spanish crown. Hernando de Soto and his army did not actually meet the Natchez, because the chief refused them entrance into his territory. They probably saw each other because the Natchez were surely part of the "armada" of large boats that chased the surviving Spaniards down the Mississippi in 1542, killing a few more of them before they reached the Gulf and escaped to Mexico.

As these Spanish explorers crossed the Southeast, legends of their behavior on their journey must have preceded them, prompting the natives' hostility to their visitors before they even met them. The legends they told about the Spaniards are lost, but the legends the Spaniards told about the peoples of La Florida were written down.

The Soto expedition was a perfect mechanism for the creation of legends (Lankford 1993). The 600 men and a few women were in a bubble of linguistic and cultural isolation moving across the land from people to people. They spoke none of the languages they heard and understood little of the cultures they were seeing. They tried to figure out these people who were neither Christians nor Spanish, but the real communication occurred in their own conversations around camp fires at night as weary soldiers tried to understand what they had seen and heard. They talked, and their anecdotes were memorates offered for comparison with their comrades' experiences. Their speculative interpretations fed the narratives and transformed them into legends. It is useful to think of legends as negotiated memory. That is what the Spanish conquistadores were doing—creating a narrative about the new reality embodied in the inhabitants of La Florida. Their fireside conversations were memorates being reborn into legends. The long-term result was a set of books, their legends written down as history to be argued about by generations after them trying to make sense of the New World of the Other they encountered (Clayton et al. 1993; Lankford 2009).

Soon after they landed in Tampa Bay, they were greeted by a "native" who turned out to be Juan Ortiz, a Spaniard who had been captured off a passing ship, enslaved, and enculturated by the natives. As he recovered his Spanish language, he told his story—how his life had been saved by the wife or daughter of a chief, an incident that may have inspired John Smith's story of how his life had been saved by Pocahontas six decades later (Clayton, et al. 1993: vol. 1, 60, 232, 255; vol.2, 63–81; Rountree 1990:38–39.). Ortiz told how he had become a successful slave, how he miraculously killed a panther with a spear while guarding a cemetery, and how he became a warrior and friend of the chief, who released him to return to his own people when Soto's army arrived. It was a grand story, and it found its way into the legendry of the army, even though Ortiz himself—like Soto—died in Arkansas. In the chronicles the details vary, but the romantic heart of the legend was preserved.

Because at the core of legends lives one or more beliefs, each narrator who passes on an evolving legend has an opportunity to add to it (or "correct it") from his own store of beliefs. That process can easily be seen in the Soto chronicles, for the medieval eyes used their belief in divine providence to see in various events evidence of the Christian God at work on their behalf. When Ortiz first saw Spanish knights, he screamed a "pious ejaculation" to the Virgin Mother, thus identifying himself as a Christian and saving himself from being skewered on a Spanish lance (Clayton et al., 1993: vol.1, 59, 225, 255; vol. 2, 114). When the army bivouacked at Casqui in the Arkansas delta, they raised a cross on a mound. All later agreed that this Christian act of faith caused the rain to fall, breaking the long drought of which the natives complained and bringing them to the Faith (Clayton et al. 1993: vol. 1, 116, 240, 300; vol. 2, 391–393).

Casqui is now a state park in Arkansas where the mound where they raised the miraculous cross can be seen (Morse 1981). By the time of Soto's journey, crosses were already known as rain-makers, one of several types of miracle by which European adventurers were seen to be (or saw themselves to be) agents of God to convert the savages. The saints' legends are no more surprising in the Soto chronicles than they are in the Venerable Bede's history of the church in England. Legends begin as conversation about experience, continue as debate about reality, and end as narratives offering evidence of incredible truths.

Hidden behind the particular belief in such legends is a deeper belief that reality is repetitious. If the Hand of God is seen in one cross and rain storm, it may be seen at work again. It may be seen in other legends of the divine work, from the arrow that split the lance of Nuño de Tovar at the battle of Mabila, turning it into a cross and saving his life, to the modern mold stain on a wall or pizza on which the faithful can see the face of Christ (Clayton et al. 1993: vol. 1, 127; vol. 2, 341).

That same reflection of firmly held beliefs about reality can be seen in another way in the legends. The last and longest of the chronicles of the Soto journey is *La Florida del Inca*, written by a half-Spaniard, half-Inca from conquered Peru. Garcilaso de la Vega, El Inca, wrote his account long after the journey on the basis of interviews with survivors, because he was not there (Clayton et al. 1993, vol. 2). He saw himself as living the struggle between Spanish and Indians in his own body, and he early set himself to be the champion of the natives of the New World. In his narrative of Soto's journey, he frequently criticized Soto for his treatment of the natives, while the stories of the behavior of the Indians—perhaps gleaned from his informants—became legends of the nobility of the natives. They tell of bravery, skill, courtesy, and honor worthy of a Spanish knight. Legend follows belief, and somewhere in the mix may be some historical fact.

Historians, though, are forced to recall that *La Florida* has been called "an early work of Chicano literature," written by a man with a bicultural mind aware that the eyes of the king were likely to read his pages (Lankford 2009:40). Garcilaso serves as a warning: The legend researcher must continually be sensitive to the possibility that behind a legend may lurk a hidden agenda, often a political, financial, or psychological goal.

Three centuries after the Soto journey, an incident occurred in the lower Mississippi Valley that illustrates the possible consequences of the cynical use of legends to serve hidden agendas. The legendary history of the "Murrell gang" was so deeply rooted in the fears of white antebellum society regarding their African slaves that the result was a major historical event. Such cases could be called "panic legends" because they emerge out of fear, feed the public panic, and end in violence (see, e.g., Victor 1993).

The historical facts are quickly told (Penick 1981). John A. Murrell, born in 1806, was sent to jail in Williamson County, Tennessee, in 1822 for horse theft. Released from jail in 1827, he moved to Wayne County, then to Madison County, where he ran a gang of robbers in west Tennessee and east Arkansas until his arrest and conviction for slave stealing in 1834. He and his men were responsible for the robbery of boat cargoes on the river and the theft and resale of horses and slaves. He was sent to prison in Nashville; the major feature of his trial was the testimony of Virgil A. Stewart, who claimed to have joined Murrell's gang as a spy to bring them to justice. In the penitentiary, Murrell became terminally ill with consumption. He was released in 1844 but died that same year. The deeds of Murrell were essentially finished in 1834.

The legends were just beginning in the world of crime on the Natchez Trace and fear of slave uprisings. While Murrell was in prison, his story grew into a "panic legend" fed by speeches, written documents, and rumors. He became an infamous man in the old Southwest. With Murrell in jail, Virgil Stewart published a pamphlet early in 1835 in which he described a huge criminal conspiracy headed by Murrell. According to Stewart, the activities of Murrell's gang began with simple robbery and murder, and then evolved into an organized system for reselling stolen slaves until they became dangerously well known, when the slaves were disemboweled and sunk in a river with stones in the cavities. Those charges escalated into a "Mystic Clan of the Confederacy" with hundreds of sworn members, many of whom (named by Stewart) were leaders in their communities. More followers were simply workers in the Clan without knowledge of the ultimate plan. That plan, as Stewart laid it out in a full book just a few months later, was to cause a huge slave insurrection that would topple the existing order in the lower Mississippi Valley (Walton 1835).

James Penick, who wrote the most recent study of the Murrell legend, observes that the Mississippi Valley region of Tennessee, Mississippi, Arkansas, and Louisiana was a dangerous place for that sort of story to occur: "Into this society that was ripe for an insurrection scare, Stewart came selling his pamphlet. Nat Turner was fresh in every Southerner's mind. . . Given the time and place, any event that suggested the existence of a white-inspired insurrection plot was bound to mean trouble. That event was the appearance and circulation of Stewart's pamphlet" (Penick 1981:108–109).

Stewart was widely believed, and his revelations had severe consequences. Criminal activities along the Mississippi River and the Natchez Trace had produced in the 1820s and 1830s a number of groups of "regulators," vigilantes who attempted to deal with crime without waiting for legal procedures. The "Murrell conspiracy" led to a wave of vigilante action in Tennessee, Mississippi, and Arkansas (see Ball 1978). Homes were burned, men were tortured for confessions and hanged, and many more were "lynched," which at the time meant a spectrum of treatment from whiplashing to tarring and feathering to being set adrift, bound and naked, in small boats on the Mississippi, to hanging. The violence took a new turn in the summer of 1835, when the regulators in central Mississippi, operating in the panic of the putative slave uprising, tortured and killed slaves and whites thought to be working with them. In July, a separate incident in Vicksburg led to a vigilante cleansing of the gamblers and prostitutes who had long been part of the life of river towns, and they, too, became part of the Murrell legend.

The final step in the evolution of the Murrell legend came with the unfortunately timed mailing of propaganda from Northern abolitionists to Southern planters, urging them to make their opposition to slavery known. The uproar in the South convinced many of the truth of the Stewart assertions, and Murrell became in the public mind a crazed abolitionist whose goal was the destruction of Southern society (Penick 1981:151–154).

By the time the panic was over, many were dead. How many will never be known. The Murrell legend became permanent. There were a few skeptical arguments raised against Stewart from the beginning, by newspaper editors, in particular. One Tennessean brought charges of theft against Stewart and published a pamphlet against him. The death of Murrell in 1844 and Stewart in 1846 diminished the public debate about the truth, but the legendry lived on. As the actual upheaval quieted, the Murrell legend became a historical narrative about the panic legend itself, but despite contemporary skepticism during and after the panic—Mississippi historian J. F. H. Claiborne observed that the whole thing was "one of the most extraordinary and lamentable hallucinations of our times" (Penick 1981:106)—the debunking of the Murrell conspiracy had to wait for full treatment until Penick's study.

African and African American

The continuing interplay of legend and history shows up in sources even closer to modern times. In the Depression-cursed 1930s the Works Progress Administration tried to assist unemployed writers by putting them to work on various public writing projects. One of them was to collect the memories of surviving antebellum slaves. In just a few years (1936–1939) an astounding number of ex-slaves—more than 2,200—were interviewed and their narratives written down. They were finally published in the 1970s (Rawick 1972, 1977, 1979). Anyone who reads all 41 volumes will find a breathtaking body of material, a mix of historical memories, legends, personal anecdotes, and disturbing cautionary tales.

I undertook that reading task while searching for information that came from people who were slaves in Arkansas, a task made difficult because the WPA collections, and therefore the published volumes, were organized by states where the interviewing was done, reflecting 1930s residences of the informants. But many people moved after freedom came. With the removal from the Arkansas collection of all those informants who had not been slaves in Arkansas, then the search through the total collection for Arkansas slaves who had moved to other states before the 1930s and addition of their interviews, it was possible to publish in a single volume the accounts of people who were slaves in Arkansas (Lankford 2006). It then seemed reasonable to examine the historical testimony of Arkansas ex-slaves via a single book.

A variety of reported episodes seemed to be family legends that likely enshrined a grain of historical truth. Two characteristics stood out: being about or from an ancestor, and being filled with uncommon details. These narratives told about a father's experience as a "waiter" or body servant with an owner in Civil War campaigns, including descriptions of the master's death (Lankford 2006:56, 58, 172, 203, 224, 241, 292); men's resistance to bad treatment, such as the man who watched his wife whipped into bloody unconsciousness, then picked up a shovel to kill the overseer, an act that would have led quickly to his death had his fellow slaves not stopped him (Rawick 1977: vol. 8:1116); special achievements, such as the grandfather who was remembered as the most respected breeder on a large plantation, having fathered 56 children (Rawick 1972: vol. 9, 3:370), or the grandmother who was renowned for her beautiful long silky hair. She became the concubine of her master, and her mistress's only available retaliation in the situation was to insist that the slave keep her hair closely cropped (Rawick 1977: vol. 6:217–218). These narratives have the sound of family history in oral tradition.

Uncommon details were another clue to possible historical accuracy. One unique claim affirmed that a Mississippi master led his slaves in weekly "secret" services in which he always prayed fervently that God would bring the American slave institution to an end (Rawick 1972: vol. 9, 3:262). The unexpectedness of this detail passed on by an ex-slave lends plausibility to the narrative. Another unusual detail was given by a significant number of informants from Virginia to Texas. They told about holding their own secret services because their masters forbade them to have religious gatherings. Because they had to be quiet to avoid getting caught, they turned a huge iron pot over, leaving room at the base for faces or even heads to be inserted under the rim into the interior for praying, singing, and shouting with little sound escaping (Perdue et al. 1976:93, 119, 139, 198, 203, 217,

242 [Virginia]; Rawick 1977: vol. 10:1815, 1926, 2096 [Mississippi]; Rawick 1972: vol. 9 [3]:256, 276 (Arkansas)]. The legendary quality of this motif is borne out by some narrator's misunderstanding of the way this worked, for they supply implausible explanations for the use of the pot: that they filled the pot with water, then submerged their heads for singing and praying, or that they put the water-filled pot in the center of the gathering. There are even some descriptions that leave the impression that the pot was operating by magic to silence the uproar of the ecstatic shouting. The long list of "pot motif" accounts in the WPA interviews, together with the variation in understanding how it worked, suggests that this was part of a legend about the tradition of the secret religious gatherings of the slaves.

There is possibly another principle at work here, though. Some years ago James Johnston, an Arkansas historian of the brutal uncivil war in the Ozarks, published an article on a peculiarity he noted while collecting memories of what are called "jayhawker" atrocities (Johnston 1976). He found that the sequence of events and details of violent raids by these nonmilitary gangs were remarkably the same in various family narratives. Johnston's explanation seems reasonable. He argued that grim reality was so widespread and the need for restoration of civil order so crucial at the end of the war that the people had tacitly created a "generic" account of a jayhawker raid so as to avoid specific historical details, such as the names of neighbors who took part in the raids. A descriptive label for this subtype is "cliché legend," because it functions like the clichéd phrase so despised by writers. It may be repetitious, it may not be creative, but it expresses so well the sense, the essence, of the experience that there is no need to be more inventive or explicit. The standard cliché-legend sums it up just right, so every family is content to tell the same story.

The problem for the historian, of course, lies in distinguishing this type of legend from an oral historical narrative, especially on the basis of a single example. That is a major reason why folklorists create archives: to provide proof that a story is in the oral tradition rather than being a single informant's invention. Good candidates for cliché-legends in the ex-slave narratives include descriptions of slave whippings and the standardized treatment of the Ku Klux Klan's night visit at a freedman's home during Reconstruction.

One final story will illustrate another possible subtype of legends. It was recorded in a 1938 interview in North Little Rock, but the story was claimed to have happened in Sumter County, Alabama, about 125 miles north of Mobile. Here is the text of this brief excerpt from a much longer interview:

> Once on [the large plantation] they took all the fine looking boys and girls that was thirteen years old or older and put them in a big

> barn after they had stripped them naked. They used to strip them naked and put them in a big barn every Sunday and leave them there until Monday morning. Out of that came sixty babies.
>
> They was too many babies to leave in the quarters for someone to take care of during the day. When the young mothers went to work, [the owner] had them take their babies with them to the field, and it was two or three miles from the house to the field. He didn't want them to lose time walking backward and forward nursing. They built a long old trough like a great long old cradle and put all these babies in it every morning when the mother come out to the field. It was set at the end of the rows under a big old cottonwood tree.
>
> When they were at the other end of the row, all at once a cloud no bigger than a small spot came up, and it grew fast, and it thundered and lightened as if the world were coming to an end, and the rain just came down in great sheets. And when it got so they could go to the other end of the field, that trough was filled with water and every baby in it was floating 'round in the water drownded. They never got nary a lick of labor and nary a red penny for any one of them babies [Rawick 1972, vol. 9 [3]:374–375].

Now that is a breathtaking story. It causes mixed feelings during the telling, from surprise to outrage, to wonder, to horror, to meditation. It was told by a 73-year-old woman who was interviewed in North Little Rock by a black interviewer, Samuel Taylor, considered by some to be the best of the Arkansas team (Taylor 1958). The event recounted could not have taken place in the narrator's lifetime, because she was born in 1865 on that Alabama plantation, so it qualifies as a legend. But is it historical?

The opening incident encouraging breeding could be true. There is an important ambiguity in the first paragraph, where the barn impregnation event is mentioned both as "once" and "every Sunday." It suggests a blunder in the telling or an error by the interviewer in writing it up. Whether the informant intends this to be a customary event or a unique one, the entire concept is a shocking procedure, but there is ample testimony in the interviews that some owners treated their slaves like prime livestock, practicing eugenics in the selection of breeding partners. The laws of the time made the children of slave women the legal property of the master, so the same concept as breeding livestock could have been readily applied. The practice of organized childcare was routine on large plantations, and the trough is reminiscent of the feeding trough used particularly in feeding the children; both are talked about in the interviews. What sounds unhistorical is the lack of several women in charge of that outdoor baby nursery, with the babies left alone.

The narrator's prosaic delivery—"just the facts"—sounds stiff, but that is a likely result of telling the story many times before. She had learned the most effective delivery for this horror story. This is probably not a historical story, and it is doubtful that she thought it was. This appears to be a case of shifting the genre from legend to something else. If it is something other than a legend, then what is it? The key lies in that terrible storm. Here is that crucial sentence again: "all at once a cloud no bigger than a small spot came up, and it grew fast, and it thundered and lightened as if the world were coming to an end, and the rain just came down in great sheets."

That line seems intended to be a challenge for the hearer. Church people are expected to recognize it as coming right out of the Elijah legend cycle in the book of Kings (1 Kings 18). In the struggle between Yahweh and Baal, Elijah competed with the 850 prophets of Baal and won when a cloud released a thunderbolt that lit his wooden altar to Yahweh. Baal's followers were slaughtered, and Yahweh's long drought was broken by the huge storm that began as a little cloud the size of a man's fist on the horizon—a "cloud no bigger than a small spot." The biblical parallel, the familiar motifs from the Elijah legend, retold in connection with the death of the babies and the great storm, proclaim God's attitude toward the institution of slavery and its practitioners. This is a sermon, and what the narrator does not provide is a genre cue, such as "Let this be a sign unto you" or "Let him who has ears, listen." This story, if told during slave times, would have had great power. It seems to be a myth told as a historical legend, which in turn became a sermon on ethics. It is legend as proclamation, as protest, as resistance, as outrage, true beyond questions of historical accuracy. Did this legendary event happen? That is probably beside the point. It is true, as myths are true.

This examination of legendary history has considered myths, historical legends, cliché-legends, saints' legends, supernatural legends, fraudulent panics, memorates, and even sermons. The process has involved material from the Natchez Indians, Spanish conquistadores, white slave owners, African American slaves, and Civil War survivors. What is the lesson? In talking about historical truth, people tell legends, and in those legends is social history—sometimes, even details of particular events, if the legends can be persuaded to yield their beliefs. A major key to using this material is to identify those beliefs and the genres. Who can predict what kinds of historical insights will emerge from creative approaches to the vast body of Southeastern legendary history?

Acknowledgment

An earlier version of this chapter was presented at the Natchez Literary and Cinema Festival in 2012.

REFERENCES CITED

Albrecht, Andrew C.
1944 The Location of the Historic Natchez Villages. *Journal of Mississippi History* 6(2):67–88.
1946 Indian-French Relations at Natchez. *American Anthropologist* 48(3):321–354.
1948 Ethical Precepts among the Natchez Indians. *Louisiana Historical Quarterly* 31(3):569–595.

Alt, Susan
1999 Spindle Whorls and Fiber Production at Early Cahokian Settlements. *Southeastern Archaeology* 18(2):124–134.
2006 The Power of Diversity: Settlement in the Cahokian Uplands, in *Leadership and Polity in Mississippian Society*, edited by B. M. Butler and P. D. Welch, Occasional Paper No. 33, Center for Archaeological Investigations, Southern Illinois University, Carbondale.

Anderson, David G.
1988 The Rise and Demise of Chiefdoms: The Mississippian and Protohistoric Periods, in *Prehistory and History along the Upper Savannah River: Technical Synthesis of Cultural Resource Investigations, Richard B. Russell Multiple Resource Area, Vol. I*, compiled by David G. Anderson and J. W. Joseph, pp. 248–320. Russell Papers 1988; National Park Service, Interagency Archaeological Services, Atlanta, GA.
1994 *The Savannah River Chiefdoms: Political Change in the Late Prehistoric Southeast.* University of Alabama Press, Tuscaloosa.

Anderson, David G., and Kenneth E. Sassaman
2012 *Recent Developments in Southeastern Archaeology.* Society for American Archaeology, Washington, DC.

Angier, Bradford
1974 *Field Guide to Edible Wild Plants.* Stackpole Books, Harrisburg, PA.

Atkinson, James
1979 A Historic Contact Indian Settlement in Oktibbeha County, Mississippi. *Journal of Alabama Archaeology* 25(1):61–82.

Baca, Keith A.
1989 Archaeological Collections of the Mississippi Department of Archives and History. *Mississippi Archaeology* 24(2):28–44.

Ball, Larry D.
1978 Murrell in Arkansas: An Outlaw Gang in History and Tradition. *Mid-South Folklore* 6(3):65–75.

Barker, Alex W., and Timothy R Pauketat (editors)
1992 *Lords of the Southeast: Social Inequality and the Native Elites of Southeastern*

North America. Archeological Papers, 3. American Anthropological Association, Washington, DC.

Barnett, James F., Jr.

1984 A New Building Location at the Fatherland Site (Grand Village of the Natchez). *Mississippi Archaeology* 19(1):2–11.

1998 *The Natchez Indians*. Mississippi Department of Archives and History, Natchez.

2007 *The Natchez Indians: A History to 1735*. University Press of Mississippi, Jackson.

Barth, Frederick (editor)

1969 *Ethnic Groups and Boundaries*. Waveland Press, Prospect Heights, IL.

Bartram, William

1792 *Travels through North and South Carolina, Georgia, East and West Florida, the Cherokee Country, the Extensive Territories of the Muscogulges or Creek Confederacy, and the Country of the Chactaws*. J. Johnson, London, UK.

Battles, Juanita

1969 One Foot in a Grave. *Journal of Alabama Archaeology* 15(1):35–38.

1972 Copper and Lithic Artifacts. *Journal of Alabama Archaeology* 18:32–35.

Beasley, Virgil Roy, III

2007 Feasting on the Bluffs: Anna Site Excavations in the Natchez Bluffs of Mississippi, in *Plaquemine Archaeology*, edited by Mark A. Rees and Patrick C. Livingood, pp. 127–144. University of Alabama Press, Tuscaloosa.

Beck, Robin A., Jr.

1997a *The Burke Phase: Late Prehistoric Settlements in the Upper Catawba Valley, North Carolina*. M.A. thesis, Department of Anthropology, University of Alabama, Tuscaloosa.

1997b From Joara to Chiaha: Spanish Exploration of the Appalachian Summit Area, 1540–1568. *Southeastern Archaeology* 16:162–169.

2013 *Chiefdoms, Collapse, and Coalescence in the Early American South*. Cambridge University Press, Cambridge, UK.

Beck, Robin A., Jr., and David G. Moore

2002 The Burke Phase: A Mississippian Frontier in the North Carolina Foothills. *Southeastern Archaeology* 21(2):192–205.

Beck, Robin A., Jr., David G. Moore, and Christopher B. Rodning

2006 Identifying Fort San Juan: A Sixteenth-Century Spanish Occupation at the Berry Site, North Carolina. *Southeastern Archaeology* 25:65–77.

Beck, Robin A., Jr., David G. Moore, and Christopher B. Rodning (editors)

2016 *Fort San Juan and the Limits of Empire: Colonialism and Household Practice at the Berry Site*. University Press of Florida, Gainesville.

Beck, Robin A., Jr., Christopher B. Rodning, and David G. Moore

2011 Resisting Resistance: Juan Pardo and the Shrinking of Spanish *La Florida*, 1566–1568, in *Enduring Conquests: Rethinking Indigenous Resistance to Spanish Colonialism in the Americas*, edited by Matthew Liebmann and Melissa Murphy, pp. 19–39. School for Advanced Research Press, Santa Fe, NM.

Bennett, Charles E.

2001 *Laudonnière and Fort Caroline: History and Documents*. University of Alabama Press, Tuscaloosa.

Bense, Judith A.

1999 Historical and Archaeological Context and Comparisons, in *Archaeology of*

Colonial Pensacola, edited by Judith A. Bense, pp. 207–229. University Press of Florida, Gainesville.

2004 Presidio Santa María De Galve (1698–1719): A Frontier Garrison in Spanish West Florida. *Historical Archaeology* 38(3):47–64.

Bettinger, Robert L., Ripan Malhi, and Helen McCarthy

1997 Central Place Models of Acorn and Mussel Processing. *Journal of Archaeological Science* 24:887–899.

Bhabha, Homi K.

1990 DissemiNation: Time, Narrative and the Margins of the Modern Nation, in *Nation and Narration*, edited by Homi K. Bhabha, pp. 291–322. Routledge, New York.

1994 *The Location of Culture*. Routledge, New York.

Biedma, Luys Hernández de

1993 Relation of the Island of Florida, in *The De Soto Chronicles: The Expedition of Hernando de Soto to North America in 1539–1543*. 2 vols., edited by Lawrence A. Clayton, Vernon J. Knight, Jr., and Edward C. Moore, translated by John E. Worth, 1:221–46. University of Alabama Press, Tuscaloosa.

Bigman, Daniel P., Adam King, and Chester P. Walker

2011 Recent Geophysical Investigations and New Interpretations of Etowah's Palisade. *Southeastern Archaeology* 30(1):38–50.

Binford, Lewis R.

1962 Archaeology as Anthropology. *American Antiquity* 28:217–225.

1965 Archaeological Systematics and the Study of Culture Process. *American Antiquity* 31:203–210.

1968 Archaeological Perspectives, in *New Perspectives in Archaeology*, edited by Sally R. Binford and Lewis R. Binford, pp. 5–32. Aldine Publishing Company, Chicago, IL.

Black, Glenn A.

1967 *Angel Site, an Archaeological, Historical, and Ethnological Study*. Indiana Historical Society, Indianapolis.

Blair, Elliot, Lorann S. A. Pendleton, and Peter Francis, Jr.

2009 *The Beads of St. Catherines Island*. American Museum of Natural History Anthropological Papers, Number 89. New York.

Blakely, Robert L.

1975 Etowah Mound C Osteological Analysis Forms. Manuscript on file, South Carolina Institute of Archaeology and Anthropology. University of South Carolina, Columbia.

Blanton, Dennis

1986 CRM: Wadley-Wallace Dam 500 KV Electric Transmission Line Corridor GP-Hk-08: Data Recovery. Report submitted to Georgia Power Company. Garrow and Associates, Atlanta, GA.

Blitz, John H.

2010 New Perspectives in Mississippian Archaeology. *Journal of Archaeological Research* 18:1–39.

Blitz, John H., and Karl G. Lorenz

2006 *The Chattahoochee Chiefdoms*. University of Alabama Press, Tuscaloosa.

Bonhage-Freund, Mary Theresa

2007 Botanical Remains, in *Archaeology of the Lower Muskogee Creek Indians,*

1715–1836, by H. Thomas Foster II, pp. 136–193. University of Alabama Press, Tuscaloosa.

Booker, Karen, Charles M. Hudson, and Robert Rankin

1992 Place Name Identification and Multilingualism in the Sixteenth-Century Southeast. *Ethnohistory* 39(4):399–451.

Bourdieu, Pierre

1977 *Outline of a Theory of Practice*. Cambridge University Press, Cambridge, UK.

Bourne, Edward G. (editor)

1904 *Narratives of the Career of Hernando De Soto*. A. S. Barnes, New York.

Bowne, Eric E.

2009 "Carryinge awaye their Corne and Children": The Effects of Westo Slave Raids on the Indians of the Lower South, in *Mapping the Mississippian Shatter Zone: The Colonial Indian Slave Trade and Regional Instability in the American South*, edited by Robbie Ethridge and Sheri M. Shuck-Hall, pp. 104–114. University of Nebraska Press, Lincoln.

Boyer, Willet A., Jr.

2005 *Nuestra Señora del Rosario de La Punta: Lifeways of an Eighteenth-Century Colonial Spanish Refugee Mission Community, St. Augustine, Florida*. M.A. thesis, Department of Anthropology, University of Florida, Gainesville.

Brain, Jeffrey P.

1971 The Natchez "Paradox." *Ethnology* X:215–222.

1978 Late Prehistoric Settlement Patterning in the Yazoo Basin and Natchez Bluffs Regions of the Lower Mississippi Valley, in *Mississippian Settlement Patterns*, edited by Bruce D. Smith, pp. 331–368. Academic Press, New York.

1979 *Tunica Treasure*. Papers of the Peabody Museum of Archaeology and Ethnology, Harvard University, Vol. 71. Cambridge, MA.

1988 *Tunica Archaeology*. Papers of the Peabody Museum of Archaeology and Ethnology, Harvard University, Vol. 78. Cambridge, MA.

Brain, Jeffrey P., and Philip Phillips

1996 *Shell Gorgets: Styles of the Late Prehistoric and Protohistoric Southeast*. Peabody Museum Press, Cambridge, MA.

Braley, Chad O.

1998 Yuchi Town (1Ru63) Revisited: Analysis of the 1958–1962 Excavations. Southeastern Archeological Services, Inc., Athens, Georgia. Report submitted to Environmental Management Division, Directorate of Public Works, U. S. Army Infantry Center, Fort Benning, GA.

Brannon, Carolyn

1931 Shell Objects from Central Alabama. *Arrow Points* 18(2):28–30.

Brannon, Peter

1935 Shell Work at the Mouth of the Tallapoosa. *Arrow Points* 20(5–6):33–35.

Brown, Ian W.

1978 *James Alfred Ford, the Man and His Works*. Southeastern Archaeological Conference Special Publication No. 4. Department of Anthropology, Memphis State University, Memphis, TN.

1979 *Early 18th Century French-Indian Culture Contact in the Yazoo Bluffs Region of the Lower Mississippi Valley*. Ph.D. dissertation, Department of Anthropology, Brown University, Providence, RI.

1982 An Archaeological Study of Culture Contact and Change in the Natchez

Bluffs Region, in *La Salle and His Legacy: Frenchmen and Indians in the Lower Mississippi Valley*, edited by Patricia K. Galloway, pp. 176–193. University Press of Mississippi, Jackson.

1985 *Natchez Indian Archaeology: Culture Change and Stability in the Lower Mississippi Valley*. Mississippi Department of Archives and History, Archaeological Report No. 15. Jackson.

1989 Natchez Indians and the Remains of a Proud Past, in *Natchez before 1830*, edited by Noel Polk, pp. 8–28. University Press of Mississippi, Jackson.

1990 Historic Indians of the Lower Mississippi Valley: An Archaeologist's View, in *Towns and Temples along the Mississippi*, edited by David Dye and Cheryl A. Cox, pp. 227–238. University of Alabama Press, Tuscaloosa.

1992 Certain Aspects of French-Indian Interaction in Lower Louisiane, in *Calumet and Fleur-de-Lys: Archaeology of Indian and French Contact in the Mid-Continent*, edited by Thomas E. Emerson and John A. Walthall, pp. 17–34. Smithsonian Institution Press, Washington, DC.

1996 B. L. C. Wailes and Mississippi Archaeology: Journals of B. L. C. Wailes, Vols. 1–13, 1852–1854. Transcribed by Nell Wailes Brandon. Manuscript on file, Gulf Coast Survey Archives, Alabama Museum of Natural History, University of Alabama, Tuscaloosa.

1998a Benjamin L. C. Wailes and the Archaeology of Mississippi. *Mississippi Archaeology* 33(2):157–191.

1998b The Eighteenth-Century Natchez Chiefdom, in *The Natchez District in the Old, Old South*, edited by Vincas P. Steponaitis, pp. 49–65. Southern Research Report No. 11. Academic Affairs Library, Center for the Study of the American South, Research Laboratories of Archaeology, University of North Carolina, Chapel Hill.

1998c Fatherland Site, in *Archaeology of Prehistoric Native America: An Encyclopedia*, edited by Guy Gibbon, pp. 269–270. Garland Publishing, New York.

1998d Plaquemine Culture, in *Archaeology of Prehistoric Native America: An Encyclopedia*, edited by Guy Gibbon, pp. 657–659. Garland Publishing, New York.

2003 *Bottle Creek: A Pensacola Culture Site in South Alabama*. University of Alabama Press, Tuscaloosa.

2007 Plaquemine Culture in the Natchez Bluffs Region of Mississippi, in *Plaquemine Archaeology*, edited by Mark A. Rees and Patrick C. Livingood, pp. 145–160. University of Alabama Press, Tuscaloosa.

Brown, James. A.

1985 The Mississippian Period, in *Ancient Art of the American Woodland Indians*, edited by David S. Brose, James A. Brown, David W. Penney, and Dirk Bakker, pp. 93–145. Harry N. Abrams, New York.

1989 On Style Divisions of the Southeastern Ceremonial Complex: A Revisionist Perspective, in *The Southeastern Ceremonial Complex: Artifacts and Analysis (The Cottonlandia Conference)*, edited by P. Galloway, pp. 183–204. University of Nebraska Press, Lincoln.

1990 Archaeology Confronts History at the Natchez Temple. *Southeastern Archaeology* 9(1):1–10.

1996 *The Spiro Ceremonial Center: The Archaeology of Arkansas Valley Caddoan Culture in Eastern Oklahoma*. Memoir No 29. University of Michigan Museum of Anthropology, Ann Arbor.

2004 The Cahokian Expression: Creating Court and Cult, in *Hero, Hawk, and*

Open Hand: American Indian Art of the Ancient Midwest and South, edited by Richard F. Townsend and Robert V. Sharp, pp. 105–123. Art Institute of Chicago, Chicago, IL.

2006 Where's the Power in Mound Building? An Eastern Woodlands Perspective, in *Leadership and Polity in Mississippian Society,* edited by Brian M. Butler and Paul D. Welch, pp. 197–213. Occasional Paper No. 33. Center for Archaeological Investigations, Southern Illinois University, Carbondale.

2007 On the Identity of the Birdman within Mississippian Period Art and Iconography, in *Ancient Objects and Sacred Realms: Interpretations of Mississippian Iconography,* edited by F. Kent Reilly III and James F. Garber, pp. 56–106. University of Texas Press, Austin.

2014 Ideological Referents of the Spiro Spirit Lodge. Paper presented at the Southeastern Archaeological Conference, Greenville, SC.

Brown, James, and John Kelly

2000 Cahokia and the Southeastern Ceremonial Complex, in *Mounds, Modoc, and Mesoamerica: Papers in Honor of Melvin L. Fowler,* edited by Steven R. Ahler, pp. 469–510. Illinois State Museum Scientific Papers 55, Springfield.

Brubaker, Rogers, and Frederick Cooper

2000 Beyond "Identity." *Theory and Society* 29(1):1–47.

Bullen, Ripley P.

1978 Tocobaga Indians and the Safety Harbor Culture, in *Tacachale: Essays on the Indians of Florida and Southeastern Georgia during the Historic Period,* edited by Jerald Milanich and Samuel Proctor, pp. 50–58. University Presses of Florida, Gainesville.

Burnett, E. K.

1945 The Spiro Mound Collection in the Museum. *Contributions from the Museum of the American Indian, Heye Foundation* 14:9–47.

Bushnell, Amy Turner

1994 *Situado and Sabana: Spain's Support System for the Presidio and Mission Provinces of Florida.* Anthropological Paper No. 74, American Museum of Natural History, New York.

Butler, Brian M., and Paul D. Welch

2006 *Leadership and Polity in Mississippian Society.* Occasional Paper No. 33. Center for Archaeological Investigations, Southern Illinois University, Carbondale, IL.

Byers, Douglas

1964 Two Textile Fragments and Some Copper Objects from Etowah, Georgia. *35th Congreso Internacional de Americanistas Actas y Memorias* 1:591–598.

Caldwell, Joseph R.

1955 Cherokee Pottery from Northern Georgia. *American Antiquity* 20(3):277–280.

Caldwell, Joseph R., and Catherine McCann

1941 *Irene Mound Site, Chatham County, Georgia.* University of Georgia Press, Athens.

Caldwell, Joseph R., and Antonio J. Waring, Jr.

1939 Some Chatham County Pottery Types and Their Sequence. *Southeastern Archaeological Conference Newsletter* 1(6):1–9.

Calhoun, Craig

1995 *Critical Social Theory: Culture, History, and the Challenge of Difference.* Blackwell, Oxford, UK.

Carr, Christopher

1995 A Unified Middle-Range Theory of Artifact Design, in *Style, Society, and Person: Archaeological and Ethnological Perspectives*, edited by Christopher Carr and Jill E. Nietzel, pp. 171–258. Plenum Press, New York.

Carr, Lucien

1895 The Food of Certain American Indians and Their Methods of Preparing It. *Proceedings of the American Antiquarian Society* 10:155–190.

Chapman, Jefferson, and Andrea Brewer Shea

1981 The Archaeobotanical Record: Early Archaic Period to Contact in the Lower Little Tennessee River Valley. *Tennessee Anthropologist* 6(1):61–84.

Charlevoix, Pierre François Xavier de

1872 *History and General Description of New France*, Vol. 6, translated and edited by John Gilmary Shea. John Gilmary Shea, New York.

Claassen, Cheryl

1989 Sourcing Marine Shell Artifacts, in *Proceedings of the 1986 Shell Bead Conference*, edited by Charles Hayes and Lynn Ceci, pp. 17–24. Rochester Museum and Science Center Research Records No. 20. Rochester, NY.

Claiborne, John F. H.

1880 *Mississippi as a Province, Territory, and State*. Power and Barksdale, Jackson, MS.

Clayton, Lawrence. A., Vernon James Knight, Jr., and Edward C. Moore (editors)

1993 *The De Soto Chronicles: The Expedition of Hernando de Soto to North America in 1539–1543*. 2 vols. University of Alabama Press, Tuscaloosa.

Clune, John James, R. Wayne Childers, William S. Coker, and Brenda N. Swann

2003 Settlement, Settlers and Survival: Documentary Evidence, in *Presidio Santa María de Galve: A Struggle for Survival in Colonial Spanish Pensacola*, edited by Judith A. Bense, pp. 25–82. University Press of Florida, Gainesville.

Cobb, Charles R.

2000 *From Quarry to Cornfield: The Political Economy of Mississippian Hoe Production*. University of Alabama Press, Tuscaloosa.

Cobb, Charles R., and Brian M. Butler

2002 The Vacant Quarter Revisited: Late Mississippian Abandonment of the Lower Ohio Valley. *American Antiquity* 67:625–641.

Cobb, Charles, and Adam King

2005 Re-Inventing Mississippian Tradition at Etowah. *Journal of Archaeological Method and Theory* 12(3):167–190.

Coe, Michael, and William Fischer

1959 Barkley Reservoir—Tennessee Portion, Archaeological Excavations, 1959. Manuscript on file, Frank H. McClung Museum, University of Tennessee, Knoxville.

Colton, Harold Sellers, and Lyndon Lane Hargrave

1937 Handbook of Northern Arizona Pottery Wares. *Museum of Northern Arizona Bulletin* 11. Flagstaff.

Cordell, Ann

2001 *Continuity and Change in Apalachee Pottery Manufacture: A Technological Comparison of Apalachee-Style and Colono Ware Pottery from French Colonial Old Mobile and Mission San Luis de Talimali*. Archaeological Monograph 9, Center for Archaeological Studies, University of South Alabama, Mobile.

Cotter, John L.

1951 Stratigraphic and Area Tests at the Emerald and Anna Mound Sites. *American Antiquity* 17(1):18–32.

Covington, James W.

1964 The Apalachee Indians Move West. *Florida Anthropologist* 17(4):221–225.

Cowan, C. Wesley

1994 The Prehistoric Use and Distribution of Maygrass in Eastern North America: Cultural Phytogeographical Implications, in *The Nature and Status of Ethnobotany*, 2nd ed. Edited by Richard I. Ford, pp. 289–300. Anthropological Papers No. 67, Museum of Anthropology, University of Michigan, Ann Arbor.

Crook, Morgan R.

1986 *Mississippi Period Archaeology of the Georgia Coastal Zone*. University of Georgia, Laboratory of Archaeology Series, Report No. 23, Georgia Archaeology Research Design Papers, No. 1. Athens.

Crown, Patricia L.

2001 Learning to Make Pottery in the Prehispanic American Southwest. *Journal of Anthropological Research* 57(4):451–469.

2007 Life Histories of Pots and Potters: Situating the Individual in Archaeology. *American Antiquity* 72(4):677–690.

Culin, Stewart

1900 The Dickeson Collection of American Antiquities. *Bulletin of the Free Museum of Science and Art of the University of Pennsylvania* 2(3):113–168.

Curren, Caleb

1984 *The Protohistoric Period in Central Alabama*. Alabama Tombigbee Regional Commission. Camden, AL.

Cutler, Hugh C., and Leonard W. Blake

2001 North American Indian Corn, in *Plants from the Past*, edited by Leonard W. Blake and Hugh C. Cutler, pp. 1–18. University of Alabama Press, Tuscaloosa.

Deagan, Kathleen

1972 Fig Springs: The Mid-Seventeenth Century in North-Central Florida. *Historical Archaeology* 6:23–46.

1973 Mestizaje in Colonial St. Augustine. *Ethnohistory* 20(1):55–65.

1978a The Material Assemblage of 16th-Century Spanish Florida. *Historical Archaeology* 12:25–50.

1978b Cultures in Transition: Fusion and Assimilation among the Eastern Timucua, in *Tacachale: Essays on the Indians of Florida and Southeastern Georgia during the Historic Period*, edited by Jerald Milanich and Samuel Proctor, pp. 89–119. University Presses of Florida, Gainesville.

1983 *Spanish St. Augustine: The Archeology of a Colonial Creole Community*. Academic Press, New York.

1987 *Artifacts of the Spanish Colonies of Florida and the Caribbean, 1500–1800*. Smithsonian Institution Press, Washington, DC.

1990 Sixteenth-Century Spanish-American Colonization in the Southeastern United States and Caribbean, in *Columbian Consequences*, Vol. 2, edited by D. H Thomas, pp. 225–250. Smithsonian Institution Press, Washington, DC.

1993 St. Augustine and the Mission Frontier, in *The Spanish Missions of La Florida*, edited by Bonnie G. McEwan, pp. 87–110. University of Florida Press, Gainesville.

Delanglez, Jean

1935 *The French Jesuits in Lower Louisiana (1700–1763)*. Loyola University, New Orleans, LA.

Densmore, Francis

1974 [1928] *How Indians Use Wild Plants for Food, Medicine and Crafts*. Dover Publications, New York.

DePratter, Chester

1979 Ceramics, in *The Anthropology of St. Catherines Island. Vol. 2: The Refuge-Deptford Mortuary Complex*, edited by David Hurst Thomas and Clark S. Larsen, pp. 109–132. Anthropological Papers of the American Museum of Natural History, 56(1). New York.

1994 The Chiefdom of Cofitachequi, in *The Forgotten Centuries: Indians and Europeans in the American South, 1521–1704*, edited by Charles Hudson and Carmen Chaves Tesser, pp. 197–226. University of Georgia Press, Athens.

DePratter, Chester (editor)

1991 *Late Prehistoric Chiefdoms in the Southeastern United States*. Garland, New York.

DePratter, Chester, and Marvin T. Smith

1980 Sixteenth-Century European Trade in the Southeastern United States: Evidence from the Juan Pardo Expeditions (1566–1568), in *Spanish Colonial Frontier Research*, edited by Henry F. Dobyns, pp. 66–77. Center for Anthropological Studies, University of New Mexico, Albuquerque, NM.

Díaz-Andreu, Margarita, Sam Lucy, Staša Babić, and David N. Edwards

2005 *The Archaeology of Identity*. Routledge, London.

Dickens, Roy S.

1976 *Cherokee Prehistory: The Pisgah Phase in the Appalachian Summit Region*. University of Tennessee Press, Knoxville.

1986 An Evolutionary-Ecological Interpretation of Cherokee Cultural Development, in *The Conference on Cherokee Prehistory*, edited by David G. Moore, pp. 81–94. Warren Wilson College, Swannanoa, NC.

Dickeson, Montroville W.

1848 American Antiquities No. III. Opening of Mounds on the Plantation of Col. A. L. Bingaman. *The Lotus* I(9):129–131.

Dietler, Michael, and Ingrid Herbich

1989 Tich Matek: The Technology of Luo Pottery Production and the Definition of Ceramic Style. *World Archaeology* 21(1):148–164.

1994 Ceramics and Ethnic Identity: Ethnoarchaeological Observations on the Distribution of Pottery Styles and the Relationship Between the Social Contexts of Production and Consumption, in *Terre cuite et société: La céramique, document technique, économique, culturel: XIV Rencontres Internationales d'Archéologie et d'Histoire d'Antibes*, edited by D. Binder and J. Courtin, pp. 459–472. Editions APDCA, Juan-les-Pins, France.

1998 Habitus, Techniques, Style: An Integrated Approach to the Social Understanding of Material Culture and Boundaries, in *The Archaeology of Social Boundaries*, edited by Miriam T. Stark, pp. 232–263. Smithsonian Institution Press, Washington, DC.

Dobres, Marcia-Anne, and Christopher R. Hoffman

1994 Social Agency and the Dynamics of Prehistoric Technology. *Journal of Archaeological Method and Theory* 1(3):211–258.

Dobres, Marcia-Anne, and John Robb
2000 Agency in Archaeology: Paradigm or Platitude? In *Agency in Archaeology*, edited by Marcia-Anne Dobres and John Robb, pp. 3–18. Routledge Press, London, UK.

Dornan, Jennifer L.
2002 Agency and Archaeology: Past, Present, and Future Directions. *Journal of Archaeological Method and Theory* 9(4):303–329.

Drooker, Penelope B.
1990 Textile Production and Use at Wickliffe Mounds (15Ba4), Kentucky. *Midcontinental Journal of Archaeology* 15(2):163–220.
1991 Mississippian Lace: A Complex Textile Impressed on Pottery from the Stone Site, Tennessee. *Southeastern Archaeology* 10(2):79–97.
1992 *Mississippian Village Textiles at Wickliffe.* University of Alabama Press, Tuscaloosa.
1993 Matting and Fabric Impressions from Bottle Creek (1Ba2), Alabama. *Journal of Alabama Archaeology* 39(1&2):115–132.
1997 *The View from Madisonville.* Memoir No. 31, Museum of Anthropology, University of Michigan, Ann Arbor.
2001a Approaching Fabrics through Impressions on Pottery, in *Approaching Textiles, Varying Viewpoints*, pp. 59–68. Seventh Biennial Symposium of the Textile Society of America, Santa Fe 2000. Textile Society of America, Earleville, MD.
2001b Leaving No Stone Unturned: Making the Most of Secondary Evidence for Perishable Material Culture, in *Fleeting Identities: Perishable Material Culture in Archaeological Research*, edited by Penelope B. Drooker, pp. 170–186. Occasional Paper No. 28. Center for Archaeological Investigations, Southern Illinois University, Carbondale, IL.
2003 Matting and Pliable Fabrics from Bottle Creek, in *Bottle Creek: A Pensacola Culture Site in South Alabama*, edited by Ian W. Brown, pp. 180–193. University of Alabama Press, Tuscaloosa.
2004a Fabrics Associated with Palettes at Etowah. Paper presented as part of a symposium, "Recent Investigations of the Mortuary Record of Etowah's Mound C," at joint meeting of Southeastern Archaeological Conference and Midwest Archaeological Conference, St. Louis, MO.
2004b Fabrics Associated with Palettes at Etowah. Report on file at Research Laboratories of Archaeology, University of North Carolina, Chapel Hill.
2007 "Octagonal Openwork" and Mississippian Boundaries. Paper presented as part of a symposium, A New Look at a Common Dilemma: Perishables and the Definition of Boundaries, at Society for American Archaeology Annual Meeting, Austin, TX.
2011 Using Replication-Related Techniques to Examine the Significance of Fabrics in Mississippian Society. *Ethnoarchaeology* 3(2):163–186.

Drooker, Penelope B., and Laurie D. Webster
2000 *Beyond Cloth and Cordage: Archaeological Textile Research in the Americas.* University of Utah Press, Salt Lake City.

Dubcovsky, Alejandra
2016 *Informed Power: Communication in the Early American South.* Harvard University Press, Cambridge, MA.

Dumont de Montigny, Jean-François-Benjamin
1753 *Mémoires historiques sur la Louisiane.* 2 vols., edited by Le Mascrier. Bauche, Paris, France.

2012 *The Memoir of Lieutenant Dumont, 1715–1747: A Sojourner in the French Atlantic.* Translated by Gordon M. Sayre; edited by Gordon M. Sayre and Carla Zecher. University of North Carolina Press, Chapel Hill.

Dunkle, John R.

1958 Population Change as an Element in the Historical Geography of St. Augustine. *Florida Historical Quarterly* 37(1):3–32.

Du Ru, Paul

1934 *Journal of Paul du Ru (February 1 to May 8, 1700), Missionary/Priest to Louisiana.* Translated by Ruth Lapham Butler. Caxton Club, Chicago, IL.

Dye, David H.

1991 Warfare in the Sixteenth Century: The de Soto Expedition in the Interior," in *Columbian Consequences,* Vol. 1, *Archaeological and Historical Perspectives on the Spanish Borderlands, West,* edited by David Hurst Thomas, 211–222. Smithsonian Institution, Washington, DC.

2002 Warfare in the Protohistoric Southeast, in *Between Contact and Colonies: Archaeological Perspectives on the Protohistoric Southeast,* edited by Cameron Wesson and Mark Rees, 126–141. University of Alabama Press, Tuscaloosa.

Early, Ann M.

1993 Hardman and Caddoan Salt Making, in *Caddoan Saltmakers in the Ouachita Valley: The Hardman Site,* edited by Ann M. Early, 223–234. Research Series No. 43. Arkansas Archaeological Survey, Fayetteville.

Eckert, Suzanne L.

2008 *Pottery and Practice: The Expression of Identity at Pottery Mound and Hummingbird Pueblo.* University of New Mexico Press, Albuquerque.

Eckert, Penelope, and Sally McConnell-Ginet

1992 Think Practically and Look Locally: Language and Gender as Community-Based Practice. *Annual Review of Anthropology* 21:461–490.

Egloff, Brian John

1967 *Analysis of Ceramics from Historic Cherokee Towns.* M.A. thesis, Department of Anthropology, University of North Carolina, Chapel Hill.

Elliott, Jack D., Jr.

1997 Of Roads and Reifications: The Interpretation of Historical Roads and the Soto Entrada. In *The Hernando de Soto Expedition: History, Historiography, and "Discovery" in the Southeast,* edited by Patricia Galloway, pp. 246–258. University of Nebraska Press, Lincoln.

Elvas, Gentleman of

1993 True Relation of the Vicissitudes That Attended the Governor Don Hernando de Soto and Some Nobles of Portugal in the Discovery of the Provence of Florida, in *The De Soto Chronicles: The Expedition of Hernando de Soto to North America in 1539–1543.* 2 vols., edited by Lawrence A. Clayton, Vernon. J. Knight, Jr., and Edward C. Moore, translated by James Robertson, 1:25–219. University of Alabama Press, Tuscaloosa.

Emerson, Thomas E.

1997 *Cahokia and the Archaeology of Power.* University of Alabama Press, Tuscaloosa.

Emerson, Thomas E., and Timothy R. Pauketat

2002 Embodying Power and Resistance at Cahokia, in *The Dynamics of Power,* edited by Maria O'Donovan, pp. 105–125. Occasional Paper No. 30. Center for Archaeological Investigations, Southern Illinois University, Carbondale.

Emerson, William K., and Morris Jacobson
1976 *The American Museum of Natural History Guide to Shells: Land, Freshwater, and Marine, from Nova Scotia to Florida.* Alfred A. Knopf, New York.

Ericksen, Annette, Kathryn Jakes, and Virginia Wimberley
2000 Prehistoric Textiles: Production, Function, Semiotics, in *Beyond Cloth and Cordage: Archaeological Textile Research in the Americas,* edited by P. B. Drooker and L. D. Webster, pp. 60–83. University of Utah Press, Salt Lake City.

Esarey, Duane
2013 *Another Kind of Beads: A Forgotten Industry of the North American Colonial Period.* Ph.D. dissertation. University of North Carolina at Chapel Hill.

Ethridge, Robbie
2003 *Creek Country: The Creek Indians and their World.* University of North Carolina Press, Chapel Hill.
2010 *From Chicaza to Chickasaw: The European Invasion and the Transformation of the Mississippian World, 1540–1715.* University of North Carolina Press, Chapel Hill.

Ethridge, Robbie, Kathryn E. Holland Braund, Lawrence A. Clayton, George E. Lankford, and Michael D. Murphy
2009 A Comparative Analysis of the De Soto Accounts on the Route to, and Events at, Mabila, in *The Search for Mabila: The Decisive Battle between Hernando de Soto and Chief Tascalusa,* edited by Vernon James Knight, Jr., pp. 153–181. University of Alabama Press, Tuscaloosa.

Ethridge, Robbie, and Charles Hudson (editors)
2002 *The Transformation of the Southeastern Indians, 1540–1760.* University Press of Mississippi, Jackson.

Ethridge, Robbie, and Sheri Shuck-Hall (editors)
2009 *Mapping the Mississippian Shatter Zone: The Colonial Indian Slave Trade and Regional Instability in the American South.* University of Nebraska Press, Lincoln.

Ewen, Charles R.
1996 Continuity and Change: DeSoto and the Apalachee. *Historical Archaeology* 30(2):41–53.

Fairbanks, Charles H.
1981 [1956] Introduction to Second Printing. In *Archeology of the Funeral Mound at Ocmulgee National Monument, Georgia,* by Charles H. Fairbanks. Archaeological Research Series Number Three, National Park Service, U.S. Department of Interior, Washington, DC.

Feathers, James K.
2006 Explaining Shell-Tempered Pottery in Prehistoric Eastern North America. *Journal of Archaeological Method and Theory* 13(2):89–133.

Feathers, James K., and Evan Peacock
2008 Origins and Spread of Shell-Tempered Ceramics in the Eastern Woodlands: Conceptual and Methodological Frameworks for Analysis. *Southeastern Archaeology* 27(2):286–293.

Feinman, Gary M.
2002 Five Points about Power, in *The Dynamics of Power,* edited by Maria O'Donovan, pp. 387–383. Occasional Paper No. 30. Center for Archaeological Investigations, Southern Illinois University, Carbondale.

Fernald, Merritt Lyndon, and Alfred Charles Kinsey
1943 *Edible Wild Plants of Eastern North America.* Idlewild Press, Cornwall-on-Hudson, NY.

Fischer, John L.
1964 Solutions for the Natchez Paradox. *Ethnology* 3:53–65.
Flannery, Kent V.
1967 Culture History v. Cultural Process: A Debate in American Archaeology. *Scientific American* 217:119–122.
Fleming, Victor Keith, and John Walthall
1978 A Summary of the Historic Aboriginal Occupations of the Guntersville Basin, Alabama. *Southeastern Archaeological Conference Special Publication* 5:30–34.
Ford, James A.
1935 Outline of Louisiana and Mississippi Pottery Horizons. *Louisiana Conservation Review* 4(6):33–38.
1936 *Analysis of Indian Village Site Collections from Louisiana and Mississippi.* Louisiana Department of Conservation, Anthropological Study No. 2. New Orleans.
Foster, H. Thomas, II
2004 Evidence of Historic Creek Indian Migration from a Regional and Direct Historical Analysis of Ceramic Types. *Southeastern Archaeology* 23(1):65–84.
2007 *Archaeology of the Lower Muskogee Creek Indians.* University of Alabama Press, Tuscaloosa.
Franquemont, Edward M.
1986 Cloth Production Rates in Chinchero, Peru, in *The Junius B. Bird Conference on Andean Textiles,* edited by Ann Pollard Rowe, pp. 309–329. The Textile Museum, Washington, DC.
French, Benjamin F. (editor)
1869 *Historical Collections of Louisiana and Florida.* J. Sabin & Sons, New York.
Fritz, Gayle
2016 People, Plants, and Early Frontier Food, in *Fort San Juan and the Limits of Empire,* edited by Robin A. Beck, Jr., Christopher B. Rodning, and David G. Moore, pp. 237–270, University Press of Florida, Gainesville.
Fritz, Gayle J., Virginia Drywater Whitekiller, and James W. McIntosh
2001 Ethnobotany of Ku-Nu-Che: Cherokee Hickory Nut Soup. *Journal of Ethnobiology* 21(2):1–27.
Galloway, Patricia
1995 *Choctaw Genesis.* University of Nebraska Press, Lincoln.
Galloway, Patricia (editor)
1989 *The Southeastern Ceremonial Complex: Artifacts and Analysis.* University of Nebraska Press, Lincoln.
2005 *The Hernando de Soto Expedition: History, Historiography, and "Discovery" in the Southeast.* 2nd ed. University of Nebraska Press, Lincoln.
Garcilaso de la Vega, the Inca
1993 La Florida, in *The De Soto Chronicles: The Expedition of Hernando de Soto to North America in 1539–1543.* 2 vols., edited by Lawrence A. Clayton, Vernon James Knight, Jr., and Edward C. Moore. Translated by Charmion Shelby, 2:25–560. University of Alabama Press, Tuscaloosa.
Gardner, Andrew
2007 *An Archaeology of Identity: Soldiers and Society in Late Roman Britain.* Left Coast Press, Walnut Creek, CA.
Gardner, Paul S.
1985 Paleoethnobotany, in *Archaeological Investigations at the Beaverdam Creek Site (9EB85) Elbert County, Georgia,* compiled by James L. Rudolph and David J. Hally,

pp. 400–411. Russell Papers 1985; National Park Service, Archaeological Services, Atlanta, GA.

1997 The Ecological Structure and Behavioral Implications of Mast Exploration Strategies, in *People, Plants and Landscapes: Studies in Paleoethnobotany*, edited by Kristen J. Gremillion, pp. 161–178. University of Alabama Press, Tuscaloosa.

Gayarré, Charles

1854 *History of Louisiana: vol. 1, The French Domination*. Redfield, New York.

Geiger, Brian S., Shaun M. Lynch, Kathryn M. Kipfer, David G. Moore, Christopher B. Rodning, and Robin A. Beck, Jr.

2011 An Archaeological Investigation of Mound Stratigraphy at the Berry Site (31BK22), Burke County, North Carolina. Poster presented at 68th Annual Meeting of the Southeastern Archaeological Conference, Jacksonville, FL.

Giddens, Anthony

1984 *The Constitution of Society: Outline of the Theory of Structuration*. University of California Press, Berkeley.

Gilmore, Melvin R.

1932a The Sacred Bundles of the Arikara. *Papers of the Michigan Academy of Science, Arts and Letters* 16:33–50, Plates III–IV.

1932b Some Chippewa Uses of Plants. *Papers of the Michigan Academy of Science, Arts, and Letters* 17:119–143.

Giraud, Marcel

1974 *A History of French Louisiana, Vol. 1: The Reign of Louis XIV, 1698–1715*. Translated by Joseph C. Lambert. Louisiana State University Press, Baton Rouge.

1991 *A History of French Louisiana, Vol. 5: The Company of the Indies, 1723–1731*. Translated by Brian Pearce. Louisiana State University Press, Baton Rouge.

Goggin, John M.

1951 Fort Pupo: A Spanish Frontier Outpost. *Florida Historical Quarterly* 30(2): 139–192.

Goody, Jack

1982 *Cooking, Cuisine, and Class: A Study in Comparative Sociology*. Cambridge University Press, Cambridge.

Gosselain, Olivier P.

1998 Social and Technical Identity in a Clay Crystal Ball, in *The Archaeology of Social Boundaries*, edited by Miriam T. Stark, pp. 78–106. Smithsonian Institution Press, Washington, DC.

2000 Materializing Identities: An African Perspective. *Journal of Archaeological Method and Theory* 7(3):187–217.

Green, John A.

1936 Governor Perier's Expedition Against the Natchez Indians. *Louisiana Historical Quarterly* 19(3):547–577.

Green, William, and Chester DePratter

2000 Ten Years of Yamasee Archaeology in South Carolina: A Retrospective and Guide for Future Research. Paper presented at the Southeastern Archaeological Conference, Macon, GA.

Greenwald, Erin M. (editor)

2013 *A Company Man: The Remarkable French-Atlantic Voyage of a Clerk for the Company of the Indies. A Memoir by Marc-Antoine Caillot*. Translated by Teri F. Chalmers. The Historic New Orleans Collection, New Orleans, LA.

Gremillion, Kristen J.
1993 Adoption of Old World Crops and Processes of Cultural Change in the Historic Southeast. *Southeastern Archaeology* 12(1):15–20.
1995 Comparative Paleoethnobotany of Three Native Southeastern Communities of the Historic Period. *Southeastern Archaeology* 14(1):1–16.
Hall, Robert L.
1997 *An Archaeology of the Soul: North American Indian Belief and Ritual.* University of Illinois Press, Urbana.
2004 The Cahokia Site and Its People, in *Hero, Hawk, and Open Hand: American Indian Art of the Ancient Midwest and South,* edited by Richard F. Townsend and Robert V. Sharp, pp. 93–103. Art Institute of Chicago, Chicago, IL.
Hally, David J.
1970 *Archaeological Investigations of the Potts Tract Site (9Mu103), Murray County, Georgia.* Laboratory of Archaeology Series 6, University of Georgia, Athens.
1986 The Cherokee Archaeology of Georgia, in *The Conference on Cherokee Prehistory,* edited by David G. Moore, pp. 95–121. Warren Wilson College, Swannanoa, NC.
1993 The Territorial Size of Mississippian Chiefdoms, in *Archaeology of Eastern North America: Papers in Honor of Stephen Williams,* edited by James A. Stoltman, pp. 143–168. Archeological Report No. 25. Mississippi Department of Archives and History, Jackson.
1994a An Overview of Lamar Culture, in *Ocmulgee Archaeology, 1936–1986,* edited by David J. Hally, pp. 144–174. University of Georgia Press, Athens.
1994b The Chiefdom of Coosa, in *The Forgotten Centuries: Indians and Europeans in the American South, 1521–1704,* edited by Charles Hudson and Carmen Chaves Tesser, pp. 227–253. University of Georgia Press, Athens.
1996 Platform Mound Construction and the Instability of Mississippian Chiefdoms, in *Political Structure and Change in the Prehistoric Southeastern United States,* edited by John F. Scarry, pp. 92–127. University Press of Florida, Gainesville.
2006 The Nature of Mississippian Regional Systems, in *Light on the Path: The Anthropology and History of the Southeastern Indians,* edited by Thomas H. Pluckhahn and Robbie Ethridge, pp. 26–42. University of Alabama Press, Tuscaloosa.
2007 Mississippian Shell Gorgets in Regional Perspective, in *Southeastern Ceremonial Complex: Chronology, Content, Context,* edited by Adam King, pp. 185–231. University of Alabama Press, Tuscaloosa.
2008 *King: The Social Archaeology of a Late Mississippian Town in Northwestern Georgia.* University of Alabama Press, Tuscaloosa.
Hally, David J., and James B. Langford, Jr.
1988 *Mississippi Period Archaeology of the Georgia Valley and Ridge Province.* University of Georgia Laboratory of Archaeology Series, Report No. 25, Georgia Archaeological Research Design Paper, No. 4, Athens.
Hally, David J., and James L. Rudolph
1986 *Mississippi Period Archaeology of the Georgia Piedmont.* University of Georgia Laboratory of Archaeology Series, Report No. 24, Georgia Archaeological Research Design Paper, No. 2, Athens.
Hally, David J., Marvin T. Smith, and James B. Langford
1990 The Archaeological Reality of de Soto's Coosa, in *Columbian Consequences, Volume 2: Archaeological and Historical Perspectives on the Spanish Borderlands*

East, edited by David Hurst Thomas, pp. 121–138. Smithsonian Institution Press, Washington, DC.

Hamel, Paul B., and Mary U. Chiltoskey

1975 *Cherokee Plants and Their Uses: A 400 Year History*. Herald Publishing, Sylva, NC.

Hammett, Julia, and Beverly Sizemore

1988 Shell Beads and Ornaments: Socioeconomic Indicators of the Past, in *Proceedings of the 1986 Shell Bead Conference*, edited by Charles Hayes and Lynn Ceci, pp. 125–135. Rochester Museum and Science Center Research Records No. 20. Rochester, NY.

Hann, John H.

1988 *Apalachee: The Land between the Rivers*. University of Florida Press, Gainesville.

1993 Visitations and Revolts in Florida, 1656–1695. *Florida Archaeology* 7. Florida Bureau of Archaeological Research, Tallahassee.

1996 *A History of the Timucua Indians and Missions*. University of Florida Press, Gainesville.

Harkin, Michael E.

2004a *Reassessing Revitalization Movements: Perspectives from North America and the Pacific Islands*, edited by Michael E. Harkin. University of Nebraska Press, Lincoln.

2004b Introduction: Revitalization as History and Theory, in *Reassessing Revitalization Movements: Perspectives from North America and the Pacific Islands*, edited by Michael E. Harkin, pp. xv–xxxvi. University of Nebraska Press, Lincoln.

Harris, Norma J.

1999 *Native Americans of Santa María de Galve, 1698–1722*. M.A. thesis, Department of History, University of West Florida, Pensacola.

2003 Native Americans, in *Presidio Santa María de Galve: A Struggle for Survival in Colonial Spanish Pensacola*, edited by Judith A. Bense, pp. 257–314. University of Florida Press, Gainesville.

2007 Eighteenth Century Native American Migration and Interaction on the Spanish Frontier: Yamassee/Apalachee and Chisca Missions of Pensacola, Florida. Paper presented at the Annual Conference of the Society for Historical Archaeology, Williamsburg, VA.

Harris, Norma J., and Krista L. Eschbach

2006 *Presidio Isla de Santa Rosa: Archaeological Investigations 2002–2004*. University of West Florida Archaeology Institute, Report of Investigations Number 133. Pensacola.

Hart, C. W. M.

1943 A Reconsideration of Natchez Social Structure. *American Anthropologist* 45:379–386.

Hart, John P., David L. Asch, C. Margaret Scarry, and Gary W. Crawford

2002 The Age of the Common Bean (*Phaseolus vulgaris* L.) in the Northern Eastern Woodlands of North America. *American Antiquity* 76:377–385.

Hassig, Ross

1991 Roads, Routes, and Ties that Bind, in *Ancient Road Networks and Settlement Hierarchies in the New World*, edited by Charles Trombold, pp. 17–27. Cambridge University Press, Cambridge, UK.

Hatch, James W.
1974 *Social Dimensions of Dallas Mortuary Patterns.* M.A. thesis, Department of Anthropology, Pennsylvania State University, University Park.
1976 *Status in Death: Principles of Ranking in Dallas Culture Mortuary Remains.* Ph.D. dissertation, Department of Anthropology, Pennsylvania State University, University Park.
Havard, V.
1896 Drink Plants of the North American Indians. *Bulletin of the Torrey Botanical Club* 23(2):33–46.
Hawkins, Benjamin
1848 *Creek Confederacy, and A Sketch of the Creek Country, by Col. Benj. Hawkins, with a Sketch of the Author, with an Appendix of Treaties.* Georgia Historical Society, Savannah.
Helms, Mary W.
1988 *Ulysses' Sail: An Ethnographic Odyssey of Power, Knowledge, and Geographical Distance.* Princeton University Press, Princeton, NJ.
Henderson, A. Gwynn
2004 Textile Structures in the Fabric-Impressed and Net-Impressed Ceramic Assemblage from the Bone Bank Site (12-PO-4), in *Bone Bank: Archaeological Rescue Investigations at a Late Mississippian Site, Posey County, Indiana,* edited by Cheryl A. Munson, Appendix III. Report prepared for Indiana Department of Natural Resources, Division of Historic Preservation and Archaeology, and National Park Service, U.S. Department of Interior.
Henry, Lisa
2004 Expressions of Identity in Tahiti, in *Reassessing Revitalization Movements: Perspectives from North America and the Pacific Islands,* edited by Michael E. Harkin, pp. 247–260. University of Nebraska Press, Lincoln.
Heye, George G., F. W. Hodge, and George H. Pepper
1918 *The Nacoochee Mound in Georgia.* Contributions from the Museum of the American Indian Heye Foundation 4(3):1–103.
Hobsbawm, Eric
1983 Introduction: Inventing Traditions, in *The Invention of Traditions,* edited by Eric Hobsbawm and Terence Ranger, pp. 1–14. Cambridge University Press, Cambridge, UK.
Hodge, Frederick W., and Theodore H. Lewis (editors)
1907 *Spanish Explorers in the Southern United States, 1528–1543.* Charles Scribner's Sons, New York.
Hoffman, Kathleen
1993 The Archaeology of the Convento de San Francisco, in *The Spanish Missions of La Florida,* edited by Bonnie G. McEwan, pp. 62–86. University of Florida Press, Gainesville.
1997 Cultural Development in La Florida. *Historical Archaeology* 31(1):24–35.
Hollenbach, Kandace D.
2008 Plant Remains from 9FN341, Fannin County, Georgia. Report submitted to Brockington and Associates, Norcross, Georgia. Archaeological Research Laboratory, University of Tennessee, Knoxville.
2009 *Foraging the Tennessee River Valley, 12,500 to 8,000 Years Ago.* University of Alabama Press, Tuscaloosa.

2010 Plant Remains from 38AK933, a Mississippian and Contact Period Site in Aiken County, South Carolina. Report submitted to Brockington and Associates, Norcross, Georgia. Archaeological Research Laboratory, University of Tennessee, Knoxville.

Holmes, William Henry

1883 Art in Shell of the Ancient Americas, in *Second Annual Report of the Bureau of American Ethnology, 1880–1881,* pp. 179–305. Smithsonian Institution, Washington, DC.

1886 Ancient Pottery of the Mississippi Valley. *Fourth Annual Report of the Bureau of American Ethnology, 1882–1883,* pp. 361–436. Smithsonian Institution, Washington, DC.

1896 Prehistoric Textile Art of the Eastern United States. *Thirteenth Annual Report of the Bureau of Ethnology, 1891–1892,* pp. 3–36. Smithsonian Institution, Washington, DC.

Honerkamp, Nicholas, and Norma Harris

2005 Unfired Brandon Gunflints from the Presidio Santa María de Galve, Pensacola, Florida. *Historical Archaeology* 39(4):95–111.

Horton, Elizabeth T.

2010 *The Ties That Bind: Fabric Traditions and Fiber Use in the Ozark Plateau.* Ph.D. dissertation, Department of Anthropology, Washington University, St. Louis, MO.

2014 Weaving for the World Beyond: Iconographic and Decorative Fabrics from Craig Mound at Spiro. Paper presented at the Southeastern Archaeological Conference, Greenville, SC.

Horton, Elizabeth, and George Sabo III

2011 Spiro Perishable Project Makes Exciting New Discovery. *Field Notes: Newsletter of the Arkansas Archeological Society* (358):9–13.

Hoyal, Suzanne D.

2005 Textiles Impressed on 40WM210 Ceramics, in *The Brentwood Library Site: A Mississippian Town on the Little Harpeth River, Williamson County, Tennessee,* edited by Michael C. Moore, pp. 533–543. Research Series No. 15, Division of Archaeology, Tennessee Department of Environment and Conservation, Nashville, TN.

Hudson, Charles

1976 *The Southeastern Indians.* University of Tennessee Press, Knoxville.

1985 De Soto in Arkansas: A Brief Synopsis. *Field Notes: Newsletter of the Arkansas Archeological Society* 205:3–12.

1994 The Social Context of the Chiefdom of Ichisi, in *Ocmulgee Archaeology, 1936–1986,* edited by David J. Hally, pp. 175–180. University of Georgia Press, Athens.

1997 *Knights of Spain, Warriors of the Sun: Hernando de Soto and the South's Ancient Chiefdoms.* University of Georgia Press, Athens.

Hudson, Charles M., Jr. (editor)

1990 *The Juan Pardo Expeditions: Explorations of the Carolinas and Tennessee, 1566–1568.* Smithsonian Institution Press, Washington, DC.

2005 *The Juan Pardo Expeditions: Exploration of the Carolinas and Tennessee, 1566–1568.* 2nd ed. University of Alabama Press, Tuscaloosa.

Hudson, Charles, Robin A. Beck, Jr., Chester B. DePratter, Robbie Ethridge, and John E. Worth

2008 On Interpreting Cofitachequi. *Ethnohistory* 55:465–490.

Hudson, Charles, Marvin T. Smith, and Chester B. DePratter
1987 The Hernando de Soto Expedition: From Apalachee to Chiaha. *Southeastern Archaeology* 19(1):18–28.
Hudson, Charles, Marvin T. Smith, Chester B. DePratter, and Emilia Kelley
1989 The Tristán de Luna Expedition, 1559–1561. *Southeastern Archaeology* 8(1):31–45.
Hudson, Charles, Marvin Smith, David Hally, Richard Polhemus, and Chester DePratter
1985 Coosa: A Chiefdom in the Sixteenth-Century Southeastern United States. *American Antiquity* 50(4):723–737.
1987 Reply to Boyd and Schroedl. *American Antiquity* 52(4):845–856.
Hulse, Frederick S.
1941 The People Who Lived at Irene, in *Irene Mound Site, Chatham County, Georgia*, edited by Joseph Caldwell and Catherine McCann, pp. 57–68. University of Georgia Press, Athens.
Ingraham, Joseph H.
1835 *The South-west, by a Yankee.* 2 vols. Harper and Brothers, New York.
Jackson, Jason Baird (editor)
2012 *Yuchi Indian Histories before the Removal Era.* University of Nebraska Press, Lincoln.
Jenkins, Ned J.
2009 Tracing the Origins of the Early Creeks, 1050–1700 CE, in *Mapping the Mississippian Shatter Zone: The Colonial Indian Slave Trade and Regional Instability in the American South*, edited by Robbie Ethridge and Sheri M. Shuck-Hall, pp. 188–249. University of Nebraska Press, Lincoln.
Jenkins, Richard
2004 *Social Identity.* Routledge, London, UK.
Jennings, Jesse D.
1940 Archeological Report on Fatherland Plantation Mound Group, Near Natchez, Mississippi. Manuscript on file, National Park Service, Southeast Regional Office, Tallahassee, FL.
1941 Chickasaw and Earlier Indian Cultures of Northeast Mississippi. *Journal of Mississippi History* 3(3):155–226.
Jeter, Marvin D.
2009 Shatter Zone Shock Waves along the Lower Mississippi, in *Mapping the Mississippian Shatter Zone: The Colonial Indian Slave Trade and Regional Instability in the American South*, edited by Robbie Ethridge and Sheri M. Shuck-Hall, pp. 365–387. University of Nebraska Press, Lincoln.
Johannessen, Sissel
1993 Food, Dishes, and Society in the Mississippi Valley, in *Foraging and Farming in the Eastern Woodlands*, edited by C. Margaret Scarry, pp. 182–205. University Press of Florida, Gainesville.
Johnson, Glenn
n.d. (pre-1980) Unpublished Leflore site field notes on file at the Cottonlandia Museum, Greenwood, MS.
Johnson, Jay K., Bryan S. Haley, and Louis G. Zachos
2014 Reassessing Mississippian Floodplain Adaptation in the Northern Yazoo Basin of Western Mississippi. Paper presented at the Southeastern Archaeological Conference, Greenville, SC.

Johnson, Jay K., John W. O'Hear, Robbie Ethridge, Brad R. Lieb, Susan L. Scott, and H. Edwin Jackson

2008 Measuring Chickasaw Adaptation on the Western Frontier of the Colonial South: A Correlation of Documentary and Archaeological Data. *Southeastern Archaeology* 27(1):1–30.

Johnson, Patrick

2012 *Apalachee Agency on the Gulf Coast Frontier.* M.A. thesis, Department of Anthropology, University of West Florida, Pensacola.

Johnston, James

1976 Jayhawker Stories: Historical Lore in the Arkansas Ozarks. *Mid-America Folklore* 4:3–10.

Jones, B. Calvin

1982 Southern Cult Manifestations at the Lake Jackson Site, Leon County, Florida: Salvage Excavation of Mound 3. *Midcontinental Journal of Archaeology* 7(1):3–44.

1994 The Lake Jackson Mound Complex (8LE1): Stability and Change in Fort Walton Culture. *Florida Anthropologist* 47(2):120–146.

Jones, B. Calvin, John Hann, and John Scarry

1991 San Pedro y San Pablo de Patale: A Seventeenth-Century Spanish Mission in Leon County, Florida. *Florida Archaeology Number 5.* Florida Bureau of Archaeological Research, Tallahassee.

Jørgensen, Dolly, and Peter Quelch

2014 The Origins and History of Medieval Wood-Pastures, in *European Wood-pastures in Transition: A Social-ecological Approach,* edited by Tibor Hartel and Tobias Pleininger, pp. 55–69. Routledge, New York.

Joyce, Rosemary and Jeanne Lopiparo

2005 PostScript: Doing Agency in Archaeology. *Journal of Archaeological Method and Theory* 12:365–374.

Kavasch, Barrie

1977 *Native Harvests: Botanicals and Recipes of the American Indian.* American Indian Archaeological Institute. Washington, CT.

Kehoe, Alice B.

1999 A Resort to Subtler Contrivances, in *Manifesting Power: Gender and the Interpretation of Power in Archaeology,* edited by T. L. Sweely, pp. 17–29. Routledge, London, UK.

2001 From Spirit Cave to the Blackfoot Rez: The Importance of Twined Fabric in North American Indian Societies, in *Fleeting Identities: Perishable Material Culture in Archaeological Research,* edited by Penelope B. Drooker, pp. 210–225. Occasional Paper No. 28. Center for Archaeological Investigations, Southern Illinois University, Carbondale.

Kelly, Arthur R.

1941 Forward, in *Irene Mound Site, Chatham County, Georgia,* edited by Joseph Caldwell and Catherine McCann, pp. v–vii. University of Georgia Press, Athens.

Kelly, John E.

2006 The Ritualization of Cahokia: The Structure and Organization of Early Cahokia Crafts, in *Leadership and Polity in Mississippian Society,* edited by Brian M. Butler and Paul D. Welch, pp. 236–263. Occasional Paper No. 33. Center for Archaeological Investigations, Southern Illinois University, Carbondale.

Kerner, Karen
1963 Magical Counterspinning: An Examination of Peruvian "Witching Veils." *International Congress of Anthropological and Ethnological Sciences* 8(3):32–35.
Kindscher, Kelly
1987 *Edible Wild Plants of the Prairie.* University Press of Kansas, Lawrence.
King, Adam
1999 De Soto's Itaba and the Nature of Sixteenth Century Paramount Chiefdoms. *Southeastern Archaeology* 18(2):110–123.
2003 *Etowah: The Political History of a Chiefdom Capital.* University of Alabama Press, Tuscaloosa.
2004 Power and the Sacred: Mound C and the Etowah Chiefdom, in *Hero, Hawk, and Open Hand: American Indian Art of the Ancient Midwest and South,* edited by Richard F. Townsend and Robert V. Sharp, pp. 150–165. Art Institute of Chicago, Chicago, IL.
2005 Deciphering Etowah's Mound C: The Construction History and Mortuary Record of a Mississippian Burial Mound. *Southeastern Archaeology* 23(2):153–165.
2007 Mound C and the Southeastern Ceremonial Complex in the History of the Etowah Site, in *Southeastern Ceremonial Complex: Chronology, Content, Context,* edited by Adam King, pp. 107–133. University of Alabama Press, Tuscaloosa.
2010 Multiple Groups, Overlapping Symbols and the Creation of a Sacred Space at Etowah's Mound C, in *Mississippian Mortuary Studies: Beyond Hierarchy and the Representationist Perspective,* edited by Lynne P. Sullivan and Robert C. Mainfort, Jr., pp. 54–73. University Press of Florida, Gainesville.
2011 Iconography of the Hightower Region of Eastern Tennessee and Northern Georgia, in *Visualizing the Sacred: Cosmic Visions, Regionalism, and the Art of the Mississippian World,* edited by George E. Lankford, F. Kent Reilly, III, and James F. Garber, pp. 279–293. University of Texas Press, Austin.
King, Adam (editor)
2007 *Southeastern Ceremonial Complex: Chronology, Content, Context.* University of Alabama Press, Tuscaloosa.
King, Julia
1984 Ceramic Variability in 17th Century St. Augustine, Florida. *Historical Archaeology* 18(2):75–82.
King, Mary E., and Joan S. Gardner
1981 The Analysis of Textiles from Spiro Mound, Oklahoma, in *The Research Potential of Anthropological Museum Collections,* edited by A. E. Cantwell, J. B. Griffin, and N. A. Rothschild, pp. 123–139. Annals of the New York Academy of Sciences, vol. 376. New York Academy of Sciences, New York.
Kneberg, Madeline
1959 Engraved Shell Gorgets and their Associations. *Tennessee Archaeologist* 15(1):1–39.
Knight, Vernon James, Jr.
1975 Some Observations Concerning Plant Materials and Aboriginal Smoking in Eastern North America. *Journal of Alabama Archaeology* 21(2):120–144.
1985 *Tukabatchee: Archaeological Investigations at an Historic Creek Town, Elmore County, Alabama, 1984.* Office of Archaeological Research, Report of Investigations No. 45. Alabama State Museum of Natural History, Tuscaloosa.

1986 The Institutional Organization of Mississippian Religion. *American Antiquity* 51(4):675–687.

1990 Social Organization and the Evolution of Hierarchy in Southeastern Chiefdoms. *Journal of Anthropological Research* 46(1):1–23.

1994 Ocmulgee Fields Culture and the Historical Development of Creek Ceramics, in *Ocmulgee Archaeology, 1936–1986*, edited by David J. Hally, pp. 181–189. University of Georgia Press, Athens.

1997 Some Developmental Parallels between Cahokia and Moundville, in *Cahokia: Domination and Ideology in the Mississippian World*, edited by Timothy R. Pauketat and Thomas E. Emerson, pp. 229–247. University of Nebraska Press, Lincoln.

2010 *Mound Excavations at Moundville: Architecture, Elites, and Social Order*. University of Alabama Press, Tuscaloosa.

Knight, Vernon J., Jr., James A. Brown, and George E. Lankford

2001 On the Subject Matter of Southeastern Ceremonial Complex Art. *Southeastern Archaeology* 20(2):129–141.

Knight, Vernon James, Jr., and Tim S. Mistovich

1984 *Walter F. George Lake: Archaeological Survey of Fee Owned Lands, Alabama and Georgia*. Office of Archaeological Research, Report of Investigations No. 42. The University of Alabama, Tuscaloosa.

Knight, Vernon James, and Vincas P. Steponaitis (editors)

2007 *Archaeology of the Moundville Chiefdom*. Reprint of the 1998 Smithsonian Institution Press edition with a new preface. University of Alabama Press, Tuscaloosa.

Kowalewski, Stephen A., and James W. Hatch

1991 The Sixteenth-Century Expansion of Settlement in the Upper Oconee Watershed, Georgia. *Southeastern Archaeology* 10(1):1–17.

Kozuch, Laura

1998 *Marine Shells from Mississippian Sites*. Ph.D. dissertation, Department of Anthropology, University of Florida, Gainesville.

Krieger, Alex D.

1940 An Analytical System for East Texas Pottery. *Southeastern Archaeological Conference Newsletter* 2(4):7–9.

Krutak, Lars

2013 The Art of Enchantment: Corporeal Marking and Tattooing Bundles of the Great Plains, in *Drawing with Great Needles: Ancient Tattoo Traditions of North America*, edited by Aaron Deter-Wolf and Carol Diaz-Granados, pp. 131–173. University of Texas Press, Austin.

Kuhnlein, Harriet V., and Nancy J. Turner

1991 *Traditional Plant Foods of Canadian Indigenous Peoples: Nutrition, Botany and Use*. Gordon and Breach Science Publishers, Philadelphia, PA.

Kurz, Don

1997 *Shrubs and Woody Vines of Missouri*. Missouri Department of Conservation, Jefferson City.

Kuttruff, Jenna Tedrick

1987 A Prehistoric Twined Bag from Big Bone Cave, Tennessee: Manufacture, Repair, and Use. *Ars Textrina* 8:125–153.

1988a *Textile Attributes and Production Complexity as Indicators of Caddoan Status*

Differentiation in the Arkansas Valley and Southern Ozark Regions. Ph.D. dissertation, Department of Textiles and Clothing, Ohio State University, Columbus.

1988b Techniques and Production Complexity of Mississippian Period Textiles from Spiro, Oklahoma, in *Textiles as Primary Sources, Proceedings of the First Symposium of the Textile Society of America,* compiled by John E. Vollmer, pp. 145–150. Minneapolis Institute of Art, Minneapolis, MN.

1991 Interpretation of Textile Production and Use by High and Low Status Caddoan Groups, in *Materials Issues in Art and Archaeology II,* edited by Pamela B. Vandiver, J. Druzik, and G. Wheeler, pp. 777–783. Materials Research Society, Pittsburgh, PA.

1993 Mississippian Period Status Differentiation through Textile Analysis: A Caddoan Example. *American Antiquity* 58(1):125–145.

Kuttruff, Jenna Tedrick, and Penelope B. Drooker

2001 Textiles from the Wickliffe Mounds Site, in *Excavations at Wickliffe Mounds,* edited by Kit W. Wesler, chapter 14 in accompanying CD-ROM. University of Alabama Press, Tuscaloosa.

Kuttruff, Jenna Tedrick, and Carl Kuttruff

1996 Mississippian Textile Evidence in Fabric Impressed Ceramics from Mound Bottom (40CH8), Tennessee, in *Native Fiber Industries from Eastern North America: Analyses of Prehistoric and Ethnographic Collections,* edited by James B. Petersen, pp. 160–173. University of Tennessee Press, Knoxville.

Kuttruff, Jenna Tedrick, Sandra G. DeHart, and Michael J. O'Brien

1998 7500 Years of Prehistoric Footwear from Arnold Research Cave, Missouri. *Science* 281(5373):72–75.

Langford, James B., Jr., and Marvin T. Smith

1990 Recent Investigations in the Core of the Coosa Province, in *Lamar Archaeology: Mississippian Chiefdoms in the Deep South,* edited by Mark Williams and Gary Shapiro, pp. 104–116. University of Alabama Press, Tuscaloosa.

Lankford, George E.

1993 Legends of the Adelantado, in *The Expedition of Hernando de Soto West of the Mississippi, 1541–1543,* edited by Gloria A. Young and Michael P. Hoffman, pp. 173–191. University of Arkansas Press, Fayetteville.

2006 *Bearing Witness: Memories of Slavery in Arkansas.* University of Arkansas Press, Fayetteville.

2007a The Great Serpent in Eastern North America, in *Ancient Objects and Sacred Realms: Interpretations of Mississippian Iconography,* edited by F. Kent Reilly III and James F. Garber, pp. 107–135. University of Texas Press, Austin.

2007b Some Cosmological Motifs in the Southeastern Ceremonial Complex, in *Ancient Objects and Sacred Realms: Interpretations of Mississippian Iconography,* edited by F. Kent Reilly III and James F. Garber, pp. 8–38. University of Texas Press, Austin.

2008 *Looking for Lost Lore: Studies in Folklore, Ethnology, and Iconography.* University of Alabama Press, Tuscaloosa.

2009 How Historical Are the De Soto Chronicles? in *The Search for Mabila: The Decisive Battle between Hernando de Soto and Chief Tascalusa,* edited by Vernon James Knight, Jr., pp. 31–44. University of Alabama Press, Tuscaloosa.

2011 The Swirl-Cross and the Center, in *Visualizing the Sacred: Cosmic Visions, Regionalism, and the Art of the Mississippian World,* edited by George E. Lankford,

F. Kent Reilly III, and James F. Garber, pp. 251–275. University of Texas Press, Austin.
Lankford, George E., F. Kent Reilly III, and James F. Garber (editors)
2011 *Visualizing the Sacred: Cosmic Visions, Regionalism, and the Art of the Mississippian World.* University of Texas Press, Austin.
Lankford, George E. (editor)
2006 *Bearing Witness: Memories of Arkansas Slavery Narratives from the 1930s WPA Collections.* 2nd ed. University of Arkansas Press, Fayetteville.
2007 *Reachable Stars: Patterns in the Ethnoastronomy of Eastern North America.* University of Alabama Press, Tuscaloosa.
2011 *Native American Legends of the Southeast: Tales from the Natchez, Caddo, Biloxi, Chickasaw, and Other Nations.* University of Alabama Press, Tuscaloosa.
Lapham, Heather
2016 Fauna, Subsistence, and Survival, at Fort San Juan, in *Fort San Juan and the Limits of Empire,* edited by Robin A. Beck, Jr., Christopher B. Rodning, and David G. Moore, pp. 271–300. University Press of Florida, Gainesville.
Larsen, Clark S., Margaret J. Schoeninger, Nikolaas J. van der Merwe, Katherine M. Moore, and Julia A. Lee-Thorp
1992 Carbon and Nitrogen Stable Isotope Signatures of Human Dietary Change in the Georgia Bight. *American Journal of Physical Anthropology* 89:197–214.
Larson, Lewis H.
1971 Archaeological Implications of Social Stratification at the Etowah Site, Georgia, in *Approaches to the Social Dimensions of Mortuary Practices,* edited by James A. Brown, pp. 58–67. Society for American Archaeology Memoir No. 25. Washington, DC.
Lave, Jeanne, and Etienne Wenger
1991 *Situated Learning: Legitimate Peripheral Participation.* Cambridge University Press, Cambridge, UK.
Lefler, Hugh T. (editor)
1967 *A New Voyage to Carolina by John Lawson.* University of North Carolina Press, Chapel Hill.
Leland, Waldo Gifford
1932 *Guide to Materials for American History in the Libraries and Archives of Paris.* Carnegie Institution of Washington, Washington, DC.
Lemonnier, Pierre
1986 The Study of Material Culture Today: Toward an Anthropology of Technical Systems. *Journal of Anthropological Archaeology* 5:147–186.
León, Juan Isidoro de
1745 Letter to Manuel de Montiano, May 21, 1745. Legajo 863, ff. 220r-229r, Santo Domingo, Archivo General de Indias, Seville, Spain.
Le Page du Pratz, Antoine Simon
1758 *Histoire de la Louisiane,* 3 volumes. Bure, Delaguette and Lambert, Paris, France.
1972 [1774] *The History of Louisiana, or of the Western Parts of Virginia and Carolina.* Claitor's Publishing Division, Baton Rouge, LA.
Leturiondo, Domingo de
1685 Visitation of the Village of Santa Maria, December 24, 1685. Legajo 2584, No. 9, ff. 93r-113v, Santo Domingo, Archivo General de Indias, Seville, Spain.

Levy, Janet E.
1999 Gender, Power, and Heterarchy in Middle-Level Societies, in *Manifesting Power: Gender and the Interpretation of Power in Archaeology*, edited by Tracy L. Sweely, pp. 62–78. Routledge, London, UK.

Levy, Janet E., J. Alan May, and David G. Moore
1990 From Ysa to Joara: Cultural Diversity in the Catawba Valley from the Fourteenth to the Sixteenth Century, in *Columbian Consequences, Volume 2: Archaeological and Historical Perspectives on the Spanish Borderlands East*, edited by David Hurst Thomas, pp. 153–168. Smithsonian Institution Press, Washington, DC.

Lewis, T. M. N.
1960 Editors' Notes: Settico Site on Little Tennessee River. *Tennessee Archaeologist* 16(2):92–103.

Lewis, Thomas M. N., and Madeline Kneberg
1946 *Hiwassee Island: An Archaeological Account of Four Tennessee Indian Peoples.* University of Tennessee Press, Knoxville.
1957 Citico Site Artifacts. *Tennessee Archaeologist* 13(2):98–99.

Lewis, Thomas M. N., Madeline Kneberg Lewis, and Lynne P. Sullivan (compilers and editors)
1995 *The Prehistory of the Chickamauga Basin in Tennessee.* 2 vols. University of Tennessee Press, Knoxville.

Liebmann, Matthew
2008 The Innovative Materiality of Revitalization Movements: Lessons from the Pueblo Revolt of 1680. *American Anthropologist* 110: 360–372.

Lightfoot, Kent, Antoinette Martinez, and Ann M. Schiff
1998 Daily Practice and Material Culture in Pluralistic Social Settings: An Archaeological Study of Culture Change and Persistence from Fort Ross, California. *American Antiquity* 63(2):199–222.

Lindsey, Mrs. E. M.
1964 Cooper Farm Salvage Project. *Journal of Alabama Archaeology* 10:22–29.

Linton, Ralph
1943 Nativistic Movements. *American Anthropologist* 45:230–240.

Litschi, Melissa
2011 *The French Natchez Settlement According to the Memory of Dumont de Montigny*. Honors thesis, Curriculum in Archaeology, University of North Carolina, Chapel Hill.

Little, Keith
2010 Sixteenth-Century Glass Bead Chronology in Southeastern North America. *Southeastern Archaeology* 29(1):222–232.

Little, Keith, and Cailup B. Curren
1981 Site 1Ce308: A Protohistoric Site on the Upper Coosa River in Alabama. *Journal of Alabama Archaeology* 27(2):117–140.

Livingood, Patrick C.
2009 Theories to Explain the Lack of Confederation among the Descendants of the Plaquemine of the Lower Mississippi Valley. Paper presented at the Plains Anthropological Conference, Norman, OK.

Loren, Diana DiPaolo
1995 *Forgotten Actors: French Interest Groups, Natchez Indians and African Slaves in*

Louisiana: 1699–1731. M.A. thesis, Department of Anthropology, State University of New York, Binghamton.

2010 *The Archaeology of Clothing and Bodily Adornment in Colonial America.* University Press of Florida, Gainesville.

Lorenz, Karl

1997 A Re-examination of Natchez Sociopolitical Complexity: A View from the Grand Village and Beyond. *Southeastern Archaeology* 16(2):97–112.

Lyman, R. Lee, Michael J. O'Brien, and Robert C. Dunnell

1997 *The Rise and Fall of Culture History.* Plenum Press, New York.

Lyon, Eugene

1976 *The Enterprise of Florida: Pedro Menéndez de Avilés and the Spanish Conquest of 1565–1568.* University Press of Florida, Gainesville.

1990 The Enterprise of Florida, in *Columbian Consequences, Volume 2: Archaeological and Historical Perspectives on the Spanish Borderlands East,* edited by David Hurst Thomas, pp. 281–296. Smithsonian Institution Press, Washington, DC.

Mainfort, Robert C., Jr.

1999 Late Period Phases in the Central Mississippi Valley: A Multivariate Approach, in *Arkansas Archeology: Essays in Honor of Dan and Phyllis Morse,* edited by Robert C. Mainfort, Jr. and M. D. Jeter, pp. 143–168. University of Arkansas Press, Fayetteville.

Marceaux, Shawn, and David H. Dye

2007 Hightower Anthropomorphic Marine Shell Gorgets and Duck River Sword-Form Flint Bifaces: Middle Mississippian Ritual Regalia in the Southern Appalachians, in *Southeastern Ceremonial Complex: Chronology, Content, Context,* edited by Adam King, pp. 165–184. University of Alabama Press, Tuscaloosa.

Marcoux, Jon Bernard

2007 On Reconsidering Display Goods Production and Circulation in the Moundville Chiefdom. *Southeastern Archaeology* 26(2):232–245.

Martin, Alexander C., and William D. Barkley

1961 *Seed Identification Manual.* University of California, Berkeley.

Mason, Carol I

2005 *The Archaeology of Ocmulgee Old Fields, Macon, Georgia.* University of Alabama Press, Tuscaloosa.

McCarthy, Donna M.

2011 *Using Osteological Evidence to Assess Biological Affinity: A Re-Evaluation of Selected Sites in East Tennessee.* Ph.D. dissertation, Department of Anthropology. University of Tennessee, Knoxville.

McCollough, Major C. R., and Quentin Bass III

1983 *Moccasin Bend: Chattanooga's First National Historic Landmark.* Chattanooga Regional Anthropological Association, TN.

McDermott, John F.

1958 *The Lost Panoramas of the Mississippi.* University of Chicago Press, Chicago, IL.

McEwan, Bonnie G. (editor)

1993 *The Spanish Missions of La Florida.* University of Florida Press, Gainesville.

McMullen, Ann M.

2004 Canny about Conflict: Nativism, Revitalization and the Invention of Tradition in Native Southeastern New England, in *Reassessing Revitalization Movements:*

Perspectives from North America and the Pacific Islands, edited by Michael E. Harkin, pp. 261–278. University of Nebraska Press, Lincoln.

McWilliams, Richebourg G. (translator and editor)

1988 *Fleur de Lys and Calumet, Being the Pénicaut Narrative of French Adventure in Louisiana.* Reprint of the 1953 edition. University of Alabama Press, Tuscaloosa.

Medsger, Oliver Perry

1972 *Edible Wild Plants.* Collier Books, New York.

Melcher, Jennifer

2011 *More Than Just Copies: Colono Ware as a Reflection of Multiethnic Interaction on the 18th-Century Spanish Frontier of West Florida.* M.A. thesis, Department of Anthropology, University of West Florida, Pensacola.

2012 Mixed Influences: Mid-18th Century Native American Ceramics from the Northern Gulf Coast. Poster presented at the 64th Annual Meeting of the Florida Anthropological Society, Tallahassee.

Menéndez, Alonso, Francisco de Ybarra, Juan de Zapala, Bernabé de Aluste, and Thomás de Yor

1657 Letter to the Spanish Crown, September 16, 1657. Legajo 235, Santo Domingo, Archivo General de Indias, Seville, Spain.

Menéndez Márquez, Francisco

1714 Inventory and valuation of the estate of Francisco de Florencia, February 14, 1714. Legajo 952, ff. 305r-308r, Contaduría, Archivo General de Indias, Seville, Spain.

Merveilleux, François Louis de

2003 *Massacre at Natchez in 1729: The Rheims Manuscript*, translated and edited by Winston De Ville. Provincial Press, Ville Platte, LA.

Meskell, Lynn

2001 Archaeologies of Identity, in *Archaeological Theory Today*, edited by Ian Hodder, pp. 187–213. Polity Press, Cambridge, UK.

Meyers, Maureen

2009 From Refugees to Slave Traders: The Transformation of the Westo Indians, in *Mapping the Mississippian Shatter Zone: The Colonial Indian Slave Trade and Regional Instability in the American South*, edited by Robbie Ethridge and Sheri M. Shuck-Hall, pp. 81–103. University of Nebraska Press, Lincoln.

Michelaki, Kostalena

2007 More than Meets the Eye: Reconsidering Variability in Iroquoian Ceramics. *Canadian Journal of Archaeology* 31(2):143–170.

Milanich, Jerald T.

1971 *The Alachua Tradition of North-Central Florida.* Contributions of the Florida State Museum, Anthropology and History, Number 17. Gainesville.

1972a Excavations at the Richardson Site, Alachua County, Florida: An Early 17th Century Potano Indian Village (with notes on Potano culture change). *Bureau of Historic Sites and Properties Bulletin* 2:35–61.

1972b Tacatacuru and the San Pedro de Mocamo Mission. *The Florida Historical Quarterly* 50(3):283–291.

1978 The Western Timucua: Patterns of Acculturation and Change, in *Tacachale: Essays on the Indians of Florida and Southeastern Georgia during the Historic Period*, edited by Jerald T. Milanich and Samuel Proctor, pp. 59–88. University Presses of Florida, Gainesville.

1999 *Laboring in the Fields of the Lord: Spanish Missions and Southeastern Indians.* Smithsonian Institution Press, Washington, DC.

Miller, Daniel, and Christopher Tilley (editors)

1984 *Ideology, Power and Prehistory.* Cambridge University Press, Cambridge, UK.

Miller Surrey, Nancy Maria

2006 *The Commerce of Louisiana during the French Regime 1699–1763.* Reprint of the 1916 edition, with an introduction by Gregory A. Waselkov. University of Alabama Press, Tuscaloosa.

Mills, Barbara J.

2002 Acts of Resistance: Zuni Ceramics, Social Identity, and the Pueblo Revolt, in *Archaeologies of the Pueblo Revolt,* edited by Robert W. Preucel, pp. 85–96. University of New Mexico Press, Albuquerque.

Minar, C. Jill

2001 Motor Skills and the Learning Process: The Conservation of Cordage Final Twist Direction in Communities of Practice. *Journal of Anthropological Research* 57(4):381–405.

Minar, C. Jill, and Patricia L. Crown

2001 Learning and Craft Production: An Introduction. *Journal of Anthropological Research* 57(4):369–380.

Mintz, Sydney W.

1985 *Sweetness and Power: The Place of Sugar in Modern History.* Viking Penguin, New York.

Mitchem, Jeffrey

1993 Beads and Pendants from San Luis de Talimali: Inferences from Varying Contexts, in *The Spanish Missions of La Florida,* edited by Bonnie G. McEwan, pp. 399–417. University Press of Florida, Gainesville.

Moerman, Daniel E.

2004 *Native American Ethnobotany: Database of Foods, Drugs, Dyes and Fibers of Native American Peoples, Derived from Plants.* Electronic document, http://herb.umd.umich.edu/, accessed February 6, 2005.

Moore, Clarence B.

1898 Certain Aboriginal Mounds of the Savannah River. *Journal of the Academy of Natural Sciences of Philadelphia* 11:167–172.

1899 Certain Aboriginal Remains of the Alabama River. *Journal of the Academy of Natural Sciences of Philadelphia* 11:289–347.

1915 Aboriginal Sites on Tennessee River. *Journal of the Academy of Natural Sciences of Philadelphia* 16:169–427.

Moore, David G.

2002 *Catawba Valley Mississippian: Ceramics, Chronology, and Catawba Indians.* University of Alabama Press, Tuscaloosa.

Moore, David G., and Robin A. Beck, Jr.

2005 Beyond Joara: Burke Phase Structures at the Ensley Site, Burke County, North Carolina. Paper presented at the 62nd Annual Meeting of the Southeastern Archaeological Conference, Columbia, SC.

Moore, David G., Robin A. Beck, Jr., and Christopher B. Rodning

2004 Joara and Fort San Juan: Culture Contact at the Edge of the World. *Antiquity* 78(299). Project Gallery. http://antiquity.ac.uk/ProjGall/moore/, accessed May 1, 2016.

2005 Joara and Fort San Juan Revisited, in *The Juan Pardo Expeditions: Explorations of the Carolinas and Tennessee, 1566–1568*, by Charles Hudson, pp. 343–349. University of Alabama Press, Tuscaloosa.

Moore, Katherine

1985 Archaeobotanical Analyses at Five Sites in the Richard B. Russell Reservoir Area, Georgia and South Carolina, in *Prehistoric Human Ecology along the Upper Savannah River: Excavations at the Rucker's Bottom, Abbeville and Bullard Site Groups*, assembled by David G. Anderson and Joseph Schuldenrein, pp. 673–693. Russell Papers 1985; National Park Service, Archaeological Services, Atlanta, GA.

Moorehead, Warren K. (editor)

1932 *Etowah Papers*. Yale University Press, New Haven, for the Phillips Academy, Andover, MA.

Morse, Dan F., and Phyllis A. Morse

1983 *Archaeology of the Central Mississippi Valley*. Academic Press, New York.

Morse, Phyllis A.

1981 *Parkin: The 1978–1979 Archeological Investigations of a Cross County, Arkansas Site*. Arkansas Archeological Survey, Research Papers 13, Fayetteville.

Muller, Jon

1966 *An Experimental Theory of Stylistic Analysis*. Ph.D. dissertation, Department of Anthropology, Harvard University, Cambridge, MA.

1984 Mississippian Specialization and Salt. *American Antiquity* 49: 489–507.

1989 The Southern Cult. In *Southeastern Ceremonial Complex: Artifacts and Analysis*, edited by Patricia Galloway, pp. 11–26. University of Nebraska Press, Lincoln.

1997 *Mississippian Political Economy*. Plenum Press, New York.

Neitzel, Robert S.

1964 The Natchez Grand Village. *Florida Anthropologist* 17(2):63–66.

1965 Archaeology of the Fatherland Site: The Grand Village of the Natchez. *Anthropological Papers* 51(1). American Museum of Natural History, New York.

1978 A Doublebarreled Detective Story, in *Codex Wauchope: A Tribute Roll*, edited by Marco Giardino, Barbara Edmonson, and Winifred Creamer, pp. 19–34. Human Mosaic No. 12. Tulane University, New Orleans, LA.

1981 A Suggested Technique for Measuring Landscape Changes Through Archaeology, in *Traces of Prehistory*, edited by Frederick H. West and Robert Neuman, pp. 57–70. Geoscience and Man 22. Baton Rouge, LA.

1983 *The Grand Village of the Natchez Revisited: Excavations at the Fatherland Site, Adams County, Mississippi, 1972*. Mississippi Department of Archives and History Archaeological Report No. 12. Jackson.

Newsom, Lee Ann

2016 Wood Selection and Technology in Structures 1 and 5, in *Fort San Juan and the Limits of Empire*, edited by Robin A. Beck, Jr., Christopher B. Rodning, and David G. Moore, pp. 150–232. University Press of Florida, Gainesville.

Niethammer, Carolyn

1974 *American Indian Food and Lore*. Macmillan, New York.

O'Brien, Michael J., and R. Lee Lyman

2000 *Applying Evolutionary Archaeology: A Systematic Approach*. Kluwer Academic/Plenum, New York.

O'Donovan, Maria

2002 Introduction, in *The Dynamics of Power*, edited by Maria O'Donovan, pp. 3–16.

Occasional Paper No. 30. Center for Archaeological Investigations, Southern Illinois University, Carbondale.

Ortner, Sherry

1984 Theory in Anthropology since the Sixties. *Comparative Studies in Society and History* 26(1):126–166.

1992 *High Religion: A Cultural and Political History of Sherpa Buddhism.* Princeton University Press, Princeton, NJ.

Oswalt, Wendall H., and Sharlotte Neely

1996 The Natchez: Sophisticated Farmers of the Deep South, in *This Land Was Theirs.* 5th ed., pp. 467–491. Mayfield Publishing, Mountain View, CA.

Ottesen, Ann I.

1979 *A Preliminary Study of Acquisition of Exotic Raw Materials by Late Woodland and Mississippian Groups.* Ph.D. dissertation, Department of Anthropology, New York University, New York.

Palmer, Edward

1871 Food Products of the North American Indians, in *Report of the Commission for 1870,* pp. 404–428. U.S. Department of Agriculture, Washington, DC.

Pappas, Christina A.

2008 *An Analysis of Textile-Impressed Ceramics from Slack Farm (15UN28), Kentucky.* M.A. thesis, Department of Anthropology, University of Kentucky, Lexington.

Parkman, Francis

1892 *France and England in North America (part third): La Salle and the Discovery of the Great West.* 12th ed. Little, Brown, Boston, MA.

Pauketat, Timothy R.

1991 *The Dynamics of Pre-State Political Centralization in the North American Midcontinent.* Ph.D. dissertation, Department of Anthropology, University of Michigan, Ann Arbor.

1992 The Reign and Ruin of the Lords of Cahokia: A Dialectic of Dominance, in *Lords of the Southeast: Social Inequality and the Native Elites of Southeastern North America,* edited by A. W. Barker and T. R. Pauketat, pp. 31–51. Archaeological Papers No. 3. American Anthropological Association, Washington, DC.

1994 *The Ascent of Chiefs: Cahokia and Mississippian Politics in Native North America.* University of Alabama Press, Tuscaloosa.

1997a Cahokian Political Economy, in *Cahokia: Domination and Ideology in the Mississippian World,* edited by Timothy R. Pauketat and Thomas E. Emerson, pp. 30–51. University of Nebraska Press, Lincoln.

1997b Specialization, Political Symbols, and the Crafty Elite of Cahokia. *Southeastern Archaeology* 16(1):1–15.

2001 Practice and History in Archaeology: An Emerging Paradigm. *Anthropological Theory* 1:73–98.

2002 A Fourth-Generation Synthesis of Cahokia and Mississippianization. *Midcontinental Journal of Archaeology* 27(2):149–170.

Pauketat, Timothy, and Thomas E. Emerson

1991 The Ideology of Authority and the Power of the Pot. *American Anthropologist* 93:919–941.

Pauketat, Timothy R., and Thomas E. Emerson (editors)

1997 *Cahokia: Domination and Ideology in the Mississippian World.* University of Nebraska Press, Lincoln.

Payne, Claudine
2002 Architectural Reflections of Power and Authority in Mississippian Towns, in *The Dynamics of Power*, edited by Maria O'Donovan, pp. 188–213. Occasional Paper No. 30. Center for Archaeological Investigations, Southern Illinois University, Carbondale.

Pearsall, Deborah M.
2000 *Paleoethnobotany: A Handbook of Procedures* 2nd ed. Academic Press, San Diego, CA.

Pearson, Charles
1977 *Analysis of Late Prehistoric Settlement on Ossabaw Island, Georgia*. Laboratory of Archaeology Series Report 12, University of Georgia, Athens.

Peeples, Matthew A.
2011 *Identity and Social Transformation in the Prehispanic Cibola World: A.D. 1150–1325*. Ph.D. dissertation, Department of Anthropology, Arizona State University, Tempe.

Penick, James Lal, Jr.
1981 *The Great Western Land Pirate: John A. Murrell in Legend and History*. University of Missouri Press, Columbia.

Perdue, Charles L., Jr., Thomas E. Barden, and Robert K. Phillips (editors)
1976 *Weevils in the Wheat: Interviews with Virginia Ex-Slaves*. University Press of Virginia, Charlottesville.

Perdue, Theda
1998 *Cherokee Women: Gender and Culture Change, 1700–1835*. University of Nebraska Press, Lincoln.

Peterson, Lee Allen
1977 *Edible Wild Plants of Eastern and Central North America*. Houghton Mifflin, New York.

Petruso, Karl M., and Jere M. Wickens
1984 The Acorn in Aboriginal Subsistence in Eastern North America: A Report on Miscellaneous Experiments, in *Experiments and Observations on Aboriginal Wild Plant Food Utilization in Eastern North America*, edited by Patrick J. Munson, pp. 360–378. Indiana Historical Society, Prehistory Research Series 6(2).

Phillips, Philip
1958 Application of the Wheat-Gifford-Wasley Taxonomy to Eastern Ceramics. *American Antiquity* 24(2):117–125.
1970a *Archaeological Survey in the Lower Yazoo Basin, Mississippi, 1949–1955*. 2 vols. Papers of the Peabody Museum of Archaeology and Ethnology, Vol. 60, Harvard University, Cambridge, MA.
1970b *Lower Mississippi Survey, 1940–1970*. Peabody Museum of Archaeology and Ethnology, Harvard University, Cambridge, MA.

Phillips, Philip, and James A. Brown
1978 *Pre-Columbian Shell Engravings from the Craig Mound at Spiro, Oklahoma*, pt. 1. Peabody Museum Press, Cambridge, MA.

Phillips, Philip, and Gordon R. Willey
1953 Method and Theory in American Archeology: An Operational Basis for Culture-Historical Integration. *American Anthropologist* 55(5, Pt. 1):615–633.

Phillips, Ruth B.
1989 Dreams and Designs: Iconographic Problems in Great Lakes Twined Bags,

in *Great Lakes Indian Art*, edited by David W. Penney, pp. 52-68. Wayne State University Press, Detroit, MI.

Pigott, Michelle

2013 Tale of Two Villages: A Study of Apalachee Culture Change in the 18th Century. Paper presented at the 70th Annual Meeting of the Southeastern Archaeological Conference, Tampa, FL.

2015 *The Apalachee after San Luís: Exploring Cultural Hybridization through Ceramic Practice.* M.A. thesis, Department of Anthropology, University of West Florida.

Plog, Fred T.

1974 *The Study of Prehistoric Change.* Academic Press, New York.

Pluckhahn, Thomas J., and Robbie Ethridge (editors)

2006 *Light on the Path: The Anthropology and History of the Southeastern Indians.* University of Alabama Press, Tuscaloosa.

Pluckhahn, Thomas J., and David A. McKivergan

2002 A Critical Appraisal of Middle Mississippian Settlement and Social Organization on the Georgia Coast. *Southeastern Archaeology* 21(2):149–161.

Polhemus, Richard R.

1982 The Early Historic Period in the East Tennessee Valley. Unpublished manuscript in possession of the author.

1987 *The Toqua Site: 40MR6: A Late Mississippian, Dallas Phase Town.* Tennessee Valley Authority, Knoxville, TN.

Powell, William Byrd

1856 *The Natural History of the Human Temperaments.* H. W. Derby, Cincinnati, OH.

Powers, Stephen

1873–4 Aboriginal Botany. *Proceedings of the California Academy of Sciences* 5:373–79.

Prentice, Guy

1987 Marine Shells as Wealth Items in Mississippian Societies. *Midcontinental Journal of Archaeology* 12(2):193–223.

Preucel, Robert W. (editor)

2002 *Archaeologies of the Pueblo Revolt.* University of New Mexico, Albuquerque.

Quimby, George I.

1942 The Natchezan Culture Type. *American Antiquity* 7(3):255–275.

1946 Natchez Social Structure as an Instrument of Assimilation. *American Anthropologist* 48:134–136.

1953 Natchez Archaeology: a Tribute to the Natchez for Their Seeming Consistency in the Production of the Fictile Fabric. *Southeastern Archaeological Conference Newsletter* 3(3):22–24.

1957 The Bayou Goula Site: Iberville Parish, Louisiana. *Fieldiana. Anthropology* 47(2):91–170.

Quinn, David B.

1985 *Set Fair for Roanoke: Voyages and Colonies, 1584–1606.* University of North Carolina Press, Chapel Hill.

Radford, Albert E., Harry E. Ahles, and C. Ritchie Bell

1964 *Manual of the Vascular Flora of the Carolinas.* University of North Carolina Press, Chapel Hill.

Rangel, Rodrigo

1993 Account of the Northern Conquest and Discovery of Hernando de Soto, in *The De Soto Chronicles: The Expedition of Hernando de Soto to North America in 1539–1543*. 2 vols., edited by Lawrence A. Clayton, Vernon. J. Knight, Jr., and Edward C. Moore. Translated by John Worth, 1:246–306. University of Alabama Press, Tuscaloosa.

Rawick, George P. (editor)

1972 *The American Slave: A Composite Autobiography*. 19 vols. Greenwood Press, Westport, CT.

1977 *The American Slave: A Composite Autobiography. Supplement, Series 1*. 12 vols. Greenwood Press, Westport, CT.

1979 *The American Slave: A Composite Autobiography. Supplement, Series 2*. 10 vols. Greenwood Press, Westport, CT.

Regnier, Amanda L.

2014 *Reconstructing Tascalusa's Chiefdom: Pottery Styles and the Social Composition of Late Mississippian Communities along the Alabama River*. University of Alabama Press, Tuscaloosa.

Reilly, F. Kent, III

2004 People of Earth, People of Sky: Visualizing the Sacred in Native American Art of the Mississippian Period, in *Hero, Hawk, and Open Hand: American Indian Art of the Ancient Midwest and South*, edited by Richard F. Townshend, pp.125–137. Art Institute of Chicago, Chicago, IL.

Reilly, F. Kent, III, and James F. Garber (editors)

2007a *Ancient Objects and Sacred Realms: Interpretations of Mississippian Iconography*. University of Texas Press, Austin.

2007b Introduction, in *Ancient Objects and Sacred Realms: Interpretations of Mississippian Iconography*, edited by F. Kent Reilly III and James F. Garber, pp. 1–7. University of Texas Press, Austin.

Reilly, F. Kent, III, and James F. Garber

2011 Dancing in the Otherworld: The Human Figural Art of the Hightower Style Revisited, in *Visualizing the Sacred: Cosmic Visions, Regionalism, and the Art of the Mississippian World*, edited by George E. Lankford, F. Kent Reilly, III, and James F. Garber, pp. 294–312. University of Texas Press, Austin.

Reitz, Elizabeth J., and C. Margaret Scarry

1985 *Reconstructing Historic Spanish Subsistence with an Example from Sixteenth-Century Spanish Florida*. Society for Historical Archaeology, Special Publications Series 3.

Renfrew, Colin

1986 Introduction: Peer Polity Interaction and Socio-Political Change, in *Peer Polity Interaction and Socio-Political Change*, edited by Colin Renfrew and John F. Cherry, pp. 1–18. Cambridge University Press, Cambridge, UK.

Rice, Orleans L., Jr.

1977 Trade Goods with a Dallas Phase Burial Salvage Archaeology at 40Mr12. *Tennessee Archaeologist* 33(1–2):17–22.

Rodning, Christopher B.

2015 *Center Places and Cherokee Towns: Archaeological Perspectives on Native American Architecture and Landscape in the Southern Appalachians*. University of Alabama Press, Tuscaloosa.

Rodning, Christopher B., Robin A. Beck, and David G. Moore

2015 Conquistadores, Colonists, and Chiefdoms in Northern La Florida. Paper presented at the 80th Annual Meeting of the Society for American Archaeology, San Francisco, CA.

Rodning, Christopher B., David G. Moore, and Robin A. Beck, Jr.

2013 Conflict, Violence, and Warfare in *La Florida*, in *Native and Spanish New Worlds: Sixteenth-Century Entradas in the American Southwest and Southeast*, edited by Clay Mathers, Jeffrey M. Mitchem, and Charles M. Haecker, pp. 231–247. University of Arizona Press, Tucson.

Rolland, Vicki

2012 The Alachua of North-Central Florida, in *Late Prehistoric Florida: Archaeology at the Edge of the Mississippian World*, edited by Keith Ashley and Nancie Marie White, pp. 126–148. University of Florida Press, Gainesville.

Rolland, Vicki, and Keith Ashley

2000 Beneath the Bell: A Study of Colonoware from Three Spanish Mission Sites in Northeastern Florida. *Florida Anthropologist* 53(1):36–61.

Romans, Bernard

1776 *A Concise Natural History of East and West-Florida*. New York.

Roth, Roman E.

2003 Towards a Ceramic Approach to Social Identity in the Roman World: Some Theoretical Considerations. *Digressus Supplement* 1:35–45.

Rountree, Helen C.

1990 *Pocahontas's People: The Powhatan Indians of Virginia through Four Centuries*. University of Oklahoma Press, Norman.

Rouse, Irving

1955 On the Correlation of Phases of Culture. *American Anthropologist* 57(4): 713–722.

Rowland, Dunbar, and Albert G. Sanders (editors and translators)

1927 *Mississippi Provincial Archives, 1729–1740, French Dominion*, Vol. 1. Mississippi Department of Archives and History, Jackson.

1929 *Mississippi Provincial Archives, 1701–1729, French Dominion*, Vol. 2. Mississippi Department of Archives and History, Jackson.

Rowland, Dunbar, Albert G. Sanders, and Patricia K. Galloway (editors and translators)

1984a *Mississippi Provincial Archives, 1729–1748, French Dominion*, Vol. 4. Louisiana State University Press, Baton Rouge.

1984b *Mississippi Provincial Archives, 1749–1763, French Dominion*, Vol. 5. Louisiana State University Press, Baton Rouge.

Sampeck, Kathryn, Jonathan Thayn, and Howard H. Earnest, Jr.

2015 Geographic Information System Modeling of De Soto's Route from Joara to Chiaha: Archaeology and Anthropology of Southeastern Road Networks in the Sixteenth Century. *American Antiquity* 80(1):46–66.

Sassaman, Kenneth E., and Wictoria Rudolphi

2001 Communities of Practice in the Early Pottery Traditions of the American Southeast. *Journal of Anthropological Research* 57(4):407–425.

Saunders, Rebecca

1992 Guale Indian Pottery: A Georgia Legacy in Northeast Florida. *Florida Anthropologist* 45(2):139–147.

2000 *Stability and Change in Guale Indian Pottery, A.D. 1300–1702*. University of Alabama Press, Tuscaloosa.

2001 Negotiated Tradition? Native American Pottery in the Mission Period in La Florida, in *The Archaeology of Traditions: Agency and History Before and After Co-*

lumbus, edited by Timothy R. Pauketat, pp. 77–93. University Press of Florida, Gainesville.

2009 Stability and Ubiquity: Irene, Altamaha, and San Marcos Pottery in Time and Space, in *From Santa Elena to St. Augustine: Indigenous Ceramic Variability (A.D. 1400–1700)*, edited by Kathleen Deagan and David Hurst Thomas, pp. 83–111. Anthropological Papers No. 90, American Museum of Natural History, New York.

2012 Deep Surfaces: Pottery Decoration and Identity in the Mission Period. *Historical Archaeology* 46(1):94–107.

Saunders, Rebecca, and Christopher T. Hays (editors)

2004 *Early Pottery: Technology, Function, Style, and Interaction in the Lower Southeast.* University of Alabama Press, Tuscaloosa.

Sawyer, Johann A.

2009 *The Mississippian Period Crib Theme: Context, Chronology, and Iconography.* M.A. thesis, Department of Anthropology, Texas State University-San Marcos, San Marcos.

Sawyer, Johann A., and Adam King.

in press Nested Bundles within Etowah's Mound C, in *Binding and Wrapping the Sacred: Sacred Bundles and Religious Communication in the Mississippian Period Eastern Woodlands*, edited by James F. Garber and F. Kent Reilly III. University of Texas Press, Austin.

Sayre, Gordon M.

2012 Introduction, in *The Memoir of Lieutenant Dumont, 1715–1747: A Sojourner in the French Atlantic*, edited by Gordon M. Sayre and Carla Zecher, pp. 1–45. University of North Carolina Press, Chapel Hill.

Scarry, C. Margaret

1993 Agricultural Risk and the Development of the Moundville Chiefdom, in *Foraging and Farming in the Eastern Woodlands*, edited by C. Margaret Scarry, pp. 157–181. University Press of Florida, Gainesville.

2003 Patterns of Wild Plant Utilization in the Prehistoric Eastern Woodlands, in *People and Plants in Ancient Eastern North America*, edited by Paul E. Minnis, pp. 50–104. Smithsonian Books, Washington, DC.

Scarry, John F.

1985 A Proposed Revision of the Fort Walton Ceramic Typology: A Type-Variety System. *Florida Anthropologist* 38:199–234.

1990 The Rise, Transformation, and Fall of Apalachee: A Case Study of Political Change in a Chiefly Society, in *Lamar Archaeology: Mississippian Chiefdoms in the Deep South*, edited by Mark Williams and Gary Shapiro, pp. 175–186. University of Alabama Press, Tuscaloosa.

1996 Stability and Change in the Apalachee Chiefdom, in *Political Structure and Change in the Prehistoric Southeastern United States*, edited by John F. Scarry, pp. 192–227. University Press of Florida, Gainesville.

Scarry, John F., and Bonnie G. McEwan

1995 Domestic Architecture in Apalachee Province: Apalachee and Spanish Residential Styles in the Late Prehistoric and Early Historic Period Southeast. *American Antiquity* 60(3):482–495.

Schneider, Jane

1977 Was There a Pre-Capitalist World-System? *Peasant Studies* 6:20–29.

Scholtz, Sandra Clements
1975 *Prehistoric Plies: A Structural and Comparative Analysis of Cordage, Netting, Basketry, and Fabric from Ozark Bluff Shelters.* Research Series, 9. Arkansas Archeological Survey, Fayetteville.

Schopmeyer, C. S. (coordinator)
1974 *Seeds of Woody Plants in the United States.* Agriculture Handbook 450. U.S. Department of Agriculture, Forest Service, Washington, DC.

Sears, William H.
1955 Creek and Cherokee Culture in the 18th Century. *American Antiquity* 21(2):143–149.

Sempowski, Martha L.
1988 Fluctuations through Time in the Use of Marine Shell at Seneca Iroquois Sites, in *Proceedings of the 1986 Shell Bead Conference,* edited by Charles F. Hayes and Lynn Ceci, pp. 81–96. Rochester Museum and Science Center Research Records No. 20. Rochester, New York.

Sempowski, Martha L., and Lorraine P. Sanders
2001 *Dutch Hollow and Factory Hollow: The Advent of Dutch Trade among the Seneca, Part One.* Rochester Museum and Science Center Research Records No. 24. Rochester, New York.

Shafer, Harry J.
1972 An Evaluation of the Natchez Occupation at the Fatherland Site. *Journal of Mississippi History* 34(3):215–235.

Sharp, Robert V., Vernon James Knight, Jr., and George E. Lankford
2011 Woman in the Patterned Shawl: Female Effigy Vessels and Figurines from the Middle Cumberland River Basin, in *Visualizing the Sacred: Cosmic Visions, Regionalism, and the Art of the Mississippian World,* edited by George E. Lankford, F. Kent Reilly III, and James F. Garber, pp. 137–198. University of Texas Press, Austin.

Sherwood, Sarah C., and Tristram R. Kidder
2011 The DaVincis of Dirt: Geoarchaeological Perspectives on Native American Mound Building in the Mississippi River Basin. *Journal of Anthropological Archaeology* 30:69–87.

Sibley, Lucy R., and Kathryn A. Jakes
1994 Coloration in Etowah Textiles from Burial No. 57, in *Archaeometry of Pre-Columbian Sites and Artifacts,* edited by D. A. Scott and P. Meyers, pp. 395–418. The Getty Conservation Institute, Los Angeles, CA.

Sibley, Lucy R., Kathryn A. Jakes, and Lewis H. Larson
1996 Inferring Behavior and Function from an Etowah Fabric Incorporating Feathers, in *A Most Indispensable Art: Native Fiber Industries from Eastern North America,* edited by James B. Petersen, pp. 73–87. University of Tennessee Press, Knoxville.

Sibley, Lucy R., M. E. Swiker, and Kathryn A. Jakes
1991 The Use of Pattern Reproduction in Reconstructing Etowah Textile Remains. *Ars Textrina* 15:179–202.

Silvia, Diane E.
2000 *Indian and French Interaction in Colonial Louisiana during the Early Eighteenth Century.* Ph.D. dissertation, Department of Anthropology, Tulane University, New Orleans, LA.

2002 Native American and French Cultural Dynamics on the Gulf Coast. *Historical Archaeology* 36(1):26–35.
Silliman, Stephen
2001 Agency, Practical Politics and the Archaeology of Culture Contact. *Journal of Social Archaeology* 1(2):190–209.
Slade, Alissa M.
2006 *An Analysis of Artifacts and Archaeology at 8JE106, A Spanish Mission Site in Florida.* M.A. thesis, Department of Anthropology, Florida State University, Tallahassee.
Smith, Anthony D.
1986 *The Ethnic Origins of Nations.* Blackwell Publishing, Oxford, UK.
Smith, Bruce D., and C. Wesley Cowan
2003 Domesticated Crop Plants and the Evolution of Food Production Economies in Eastern North America, in *People and Plants in Ancient Eastern North America,* edited by Paul E. Minnis, pp. 105–125. Smithsonian Books, Washington, DC.
Smith, Marvin T.
1976 The Route of De Soto through Tennessee, Georgia, and Alabama: The Evidence from Material Culture. *Early Georgia* 4:27–48.
1987 *The Archaeology of Aboriginal Culture Change in the Interior Southeast: Depopulation during the Early Historic Period.* University Presses of Florida, Gainesville.
1995 Woods Island Revisited. *Journal of Alabama Archaeology* 41:93–106.
2000 *Coosa: The Rise and Fall of a Southeastern Mississippian Chiefdom.* University Press of Florida, Gainesville.
2001 The Rise and Fall of Coosa, A.D. 1350–1700, in *Societies in Eclipse: Archaeology of the Eastern Woodlands Indians, A.D. 1400–1700,* edited by David S. Brose, C. Wesley Cowan, and Robert C. Mainfort, Jr., pp. 143 155. Smithsonian Institution Press, Washington, DC.
2005 Foreword, in *The Archaeology of Ocmulgee Old Fields, Macon, Georgia,* by Carol I. Mason, pp. ix–xvii. University of Alabama Press, Tuscaloosa.
Smith, Marvin T., and David J. Hally
1992 Chiefly Behavior: Evidence from Sixteenth Century Spanish Accounts. *Archaeology Papers of the American Anthropological Association* 3(1):99–109.
Smith, Marvin T., Vernon J. Knight, Julie B. Smith, and Ken Turner
1993 The Milner Village (1Et1): A Mid Seventeenth-Century Site near Gadsden, Alabama, in *Archaeological Survey and Excavations in the Coosa River Valley, Alabama,* edited by Vernon. J. Knight, Jr., pp. 49–61. Bulletin 15. Alabama Museum of Natural History, Tuscaloosa.
Smith, Marvin T., and Julie B. Smith
1989 Engraved Shell Masks in North America. *Southeastern Archaeology* 8(1):9–18.
Somers, Margaret R.
1994 The Narrative Constitution of Identity: A Relational and Network Approach. *Theory and Society* 23(5):605–649.
Somers, Margaret R., and Gloria D. Gibson
1994 *Reclaiming the Epistemological "Other": Narrative and the Social Constitution of Identity.* CSST Working Papers, University of Michigan, Ann Arbor.
South, Stanley A., Russell K. Skowronek, and Richard E. Johnson
1988 *Santa Elena.* South Carolina Institute for Archaeology and Anthropology, Archaeology Series 7, Columbia.

Spanos, Mary

2006 *Mississippian Textiles at Beckum Village (1CK24), Clarke County, Alabama.* M.A. thesis, Department of Anthropology, University of Alabama, Tuscaloosa.

Spencer-Wood, Suzanne M.

1999 Gendering Power, in *Manifesting Power: Gender and the Interpretation of Power in Archaeology*, edited by Tracy L. Sweely, pp. 175–183. Routledge, London, UK.

Stark, Miriam T.

1998 Technical Choices and Social Boundaries in Material Culture Patterning: An Introduction, in *The Archaeology of Social Boundaries*, edited by Miriam T. Stark, pp. 1–11. Smithsonian Institution Press, Washington, DC.

Stathakis, Steven A.

1996 *Analysis of Fabric-Impressed Pottery from the Great Salt Spring in Gallatin County Illinois: Social Status and Salt Production during the Mississippian Period.* M.A. thesis, Department of Anthropology, Southern Illinois University at Carbondale.

Steponaitis, Vincas P.

1978 Location Theory and Complex Chiefdoms: A Mississippian Example, in *Mississippian Settlement Patterns*, edited by Bruce D. Smith, pp. 417–453. Academic Press, New York.

1991 Contrasting Patterns of Mississippian Development, in *Chiefdoms: Power, Economy, and Ideology*, edited by Timothy K. Earle, pp. 193–228. Cambridge University Press, Cambridge, UK.

2009 *Ceramics, Chronology, and Community Patterns: An Archaeological Study at Moundville.* Reprint of the 1983 Academic Press edition with a new preface. University of Alabama Press, Tuscaloosa.

Steponaitis, Vincas P., Jeffrey P. Brain, and Ian W. Brown (editors)

1983 *The Grand Village of the Natchez Revisited: Excavations at the Fatherland Site, Adams County, Mississippi*, by Robert S. Neitzel. Archaeological Report 12. Mississippi Department of Archives and History, Jackson.

Steponaitis, Vincas P., Joseph V. Frank III, and Elizabeth Jones

2006 Broutin's 1723 Map of the French Colony at Natchez. Paper presented at the Annual Meeting of the Southeastern Archaeological Conference, Little Rock, Arkansas. Abstract Published in *Southeastern Archaeological Conference Bulletin* 49:47. Fayetteville, AR.

Steponaitis, Vincas P., Samuel E. Swanson, George Wheeler, and Penelope B. Drooker

2011 The Provenance and Use of Etowah Palettes. *American Antiquity* 76(1):81–106.

Stern, Theodore C.

1977 The Natchez, in *The Native Americans*, 2nd ed., edited by Robert F. Spencer and Jesse D. Jennings, pp. 414–424. Harper and Row, New York.

Stoltman, James B.

1978 Temporal Models in Prehistory: An Example from Eastern North America. *Current Anthropology* 19(4):703–746.

Strong, John A.

1989 The Mississippian Bird-Man Theme in Cross-Cultural Perspective, in *The Southeastern Ceremonial Complex: Artifacts and Analysis (The Cottonlandia Conference)*, edited by Patricia Galloway, pp. 211–238. University of Nebraska Press, Lincoln.

Sullivan, Lynne P.

2007 Shell Gorgets, Time, and the Southeastern Ceremonial Complex in Southeastern Tennessee, in *Southeastern Ceremonial Complex: Chronology, Content, Context*, edited by Adam King, pp. 38–56. University of Alabama Press, Tuscaloosa.

Swanton, John R.

1911 *Indian Tribes of the Lower Mississippi Valley and Adjacent Coast of the Gulf of Mexico.* Bureau of American Ethnology Bulletin 43. Washington, DC.

1946 *The Indians of the Southeastern United States.* Bureau of American Ethnology Bulletin 137. Government Printing Office, Washington, DC.

Sweely, Tracy L.

1999 Introduction, in *Manifesting Power: Gender and the Interpretation of Power in Archaeology*, edited by Tracy L. Sweely, pp. 1–14. Routledge, London, UK.

Sweeney, Alex

2005 Identifying Pocotaligo, an Upper Yamasee Town in Jasper County, South Carolina. Paper presented at the 62nd annual meeting of the Southeastern Archaeological Conference, Columbia, SC.

2009 The Archaeology of Indian Slavers and Colonial Allies: Excavations at the Yamasee Capital of Altamaha Town. Paper presented at the Annual Conference of the Society for Historical Archaeology, Toronto, Canada.

Sydnor, Charles S.

1938 *A Gentleman of the Old Natchez Region, Benjamin L. C. Wailes.* Duke University Press, Durham, NC.

Talalay, Laurie, Donald R. Keller, and Patrick J. Munson

1984 Hickory Nuts, Walnuts, Butternuts, and Hazelnuts: Observations and Experiments Relevant to Their Aboriginal Exploitation in Eastern North America, in *Experiments and Observations on Aboriginal Wild Plant Food Utilization in Eastern North America*, edited by Patrick J. Munson, pp. 338–359. Indiana Historical Society, Prehistory Research Series 6(2).

Taylor, Orville

1958 *Negro Slavery in Arkansas.* University of North Carolina Press, Chapel Hill.

Teague, Lynn S.

1998 *Textiles in Southwestern Prehistory.* University of New Mexico Press, Albuquerque.

Thomas, Cyrus

1891 *Catalogue of Prehistoric Works East of the Rocky Mountains.* Bureau of Ethnology Bulletin 12, Washington, DC.

1894 Report on the Mound Explorations of the Bureau of American Ethnology, in *Twelfth Annual Report of the Bureau of American Ethnology, 1890–1891*, pp. 3–742. Washington, DC.

Thomas, David H.

2008 Melding the Ceramic and Radiocarbon Chronologies, in *Native American Landscapes of St. Catherines Island, Georgia II: The Data*, edited by David H. Thomas, pp. 404–434. American Museum of Natural History, Anthropological Papers, Number 88. New York.

Thomas, David Hurst (editor)

1990 *Columbian Consequences, Volume 2: Archaeological and Historical Perspectives on the Spanish Borderlands East.* Smithsonian Institution Press, Washington, DC.

Thomas, Larissa
2001 The Gender Division of Labor in Mississippian Households, in *Archaeological Studies of Gender in the Southeastern United States*, edited by Jane M. Eastman and Christopher B. Rodning, pp. 27–56. University Press of Florida, Gainesville.

Thompson, Stith
1956–1960 *Motif Index of World Literature*. 6 vols. Indiana University Press, Bloomington.

Tilly, Charles
2005 *Identities, Boundaries, and Social Ties*. Paradigm Publishers, Boulder, CO.

Tite, M. S.
1999 Pottery Production, Distribution, and Consumption: The Contribution of the Physical Sciences. *Journal of Archaeological Method and Theory* 6(3):181–233.

Tooker, Elizabeth
1963 Natchez Social Organization: Fact or Anthropological Folklore? *Ethnohistory* 10:358–372.

Townsend, Richard F., and Robert V. Sharp (editors)
2004 *Hero, Hawk, and Open Hand: American Indian Art of the Ancient Midwest and South*. Art Institute of Chicago, Chicago, IL.

Trocolli, Ruth
2002 Mississippian Chiefs: Women and Men of Power, in *The Dynamics of Power*, edited by Maria O'Donovan, pp. 168–187. Occasional Paper No. 30. Center for Archaeological Investigations, Southern Illinois University, Carbondale.

Truett, Randle B.
1938 The Fatherland Mounds, Adams County, Mississippi: A Preliminary Report. Unpublished manuscript, File 740–04.4, National Park Service, Southeast Regional Office, Tallahassee, FL.

Twiss, Katheryn C.
2007 We Are What We Eat, in *The Archaeology of Food and Identity*, edited by Katheryn C. Twiss, pp. 1–15. Center for Archaeological Investigations, Occasional Paper 34. Southern Illinois University, Carbondale.

Ulmer, Mary, and Samuel E. Beck (editors)
1951 *Cherokee Cooklore: Preparing Cherokee Foods*. Museum of the Cherokee Indian, Mary and Goingback Chiltoskey, Cherokee, NC.

U.S. Department of Agriculture, Agricultural Research Service, Nutrient Data Laboratory
2004 *USDA National Nutrient Database for Standard Reference, Release 17*. Electronic document, http://www.nal.usda.gov/fnic/foodcomp, accessed January 30, 2005.

U.S. Department of Agriculture, Natural Resources Conservation Service
2014 *The PLANTS Database*. National Plants Data Center, Baton Rouge, Louisiana. Electronic document, http://plants.usda.gov, accessed February 2010.

VanDerwarker, Amber M., and Kandace R. Detwiler
2000 Plant and Animal Subsistence at the Coweeta Creek Site (31Ma34), Macon County, North Carolina. *North Carolina Archaeology* 49:59–77.

VanDerwarker, Amber M., C. Margaret Scarry, and Jane M. Eastman
2007 Menus for Families and Feasts: Household and Community Consumption of Plants at Upper Saratown, North Carolina, in *Archaeology of Food and Identity*, edited by K. Twiss, pp. 16–49. Center of Archaeological Investigations, Southern Illinois University, Carbondale.

VanDerwarker, Amber M., and Bill Stanyard
2009 Bearsfoot and Deer Legs: Archaeobotanical and Zooarchaeological Evidence of a Special-Purpose Encampment at the Sandy Site, Roanoke, Virginia. *Journal of Ethnobiology* 29(1):129–148.
Vernon, Richard
1988 17th Century Apalachee Colono-Ware as a Reflection of Demography, Economics, and Acculturation. *Historical Archaeology* 22(1):76–82.
Vernon, Richard, and Ann S. Cordell
1993 A Distributional and Technological Study of Apalachee Colono-Ware from San Luís de Talimali, in *The Spanish Missions of La Florida*, edited by Bonnie G. McEwan, pp. 418–441. University of Florida Press, Gainesville.
Victor, Jeffrey S.
1993 *Satanic Panic: The Creation of a Contemporary Legend.* Open Court, Chicago, IL.
Villiers, Marc de
1931 L'établissement de la province de la Louisiane avec les moeurs des sauvages, leurs danses, leurs religions, etc. Poème composé de 1728 à 1742 par Dumont de Montigny. *Journal de la Société des Américanistes* 23(2):273–440.
Vokes, Richard
2007 Rethinking the Anthropology of Religious Change: New Perspectives on Revitalization and Conversion Movements. *Reviews in Anthropology* 36(4): 311–333.
Voragine, Jacobus de
1941 *The Golden Legend of Jacobus de Voragine.* Longmans, Green, & Co., New York.
Wagner, Gail E., and Jamie Civitello
2000 *Ancient Gardening in South Carolina, 10,000 B.C.–A.D. 1700.* Electronic document, http://www.cas.sc.edu/anth/gardening/ancientgardening.html#c, accessed January 10, 2008.
Wailes, Benjamin L. C.
1843–1862 Papers, 1843–1862. Manuscript. Rubenstein Library, Duke University, Durham, NC.
1852–1854 Wailes (B. L. C.) Papers. Manuscript. Mississippi Department of Archives and History, Special Collections Z0076.000 (manuscript diaries) and Z0076.001 (typescripts of all 36 volumes from MDAH and Duke University). Jackson.
Wallace, Anthony F. C.
1956 Revitalization Movements. *American Anthropologist* 58(2):264–281.
2004 Forward, in *Reassessing Revitalization Movements: Perspectives from North America and the Pacific Islands*, edited by Michael E. Harkin, pp. vii–xi. University of Nebraska Press, Lincoln.
Walton, Augustus Q.
1835 *A History of the Detection, Conviction, Life and Designs of John A. Murel, the Great Western Land Pirate.* George White, Athens, TN.
Ward, H. Trawick, and R. P. Stephen Davis, Jr.
1993 *Indian Communities on the North Carolina Piedmont A.D. 1000 to 1700.* Monograph 2. Research Laboratories of Anthropology, University of North Carolina at Chapel Hill.
1999 *Time before History: The Archaeology of North Carolina.* University of North Carolina Press, Chapel Hill.
Waring, Antonio J.
1968 The Southern Cult and Muskhogean Ceremonial, in *The Waring Papers: The*

Collected Works of Antonio J. Waring, Jr., edited by S. Williams, pp. 30–69. Papers of the Peabody Museum of Archaeology and Ethnology 58. Harvard University, Cambridge, MA.

Waring, Antonio J., and Preston Holder

1945 A Prehistoric Ceremonial Complex in the Southeastern United States. *American Anthropologist* 47(1):1–34.

Waselkov, Gregory A.

1989 Seventeenth-Century Trade in the Colonial Southeast. *Southeastern Archaeology* 8:117–133.

Waselkov, Gregory A., and Ashley A. Dumas

2009 Archaeological Clues to a Seventeenth-Century Pan-Southeastern Revitalization Movement. Paper presented at the Annual Meeting of the Southeastern Archaeological Society, Mobile, AL.

Waselkov, Gregory A., and Bonnie L. Gums

2000 *Plantation Archaeology at Rivière Aux Chiens, ca. 1725–1848.* Archaeological Monograph 7, Center for Archaeological Studies, University of South Alabama, Mobile.

Waselkov, Gregory A., and Craig T. Sheldon, Jr.

1987 *Cataloguing and Documenting the Historic Creek Archaeological Collections of the Alabama Department of Archives and History: A Final Report to the National Science Foundation.* Auburn University and the Alabama Department of Archives and History, Montgomery, AL.

Waters, Gifford

2005 *Maintenance and Change of 18th Century Mission Identity: A Multi-Ethnic Contact Situation.* Ph.D. dissertation, Department of Anthropology, University of Florida, Gainesville.

2009 Aboriginal Ceramics at Three 18th-Century Mission Sites in St. Augustine, Florida, in *From Santa Elena to St. Augustine: Indigenous Ceramic Variability (A.D. 1400 – 1799)*, edited by Kathleen Deagan and David Hurst Thomas, pp. 165–176. Anthropological Papers No. 90, American Museum of Natural History, New York.

Watson, Patty Jo, and Richard A. Yarnell

1966 Archaeological and Paleoethnobotanical Investigations in Salts Cave, Mammoth Cave National Park, Kentucky. *American Antiquity* 31(6):842–849.

Webb, Clarence H., and Ralph R. McKinney

1975 Mounds Plantation (16CD12), Caddo Parish, Louisiana. *Louisiana Archaeology* 2:39–127.

Webb, William S., and Charles Wilder

1951 *An Archaeological Survey of Guntersville Basin on the Tennessee River in Northern Alabama.* University of Kentucky Press, Lexington.

Weinstein, Richard A., and Ashley A. Dumas

2008 The Spread of Shell-Tempered Ceramics along the Northern Coast of the Gulf of Mexico. *Southeastern Archaeology* 27(2):202–221.

Welch, Paul D.

1991 *Moundville's Economy.* University of Alabama Press, Tuscaloosa.

Welch, Paul D., and Brian M. Butler

2006 Borne on a Litter with Much Prestige, in *Leadership and Polity in Mississippian Society*, edited by Brian M. Butler and Paul D. Welch, pp. 1–15. Occasional Paper No. 33. Center for Archaeological Investigations, Southern Illinois University, Carbondale.

Wenger, Etienne
1998 *Communities of Practice: Learning, Meaning, and Identity*. Cambridge University Press, Cambridge, UK.
Wesson, Cameron B.
2008 *Households and Hegemony: Early Creek Prestige Goods, Symbolic Capital, and Social Power*. University of Nebraska Press, Lincoln.
Wheat, Joe Ben, James C. Gifford, and William W. Wasley
1958 Ceramic Variety, Type Cluster, and Ceramic System in Southwestern Pottery Analysis. *American Antiquity* 24(1):34–47.
White, Andrea P.
2002 *Living on the Periphery: A Study of an Eighteenth-Century Yamasee Mission Community in Colonial St. Augustine*. M.A. thesis, Department of Anthropology, College of William and Mary, Williamsburg, VA.
White, Douglas R., George P. Murdock, and Richard Scaglion
1971 Natchez Class and Rank Reconsidered. *Ethnology* 10:369–388.
Whiteford, Andrew Hunter
1977a Fiber Bags of the Great Lakes Indians, I. *American Indian Art* 2(3):55–64, 85.
1977b Fiber Bags of the Great Lakes Indians, II. *American Indian Art* 3(1):40–47, 90.
Whitley, Thomas G.
2009 Conflict and Confusion on the Middle Savannah: The 17th to 18th Century Occupation at Riverfront Village (38AK1933), Aiken County, South Carolina. Paper presented at the 74th Annual Meeting of the Society for American Archaeology, Atlanta.
2013 *Archaeological Data Recovery at Riverfront Village (38AK933): A Mississippian/Contact Period Occupation, Aiken County, South Carolina*, with contributions by Jana Futch, Kandace D. Hollenbach, Jon Marcoux, Kim Wescott, Maggie Needham, and Jessica L. Allgood. Submitted to Davis and Floyd, Greenwood, South Carolina, and South Carolina Department of Transportation, Columbia. Brockington and Associates, Atlanta, GA.
Wiessner, Polly
1983 Style and Social Information in Kalahari San Projectile Points. *American Antiquity* 48:253–276.
Willey, Gordon R.
1949 *Archaeology of the Florida Gulf Coast*. Smithsonian Miscellaneous Collections. Vol. 113. Washington, DC.
Willey, Gordon R., and Philip Phillips
1958 *Method and Theory in American Archaeology*. University of Chicago Press, Chicago, IL.
Williams, Mark, and Gary Shapiro
1990 *Lamar Archaeology: Mississippian Chiefdoms in the Deep South*. University of Alabama Press, Tuscaloosa.
Williams, Stephen
1962 Historic Archaeology in the Lower Mississippi Valley. *Southeastern Archaeological Conference Newsletter* 9(1):53–63.
1966 Historic Archaeology, Past and Present. *School of American Research Annual Report for 1966*, pp. 23–26. Santa Fe, NM.
1980 Armorel: A Very Late Phase in the Lower Mississippi Valley. *Southeastern Archaeological Conference Bulletin* 22:105–109.
1990 The Vacant Quarter and Other Late Events in the Lower Valley, in *Towns and*

Temples along the Mississippi, edited by David H. Dye and Cheryl Anne Cox, pp. 170–181. University of Alabama Press, Tuscaloosa.

2003 Introduction to 2003 Edition: Phillips, Ford, and Griffin's Lower Valley Survey, in *Archaeological Survey in the Lower Mississippi Alluvial Valley, 1940–1947*, by Philip Phillips, James A. Ford, and James B. Griffin, edited by S. Williams, pp. xi–xxxii. University of Alabama Press, Tuscaloosa.

Willoughby, Charles C.

1952 Textile Fabrics from the Spiro Mound. *Missouri Archaeologist* 14:107–118.

2000 Notes on the History and Symbolism of the Muskhogeans and the People of Etowah, in *Exploration of the Etowah Site in Georgia: The Etowah Papers*, edited by Warren K. Moorehead, pp. 7–66. Reprint of 1932 edition. University Press of Florida, Gainesville.

Wilson, Gilbert Livingstone

1917 Agriculture of the Hidatsa Indians: An Indian Interpretation. *Bulletin of the University of Minnesota, Studies in the Social Sciences*, No. 9. University of Minnesota, Minneapolis. Electronic document, http://digital.library.upenn.edu/women/buffalo/garden/garden.html, accessed January 10, 2008.

Wilson, Gregory D., Jon Marcoux, and Brad Koldehoff

2006 Square Pegs in Round Holes: Organizational Diversity between Early Moundville and Cahokia, in *Leadership and Polity in Mississippian Society*, edited by Brian M. Butler and Paul D. Welch, pp. 43–72. Occasional Paper No. 33. Center for Archaeological Investigations, Southern Illinois University, Carbondale.

Wilson, Samuel, Jr.

1969 Ignace François Broutin, in *Frenchmen and French Ways in the Mississippi Valley*, edited by John Francis McDermott, pp. 231–294. University of Illinois Press, Urbana.

1982 French Fortification at Fort Rosalie, Natchez, in *LaSalle and His Legacy*, edited by Patricia Kay Galloway, pp. 194–210. University of Mississippi Press, Jackson.

Wilson, William A.

1979 Folklore and History: Fact amid the Legends, in Jan Harold Brunvand, editor, *Readings in American Folklore*, pp. 449–466. W. W. Norton, New York.

Winters, Howard D.

1974 Some Unusual Grave Goods from a Mississippian Burial Mound. *Indian Notes* 10(2):34–46.

Wobst, H. Martin

1977 Stylistic Behavior and Information Exchange, in *For the Director: Research Essays in Honor of James B. Griffin*, edited by C. E. Cleland, pp. 317–342. Anthropological Papers No. 61. Museum of Anthropology, University of Michigan, Ann Arbor.

1999 Style in Archaeology or Archaeologists in Style, in *Material Meanings: Critical Approaches to the Interpretation of Culture*, edited by Elizabeth Chilton, pp. 118–132. University of Utah Press, Salt Lake City.

Wolf, Eric R.

1990 Facing Power—Old Insights, New Questions. *American Anthropologist* 92(3):586–596.

Worth, John E.

1988 *Mississippian Occupation on the Middle Flint River*. M.A. thesis, Department of Anthropology, University of Georgia, Athens.

1992 *The Timucuan Missions of Spanish Florida and the Rebellion of 1656.* Ph.D. dissertation, Department of Anthropology, University of Florida, Gainesville.

1994 Late Spanish Military Expeditions in the Interior Southeast, 1597–1628, in *The Forgotten Centuries: Indians and Europeans in the American South, 1521–1704,* edited by Charles Hudson and Carmen Chaves Tesser, pp. 104–122. University of Georgia Press, Athens.

1995 *The Struggle for the Georgia Coast: An Eighteenth-Century Spanish Retrospective on Guale and Mocama.* Anthropological Papers of the American Museum of Natural History, Number 75. American Museum of Natural History, New York.

1997a The Eastern Creek Frontier: History and Archaeology of the Flint River Towns, ca. 1750–1826. Paper presented in the symposium "Recent Advances in Lower Creek Archaeology" at the annual conference of the Society for American Archaeology, Nashville, TN.

1997b Integrating Ethnohistory and Archaeology among the Timucua: An Overview of Southeast Georgia and Northeast Florida. Paper presented in the symposium "Late Prehistoric through Mission Period Research in the Coastal Timucuan Region" at the 54th annual meeting of the Southeastern Archaeological Conference, Baton Rouge, LA.

1998a *The Timucuan Chiefdoms of Spanish Florida,* Vol. I: *Assimilation.* University of Florida Press, Gainesville.

1998b *The Timucuan Chiefdoms of Spanish Florida,* Vol. II: *Resistance and Destruction.* University of Florida Press, Gainesville.

2000 The Lower Creeks: Origins and Early History, in *Indians of the Greater Southeast: Historical Archaeology and Ethnohistory,* edited by Bonnie G. McEwan, pp. 265–298. University of Florida Press, Gainesville.

2004 Yamasee, in *Handbook of North American Indians, Volume 14: Southeast.* Raymond D. Fogelson, vol. ed.; William C. Sturtevant, gen. ed., pp. 245–253. Smithsonian Institution Press, Washington, DC.

2007 [1995] *The Struggle for the Georgia Coast.* University of Alabama Press, Tuscaloosa.

2009a Explaining Native American Ceramic Variability in the Early Historic Southeast. Paper presented at the Annual Conference of the Society for Historical Archaeology, Toronto, Canada.

2009b Ethnicity and Ceramics on the Southeastern Atlantic Coast: An Ethnohistorical Analysis, in *From Santa Elena to St. Augustine: Indigenous Ceramic Variability (A.D. 1400–1700),* edited by Kathleen Deagan and David Hurst Thomas, pp. 179–207. American Museum of Natural History Anthropological Papers No. 90. New York.

2010 Explaining Ceramic Stylistic Variability during the Late Mississippi Period in Northwest Georgia: A Design Type Analysis of Lamar Bold Incised Pottery. Paper presented at the 67th Annual Meeting of the Southeastern Archaeological Conference, Lexington, KY.

2012 An Overview of the Suwannee Valley Culture, in *Late Prehistoric Florida: Archaeology at the Edge of the Mississippian World,* edited by Keith Ashley and Nancy Marie White, pp. 149–171. University of Florida Press, Gainesville.

2013a Inventing Florida: Constructing a Colonial Society in an Indigenous Landscape, in *Native and Spanish New Worlds: Sixteenth-Century Entradas in the American Southwest and Southeast,* edited by Clay Mathers, Jeffrey M. Mitchem, and Charles M. Haecker, pp. 189–201. University of Arizona Press, Tucson.

2013b Catalysts of Assimilation: The Role of Franciscan Missionaries in the Colonial System of Spanish Florida. *Proceedings of the Conference "From La Florida to La California: The Genesis and Realization of Franciscan Evangelization in the Spanish Borderlands."* Academy of American Franciscan History, Berkeley, CA.

2014 *Discovering Florida: First-Contact Narratives from Spanish Expeditions along the Lower Gulf Coast.* University Press of Florida, Gainesville.

Worth, John E., Norma J. Harris, and Jennifer Melcher

2011 San Joseph de Escambe: A 18th-Century Apalachee Mission in the West Florida Borderlands. Paper presented at the 2011 Conference of the Society for Historical Archaeology, Austin, TX.

Worth, John E., Norma J. Harris, Jennifer Melcher, and Danielle Dadiego

2012 Exploring Mission Life in 18th-Century West Florida: 2011 Excavations at San Joseph de Escambe. Paper presented at the 2012 Conference of the Society for Historical Archaeology, Baltimore, MD.

Yanovsky, Elias

1936 *Food Plants of the North American Indians.* U.S. Department of Agriculture, Miscellaneous Publication No. 237. Washington, DC.

Yarnell, Richard A.

1982 Problems of Interpretation of Archaeological Plant Remains of the Eastern Woodlands. *Southeastern Archaeology* 1(1):1–7.

1993 The Importance of Native Crops during the Late Archaic and Woodland Periods, in *Foraging and Farming in the Eastern Woodlands,* edited by C. Margaret Scarry, pp. 13–26. University Press of Florida, Gainesville.

Yarnell, Richard A., and M. Jean Black

1985 Temporal Trends Indicated by a Survey of Archaic and Woodland Plant Food Remains from Southeastern North America. *Southeastern Archaeology* 4(2):93–106.

CONTRIBUTORS

Robin A. Beck is an associate professor of anthropology and associate curator of North American archaeology (Museum of Anthropological Archaeology) at the University of Michigan. He is the author of *Chiefdoms, Collapse, and Coalescence in the Early American South*, editor of *The Durable House: House Society Models in Archaeology*, and coeditor of *Fort San Juan and the Limits of Empire: Colonialism and Household Practice at the Berry Site.*

Ian W. Brown is a professor and the chair of the Department of Anthropology at the University of Alabama. Educated at Harvard and Brown, he has been with the Crimson Tide since 1991. Research interests include the ethnohistory and prehistory of the Southeast, especially the lower Mississippi Valley, anthropology of salt, and cemeteries.

Penelope B. Drooker, author of *Mississippian Village Textiles at Wickliffe* and *The View from Madisonville: Protohistoric Western Fort Ancient Interaction Patterns*, is curator of anthropology emerita, New York State Museum, Albany.

Robbie Ethridge is a professor of anthropology at the University of Mississippi. She is the author of *Creek Country: The Creek Indians and Their World, 1796–1816* and *From Chicaza to Chickasaw: The European Invasion and the Transformation of the Mississippian World, 1540–1715*. Her current research is on the rise and fall of the pre-Columbian Mississippian world.

Kandace D. Hollenbach is a research associate professor in the Department of Anthropology at the University of Tennessee, Knoxville, where she studies the foodways of prehistoric and historic peoples of the Southeastern United States.

Adam King is a research associate professor in the South Carolina Institute of Archaeology and Anthropology at the University of South Carolina. His research uses traditional archaeological excavation coupled with remote sensing and the study of ancient imagery to understand how Mississippian societies (A.D. 1000–1600) came into being and changed over the course of their individual histories.

George E. Lankford is a professor emeritus of folklore at Lyon College in Batesville, Arkansas. His recent research publications are studies of the relationship of visual art and myth as focused in iconographic puzzles. Two recent books include *Reachable Stars* and *Looking for Lost Lore.*

David G. Moore is a professor of anthropology at Warren Wilson College. He is the author of *Catawba Valley Mississippian: Ceramics, Chronology, and Catawba Indians* and coeditor, with Robin A. Beck and Christopher B. Rodning, of *Fort San Juan and the Limits of Empire: Colonialism and Household Practice at the Berry Site.*

Christopher B. Rodning is an associate professor of anthropology at Tulane University in New Orleans, Louisiana. He is the author of *Center Places and Cherokee Towns: Archaeological Perspectives on Native American Architecture and Landscape in the Southern Appalachians* and a coeditor, with Robin A. Beck and David G. Moore, of *Fort San Juan and the Limits of Empire: Colonialism and Household Practice at the Berry Site.*

Rebecca Saunders, an associate professor and associate curator of anthropology at Louisiana State University in Baton Rouge, has worked on the Georgia coast since the 1980s. She has an abiding interest in the changes wrought by culture contact in late prehistoric and early historic cultures.

Johann A. Sawyer completed a Ph.D. in anthropology at the University of South Carolina. His dissertation is "Cults and Bradenization: Tracking the Braden Style and Iconographic Variability throughout the Mississippian Period." His research interests lie in the ethnohistory and archaeology of the Southeast, with emphasis on Mississippi-period iconography and ritual practices.

Marvin T. Smith recently retired as a professor of anthropology at Valdosta State University in Georgia. He is the author of more than 70 scholarly publications, including *The Archaeology of Aboriginal Culture Change in the Interior Southeast: Depopulation during the Early Historic Period* and *Coosa: The Rise and Fall of a Southeastern Mississippian Chiefdom.* In 1992 he received the C. B. Moore Award for Excellence presented by the Lower Mississippi Survey at the annual meeting of the Southeastern Archaeological Conference.

Vincas P. Steponaitis is the director of the Research Laboratories of Archaeology, the chair of the Curriculum in Archaeology, and a professor of anthropology at the University of North Carolina at Chapel Hill. His research focuses principally on the Late Woodland and Mississippian cultures of the Deep South. His most recent book is *Rethinking Moundville and Its Hinterland* (coedited with C. Margaret Scarry).

Gregory A. Waselkov, a professor of anthropology at the University of South Alabama in Mobile, directs the Center for Archaeological Studies and writes on Southeastern Indians, French colonists, and shell middens. Recent books include *A Conquering Spirit: Fort Mims and the Redstick War of 1813–1814* and *Archéologie de l'Amérique coloniale française* (with Marcel Moussette).

John E. Worth is an associate professor of historical archaeology in the Department of Anthropology at the University of West Florida in Pensacola, where he specializes in archaeology and ethnohistory focusing on the Spanish colonial era in Southeastern North America.

INDEX